CW00969221

Implicit Parallel Programming in *pH*

About the Authors

Rishiyur Nikhil is the director of software at Sandburst Corporation, where he manages the development of software for hardware synthesis from declarative specifications. Previously, as a researcher at the Cambridge Research Laboratory of Digital Equipment Corporation and Compaq Computer Corporation, and as a professor at the Massachusetts Institute of Technology in the electrical engineering and computer science department, he conducted research on the design and implementation of functional programming languages, high-level parallel programming languages and systems, multithreaded languages and implementations, and dataflow and multithreaded computer architectures. He participates actively in the research community, publishing in leading conferences and journals and serving on program committees. He received his M.S.E. and Ph.D. degrees in computer and information sciences from the University of Pennsylvania, and his B.Tech. degree in electrical engineering from the Indian Institute of Technology, Kanpur, India. He is a member of the ACM, IEEE, and IFIP Working Group 2.8 on Functional Programming.

Arvind is the Johnson Professor of Computer Science and Engineering at the Massachusetts Institute of Technology. His recent work centers on high-level specification and description of architectures and protocols using Term Rewriting Systems, encompassing both hardware synthesis and verification of implementations against TRS specifications. In 2000, Arvind founded a new style chips company called Sandburst Corporation to exploit these ideas. Previously, he contributed to the development of dynamic dataflow architectures, the implicitly parallel programming languages Id and *pH*, and compilation of these languages on parallel machines. In 1992, Arvind's group at MIT, in collaboration with Motorola, built a dozen Monsoon dataflow machines and associated software. Arvind has served on editorial boards, chaired professional conferences, and consulted for many computer companies. In 1994, he became an IEEE Fellow and was awarded the Charles Babbage Outstanding Scientist Award. In 1999 he received the Distinguished Alumni Award from the Indian Institute of Technology, Kanpur.

Implicit Parallel Programming in *pH*

Rishiyur S. Nikhil
Sandburst Corporation

Arvind
MIT

MORGAN KAUFMANN PUBLISHERS

AN IMPRINT OF ACADEMIC PRESS
A Harcourt Science and Technology Company

SAN FRANCISCO   SAN DIEGO   NEW YORK   BOSTON
LONDON   SYDNEY   TOKYO

Senior Editor	Denise E. M. Penrose
Publishing Services Manager	Scott Norton
Production Editor	Howard Severson
Editorial Coordinator	Emilia Thiuri
Cover Design	Yvo Riezebos
Cover Image	Grant's zebras, Kenya; © Art Wolfe/Tony Stone images
Text Design	Mark Ong/Side By Side Studios
Composition and Illustration	Windfall Software, using ZzTEX
Copyeditor	Ken DellaPenta
Proofreader	Ruth Stevens
Indexer	Ty Koontz
Printer	Courier Corporation

Designations used by companies to distinguish their products are often claimed as trademarks or registered trademarks. In all instances in which Morgan Kaufmann Publishers is aware of a claim, the product names appear in initial capital or all capital letters. Readers, however, should contact the appropriate companies for more complete information regarding trademarks and registration.

Morgan Kaufmann Publishers
340 Pine Street, Sixth Floor, San Francisco, CA 94104-3205
http://www.mkp.com

ACADEMIC PRESS
A Harcourt Science and Technology Company
525 B Street, Suite 1900, San Diego, CA 92101-4495, USA
http://www.academicpress.com

Academic Press
Harcourt Place, 32 Jamestown Road, London, NW1 7BY, United Kingdom
http://www.academicpress.com

Library of Congress Cataloging-in-Publication Data
Nikhil, Rishiyur S.
    Implicit parallel programming in pH / Rishiyur S. Nikhil, Arvind.
      p. cm.
    Includes bibliographical references and index.
    ISBN 1-55860-644-0
    1. Parallel programming (Computer science)   2. pH (Computer program language)   I.
Arvind, 1947–   II Title.
QA76.58 .N55 2002
005.2'75—dc21   2001029379

This book is printed on acid-free paper.

To the many veterans of CSG, 6.847, and 6.827
— R.S.N. and A.

To Amma, Appa, and the spirit of Ranjana and Jagadambal Street
— R.S.N.

To Amma and Papa
— A.

Contents

▼ Indicates advanced or optional material that may be skipped in the interest of time.

Preface

Parallel machines in the form of small symmetric multiprocessors (SMPs) containing two to four processors are now becoming affordable and available to many users. Until recently, four-processor SMPs were considered "enterprise" servers; today, they are manufactured and sold as commodity items. Unfortunately, when upgrading to an SMP, we do not see a jump in application performance in the same way as we expect when upgrading our machines with a faster processor or a better memory system. The reason is that, to date, most application programs have been written as sequential programs in sequential languages, and these programs cannot directly exploit more than one processor. Even if it were possible to recompile some of these applications, it is unlikely to be of much use, since it is very hard for a compiler to extract a usefully parallel program from traditional sequential source code.

The traditional approach to parallel programming has been to extend a sequential language with constructs for parallelism. For SMPs this has usually meant adding a mechanism for creating threads/processes/tasks, plus some synchronization mechanisms such as locks or monitors, and, if you are sufficiently brave to attempt to scale beyond a single SMP to a cluster of workstations or SMPs, you might try message-passing. But these approaches to parallel programming are quite daunting—the domain of the expert programmer—and not to be undertaken lightly.

We have a vision of the future in which parallel programming is the default, and sequential programming is a special case. The very first programs written by high school and undergraduate students will be parallel, and they will only later learn why it may be necessary to sequentialize some parts of it, and how. The foundation of this vision is an *implicitly parallel programming language* that is highly expressive even without the concept of updatable state, which is the fundamentally hard concept in parallel programming. *Functional programming languages* are perfectly suited for this purpose, by offering a model of computation with pure functions and values and absent of any notion of updatable variables. Modern functional languages, with higher-order functions and polymorphic type systems, have proven to be very expressive, and most, if not all, of the work of many applications can be done completely in the functional paradigm.

The advanced student will eventually want to go beyond the purely functional paradigm for two reasons. First, certain structures such as hash tables and graphs have asymptotically better efficiency with updatable state. Second, certain applications are either inherently nondeterministic or have more parallelism when they exploit nondeterminism. The two are not unrelated, since introducing updatable, observable state into a parallel language also enables nondeterminism. Traditionally, updatable state has been introduced into functional languages only in conjuction with complete sequentialization (e.g., Lisp, Scheme, SML). Instead, it is possible to retain the abundant implicit parallelism of a functional language by introducing *implicitly synchronized* updatable state—state in which the act of reading or writing a value is combined implicitly with a synchronization. This implicit synchronization greatly simplifies the management of shared updatable state in a parallel language.

In this book we advocate this vision for parallel programming, using the language *pH* as our vehicle. *pH* is a result of over two decades of experience with the functional programming language *Id* and several implementations of *Id* on dataflow and conventional architectures. *pH* is a modern incarnation of *Id* that uses the standard nonstrict purely functional language Haskell for its functional core, and so *pH* is a parallel dialect and extension of Haskell. The implicit parallelism in *pH* makes it easy to compile parallel code for an SMP.

Although our research in *Id* and *pH* has been motivated primarily by parallelism for speed, implicit parallelism also encompasses concurrent programming, that is, for programs that combine computation with reaction to multiple asynchronous events.

This book is completely self-contained and is suitable for several audiences including the following:

◆ General software professionals and researchers who would like to learn about implicit parallelism and its possibilities.

◆ Haskell programmers who want to understand how their programs can run in parallel without modification. In fact, Chapters 2 through 7 can be used as a general tutorial on Haskell, along with an understanding of how Haskell programs can be automatically executed in parallel. Chapter 8 covers Haskell's monadic I/O, but also introduces explicit sequencing, the first of *pH*'s extensions to Haskell (the remaining extensions are covered in Chapters 9 and 10).

This book is not a primer—it requires prior familiarity and experience with programming. It will challenge the reader, even the expert in traditional programming languages, into new ways of thinking about programming and parallelism. We have taught courses for about 10 years using successive drafts of this book—every Fall, in a semester-long graduate course taught by the second author at the Massachusetts Institute of Technology, and in several shorter courses taught by both authors at other locations. In the semester-long course, this book is self-contained and covers about the first 80 percent of the material, with the rest of the time devoted to compiler and implementation issues. The course has been taken by advanced undergraduates, junior graduate students, and software professionals. We recommend reading the material in its entirety in the order presented, but just in case you need to catch a plane or save the free world, we have marked a few sections with "▼" indicating that they may be skipped without loss of continuity.

A production implementation of any programming language requires a vast engineering effort: to implement the main compiler, to implement a comfortable program development environment, and to implement interoperability mechanisms and the numerous libraries necessary to work in today's complex and heterogeneous software environment. A research implementation of *pH* exists at MIT and is available. We hope this book will inspire potential language implementors to improve, extend, and widen the current implementation.

Acknowledgments

This book has been years in the making, taking shape concurrently with substantial evolution of the *pH* language itself and its predecessor *Id*, based on our research at MIT Laboratory for Computer Science and Compaq's

Cambridge Research Laboratory (CRL). At MIT the research was supported by the Defense Advanced Research Projects Agency (DARPA) and took place in the Computation Structures Group. At CRL, the work was supported by Digital Equipment Corporation and Compaq Computer Corporation. During that time, a steady stream of extremely bright and talented students helped shape the language, its implementation, and this book with their research contributions and their involvement in MIT's 6.847, 6.827, and 6.83s courses. There are too many to name, but we would particularly like to recognize Shail Aditya, Zena Ariola, Paul Barth, Alex Caro, Derek Chiou, David Culler, Steve Heller, Jamey Hicks, Bob Iannucci, Vinod Kathail, Mieszko Lis, Jan-Willem Maessen, Dinarte Morais, Greg Papadopoulos, Keshav Pingali, Jacob Schwartz, Andy Shaw, Richard Soley, and Ken Traub. We also received useful feedback from attendees of courses we taught at Los Alamos National Laboratories, at the Indian Institute of Science Bangalore, at the Supercomputing 1989 conference, and in Japan. We have benefited from technical collaborations on *Id* and *pH* with researchers such as Lennart Augustsson (Chalmers Institute of Technology, Sweden); Wim Bohm (Colorado State University); K. Ekanadham (IBM Research); Cormac Flanagan (Rice University); Jamey Hoch (Sandia); Olaf Lubeck (Los Alamos National Laboratory); Klaus Schauser, Thorsten von Eicken, and Seth Goldstein (U.C. Berkeley); and Joe Stoy (Oxford University). The decision to transform *Id* into *pH* was taken shortly after both authors served on the original Haskell committee, and the transformation was helped particularly by our discussions with the committee members about functional arrays and accumulators. We have also benefited from many substantial discussions about parallel functional languages with Simon Peyton Jones of Glasgow University and Microsoft Research. Wim Bohm, Marc Feeley (Université de Montréal), Simon Peyton Jones, and Toru Nakagawa (Fujitsu Laboratories) carefully read and commented on drafts of the book. Finally, our sincere thanks to Denise Penrose, our editor at Morgan Kaufmann Publishers, for her constant encouragement and support and, in particular, her infinite patience during the long "last mile."

From Sequential to Implicit Parallel Programming

Wouldn't it be great if our programs ran twice as fast merely by upgrading our workstation from one to two processors, or from two to four? Wouldn't it be great if doubling the number of processors meant that it took only half as long to evaluate alternative designs using CAD tools, to complete a modeling run for tomorrow's weather, or to search a large database? We are all very used to the idea of gaining increased performance by upgrading our workstation with a faster processor, or with a larger or faster memory system. Unfortunately we do not see this kind of automatic improvement when we upgrade to a multiprocessor. Although a multiprocessor often allows us to run more programs simultaneously, it seldom allows us to complete a given program in less time, or to run a larger program in a given amount of time, without extraordinary effort.

The problem is that most application programs are written in sequential programming languages, and these programs cannot exploit the extra processors available in a multiprocessor. We can run separate programs on the different processors to increase the overall throughput of the system, but no single program runs faster by dividing its work among multiple processors the way a parallel program could.

Why are most programs sequential? The answer has a number of dimensions, one of which is historical—it was only in the late 1990s that multiprocessors began to be commonly affordable and available as commodity hardware, and so until recently there was no widespread interest in writing parallel programs.[1] But, in addition, most existing approaches to producing parallel programs are very hard, whether they involve automatically converting existing sequential programs into parallel ones, or whether they involve the programmer explicitly writing parallel programs.

In this chapter we will explore the question of what makes parallel programming so hard, and we will end with an overview of the *pH* solution. First, we will see that many programs, when viewed at a suitable level of algorithmic abstraction, in fact contain abundant parallelism. Most of this parallelism is obscured and eliminated by the time we write the code in a concrete sequential programming language. We will see why it is very difficult for an automatic system to recover this obscured parallelism.

If parallelism is not recoverable from our existing sequential programs, an alternative is to rewrite our programs with parallelism in mind. Three approaches suggest themselves:

- We can write our programs in sequential languages in certain stylized ways and with certain annotations that make it easy for a compiler to generate parallel code. The design of these idioms and annotations is influenced by our insights into what makes automatic parallelization of legacy sequential programs difficult. Examples of programming languages in this category are High Performance Fortran [29] and OpenMP [48]. Unfortunately this approach is not truly general purpose in that only a certain class of applications fits this paradigm.
- We can abandon automatic parallelization and extend our existing sequential languages with *explicit* constructs to initiate parallel activ-

---

1. Parallel programming has long been of interest to programmers of operating systems because even on a uniprocessor an operating system juggles a number of activities "simultaneously."

ities and to coordinate their interactions. There are a large number of programming languages in this category, including POSIX threads (pthreads) [33], Java [8], PVM [24] and MPI [40], Modula [77], Multilisp [28], Cid [45], Cilk [15], Split-C [19], and Linda [3].

- ◆ We can write our programs in a new programming language where parallelism is *implicit*. This is the approach advocated in this book, and *pH* is such a language. *pH* is parallel from the ground up—there is no sequential core. Its approach is quite the opposite from the previous ones—the very first, simplest programs that a *pH* programmer writes are parallel, and it is only later that an advanced *pH* programmer learns judiciously to introduce a little explicit sequencing. As such, exploiting multiple processors is almost trivial in *pH*.

  pH builds on over two decades of experience with dataflow and functional programming languages. *pH* is a modern successor to the Id dataflow language [10, 47, 43, 46], adopting the notation and type system of the standard nonstrict pure functional language Haskell [53] (the name "pH" can be read as "parallel Haskell").

When discussing parallel programming, it is important also to keep a proper perspective on expectations of *scaling*. Parallel computers today come in a wide range of sizes, from uniprocessors to thousands of processors. It is, in general, unreasonable to expect that a program's speed will automatically scale across such a diversity of platforms. In very large machines a processor may experience several orders of magnitude variation in access times for data that is "near" to the processor versus "far." This fundamental change in cost model may require algorithms to be redesigned: how we map work to different processors, how we place data in the machine's memory relative to processors, and how we schedule activities. None of the above approaches to parallel programming can completely insulate us from these considerations. However, it is reasonable to expect that scaling should happen automatically without programmer intervention for the kinds of parallel machines that are likely to be in the vast majority as commodity machines—small symmetric multiprocessors (SMPs), with perhaps 2 to 16 processors, all having more or less uniform access to a shared memory (a uniform cost model). At the end of this chapter we will have a few more remarks on the effect of architectures on programming.

1.1   How Sequential Languages Obscure Parallelism

Many problems, when viewed abstractly, appear to be abundantly parallel. However, this parallelism gets obscured when the problem is expressed in a sequential language. Even the most sophisticated compilers are able to recover only a small part of the obscured parallelism. We illustrate this with the problem of matrix multiplication.

1.1.1   Parallelism in Matrix Multiplication

Matrix multiplication is a computation at the heart of many problems such as scaling, rotation, and displacement transformations in computer graphics. A matrix is just a two-dimensional grid containing numbers in every slot. Given two $n \times n$ matrices A and B, their product $C = A \times B$ is another $n \times n$ matrix, such that

$C_{ij} = $ inner product of A's row i with B's column j

which can be visualized as shown in Figure 1.1. A's row i and B's column j are called *vectors*—one-dimensional grids of numbers. The inner-product computation can be expressed as

$$C_{ij} = \sum_{k=1}^{n} A_{ik} \times B_{kj}$$

which can be visualized as shown in Figure 1.2, where we have laid B's column j on its side for clarity.

What can be computed in parallel, and what must be done sequentially? First, it should be clear from Figure 1.1 that each component of C is independent of all other components of C. Thus, we can compute C_{11} in parallel with C_{12} in parallel with C_{21} . . . and so on, that is, n^2 inner products in parallel. For example, if we put up the three matrices on a large blackboard and employed n^2 lieutenants, one per slot in C, each lieutenant could compute his assigned inner product independently of the others, after which he could walk up and write his answer in his assigned slot of C.

From Figure 1.2, it should be clear that all the multiplications can be done in parallel. However, the additions must be done sequentially because each addition needs the result of a previous one. In other words, each inner-product lieutenant could hire n ensigns to perform one multiplication each

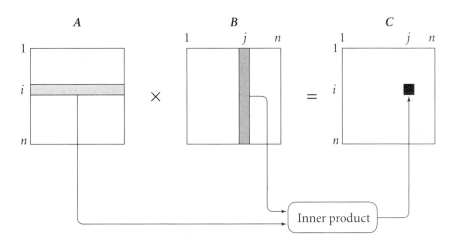

Figure 1.1 Matrix multiplication.

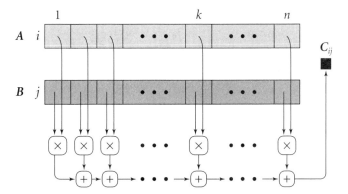

Figure 1.2 Inner product of two vectors.

and n ensigns to perform one addition each; all the multiplier ensigns would compute in parallel, but the plus ensigns would resemble a relay race.

There is more parallelism available if we recognize that "+" is associative, namely, that $(x + (y + z)) = ((x + y) + z)$—the order of the additions does not matter.[2] The new computation structure is shown in Figure 1.3.

---

2. Arithmetic in computers is often done with *floating-point* numbers, for which "+" is not associative, but let us ignore this problem for the moment.

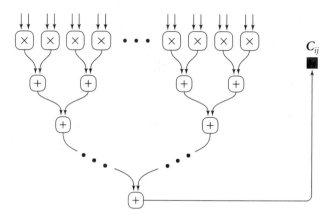

Figure 1.3 Tree summation in inner product.

The "+" ensigns, instead of being organized as a linear relay, are now organized as a tree. It is clear that all the "+" ensigns at the leaves of the tree (top row) can operate in parallel, after which all the "+" ensigns at the next level can operate in parallel, and so on until the ensign at the root of the tree produces the final sum. A little calculation shows that the N additions, instead of taking N steps, now take only $\log_2(N)$ steps (the height of the tree).

It turns out that there is another way to obtain parallelism, which is perhaps not so useful in this example, but we mention it here for completeness. By recognizing that "+" is also commutative, namely, that $(x + y) = (y + x)$, we could also structure the inner product as shown in Figure 1.4. Here, the lieutenant employs n ensigns to do the multiplications in parallel, as before. Meanwhile, the lieutenant keeps a running total, initially zero. He also keeps a tally of how many multiplication ensigns have checked in, initially zero. As each ensign finishes his multiplication, he sends a token to the lieutenant, reporting his result. The lieutenant adds it to his running total and increments his tally. When his tally reaches n, the lieutenant knows that all multiplication ensigns have been accounted for, and delivers the final total, which is C_{ij} (for which presumably he receives a token medal).

Observe that the additions occur in a nondeterministic order, as and when product tokens arrive. In both our previous versions of the inner product, the summation was deterministic. Now, the summation is again sequential because only one addition happens at a time. However, unlike

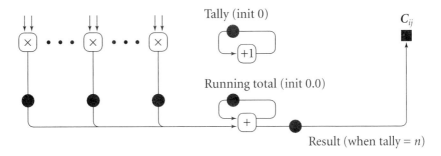

Figure 1.4   Nondeterministic summation in inner product.

the previous versions, if the multiplication ensigns took widely varying times (alas, in these days of voluntary service the quality of ensigns is very uneven), ensigns who are slow will not hold back the summation of products delivered by fast ensigns; in some situations, this may be preferable to the tree summation.

1.1.2   Matrix Multiplication in a Sequential Language

We have seen that matrix multiplication has abundant parallelism at the algorithmic level. Now let us consider a Fortran program for matrix multiplication. (The choice of Fortran here is unimportant; our discussion applies equally to C, C++, Pascal, and other languages.)

```
integer i, j, k
real A(N,N), B(N,N), C(N,N), s

do i = 1,N
    do j = 1,N
        s = 0.0
        do k = 1,N
            s = s + A(i,k) * B(k,j)
        end do
        C(i,j) = s
    end do
end do
```

This program is totally sequential: exactly one operation is performed at a time, as depicted schematically in the schedule below (imagine time flowing downwards):

```
i=1
    j=1
        s=0.0
            k=1
                s = s + A(1,1) * B(1,1)
            k=2
                s = s + A(1,2) * B(2,1)
                .
                .
                .


                .
                .
                .
            k=N
                s = s + A(1,N) * B(N,1)
                                        C(1,1) = s
    j=2
        s=0.0
            k=1
                s = s + A(1,1) * B(1,2)
            k=2
                s = s + A(1,2) * B(2,2)
                .
                .
                .
            k=N

                .
                .
                .
                s = s + A(1,N) * B(N,2)
                                        C(1,2) = s
    .
    .
    .
```

In other words, *while the abstract solution had abundant parallelism, we discarded it completely when we encoded it into a sequential programming language.*

So, what makes it difficult to execute our existing programs in parallel? The principal difficulty has to do with *state*, which manifests itself in the *reuse of storage*, which, in turn, leads to nondeterminism (or *races*) if executed in parallel. In our example program, the variable s initially contains 0.0, which is replaced by

(*current value of* s) + A(1,1) * B(1,1)

which, in turn, is replaced by

(*current value of* s) + A(1,2) * B(2,1)

and so on. In other words, s is a storage location into which we can read and write values. At any point in time, it contains the most recent value written. Languages that model state by reuse of storage are also known as *imperative* languages.

As long as our programming languages have this notion of state, it is not trivial to execute things in parallel. In our matrix multiplication program, suppose we indicate that the i and j loops should run in parallel (by using the popular doall notation):

```
integer i, j, k
real A(N,N), B(N,N), C(N,N), s

doall i = 1,N
    doall j = 1,N
        s = 0.0
        do k = 1,N
            s = s + A(i,k) * B(k,j)
        end do
        C(i,j) = s
    end do
end do
```

Conceptually, we now have the following computations running in parallel:

```
comment (i,j) = (1,1)              comment (i,j) = (1,2)
    s = 0.0                            s = 0.0
    do k = 1,N                         do k = 1,N
        s = s + A(1,k) * B(k,1)            s = s + A(1,k) * B(k,2)
    end do                             end do
    C(1,1) = s                         C(1,2) = s
```

and so on, for each of the N^2 combinations of (i, j). Unfortunately, there is a problem, called a *race* condition. Consider the simultaneous execution of the following two statements:

```
s = s + A(1,1) * B(1,1)    and    s = s + A(1,1) * B(1,2)
```

which occur in the apparently independent inner-product computations for C_{11} and C_{12}, respectively. Each statement reads a value from storage location s, adds a value to it, and stores it back. If the reads and writes from different parallel statements are interleaved arbitrarily, these statements will interfere with each other—they continually clobber each other's s values.

The values ultimately computed for matrix C are likely to be utterly wrong. Unfortunately, this error may not be easily detectable because the error may not be visually apparent (which of us could eyeball large A, B, and C matrices and recognize immediately that the product has been miscalculated?), or because the computation may be buried deep inside a large program and the error ultimately surfaces elsewhere. Debugging a program with a race condition is a nightmare because the aberrant behavior is often not reproducible, since it is so time dependent.

Suppose, instead, we had written our program this way:

```
integer i, j, k
real A(N,N), B(N,N), C(N,N)

doall i = 1,N
    doall j = 1,N
        C(i,j) = 0.0
        do k = 1,N
            C(i,j) = C(i,j) + A(i,k) * B(k,j)
        end do
    end do
end do
```

Here, we have eliminated the variable s and used C(i,j) itself as the location to hold the partial sum of the inner product. Now, our concurrent statements are

```
C(1,1) = C(1,1) + A(1,1) * B(1,1)      and
C(1,2) = C(1,2) + A(1,1) * B(1,2)
```

and there is no longer any interference—the two inner products use two separate locations to hold their partial sums, so there is no danger of them reading and writing each other's values.

This illustrates the difficulties encountered when concurrent computations simultaneously access a shared, updatable storage location. It also illustrates how sensitive the parallelism can be to the original coding style. In fact, a skilled programmer may well prefer the first version because a compiler would (1) find it easier to keep s in a register than C(i,j) and (2) find it easier to avoid repeated calculations of the address of C(i,j).

A powerful argument for sequential languages, therefore, is that the programmer does not have to worry about such race conditions—the sequential semantics of Fortran enforces a particular, easy-to-understand schedule on the reads and writes to shared locations. This enables the programmer to reason about the state manipulation behavior of programs and, for debugging, to reproduce the behavior of errant programs exactly.

1.2   How to Achieve Parallel Execution?

Since it is hazardous and nontrivial for a programmer to take an existing sequential program and simply annotate some parts of it (such as loops) to run in parallel, what alternatives are open to us? There are several approaches that have been or are being pursued.

One approach is automatic parallelization. We could retain existing sequential languages (for ease of programming and familiarity) and rely on an automatic system such as a compiler to analyze and transform our sequential programs *safely* into parallel ones—for example, to convert our original matrix multiplication program automatically into the final version. Because it is systematic, it would presumably not accidentally introduce race conditions the way a human might.

One popular variant of this approach is to make parallelization relatively easy for the compiler by providing "data parallel" extensions in an existing sequential language. These primitives package up common paradigms for manipulating large data collections such as arrays.

Another possibility is explicit parallelism. We could shift the burden of specifying parallel execution to the programmer. There are two major approaches:

- *Shared-memory programming with parallel threads and locks:* We could ask the programmer to specify what should be executed in parallel (like our doall loop above), but we could give the programmer tools and methodologies that permit manipulation of shared state in a disciplined way, thereby preventing unwanted race conditions.
- *Message-passing:* We could move to a radically different model of parallelism, where a parallel program consists of N totally independent, conventional, sequential programs, augmented with communication primitives that allow them to send messages to each other. Since the N programs are independent, they never directly manipulate each

other's state. (However, it is still possible to have race conditions because a processor can indirectly read and write locations in another processor by sending it messages requesting it to do so.)

A third option open to us is implicit parallelism, using state-free or declarative languages. We could pursue programming notations that avoid the notion of state entirely, thereby avoiding parallelization problems. After all, the mathematical description of matrix multiplication says nothing about state; it was only our encoding into a programming notation that introduced it—perhaps we could move to programming notations that are closer to mathematical notation. A related question is, Are such state-free notations adequate to express all programming tasks?

And, of course, we could attempt a mixture of these approaches. The rest of this chapter outlines all these approaches. We will end with a discussion of *pH*, which may be regarded as a mixture of two approaches: it is predominantly a declarative language (in fact, a *functional language*), but it also permits disciplined use of shared state when necessary.

1.3   Automatic Parallelization of Sequential Programs

The goal of taking programs in traditional sequential programming languages and converting them automatically into parallel programs has been pursued by researchers since the early 1970s. That goal remains elusive; however, the insights, terminology, and technology that emerged from that research have proven to be quite valuable.

We start by developing a deeper understanding of how reuse of storage prevents parallel execution. Consider the following sequence of assignment statements:

```
x = a + b              % S₁
```
$\quad\quad$ % S_1

```
y = 2 * x              % S₂
```
$\quad\quad$ % S_2

```
x = a - b              % S₃
```
$\quad\quad$ % S_3

```
print(x+y)             % S₄
```
$\quad\quad$ % S_4

We focus on the variable x. Statements S_1 and S_3 are called *defs* of x (for *definitions*), and statements S_2 and S_4 are called *uses* of x.

We say that there is a true *data dependence* from S_1 to S_2 and from S_3 to S_4 due to x (this is also called a *flow dependence* or *def-use dependence*). In each case, a value is communicated (via x) from one statement to the next, and so, clearly S_1 must be executed before S_2, and S_3 must be executed before S_4.

Consider S_2 and S_3: there is no value being communicated, but, since x is being reused, we must execute them in order so that S_2 reads the old value of x before S_3 clobbers it with a new value. This situation, where no value is communicated, but where statements must still be ordered because of reuse of storage, is called an *antidependence* (or a *use-def dependence*). Similarly, there is also the notion of a *def-def dependence* (or *output dependence*), but we need not explore that further here. The fourth case (*use-use*) is clearly not a problem for parallelism.

It is important to note that an antidependence can be eliminated by introducing new storage locations. For example, we can change our program fragment so that S_3 uses a new variable z instead (and we also have to change S_4 correspondingly):

```
x = a + b               % S₁

y = 2 * x               % S₂

z = a − b               % S₃

print(z+y)              % S₄
```

Now, S_3 is no longer restricted to follow S_2, or even S_1, for that matter. By eliminating antidependencies, we obtain more parallelism. In fact, this was exactly what happened in our matrix multiplication program—the conflict on variable s was an antidependency, and by eliminating it (by replacing s with C(i,j)), we obtained more parallelism.

This method is known in the literature as *renaming*. We can now phrase our question more technically: Is it possible for a compiler to take a sequential program and automatically perform renaming transformations to convert it into a parallel program?

In order to do this, a compiler would first have to identify all antidependencies. This seems trivial in our four-line program fragment above, but it gets very complicated when we encounter *aliasing*—the fact that the same storage location may be referred to by syntactically distinct names. For example, let us package our four-line fragment into a larger context:[3]

```
subroutine foo(x,z, a,b)
x = a + b              % S₁
y = 2 * x              % S₂
z = a - b              % S₃
print(z+y)             % S₄
end


program bar
call foo(w,w, 6.001, 6.002)
stop
end
```

Now, variables x and z actually refer to the same location (corresponding to w) in the main program, and we have our antidependency all over again.[4] Note that the antidependence may not exist for other calls, such as

```
call foo(v,w, 6.003, 6.004)
```

where v and w are distinct variables. It gets even more complicated when variable locations are *computed*, as in indexed arrays:

```
program glurph
real U(10)     % (U is an array of 10 elements)
   .
   .
   .
read(i,j)
call foo(U(i), U(j), 6.003, 6.004)
   .
   .
   .
```

---

3. For those more familiar with C, the subroutine header and the call correspond to

```
void function foo(float *x, float *z, float a, float b)
```

and

```
foo(&w, &w, 6.001, 6.002);
```

respectively, and instances of x and z in the subroutine body need to be replaced by *x and *z, respectively. For those more familiar with Pascal, the subroutine header is

```
Procedure foo(var x, z: real; a, b: real)
```

4. Technically, it is illegal in Fortran to pass duplicate parameters like this, but compilers typically do not enforce this. In any case, our point still stands because there are many other ways for aliasing to occur.

Now, the antidependence exists if $i = j$, and since these values are read from the input during program execution, the compiler has no hope of deciding the issue. Or, consider this context:

```
do i = 1,10
    do j = 1,10
        call foo(U(i), U(j), 6.003, 6.004)
    end do
end do
```

Here, the antidependence occurs only in 10 percent of the iterations (whenever $i = j$). But, to be conservative, the compiler must assume the antidependence, and force S_3 to be sequenced after S_2. One might imagine that the compiler produces two versions of the body of foo, one sequential and the other parallel; at the entry to foo, it could insert code that will test for aliasing and invoke the appropriate body. However, note that this test would be executed a hundred times, once per call to foo, which is a significant overhead.

The last example also introduces the idea that, in general, the compiler has to perform *subscript analysis* to recognize dependences. For example, in this loop,

```
do i = 1,N
    do j = 2,N
        Q(i,j) = P(j) + Q(i,j-1)
    end do
end do
```

the compiler would have to realize that there is a dependence from one *j* iteration to the next, but not from one *i* iteration to the next (so, the *i* iterations can be executed in parallel, but within each such iteration, the *j* loop must execute sequentially). Further, *loop transformations* can sometimes eliminate dependences. For example,

```
s = 0.0
do 10 i = 1,N
    P(i) = s
    s = s + 5.0
end do
```

appears to be a sequential loop because there is a dependence on s from one iteration to the next, but the loop can be transformed, using a technique called *induction variable analysis*, which recognizes that s "tracks" i; that is, it is a function of i. Here is a transformed version of the loop:

```
do i = 1,N
    P(i) = (i-1) * 5.0
end do
s = N * 5.0
```

Now, there is no dependence from one iteration to the next, and the iterations can be executed in parallel.

Subscript analysis, and aliasing detection in general, are *undecidable problems;* that is, a compiler can only hope to obtain approximate information and must conservatively assume the worst whenever the information is inexact. For example, if a compiler cannot prove that x and y point to different objects, then it must assume that they may point to the same object. Despite over two decades of research on this topic (which originally began with so called "vectorizing compilers"), the goal of automatic parallelization has been achieved only on programs with relatively simple structure (simple loops containing matrix computations with simple index expressions; this includes matrix multiplication). In fact, one of the effects of this research has been that, instead of training compilers to recognize parallelism in arbitrary programs, *it has trained people to write programs conforming to the structured parallelism that compilers can recognize automatically.*

The problem is even more difficult for arrays with complex index structures, such as sparse matrix computations, and for other data structures such as trees, graphs, and queues that are common in nonnumerical, symbolic programs. The additional difficulty arises because the data structures are often dynamically allocated (and so, not directly visible to the compiler), often recursive, and rife with shared (aliased) substructures. Instead of subscript analysis, one needs some kind of "path analysis" to keep track of paths through chains of links between data structures and, in some sense, to approximate at compile time the structure of the complex data structure that will be built at run time. Research in this area is still in its infancy, and there are many who believe that the problem is intractable. One promising new approach is "commutativity analysis" [56], which takes advantage of the encapsulation of state provided in object-oriented languages. Because of this encapsulation, the only code that can modify a particular object is in the methods of that object. The basic idea of the analysis is to look at the methods associated with an object and see if they commute pairwise, that is, if a method call f followed by a method call g is equivalent to g followed by f. If they commute, the methods can be called in parallel instead of sequentially.

1.4 ▼   Data Parallel Programming Languages

Data parallel languages are typically sequential languages extended with constructs that, by definition, permit parallel operations on large homogeneous collections of data. The principal examples today are Fortran 90 and High Performance Fortran (HPF) [29].

Consider the assignment statement

```
A = B + C
```

When A, B, and C are integers or floating-point numbers, this statement has the usual meaning. However, in Fortran 90, this statement has a different meaning if the variables were vectors, for example, declared as follows:

```
REAL, DIMENSION(1:100) :: A, B, C
```

Now, the meaning of the assignment statement is, for all $1 \le i \le 100$, A[i] = B[i] + C[i], that is, a complete vector addition. Or, suppose C was a scalar:

```
REAL C
REAL, DIMENSION(1:100) :: A, B
```

Then the meaning of the assignment statement is to execute 100 assignments of the form A[i] = B[i] + C. Conceptually one can think of C as being promoted to a vector containing 100 copies of its value, followed by a vector addition.

These concepts generalize to multiple dimensions—the variables may, in general, be n-dimensional matrices, and lower-dimensional variables are automatically promoted to higher dimensions before performing the element-wise operations.

The assignment statements can be more sophisticated in picking which elements of an array are involved. For example:

```
A(4:100:2) = B(1:49) + 1.0
```

Here, the first 49 elements of B are selected, and incremented values are stored into A[4], A[6], . . . , A[100] (the remaining locations of A are untouched).

In data parallel assignment statements, all the element-wise computations can be done in parallel. This is *by definition*, and not merely an observation inferred by reasoning about the statements. The following example illustrates the subtlety:

```
A(1:99) = A(2:100) - 1
```

Consider two of the element-wise assignments involved: `A[1] = A[2] - 1` and `A[2] = A[3] - 1`. The first one reads `A[2]` and the second one writes `A[2]`. If executed in parallel without care, there is a race condition—the first statement may read the old or the new value of `A[2]`, depending on how things are scheduled. The language definition eliminates this ambiguity by defining the semantics of the statement as (conceptually) performing *all* reads on the right-hand sides before *any* of the writes on the left-hand sides. In the general case, the implementation may have to allocate temporary storage for all the results before doing any of the final assignments to the left-hand side array, for example, transform the above assignment into

```
REAL, DIMENSION(1:99) :: TEMP

TEMP(1:99) = A(2:100) - 1
A          = TEMP
```

A clever compiler may of course avoid introducing such temporary storage for a particular assignment statement if it sees that there is no danger of a race (as in the assignment statements earlier in this section).

In addition to these data parallel assignments, Fortran 90 also has data parallel loops (which may contain several assignment statements) and a variety of operators to perform reduction operations on arrays, such as finding the sum of elements in an array, or the maximum element, and so on. Since these operators are primitives, they may be implemented by the compiler using parallel algorithms—the programmer is essentially specifying the parallelism at a very high level, leaving it up to the compiler to manage all the tedious coding details.

Fortran 90 was originally developed for *vector supercomputers*, machines with hardware support to perform element-wise operations on arrays in parallel. However, nowadays the more common computing workhorses are clusters and multicomputers, which are distributed memory machines. In such machines it is very important to have a good *data distribution*—a partitioning of the data into pieces that are distributed across the individual computers of the parallel machine. A bad distribution can result in a lot of communication, and, since communication is quite expensive in these machines, this results in poor performance.

HPF was developed to address this problem. It extends Fortran 90 with directives by which the user can specify how an array is to be partitioned across a parallel machine and how pieces of different arrays are to be "aligned," or colocated. For example,

```
REAL,  DIMENSION(100,100) :: A, B

!HPF$  ALIGN A(I,J) with B(J,I)

!HPF$  PROCESSORS P(4)

!HPF$  DISTRIBUTE  A(BLOCK, *) ONTO P
```

The second line specifies that for $1 \leq i \leq 100$, $1 \leq j \leq 100$, each element A_{ij} should be on the same processor as B_{ji}. The third line specifies that conceptually there are four processors. The last line specifies that the rows of A should be distributed in *blocks* over the four processors. In particular, the chunk $A_{1,1}$ through $A_{25,100}$ should be on processor P_1, the chunk $A_{26,1}$ through $A_{50,100}$ should be on processor P_2, the chunk $A_{51,1}$ through $A_{75,100}$ should be on processor P_3 and the chunk $A_{76,1}$ through $A_{100,100}$ should be on processor P_4. By the ALIGN directive, this, in turn, places requirements on how B should be distributed. This is illustrated in Figure 1.5.

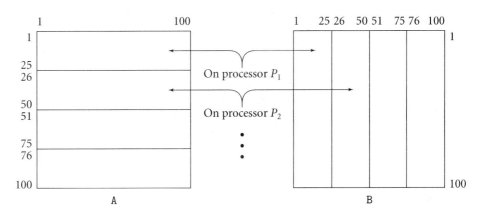

Figure 1.5 HPF array layouts.

From this programmer-supplied information, an HPF compiler does two things. First, it decides how to distribute work across the processors. For example, given an assignment statement

```
A = A + 1
```

it may decide to perform the 2500 assignments for $A_{1,1}$ through $A_{25,100}$ on processor P_1, the 2500 assignments for the next chunk on processor P_2, and so on.

Second, it decides what communication, if any, is necessary and generates the necessary code. In the above assignment statement, no communication at all is necessary since, for each assignment, both the left- and right-hand side data are always on the same processor. However, consider

```
A(1:100,1:99) = A(1:100,2:100) + 1

A(1:99,1:100) = A(2:100,1:100) + 1
```

The first statement, again, needs no communication, but the second one does. For example, consider any element assignment A(25,j) = A(26,j) + 1. The right-hand side element is on processor P_2, whereas the left-hand side is on processor P_1. Consequently, every element in row 26 needs to be communicated from processor P_2 to processor P_1.

HPF compilers detect such communication requirements and typically generate appropriate message-passing code. In fact, they typically go further and try to produce a single send-receive of the entire 26th row of 100 elements, rather than 100 individual sends and receives, since the former is typically much cheaper on most multicomputers (less fixed overhead).

Choosing a good data distribution is not easy. In one part of the computation, it may be appropriate to align A with B in one particular way; in another part of the computation, another alignment may be better. A good alignment of A with B may suggest one distribution across processors, whereas a good alignment of A with C may suggest another. Arrays may be redistributed dynamically to alleviate such conflicting requirements, but redistribution is not free and its cost has to be weighed against not redistributing but paying more for communication somewhere else. Many researchers are skeptical that such *data distribution optimization* can be done manually by programmers and are working hard to devise automated means to insert HPF data distribution annotations into plain Fortran 90 code.

Although HPF and Fortran 90 are the principal examples of data parallel programming languages, the same ideas can of course be embedded in other languages. For example, the language Split-C is a data parallel programming language from the University of California at Berkeley and is an extension of C [19]. It is a lower-level language because, unlike HPF, the programmer is aware of separate threads executing on different processors and of the distinction between local data (on the same computer as a thread) and global data (on a different computer). The language NESL is a purpose-built data parallel language from Carnegie-Mellon University allowing nested data parallelism [14].

We close this section by noting that this style of data parallel programming only addresses a certain class of applications, namely, those based on dense rectangular arrays with simple, nested loop parallelism. Like automatic parallelization in general, these methods are not very appropriate for applications based on sparse matrices or those based on other data structures such as trees and graphs.

1.5 Explicit Parallelism: Shared-Memory Programming with Threads and Locks

A well-known method for parallel programming is to extend a sequential language with *threads*. These may be regarded as multiple sequential programs that have the same view of all data—two threads may hold the address of the same variable, and they both access the contents of the variable with the standard notations for variable access. Local variables of a procedure invocation in one thread are private, or inaccessible to other threads, in much the same way that each recursive invocation of a procedure in a sequential program refers to its own copy of local variables.

1.5.1 Threads

One notation to express creation of a new thread replaces a function call with a **fork**:

F(i)   replaced by   **fork** F(i)

When the machine encounters a normal procedure call, it suspends execution at that point, executes F to completion, returns, and continues execution of the sequel. When the machine encounters a **fork**, on the other

hand, it simultaneously executes F and the sequel. The two threads are
called the "parent" and "child" threads, respectively. For example, we could
express a parallel loop as follows (we switch from Fortran to C notation, because thread-and-lock-based programming is more common in C than in
Fortran):

```
int main (...)
{
    float A[N];

    for (i = 0; i < N; i++) {
        fork BODY(i, A);
    }
    .
    .
    .
}

void BODY (int i, float A[])
{
    A[i] = f(A[i]);
}
```

At the end of the for loop, we have *N* child threads running in parallel, executing BODY(0,A), . . . , BODY(N–1,A), respectively. Each one, in parallel,
computes with one element of A. Note that each thread has its copy of i,
but, because of C's procedure call semantics, A refers to the same array for
all of them.

A fundamental problem with explicit threads is the choice of *thread
granularity;* that is, where should the programmer place **fork** calls for
maximum advantage? The cost of a **fork** is typically hundreds to thousands of times the cost of a procedure call. If the program generates too
many threads, it may slow down because of the overhead of thread creation
and context switching between threads. If the program generates too few
threads, then processors may remain idle. In many programs, particularly
recursive programs, it is difficult for the programmer to find the right balance by placing **fork**s in just the right places. The task is complicated by
the fact that the right placement may depend on input data, it may depend
on the number of processors in the machine on which the program is run,
it may depend on the other load on those processors, and so on; there is
no single "correct" solution. Programmers sometimes deal with this issue
by writing all kinds of conditional code that, at run time, chooses between

a **fork** or an ordinary procedure call based on querying the load on the system. This greatly obscures the original clarity of the program.

1.5.2 Locks

When there is a danger of a race condition, data that is shared by multiple threads is usually protected by a *lock* data structure: a thread acquires the lock, manipulates the shared data, and then releases the lock. When a thread tries to acquire a lock, the implementation forces it to wait if the lock is currently held by another thread. When the lock is released, only one of possibly many waiting threads is allowed to acquire it. This ensures that the shared data is not simultaneously manipulated by multiple threads and so there are no race conditions. Normally, only one thread may hold the lock at a time, although there are many variations: for example, read-write locks permit many threads that merely read the shared data to hold the lock simultaneously, while any thread that updates the shared data must acquire the lock exclusively.

Let us illustrate the use of locks by extending the above example. In the above code, the parent thread has no way of knowing when the child threads have completed; the loop simply forks the child threads and the parent goes on. Thus, the parent does not know when it is safe to assume that all the new values in A are ready. One solution is to have a counter, initialized to N, that is decremented by each loop iteration when it has completed its work. The parent thread, observing the counter drop to zero, infers that all child threads have completed and that A is ready.

```
int main (...)
{
    float A[N];
    int counter = N;

    for (i = 0; i < N; i++) {
        fork BODY(i, A, & counter);
    }
    .
    .
    .
    while (counter > 0) { /* spin */ };
    .
    .   Now, A is ready
    .
}
```

```
void BODY(int i, float A[], int *counter)
{
    A[i]     = f(A[i]);
    *counter = *counter - 1;
}
```

Unfortunately, there is a race condition: each thread, in trying to decrement the counter, reads it, subtracts one, and stores it. Now, it is possible that two threads simultaneously read it, subtract one, and store it. In this case the counter, instead of being decremented by two, is only decremented by one. The counter will thus never reach zero and the parent thread will be stuck in its spin loop.

Things could be even worse. Depending on the processor architecture and the compiler, the counter-decrement statement of BODY may not compile into a single read followed by a single write. For example, counter may have a 4-byte representation, and the compiler may produce two 2-byte reads and two 2-byte writes. If these finer-granularity operations from different threads are interleaved, there could be even more possibilities for the actual value stored and read in the counter variable.

We introduce a lock to avoid this:

```
int main (...)
{
    float A[N];
    int counter = N;
    lock   lk;

    for (i = 0; i < N; i++) {
        fork BODY(i, A, & counter, & lk);
    }
    :
    :   May do other work, unrelated to A
    :
    while (counter > 0) { /* spin */ };
    :
    :   Now, A is ready for use
    :
}

void BODY(int i, float A[], int *counter, lock *lk)
{
    A[i]     = f(A[i]);
    wait(lk);                           acquire the lock
    *counter = *counter - 1;
    signal(lk);                         release the lock
}
```

The lock operations ensure that the entire read-decrement-write sequence of the enclosed statement is performed in its entirety by one thread before another thread can attempt it. This eliminates the race condition.

Threads (or processes, or tasks) and locks have been used for parallel programming for decades. They were originally developed for operating systems, even on uniprocessor machines, in order to express computations that are conceptually if not physically parallel. For example, an operating system must "simultaneously" execute many users' programs, as well as respond to unpredictable events from disks, networks, printers, terminals, and so on. This is most easily expressed as a parallel program, even though the threads may be time-multiplexed on a single processor.

While threads and locks have long been used in operating systems, they started becoming visible in users' programs since the early 1980s when so-called bus-based shared-memory multiprocessors started becoming available. In these machines, a small number of processors (typically less than a dozen) are plugged into a common bus sharing a common memory system. Users could now write parallel programs that ran faster because they actually ran in parallel on multiple processors, without time-multiplexing.

1.5.3 Higher-Level Constructs for Shared-Memory Programming

Coordinating the interaction of parallel threads (e.g., by protecting shared data with locks) is called *synchronization* of a parallel program. It is somewhat tricky to be convinced that a thread-based parallel program has adequate synchronization. For example, a purist may complain that access to the counter in the spin loop (`while`) in the parent thread has not been protected by lock acquisition. Fortunately, in this case, the omission is benign; since the loop only reads the counter, and since the counter value decrements monotonically from N down to zero, reading a zero value is still a correct guarantee that the child processes have completed.[5] In

---

5. Actually, some C compilers perform "optimizations" that may prevent the parent thread from *ever* reading zero! Because reading the `counter` variable is not protected by a lock, some C compilers might feel free to make a copy of `counter` that is "closer" to the parent thread (e.g., in a register or some other nearby memory). In this case, the decrements down to zero are never seen in the local copy. Declaring the variable `counter` to be `volatile` can sometimes prevent this behavior.

general, however, all accesses to shared data should be protected by lock acquisition.

To prevent inadvertent synchronization errors, many languages provide higher-level constructs to package up common parallel paradigms. For example, the paradigm of executing iterations of a loop in parallel and waiting for all iterations to complete (also called a *barrier*) is so common that some languages introduce a special parallel loop construct (we first saw this in Section 1.1.2):

```
doall i = 1, N
    A(i) = f(A(i))
end do
```

The compiler now manages all the details and will often use a more sophisticated and efficient barrier implementation than the simple counter described above.

Another common language construct is the *monitor* [30]. Here, the programmer declares a shared data structure along with a collection of procedures to manipulate it. The data structure is not directly visible to the rest of the program, so it can only be manipulated by calling the monitor procedures. The compiler ensures that these procedures implicitly acquire a lock on entry when they are called and release the lock on exit just before returning, ensuring one-at-a-time access to the shared data. This approach to structured synchronization is used in the language Modula [77], in the POSIX threads extensions to C and Fortran [33], and most recently in *synchronized methods* in Java [8].

Another popular language construct is the *future* (for example, in the language Multilisp [28]). In parallel programs, we often encounter the following scenario: we wish to fork a function, which will ultimately return some result, but we do not need the result immediately, since there is other useful work to be done before we need the result. However, when we eventually do need the result, we need some way of waiting for it, since it may not be ready yet. Futures are a notation to express this. For example, suppose we want a program that recursively traverses a binary tree, adding up some integer information available at each tree node. We can express this using futures, as follows:

```
typedef struct tree {
    int info;
    struct tree *left, *right; } *treeptr;
```

```
int tree_Add(treeptr  tp)
{
    future int x;
    int        y;

    if (tp == NULL)
        return 0;
    else {
        future x = tree_Add (tp->left);
        y        = tree_Add (tp->right);
        return touch (x) + y + tp->info;
    }
}
```

The declaration `future int x` conceptually declares x to be an integer together with a lock that is initially in the locked state. If the tree is not empty, the `future` call forks a call to traverse the left subtree. This forked call will ultimately deliver its integer result into the integer component of x and signal the lock indicating that the x is ready. Meanwhile, the parent thread goes on to traverse the right subtree. Note that this happens recursively at every level of the tree and so it can generate threads exponentially. After the right subtree's value has been computed (y), we wait for the result x by executing `touch(x)`, which waits for the lock to be signaled and then returns the integer value in x. This is combined into the final answer and returned.

Constructs like `doall`, monitors, and futures make it easier to write robust parallel programs because they hide the details of lock manipulation completely; one is less likely to forget inadvertently to protect shared data access with suitable lock operations.

Recently, two languages, Jade [57] and Cilk [15], have gone further. Both rely on programmer annotations to indicate what can be executed in parallel, but both provide a guarantee that parallel execution is faithful to the semantics of sequential execution (where the parallelism annotations are ignored). This is a powerful guarantee because it allows one to debug the program in sequential mode using standard tools. In Jade, the programmer specifies that a section of code can be executed in parallel (analagous to forking it), but must also declare what data is accessed by the section and how (read or write). This declaration is executable, so that it can handle dynamic data structures. The run-time system checks that data accesses by the parallel code indeed conform to the declarations and introduces all the synchronization necessary to preserve the sequential semantics. Cilk provides extensions to C for forking threads and to wait for their completion. A thread-fork is basically an annotation on a procedure call. This induces a certain precedence between the parallel activities of a program— it is a *directed acyclic graph* (DAG) or partial order. The scheduler in Cilk's run-time system is carefully designed so that threads access memory according to this partial order, preserving the sequential semantics.

1.6 ▾   Explicit Parallelism: Message-Passing

So far, we have seen that automatic parallelization of sequential programs is hard because precise dependence analysis is hard; data parallel programming languages have a limited application space and choosing good data distributions is hard; and programming with explictly parallel threads and locks is difficult because it is hard to avoid races.

The message-passing model for parallel programming consists of a collection of conventional sequential programs that can communicate by sending and receiving messages. This model is popular because it closely mirrors many parallel machines available today, called "multicomputers" and "clusters," which consist of a collection of conventional computers each of which contains an input-output device that is connected to a shared network. Each computer is either a traditional uniprocessor or a small SMP (symmetric multiprocessor), typically with four processors or less. Some multicomputers have been designed as parallel machines and have very sophisticated, fast interconnection networks, but even a collection of workstations on a local-area network—a configuration found in most offices today—can be regarded as a multicomputer.

In a multicomputer, since each computer (or *node*) is independent, a program on node Nd_2 has no way directly to read a variable x on node Nd_1. Instead, node Nd_1 can *communicate* the value in variable x to node Nd_2. The program on node Nd_1 executes

```
send(Nd₂, x)
```

while the program on node Nd_2 executes

```
receive(Nd₁, y)
```

as a result of which a chunk of data is effectively copied from variable x in node Nd_1 into variable y in node Nd_2. For the moment, think of send as depositing a message into the network, which will ultimately be delivered to the recipient; in particular, after executing send, a node in the multicomputer can continue to compute, even though the recipient may not yet have attempted to execute receive. These are called "nonblocking" or "asynchronous" sends (we will discuss this issue in Section 1.6.2). The receive call is blocking; that is, execution waits at that statement until a message is actually received.

1.6.1 Matrix Multiplication with Message-Passing

Let us reconsider matrix multiplication of $n \times n$ matrices. Assume that our multicomputer has exactly $n \times n$ nodes, and assume that the (i, j)th node contains the variables A_{ij}, B_{ij}, and C_{ij}, as shown in Figure 1.6. One could

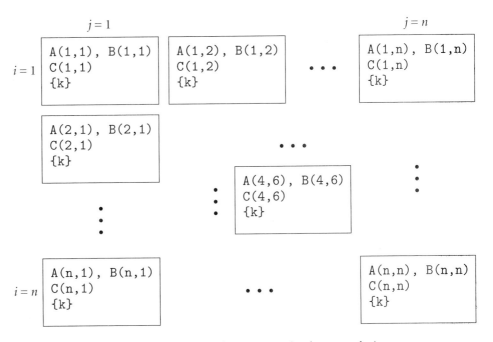

Figure 1.6 Layout of matrices in a multicomputer (each rectangle is a separate computer).

imagine that each node computes an inner product; let us concentrate on
the node $(4, 6)$:

```
private real k      % (each node has a private variable k)
C(4,6) = 0.0
do k = 1,n
     C(4,6) = C(4,6) + A(4,k) * B(k,6)
end do
```

Unfortunately, in the message-passing model, this node $(4, 6)$ cannot directly access components that it needs: `A(4,1)`, `B(1,6)`, `A(4,2)`,
`B(2,6)`, . . . So, the system is organized as in Figure 1.7. Every node has
variables called `aij` and `bij`, which we assume have been preloaded with
the appropriate matrix components, and variable `cij`, which will contain C_{ij} after the matrix multiplication. Each node also has variables `my_i`
and `my_j`, which we assume have been preloaded with the node's indices. Finally, assume that each node contains two $1 \times n$ vectors called `ai`
and `bj`.

We assume that nodes can communicate as shown in the figure; that is,
node (i, j) communicates with nodes $(i - 1, j)$, $(i + 1, j)$, $(i, j - 1)$, and
$(i, j + 1)$, which we will henceforth abbreviate as up, down, left, and right,
respectively. We assume the communication "wraps around" at the edges
so that, for example, the "up neighbor" of a node in the top row is the corresponding node in the same column in the bottom row. It is important
to be aware that this does not mean that the machine's physical communication network has this two-dimensional topology, just that nodes are
capable of communicating in this pattern. In general, a machine's physical
network topology has very little to do with a program's abstract communication patterns.

The first thing we do is to collect, in each node, a copy of its entire row of
matrix A, using the vector `ai`. Here is the code (all nodes execute this code
simultaneously):

```
j     = my_j
ai(j) = aij

do jj = 1, n-1
     send(left, ai(j))
     j = j + 1
     if (j.gt.n) j = 1
```

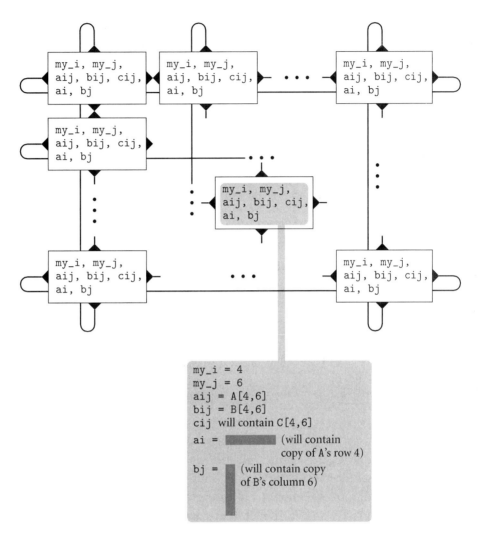

Figure 1.7 Multicomputer matrix multiplication, local memories only.

```
        receive(right, ai(j))
    end do
```

The net effect is to "slide" matrix A to the left (with wraparound at the edge). Each node, when it receives a component of A from its east, deposits it into the right slot of ai. In particular, node (i, j) receives $A_{i,j+1}$, $A_{i,j+2}$, $A_{i,j+3}$, ... in turn.

Similarly, we can slide matrix B upward (with wraparound at the edge). As each node receives a component of B from below, it is incorporated into bj. In particular, node (i, j) receives $B_{i+1,j}$, $B_{i+2,j}$, $B_{i+3,j}$, ... in turn. Here is the code (all nodes execute this code simultaneously):

```
i = my_i
bj(i) = bij

do ii = 1, n-1
    send(up, bj(i))
    i = i + 1
    if (i.gt.n) i = 1
    receive(down, bj(i))
end do
```

At this point, the (i, j)th node contains, in its ai and bi variables, the ith row of A and jth column of B. It can now perform the inner product (for which no communication is needed—it is a purely local computation):

```
cij = 0.0
do k = 1,n
    cij = cij + ai(k) * bj(k)
end do
```

The cijs now represent the desired result matrix.

Message-Passing Matrix Multiplication, Version 2

If one regards communication as the dominant time-consuming operation (as indeed was the case in first-generation parallel machines), then our program takes about $2N$ time steps: N steps in each of the two loops that shifted A and B. In fact, they can be performed together in a single loop:

```
i      = my_i
bj(i) = bij

j      = my_j
ai(j) = aij

do iijj = 1, n-1
    send(up, bj(i))
    send(left, ai(j))
    i = i + 1
    if (i.gt.n) i = 1
    j = j + 1
```

```
        if (j.gt.n) j = 1
        receive(down, bj(i))
        receive(right, ai(j))
    end do
```

Assuming that the two sends upward and leftward take place in parallel, this combined loop takes only N communication time steps.

A small optimization can replace the two vectors ai and bj in each node by a single vector ab. We initialize all components to 1.0. For each value received from the south, the node multiplies it into ab(i). For each value received from the east, the node multiplies it into ab(j). At the end of the communication phase, ab will contain all the individual products in the inner product. These can now be summed for the final value of C_{ij}.

Message-Passing Matrix Multiplication, Version 3

The matrix multiply programs still use storage proportional to n^3, since there are n^2 nodes and each node contains a vector or two of size n. A very clever optimization that reduces this down to n^2 storage is possible if we observe that the additions in the inner product can be performed in a different order without changing the final result of the computation.

We first show the solution and then convince ourselves that it is correct. To avoid getting buried in subscripts and ellipses, we will work specifically with 4×4 matrices. Figure 1.8 shows the initial configuration. This configuration can always be achieved from that of Figure 1.7 by writing a prelude that rotates the four rows of A to the left by 0, 1, 2, and 3 steps, respectively, and rotates the four columns of B upward by 0, 1, 2, and 3, respectively. Each node now executes the following code:

```
cij = aij * bij
do k = 1, n-1
    send(left, aij)
    send(up, bij)
    receive(right, aij)
    receive(down, bij)
    cij = cij + aij * bij
end do
```

To convince ourselves that this works, let us focus on the node computing C_{23} (highlighted in the figure). Initially,

```
cij = A₂₄  ×  B₄₃
```
$$\text{cij} = A_{24} \times B_{43}$$

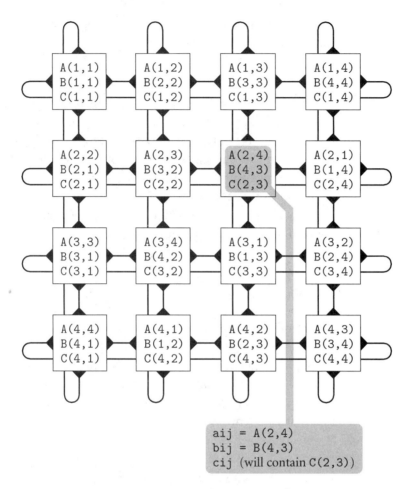

Figure 1.8 Multicomputer matrix multiplication, n^2 storage.

In the first iteration of the loop, we slide all A values left and all B values up. So, this node receives A_{21} and B_{13} from the right and below, respectively, and the next partial sum is

cij = $(A_{24} \times B_{43}) + (A_{21} \times B_{13})$

In the next iteration, the node receives A_{22} and B_{23} from the right and below, respectively, and the next partial sum is

cij = $(A_{24} \times B_{43}) + (A_{21} \times B_{13}) + (A_{22} \times B_{23})$

In the final iteration, the node receives A_{23} and B_{33} from the right and below, respectively, and the final sum is

$$\text{cij} = (A_{24} \times B_{43}) + (A_{21} \times B_{13}) + (A_{22} \times B_{23}) + (A_{23} \times B_{33})$$

which is clearly the same as the inner product, which is usually written with the summands in the following order:

$$C_{23} = A_{21} \times B_{13} + A_{22} \times B_{23} + A_{23} \times B_{33} + A_{24} \times B_{43}$$

$$= \sum_{k=1}^{4} A_{2k} \times B_{k3}$$

This solution is sometimes called a "systolic" solution, because its behavior suggests the pumping of the heart: all nodes communicate, then compute, then communicate, then compute, and so on.[6]

1.6.2 Communication Issues and Their Effect on Programming

Multicomputer systems have many variations in the semantics of communication. One aspect is synchronicity. At one extreme, even if node Nd_1 attempts to send a message very early, it is not allowed to proceed until node Nd_2 attempts to receive. This is called "synchronous communication," or "blocking sends," and is analogous to handing a letter directly in person to someone—if that person is not ready yet, we have to wait. At the other extreme, node Nd_1 can send a message at any time and proceed, with the network undertaking to transport and hold on to the message until Nd_2 eventually tries to receive it. This is called "asynchronous communication," or "nonblocking sends," and is analogous to a pipe of unbounded capacity through which we send letters to the addressee. In between these extremes, the network may bound the number of messages allowed in transit between nodes to some threshold c. Nd_1 can send up to c messages before other nodes attempt to consume them; however, any attempt to send more messages will cause Nd_1 to block until other nodes drain the network by receiving messages.

In the program examples above, we assumed asynchronous communications. Suppose, instead, the network only allowed one message to be

---

6. It is also sometimes called the "just in time," or "kan-ban," or "zero inventory" solution!

in transit between nodes; once a node has done a send, it cannot do another send until the first message has been consumed by a receive. Unfortunately, our program will get stuck (or *deadlock*): every node sends to the left and then tries sending upward, but since no node is yet trying to receive from the right, none of the original leftward sends can complete, and all the nodes will wait forever. So, we have to rewrite our program as follows:

```
cij = aij * bij
do k = 1, n-1
    send(left, aij)
    receive(right, aij)
    send(up, bij)
    receive(down, bij)
    cij = cij + aij * bij
end do
```

and this solves the problem.

Other variations in network properties include whether two consecutive messages sent from Nd_1 to Nd_2 will arrive in the same order; whether messages are always delivered (or sometimes lost); whether they are sometimes duplicated; whether they are sometimes corrupted (for example, a message transmitted via a modem over a phone line or over a satellite link is often corrupted), and so on. Another concern is protection—if two independent parallel programs are running simultaneously on the same parallel machine, some mechanism is necessary to ensure that one program's messages are not delivered to the other program and vice versa. Most of these variations are architecture specific and not of direct concern to the programmer because they are usually hidden under layers of "protocol" software that provide the illusion of a reliable, private, nonblocking, order-preserving network. These layers of software can add significant overhead to sending and receiving a message.

Communication overhead usually has two components—a fixed overhead that is paid whether we send 1 byte or 1000 bytes, and a per-byte overhead. Existing multicomputers vary greatly in the overheads they impose, particularly the fixed overhead. For workstations using standard network communications (e.g., TCP over Ethernet), the fixed overhead can cost 10^5–10^6 instructions; almost all of this overhead is typically in operating-system-mediated communication protocol software, not in actual transit time on the network. On special-built multicomputers and clusters, which often have custom-built networks and network interfaces and much leaner, custom communication software, the fixed overhead can still cost 10^2–10^3 instructions.

Per-byte overheads are visible as limitations on bandwidth: the number of bytes per second that can be pushed through a channel. Bandwidths of standard local-area networks have been improving (from 10 Mbits/s to 100 Mbits/s and, soon, to 1 Gbits/s). Multicomputer networks have also continually improved, with bandwidths typically an order of magnitude greater than current local-area network technology. However, even these bandwidths are lower than main memory bandwidths by another order of magnitude.

These performance properties are impossible to hide, and they have a profound impact on how we program multicomputers. It should be clear that the only programs that will successfully see a performance improvement by executing on a multicomputer are those programs that achieve a "good" computation-to-communication ratio. In other words, each node needs to perform a lot of computation for each communication, in order that the communication overhead is amortized over a lot of useful work. This naturally leads to "blocked" program structures where each node works on large blocks of data and communicates infrequently in large blocks of data.[7]

For matrix multiplication, chunking up the data is particularly easy, leading to a so-called "blocked" matrix multiply program. Consider the 4×4 matrix multiplication shown in Figure 1.9. An example component in the result is x with value

$$x = ap + bq + cr + ds$$

However, it is also possible to view it as shown in Figure 1.10, where

$$X = A \times P + C \times R$$

and "$\times$" and "$+$" are themselves matrix multiplication and addition on 2×2 matrices, respectively. (We leave it as an exercise to the reader to verify that x still has the value $ap + bq + cr + ds$.)

---

7. This use of the word "block" refers to the fact that we are dealing with a chunk, or block of data, and is unrelated to its use in phrases like "blocking sends," where it means that the program is blocked, or stuck, until the send operation completes.

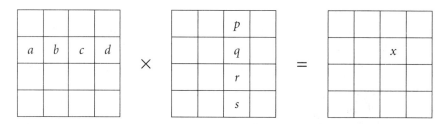

Figure 1.9   A 4 × 4 matrix multiplication.

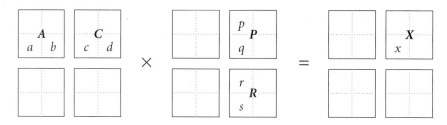

Figure 1.10   Viewing 4 × 4 matrices as 2 × 2 blocks.

This insight allows us to generalize our systolic matrix multiplication program trivially to work on blocks of size N, instead of individual words:

```
real aij(N,N), bij(N,N), cij(N,N)
cij = matmult(aij, bij, N)
do k = 1, n/N - 1
    send(left, aij,      N*N)
    send(up, bij,        N*N))
    receive(right, aij, N*N))
    receive(down, bij, N*N))
    cij = matadd(cij,
            matmult(aij, bij, N),
            N)
end do
```

This kind of "blocking" has two advantages. First, the fixed communication overhead for each send is amortized over four elements, instead of one. Second, each element that is received by a node is used N times without further communication, once for each of the N local inner products that it participates in.

Now, the loop does an $N \times N$ matrix multiplication and addition for every two sends and receives. By making N sufficiently large, clearly we can make the computation to communication ratio as high as we want. Of course, the question arises, Does the application program really need such large matrices? And the answer is, Yes, the usual reason for turning to parallel processing in the first place is for speed on large data sets.

In closing, we observe that although we have described blocking as an important consideration in programming multicomputers, it turns out to be important even on uniprocessors and on conventional bus-based shared-memory multiprocessors. The reasons, at a certain abstract level, are the same—minimizing data movement between "near" and "far" memory. Modern uniprocessors and bus-based multiprocessors typically have a *memory hierarchy:* disks (for paging virtual memory), main memory, and one or more levels of caches. Data is moved automatically on cache misses and page faults, and these movements have overheads. By using a blocked algorithm, since elements of a subblock may be used multiple times, the number of cache misses and page faults is reduced, thereby improving performance, often dramatically.

1.6.3 Message-Passing Programming Is Not Easy

We hope the reader will agree that obtaining the final, efficient message-passing program from the original mathematical specification of matrix multiplication was nontrivial. It takes careful study to convince oneself that the final solution actually works.

If this is the case even for something as simple, structured, and straightforward as matrix multiplication, one can imagine how difficult it is to write programs with more complicated, dynamically unfolding, unpredictable structure, such as sparse matrix programs, or symbolic programs that use graphs and trees instead of matrices.

1.7 Implicit Parallel Programming: Declarative Programming Languages

Since dealing with state (reuse of storage) causes so much difficulty for parallel execution, we can ask if there are programming notations that avoid the notion of state completely, and whether such notations are adequate for general-purpose programming. The answer to the first question is yes—such languages are called *declarative languages*—but the answer to the second question is no—some programming tasks are difficult, if not impossible, to express declaratively. The efficient implementation of pure declarative languages is also very difficult. (Curiously, the implementation problem is the dual of the automatic parallelization problem, an observation that we will return to shortly.) Nevertheless, declarative languages are an excellent basis for more complete parallel programming languages, and indeed *pH*, the language advocated in this book, is based on this idea.

A well-known class of declarative languages is that of *functional programming languages*, such as Lisp [63], SML [27, 42], and Haskell [53]. Hughes provides an excellent articulation of the advantages of functional programming in [32]. A second well-known class is that of *logic programming languages*, such as Prolog [18] and KL1 [69], and their more modern derivatives, *constraint logic programming languages*, such as Oz [62]. We will mainly discuss functional languages here (because of their relationship to *pH*), but many of our remarks also apply to the latter.

As an aside, we note that the adjective "declarative" is subjective. Intuitively it means that the program describes *what* is to be computed rather than *how* to compute it. Such a description is "higher level," or more "abstract," and hence presumably easier for humans to write and comprehend. However, no programming language can ever get away completely from the *how* of problem solving. The most abstract descriptions of computations may not even be executable (such descriptions are the purest form of *specifications*). For example, an abstract description of the square root function is "the function that, for argument n, produces x such that $x^2 = n$." An abstract description of a sorting function is "the function that, for argument sequence xs, produces the sequence ys that is a permutation of xs and in which $y_i < y_{i+1}$." It is unreasonable to expect any interpreter/compiler to actually execute these specifications systematically and efficiently. Thus, all programming, no matter how high level, fundamentally concerns *algorithms*, which specify *how* to compute an answer. So, the adjective "declarative" is mainly an assessment of how much non-problem-specific detail can be supressed in a programming language. At one extreme (least declarative) is architecture-specific assembler, where the programmer is intimately concerned with managing storage layout, movement of data between registers and memory, and sequencing. Most architecture-independent programming languages such as C, Pascal, and Fortran abstract away from some storage layout details and provide higher-level control structures such as if-then-elses, loops, and recursive procedures. Some object-oriented languages like Java provide even higher-level structures such as data abstraction and inheritance and further relieve the programmer from storage management details by managing storage deallocation automatically. Declarative languages like functional and logic programming languages abstract away from storage layout and storage management details *completely* and also abstract away from many sequencing details.

1.7.1 Implicit Parallelism Due to Lack of Antidependences

In functional languages, there is no such thing as a variable whose value can change during the computation. Rather, a variable behaves like a mathematical variable, having a unique *value* that is computed (or "solved") by the program. Multiple definitions of a variable are simply not allowed, and *all* computations are expressed in terms of computing new values from old. For example, given A, a vector of numbers, suppose we want to scale it by 5; that is, the result should be a vector whose ith component should be $5A_i$. In Fortran, we might say

```
do i = 1,N
      A(i) = 5 * A(i)
   end do
```

and A itself contains the result. Further, the old value of A is no longer available. In functional languages, such a concept does not exist; instead, we define a *new vector* based on the old. For example, in *pH:*

```
b = array (1,n)
              [ (i, 5 * a!i)  | i <- [1..n] ]
```

This defines b, a new vector with index range 1 to n, such that $b_i = 5a_i$. Nothing has happened to a—it still means exactly what it used to mean. For example, we could now produce a third vector c that is the vector sum of a and b:

```
c = array (1,n)
              [ (i, a!i +b!i) | i <- [1..n] ]
```

Matrix multiplication may be expressed in *pH* as follows:

```
matmult a b =
    matrix ((1,1), (n,n))
              [ ((i,j), ip A i B j) | i <- [1..n], j <- [1..n] ]
```

```
ip A i B j =
    let
        s = a!(i,1) * b!(1,j)
    in
        for k <- [2..n] do
            next s = s + a!(i,k) * b!(k,j)
        finally s
```

The first part defines the function `matmult`, which takes two arguments—the matrices a and b.[8] It produces a new $n \times n$ matrix whose (i, j)th component is the inner product of the ith row of a with the jth column of b.

The second part defines the inner product function `ip`. The **let** statement binds the value of $a_{i1} \cdot b_{1j}$ to a variable s. Although the loop may superficially look like the corresponding Fortran loop, it is fundamentally different—it expresses the idea of n separate and concurrent computations:

```
s₁ =         a!(i,1) * b!(1,j)
s₂ = s₁ + a!(i,2) * b!(2,j)
s₃ = s₂ + a!(i,3) * b!(3,j)
  .
  .
  .
sₙ = sₙ₋₁ + a!(i,n) * b!(n,j)
```

The first computation is the one outside the loop (the **let**-binding), and s_n, the final s, is the value of the entire loop. In other words, there are n different values of s; the **next** notation simply relates each s_k to its corresponding s_{k-1}; and the **finally** term just specifies which s is returned as the result value of the whole loop (and, in turn, the function). The statements of a loop are all executed concurrently, limited only by data dependencies (although the data dependencies in this particular loop do not admit much parallelism other than doing the multiplications in parallel). Thus, it is not the case that s is a variable that is being updated, as in the Fortran loop—each variable still has a unique definition.

The *pH* program for matrix multiplication *directly* expresses the structures in Figures 1.1 and 1.2. In particular, it takes no position on the order in which computations are done, beyond the natural ordering of data

---

8. *pH* permits us to extract size information from a matrix, but since this representation choice is orthogonal to whether a language is functional or not, and since we want to keep the example simple, we assume that a and b are $n \times n$ matrices.

dependencies. Since variables never change, there cannot ever be any anti-dependencies. It is for this reason that functional languages are considered to be "naturally parallel" languages.

Implicit Producer-Consumer Parallelism

Most of the parallelism in matrix multiplication comes from data parallelism—an independent inner product is computed at each of the n^2 components of the result matrix. Another kind of parallelism that is very important is *producer-consumer* parallelism, and this arises naturally in functional languages with *nonstrict* data structures. Suppose, instead of scaling vector a by 5, we have a more complicated mapping function f:

```
b = array (1,n)
            [ (i, f (A!i))  | i <- [1..n] ]
```

The computation of all elements of b may be done in parallel, but they may take widely differing times. In languages with strict data structures (most existing programming languages), a consumer of b must wait until all components have been defined (i.e., until the slowest component computation has completed) because b is simply not available to the consumer until it is fully defined. In languages like *pH* with nonstrict data structures, on the other hand, a consumer may be given a reference to b as soon as it is allocated and may attempt to read its components immediately. These reads automatically wait as long as the components are empty and automatically resume as they become filled. Thus, the consumer can overlap some of its work with the computation of b's components.

For a more dramatic example of producer-consumer parallelism, suppose we have one computation that produces a list of sample readings (perhaps obtaining them from some measuring instrument) and another computation that analyzes these readings looking for interesting events. In *pH*,

```
producer instrument =
    if no_more_readings(instrument)
    then []
    else
        let
            x = get_reading(instrument)
        in
            x : producer (instrument)
```

```
analyzer   []     = []
analyzer   (x:xs) = if is_interesting(x)
                    then x : analyzer(xs)
                    else analyzer(xs)
```

The notation "x:xs" is pronounced "*x* cons *xs*" and represents a list with x in front, followed by the remaining list, xs. The notation [] represents an empty list. The producer function gets a reading x from the instrument and produces a list containing x followed by more readings, until the instrument indicates that there are no more readings. The analyzer function handles two cases, and this is indicated by matching the actual argument against one of the two patterns [] and (x:xs). In the former case, it returns an empty list of interesting readings. In the latter case, it checks if the first reading x is interesting. If so, it returns it, followed by the result of analyzing the remaining readings xs. Otherwise, it discards x and simply returns the result of analyzing the remaining readings.

Now, the interesting producer-consumer parallelism occurs when we plug these functions together:

```
events = analyzer (producer (a_particular_instrument))
```

Suppose the instrument yielded a reading every 10 seconds, there are 100 readings, and it takes 5 seconds to analyze each reading. With conventional ("strict") data structures, the producer function would, after 1000 seconds or so, return a list of 100 elements. At this point, the analyzer would begin its work and, about 500 seconds later, eventually return a list of interesting readings. Overall, the computation takes 1500 seconds or more.

With nonstrict data structures, however, as soon as the instrument has yielded its first reading, the producer can return the first element of the list, leaving the "tail" of the list temporarily *empty*, to be filled in later when it gets the next reading. Having returned this first reading, the analyzer can examine it immediately. If it is interesting, the analyzer, in turn, can immediately return the first element of its result list, leaving its tail empty, to be filled in later. There is an implicit synchronization necessary here. In particular, the analyzer, having examined the first reading, may attempt to proceed to the next reading, which may not be available yet. The semantics of nonstrict data structures specify that the analyzer automatically blocks until the tail of its input list is no longer empty (i.e., has been filled in by the producer). One can visualize this as a chain that is gradually produced by the producer and incrementally consumed by the analyzer as it becomes available. The work of the analyzer and producer can thus be *overlapped*, instead of being run seriatim. Thus, each 5-second activity of the analyzer can take place *during* the 10-second wait for the next instrument reading, and the overall computation can be completed in about 1000 seconds.

Although we have illustrated producer-consumer parallelism with a simple, linear data structure (a list), the same principle applies to arbitrary data structures in *pH* and nonstrict functional languages. For example, the producer may organize the instrument readings in a sorted tree. The picture changes to one where the fringe, or frontier, of the tree grows incrementally as readings arrive. The analyzer, in parallel, pursues all branches up to the current fringe, consuming values at the fringe as it moves outward. Similarly, the production of different elements of an array may take varied times, and a consumer of the array can simultaneously pick up those values that are ready at any given point in time.

1.7.2   Limitations of Functional Languages

So, why aren't we all using functional languages yet? Despite the strengths of functional programming languages, they are not adequate to express all programming tasks. In part, this has to do with their inability to express nondeterministic computations; in part, some programs are simpler when expressed with state; and, in part, it has to do with efficiency (these issues are explored in greater detail in Chapter 10).

Some computing tasks are inherently nondeterministic. For example, when we benchmark programs, we expect that the timer readings taken before and after the computation will change, depending on the machine configuration, load, quality of compiled code, and so on. Some computations, such as communication protocols, use explicit time-outs in a fundamental way. Storage allocators, such as the one that finds a free disk block when we write to a file, generally do not care *which* disk block is returned for use. None of these can be expressed in a functional language because the values returned by these operations are fundamentally not functions of inputs.

Although the nondeterminism of parallel access to shared state is usually an obstacle to parallelism, there are a number of situations where this nondeterminism may be exploited usefully to *enhance* parallelism and to enhance the clarity of the program. An example is the nondeterministic summation discussed earlier in the inner product of matrix multiplication. It is a specific case of "accumulation" programs where the order of accumulation does not matter. Computing histograms is another example: the order in which samples are tallied in a histogram does not matter. Another useful class of problems is nondeterministic search; for example, a robot motion-planning program may evaluate several alternative strategies in parallel and choose the best one it can find within a given time limit—there is no a priori way to predict which alternative will be chosen.

Some programs are simpler (and, counterintuitively, more parallel!) when they use state explicitly. An example is graph traversal. Suppose we were exploring a maze and we have to find a path from the entrance to the exit. Suppose we had an army of lieutenants and we sent them down different paths in parallel. In order to prevent duplication of work (and to avoid going round in circles), each lieutenant is provided with a stick of chalk, and he marks every corner that he visits. When he arrives at a marked corner he retreats, knowing that some other lieutenant (or even himself, if he walked in a circle) has already been there. Unfortunately, there is no way of expressing this intuitive algorithm in a pure functional language. Every corner has state—it is either marked or unmarked—and this cannot be expressed functionally. Instead, the functional program looks like this: we have only *one* lieutenant, who carries a log book in which he records every corner that he visits. More precisely, at every visited corner, he constructs a new log book that differs from the old log book by one additional entry—the entry for that corner. At each corner, he consults his log book to check whether he has been there before. Not only is this solution totally sequential (just one lieutenant), it is potentially expensive (constructing and consulting log books), and it is also much less intuitive than the solution that uses state.

There is simply no way to express any of these nondeterministic programs in a functional language. This is true by definition; in fact, functional languages are so named because programs behave like mathematical functions—outputs are uniquely determined by inputs.

Functional languages are generally less efficient than imperative languages. Much of this inefficiency comes from two factors: storage management overhead and unnecessary copying. At the beginning of this section, we showed both Fortran and *pH* code to scale a vector by 5. The Fortran code simply overwrote the existing array with the new contents, whereas the *pH* version created an entirely new vector; that is, it has to pay the extra cost of allocating a new vector. And, since computers have finite storage and functional languages continually allocate new storage for new objects, there has to be a corresponding deallocation process (usually called "garbage collection") that recycles storage for objects that are no longer necessary in the computation—this also adds to storage management overhead. Java is an example of a newer imperative language where the designers have appreciated the value of garbage collection (automatic storage management) and incorporated it as a standard part of the language.

Unnecessary copying occurs whenever we compute a new data structure from an old one, in which many of the component values are unchanged. For example, suppose we want to scale only the seventh component of vector A by 5. In Fortran, we could say

```
A(7) = 5 * A(7)
```

and A contains the result. In a functional language we must, as always, define a new array for the result:

```
b = array (1,n)
        [ (i, if i == 7
              then 5 * a!i
              else a!i    ) | i <- [1..n] ]
```

The new array b is mostly a copy of a, except at index 7. In Fortran, the operation performs a fixed (constant) amount of work (one read, one multiplication, one write), whereas the functional program performs work proportional to the size of the array (N reads, one multiplication, and N writes).

Nonstrict languages have additional "synchronization" overheads. First, when a data structure is allocated, the implementation has to *initialize* all the components of the new structure to be "empty" because it cannot predict whether or not a consumer will attempt to read a component before it is filled (the filling computation may be arbitrarily complicated, and, moreover, the filling computations for some components may depend on the values in other components). Second, when a computation attempts to read a data structure component, it has to check whether the data is available yet and, if not, it has to be suspended and resumed when the data does become available. To illustrate why it is difficult for a compiler to eliminate this overhead, consider the following rather innocent-looking function definition that takes two arguments and returns two results:

```
f (x,y)  =  (x+5, y+10)
```

It appears straightforward to generate efficient code for this—simply add 5 and 10 to the first and second arguments, respectively, and return them. However, consider the following two contexts in which f may be called:

```
(c, d)  =  f (23,  c)        -- (A)

(c, d)  =  f (d ,  23)       -- (B)
```

In (A), when f is called, we know x = 23; it can compute and return x+5. This defines c = 28, at which point f's second argument is known, and f can finish its work, computing and returning y+10 as its second result; this defines d = 38. On the other hand, in (B), when f is called, we know y = 23; it can compute and return y+10. This defines d = 33, at which point f's first argument is known, and f can finish its work, computing and returning x+5 as its first result; this defines c = 38. In other words, a compiler cannot even schedule the order in which x+5 and y+10 are to be computed; instead, it has to produce code that allows this to be determined dynamically. This adds additional overhead to the execution.

The efficiency issue is quite slippery because it is tied to parallelism. First, in situations where we do need both the old and the new values of the array for parallel access, or where we do need producer-consumer parallelism and so on, the Fortran programmer would have to replicate, manually, what the functional programmer does naturally; here, it is possible that the functional language compiler produces a more efficient implementation than storage management and synchronization code written manually by the Fortran programmer. Second, a smart functional language compiler may recognize that the array a is no longer needed after the above scaling computation, and so it may choose to reuse a's storage for b and do a single update at index 7, just like the Fortran code. This not only eliminates the storage management overhead, it also eliminates the unnecessary copying.

Interestingly, the problem of determining when storage *can* be reused safely by the system also requires exact information about when two expressions refer to the same object. It is exactly the same aliasing problem that makes automatic parallelization of sequential languages difficult—this is the *duality* that we mentioned earlier. The analysis is the same, but the solutions are duals of each other in the sense that the automatic parallelizer, to be conservative, *must reuse storage* and avoid parallelism, whereas the functional language compiler, to be conservative, *must not reuse storage* and must avoid sequentiality. This is why, in imperative languages, it is easy to write sequential programs and difficult to write parallel ones, whereas in functional languages, it is easy to write highly parallel programs and difficult to write sequential ones. In fact, one might observe that sequentializing a nonstrict functional program is as hard a problem (some would say, as intractable) as parallelizing a sequential imperative program.

1.7.3   Prominent Functional Languages

There are three major families of functional languages: the Lisp family (including Common Lisp [63] and Scheme [35]), the ML family (including SML [42]), and the lazy functional languages family, including Haskell [53]. These families differ primarily in their choice of static versus dynamic type checking, whether or not they are pure—that is, without side-effecting operations (state)—and whether they have strict or nonstrict semantics.

Lisp is dynamically typed, whereas SML and Haskell are statically typed and have a rich data type system based on the Hindley-Milner type system [41]. These choices are orthogonal to issues of parallelism; type system choices are usually made on other considerations such as expressive power, program robustness, and software engineering. Since *pH* has a static type system similar to Haskell's, we will be discussing type issues in great detail as we progress through the book.

While it is possible to do pure functional programming in Scheme and SML, both are impure functional languages; that is, they both have side-effecting operations and a notion of state, motivated by efficiency and expressivity concerns such as those discussed in the previous section. Haskell, on the other hand, is a pure functional language with no side-effecting operations whatsoever.

Being a pure functional language, Haskell has an additional efficiency concern beyond those that it shares with Lisp and SML—the overhead of allocating and copying data structures as we "update" them. Researchers in this community have worked hard to address this. The key insight is that, when we "update" a functional data structure, if there are no other references to its old value, then the implementation can safely perform the update in situ and avoid copying the data structure. There are several ways to achieve this. At run time, we could maintain a *reference count* for each data structure, which is an integer counter associated with each data structure that counts the number of references to it. During an "update" operation, if the implementation sees that this value is 1, it can perform the update in place, on the old data structure. Alternatively (or in addition to dynamic reference counts) we can statically analyze the program to prove that the reference count during a particular update will be 1; if so, we can generate code that directly performs the update in place and avoids the reference count check entirely. A further alternative is to invent a type system that guarantees that certain things have unit reference counts; various systems called "linear types," "unique types," and so on have been proposed and prototyped. In recent years, a system called *monads* has gained currency in the Haskell community to address this issue. Briefly, monads provide a way to package up a sequence of computations on a data structure in such a way that, *by construction*, there is always exactly one reference to the data structure. In essence, the data structure is "single-threaded" through the computation. This allows all functional "updates" on that data structure safely to be implemented with in-place updates, avoiding copying. Of course, this does not at all address the issue of *parallel* updates to a data structure. Monads are discussed in Chapter 8.

The final dimension along which these functional languages differ is strictness: Lisp and SML are strict languages, whereas Haskell is non-strict. This choice is not entirely independent of the choice of purity. Raw (unsynchronized) side effects usually need a sequencing context to be meaningful, and strictness imposes more sequencing constraints than non-strictness. SML's language definition specifies sequencing totally and precisely; it is strict by implication because the sequencing specifies that arguments are evaluated before performing function calls, and data structure components are evaluated before the data structure itself is constructed. Common Lisp's language definition also specifies sequencing completely, and it is also strict by implication. Scheme, in the Lisp family, is also strict, even though it leaves some sequencing questions open (such as the order of evaluation of arguments).

Haskell is a nonstrict language, and most implementations use *lazy evaluation* to implement this. Lazy evaluation is a totally sequential evaluation mechanism that works backward from the final result expression to determine exactly what needs to be computed in order to realize the final result, and computes it.

Until recently functional languages have made little headway in the wider professional software development programming community, primarily because of certain perceptions about their inefficiency. Even though Lisp is as old as Fortran, many features of functional languages have long been regarded as having an unacceptable run-time cost; these features include heap-allocated storage with automatic garbage collection and complete type safety (including safe pointers and array bounds-checking). Somehow, arguments about increased programmer productivity, more robust programs, simpler and cleaner coding, and so on were not sufficient to persuade many professionals or organizations to adopt functional languages.

The advent of Java has done much to dismantle this barrier. Java was not originally promoted as a universal application programming language. Its main attractions were portable, secure Internet programming with the support of byte-code interpretation and dynamic loading. Nevertheless, its success has led to a broadening of its scope to the point where many projects are now choosing Java as their implementation language, whether related to portable Internet programming or not. In the process, many people have for the first time directly experienced and realized the benefits of automatic garbage collection and complete type safety. It is possible that this revolution will also make people more receptive to functional programming languages (indeed many functional programming languages have implementations that are more efficient than current Java implementations). An example of this change in thinking is the telephone equipment company L.M. Ericsson of Sweden, which has begun to use a simple concurrent functional language called Erlang for new telephone switch codes after finding it difficult to produce robust software with C++ [7, 6].

1.8   *pH*: An Implicitly Parallel, Declarative Language

pH is a parallel dialect of Haskell. It is primarily a functional language because we believe that functional languages are the best starting point for parallel programming languages. Ultimately, we need massive parallelism to exploit all the varieties of parallelism in real machines, and functional languages allow us to express vast amounts of parallelism implicitly and effortlessly. Moreover, this parallelism is not restricted to dense rectangular arrays and loops, but to arbitrary recursive and loop computations on arbitrary linked data structures. However, recognizing the limitations of pure functional programming described above, *pH* also provides constructs for explicit expression and manipulation of state. It is convenient to view *pH*

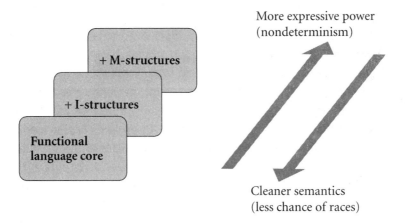

Figure 1.11 Layers of *pH*.

as a language with three layers, as depicted in Figure 1.11. We will discuss each of these layers in the following sections.

pH is based on over two decades of research with several versions of the functional language Id [10, 47, 43] and experience with their implementation on dataflow and conventional architectures [67, 11, 49, 44]. A few years ago, recognizing the semantic similarity between the functional core of Id and the standard nonstrict functional language Haskell, the authors decided to adopt Haskell for the functional core, extending it as necessary with I-structure and M-structure constructs. The Haskell basis should make *pH* familiar to a much larger audience and should make exploitation of parallelism an easy step for programmers already familiar with Haskell.

1.8.1   The Functional Layer

A large subset of *pH* is its *functional core*, whose syntax and nonstrict semantics are exactly those of the pure functional language Haskell. The major programming style in *pH* is functional, and a large part of this book (Chapters 2 through 7) is devoted to functional programming. Because there is no notion of state, it is trivial to write parallel programs without races in the functional core. In fact, it is *impossible* to write a program with races; functional programs are guaranteed to be deterministic.

A central feature of the functional core is the *higher-order function*. The key idea is that functions themselves can be treated as values. Higher-order functions increase the parametric power of a language and, consequently, allow us to write shorter, more abstract programs. For example, a function to sort a list can take, as one of its arguments, the function used to decide the relative order of any pair of elements in the list. Then, the same sorting function can be used to sort a list of integers both in ascending and descending orders, simply by passing in the "<" or ">" functions, respectively. Or, the same sorting function can be used to sort a list of strings in lexicographic order, by passing in the appropriate string comparison function. The experienced functional programmer uses higher-order functions like oxygen—they are an essential part of one's toolkit. We will introduce higher-order functions within the first few pages of the next chapter.

We have already mentioned the notion of *nonstrictness*, another central feature of *pH*. Functions can be executed before arguments are available (unless restricted by data dependencies) and can even return results before the body has completed computing. Similarly, any component of a data structure may be *empty* for an indefinite period, allowing producers and consumers to compute concurrently. We motivated this idea from the point of view of producer-consumer parallelism, but this feature also fundamentally adds expressive power to the language, allowing us to write certain recursive definitions of data structures that would otherwise be awkward to express.[9]

Pervading the entire language is the notion of *types* and *static type checking*, although this is orthogonal to parallelism. Every phrase in *pH* (variable, expression, function, and so on) must have a well-defined data type, and this property is checked statically (i.e., by the compiler) before running the program. Static types facilitate the construction of robust programs because many simple programming errors are caught at compile time, and because they give a convenient framework in which to organize the program. Static types have sometimes earned a bad reputation for increasing the "bureaucracy" that the programmer has to deal with; however, there are three aspects of *pH*'s type system that make it easy to use compared

---

9. Recent studies indicate that the practical advantages of nonstrictness (producer-consumer parallelism, definition of cyclic data structures) may accrue even with strict functions, as long as data structures are nonstrict. This could have significant performance advantages—not only can strict function calls be implemented more efficiently, but they also permit better compiler analysis of function bodies, resulting in better code therein. This is still an open area of research and is a possible future for *pH*.

to, say, the static type system of Pascal. The first is *polymorphism:* for example, we can write a single function that computes the length of a list, no matter what the list contains (integers, strings, and so on), whereas in Pascal we would have to write several (nearly identical) functions for this purpose, one for integer lists, one for string lists, and so on. The second convenient feature is *type inference:* the programmer is relieved of the tedium of having to predeclare the type of *every* variable used in the program. Instead, the compiler infers these types automatically, and, in fact, it is perfectly safe for the programmer to omit *all* type declarations (although it is highly recommended that the programmer declare the types of at least the top-level functions). The third convenience is *overloading:* for example, we can write a single function to multiply two integer or floating-point matrices, whereas in Pascal we would have to write two (nearly identical) functions for this purpose. Overall, the static type system is invaluable in structuring the way we think about and design programs. Types are introduced immediately (in Chapter 2) and are elaborated thereafter throughout the book.

1.8.2   The I-structure Layer

The second layer of *pH* adds "I-structures" to the functional core, and these are introduced in Chapter 9. I-structures are a limited but benign form of state—benign, because it is still impossible to write a program with a race condition and programs are still guaranteed to be determinate. Data structures in *pH* can contain I-structure components. What this means is that when the data structure is allocated, the component is initially left empty. Later, a computation can *assign* a value into that component, making it full. Any other computation that tries to read that component automatically blocks until the value is available. We have already mentioned this type of synchronization in the context of producer-consumer parallelism in nonstrict functional data structures. The difference here is this: in functional data structures, the allocation of the data structure and the values that fill its components are always specified syntactically together, as a single construct. For this reason, in functional data structures we never even think of the action of filling in of a component as an assignment—that is something inside the implementation. In I-structures, on the other hand, the computation that fills in an empty component may be in some syntactically unrelated part of the program and is thus always expressed explicitly as an assignment.

One common use of I-structures is to implement pure functions efficiently. For example, most functional languages provide a `map_array` primitive that transforms one array into another by applying a given function to each element and a `foldl_array` primitive that computes some overall property of an array, such as the sum of all elements, or the maximum element. Now, suppose we want to both transform an array as well as compute an overall property. This `map_foldl` operation is a perfectly well-defined, pure function, and it is of course possible to define it by simply applying both the map and the fold primitives; however, this involves two array traversals. With I-structures, it is possible for the programmer to implement this function directly as a new primitive, using a single array traversal. These ideas are also discussed in Chapter 9.

I-structures retain determinacy in *pH* precisely because of their "write-once" semantics: an I-structure component makes a single transition from empty to full with a value, and no computation can observe this transition because any attempt to read an empty component will simply block the computation until the component is full and then return the value. In other words, there is only one possible value that can be obtained by reading an I-structure component, and so there is no chance of nondeterminism.

I-structures are closely related to *logic variables* in *logic programming languages*. In fact, I-structures may be used in the same way that logic variables are often used—to implement difference lists, mailboxes, and so on.

1.8.3   The M-structure Layer

The final level of *pH* adds "M-structures" to the functional and I-structure layers. M-structures, introduced in Chapter 10, allow reuse of storage and, thus, arbitrary manipulation of state. However, the main difference from assignment statements in imperative languages is that access to M-structure data is implicitly synchronized. This has two advantages—first, it permits more economical expression of shared state manipulation and, second, it can usually be implemented more efficiently. For example, consider many parallel computations that are all updating components of a shared array h. With explicit synchronization (e.g., with threads and locks), each update would be expressed as follows:

```
wait(locks[j]);
H[j] = f(H[j]);
signal(locks[j]);
```

In other words, we wait for exclusive access to the jth component, using a companion array of locks. After performing the update, we release the lock to allow other similar parallel computations to proceed. In *pH*, we express it as follows:

```
h!j := f (h !& j)
```

where the `h!&j` notation means "wait until Full, read, and leave Empty," and the assigment means "write, and make Full." In addition to simplifying the notation (we don't have to declare an array of locks and explicitly perform waits and signals), the implementation can also be more efficient because of the combined synchronization and data access. For example, in the conventional imperative language code, each of the operations—wait, update h, and signal—is likely to be a separate transaction with memory. In the M-structure version, the wait and read h can be combined into a single transaction, as can the write h and signal, resulting in two transactions, the minimum possible.

In the functional and I-structure layers, there is no sequencing of operations other than that which is naturally implied by data dependencies. With M-structures, however, sequencing may be necessary to control non-determinism. For example, if we want to ensure that a bank deposit computation completes before we perform a withdrawal computation on a shared M-structure, data dependencies are no longer adequate; for this, *pH* provides ways to explicitly sequence computations.

As discussed earlier, several languages such as ML and Scheme also have purely functional cores augmented with operations to manipulate state. However, in those languages, state manipulation comes at the expense of parallelism; unwanted race conditions are made into a nonissue by making the *entire* language strict and totally sequential. Of course, many researchers have reintroduced limited, user-specified parallelism by extending these languages with traditional parallel constructs such as threads, locks, and message-passing. Also, as discussed earlier, a recent development in nonstrict functional languages such as Haskell is a technique called *monads*, which is a way to encapsulate state manipulation. While this is done without making the entire language sequential, the state manipulation operations are still completely sequenced, so that one cannot have a parallel, state-manipulating program. We discuss monads and explicit sequencing in *pH* in Chapter 8.

In *pH*, on the other hand, despite the addition of M-structures, the overall programming style remains implicitly parallel unless otherwise specified. Unlike other parallel languages that are implicitly sequential unless otherwise specified, the difference is qualitative, but noticeable—implicit parallelism makes it significantly easier to write massively parallel programs.

The parallelism in *pH* is pervasive. Not only does it occur at a very fine grain (e.g., reading the head and tail fields of a list record proceed in parallel), but also at a larger grain (e.g., two functions or loop iterations can execute in parallel). Both of these are important for parallel computer architectures. The large-grain parallelism allows easy distribution of work across the multiple processors of a parallel machine. The fine-grain parallelism allows each processor to exploit *instruction-level parallelism* (i.e., the ability to execute instructions of a thread in parallel) and *multithreading* (i.e., the ability to execute another fine-grain thread while one of its fine-grain threads has to wait, perhaps to access a datum on a different processor).

We know of no other programming language that exposes as much parallelism as effortlessly as *pH*.

1.9   The Effect of Architecture on Programming

While this book is mainly about parallel programming, it is important to recognize that computer architecture can have a major effect on our programming languages and on our programming methodology.

For example, early computers (and even some as recent as the Intel 8086) had small physical address spaces and no architectural support for virtual memory. On these machines, it was still possible to write programs that manipulated huge data structures that would not fit into memory at once. In effect, the programmer could mimic a virtual memory system by manually moving pieces of the array between disk and main memory. This kind of programming was the domain of experts who understood the architecture thoroughly.

Eventually, tools came into existence to automate some of this effort for large-memory programming, using a method called "overlays." However, these tools were never even close to being able *automatically* to translate an arbitrary program that assumed large memory into code that could work in limited memory. In other words, the architectural limitation simply could not be hidden from programmers.

Ultimately, it required architectural support for virtual memory before the situation changed. Finally, everyday programmers could write programs that were not limited by the processor's physical address space.

A similar situation exists with parallel computers today. A universal requirement of (large) parallel architectures is that, in order to be physically scalable, they must have distributed memories—the machine's memory must be divided into several independent modules, and there must be many independent paths from processors to memory modules. The first generation of commercially viable large parallel computers achieved this by simply interconnecting large numbers of conventional sequential computers; each *node* of the machine consists of a conventional processor with memory and a means to communicate with other nodes. These *multicomputers* can be programmed with message-passing, which exactly mirrors the architectural organization. But we have seen how difficult it is to program using the message-passing model; so, while extremely useful and effective programs have been (and continue to be) written this way, it remains the domain of experts. Just as yesterday's large-memory programming was only feasible for those who understood thoroughly how to manage movement of data between memory and disk, today's parallel programming with message-passing is only feasible for those who understand thoroughly how to manage movement of data between processing nodes of a multicomputer.

HPF can be seen as an attempt to automate some of this. But, just as with yesterday's tools for overlays in small-memory machines, today's HPF programmer has to be sophisticated about data distributions, and in any case these tools can't handle arbitrary, general-purpose programs.

It is our belief that shared-memory parallel programming today is the analog of virtual-memory programs of yesterday—it is the only model feasible for general-purpose programs written by ordinary programmers (and hence for widespread use). Further, it will not become viable without architectural support. Even though the virtual-memory illusion is mostly implemented in operating system software, it required some architectural support before it became efficient enough that the average programmer no longer had to think about it (translation lookaside buffers, page faults). Similarly, even though the shared-memory illusion may be implemented mostly in run-time system software, some architectural support is needed to make it efficient enough that the average parallel programmer no longer needs to think about it. (This is not to imply that message-passing must be completely hidden from the programmer; carefully hand-crafted message-passing algorithms are still likely to be advantageous. We simply mean that, by and large, the programmer would prefer a shared-memory programming model.)

To date, there is no consensus on exactly what architectural support is necessary to support the shared-memory illusion on a distributed-memory parallel machine (even though there are some commercial products that choose particular approaches). The question is further complicated because the required architectural support depends on what parallel programming models one wishes to support, and there is no consensus on that either. (The situation was easier with virtual memory—at least the user-level programming model was not an issue.) Architectural support for distributed shared-memory is a hot topic of research in many academic, industrial, and government groups all over the world.

We believe that in the long run, for *general-purpose* parallel programming (i.e., arbitrary programs written by ordinary programmers), the language must make it effortless to express huge amounts of parallelism. The reasons are twofold:

- No matter what architectural support there may be for shared memory, movement of data across the machine will always be slow, compared to instruction execution times and local memory access times. Abundant parallelism permits the processor to perform useful work on one thread while another may be waiting for data to be moved. This is analogous to the situation in operating systems today: when one process encounters a page fault, the processor switches to another process while the first one waits for the page to arrive from disk.
- In arbitrary parallel programs, synchronization waits (waiting to acquire a lock) are as unpredictable as nonlocal memory accesses. Again, we need an adequate number of threads so that the processor can continue useful work while some are waiting for synchronization events.

Since manual synchronization in the face of massive parallelism is too tedious to be feasible (except for programs with extremely simple, rigid structures), this, too, is something that the programmer should not have to manage explicitly.

The bottom line is that for general-purpose, scalable, parallel computing, architectures need to support fine-grain threads with fine-grain synchronization, and programming languages and implementations need to exploit this capability. Although these architectural features will benefit all parallel programming languages, existing languages do not make it easy to express or to exploit fine-grain parallelism. Declarative programming languages such as *pH* appear to be the most promising approach toward this goal.

Functions and Reduction

Function space available. Apply inside.

—*Sign in a restaurant window*

We are all familiar with the following simple notion of computation. Given an expression like this:

    (2 + 3) + 4

we can replace the expression (2 + 3) by the equivalent but simpler expression 5, giving

    5 + 4

which in turn can be further simplified to

    9

At this point, no further simplification can take place; hence we say that this is the "result" of the computation.

   This simple principle is the basis of computation in functional languages such as *pH*. Each step is called a *reduction*. The allowable reductions are specified by *rewrite rules*. *pH* has some built-in rewrite rules for arithmetic operations. So, for example, (2 + 3) ⟶ 5.

In addition to the built-in rewrite rules, the programmer may specify additional rewrite rules through *function definitions*. We begin with a simple example. The function doesn't do much—it simply takes two arguments, adds them up, and returns the result.

```
plus x y = x + y
```

The name of the function being defined (plus) is followed by names for the arguments (x and y). On the right-hand side of the "=" is the *body* of the function, which is an expression representing the value returned by the function. The identifiers x and y are called *formal parameters* because they are just dummy names that stand for the *actual parameters* that will be supplied when this function is used. Unlike other programming languages, there is no punctuation around the formal parameters (such as parentheses, commas, or semicolons).

The function can be read as a rewrite rule; that is, whenever we see an expression that matches the left-hand side:

```
plus e₁ e₂
```

where e_1 and e_2 are any expressions, we can reduce it as specified by the right-hand side, to

$$e_1 + e_2$$

Suppose we were given the expression "plus 2 3". We can perform the rewrites as follows:

$$\text{plus } 2\ 3 \longrightarrow 2 + 3 \longrightarrow 5$$

In the second step, we use the built-in rewrite rule for "+".

A function application is written by simply juxtaposing the function with its arguments. There is no additional punctuation for application, such as parentheses or commas.

A more complicated example:

```
      plus (2 * 3) (plus 2 3)
 ⟶  plus 6 (2 + 3)
 ⟶  plus 6 5
 ⟶  6 + 5
 ⟶  11
```

In general, whenever we see any expression that matches the left-hand side of a function definition, we can replace it by the right-hand side, substituting formal parameters by actual parameters. By repeatedly performing such rewrites, we reduce the program expression to its result—an expression that cannot be rewritten any further.

Please remember this definition of `plus`; we will be using it often in later examples.

Exercise 2.1   Write a function "`sqr`" that takes one argument x and returns the value of x^2 by multiplying it by itself.   ∎

Exercise 2.2   Write a function "`discriminant`" that takes three arguments a, b, and c and returns the value of $b^2 - 4ac$.   ∎

2.1   Basics

The central constructs of *pH* are *expressions* and *functions*. The simplest expressions are constants, such as numbers and identifiers. More complex expressions are constructed by applying functions or operators to other expressions. Indeed, a function is itself an abstraction of an expression, such as an expression that has been parameterized with respect to one or more identifiers used in the expression.

2.1.1   Numbers and Identifiers

Here are some examples of numeric constants in *pH*.

```
255
0.6667
1.45
2.56e4
3.0e-3
```

The first number is an integer, and the remaining numbers are floating-point numbers. In a floating-point number, the decimal point must be preceded and followed by at least one digit. The radix is always 10. A floating-point number can be followed by an exponent, as in the last two examples. In an exponentiated number, the base is always 10. For example, `3.0e-3` denotes 3.0×10^{-3}, or 0.003.

An identifier in *pH* consists of a lowercase letter (a–z) followed by zero or more letters (A–Z, a–z), digits (0–9), underscores (_), and single quotes (').

However, reserved words (such as **if**, **then**, **else**, etc.) may not be used as identifiers. Examples of identifiers: `desmond_2_2`, `tax_1989`, `x'`, `x''`.

Upper- and lowercase letters are distinct, so, for example, `first_x` and `first_X` represent two distinct identifiers.

2.1.2   Function Application

The application of a function to its arguments is written merely by juxtaposing them, unlike notations in other programming languages that require parentheses around the arguments and commas or semicolons between them. As in conventional algebraic notation, parentheses are used in *pH* almost exclusively for grouping. For example, we are all used to the idea that the parentheses are necessary in

$$a \times (b + c)$$

and that they are unnecessary, but acceptable, in

$$(a \times b) + c$$

This is because, by convention, we say that $\times$ has higher precedence than $+$; that is, multiplication binds more tightly than addition.

Similarly, in *pH*, application has the highest precedence. Thus, parentheses are necessary in

```
plus 2 (3 * 5)
```

and unnecessary, but acceptable, in

```
(plus 2 3) * 5
```

2.1.3   Spaces and Formatting

pH follows the so-called free format convention, whereby multiple spaces are equivalent to one space, and "whitespace" characters such as carriage returns, line feeds, tabs, and form feeds are also treated as spaces. Thus, the programmer should feel free to use multiple pages and lines with extra spaces and especially *indentation* to improve readability.

2.1.4   Comments

Comments in *pH* programs may be written with two dashes ("--") followed by any text up to and including the end of the line. In parsing a *pH* program, a comment is treated as just another space.

2.1.5   Operators

pH has a number of infix *operators*, such as "+" and "−" for addition and subtraction, "∗" and "/" for multiplication and division, and so on. We will introduce other operators as we go along.

Associativity of operators is another device to minimize the number of parentheses. For example,

    a^b^c   and   a*b*c

stand for, respectively,

    a^(b^c)   and   (a*b)*c

because the exponent operator "^" associates to the right and multiplication associates to the left. Still, as in conventional algebra, the programmer should feel free to use extra parentheses if there is any doubt about the grouping or if it improves readability.

2.2   Higher-Order Functions and Currying

Suppose we have the following definition:

    f = plus 1

and we now try to evaluate the expression

    f 3

That is, let "f" name the value of the expression "plus 1"; using this name, compute the value of the expression "f 3".

Is the expression "plus 1" meaningful? Is there an argument missing? In *pH*, we treat "plus 1" as an expression whose value is itself a function of one argument; that is, "f" represents a function that adds one to its argument and returns the sum.

As before, the definition can be used as a rewrite rule:

       f 3
⟶ (plus 1) 3   *using the definition of* f

Now, application by juxtaposition associates to the left, so we can drop the parentheses.

⟶ plus 1 3

Continuing,

$\longrightarrow$ plus 1 3
$\longrightarrow$ 1 + 3   *using the definition of* plus
$\longrightarrow$ 4   *using the built-in rule for* +

In general, whenever we see an application of the form

f e_1 e_2 ... e_n

it should be read as

$(...((f\ e_1)\ e_2)...e_n)$

That is, f applied to e_1, the result of which is applied to e_2, the result of which is applied to e_3, and so on.

This notation, whereby "plus e_1" can itself be treated as a function, is a very clever and powerful notation found in functional languages and is called "currying" after Haskell B. Curry, a famous logician who popularized it in the 1950s (the programming language Haskell is named after him). We will make much use of this notation in this book.

A *higher-order function* is a function that has an argument or result that is itself a function. More generally, its arguments and result may also be data structures that contain functions.

Exercise 2.3   *pH* has an exponent operator "^" such that a^b raises a to the bth power. Suppose we write

f n x = x^n

What do the following expressions represent?

f 2 3   and   (f 2)   and   (f 3)   ∎

Exercise 2.4   Suppose we defined

g x n = f n x

What do the following expressions represent?

g 2 3   and   (g 2)   and   (g 3)   ∎

The idea that there are *values* that are functions, and that there are expressions whose values are functions, is made more explicit by a notation known as *lambda abstraction*. The following expression:

\y -> (1 + y)

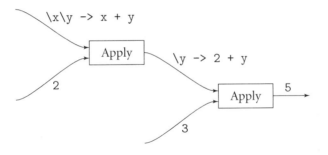

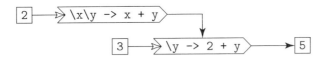

Figure 2.1 Two visualizations of: (\x->\y-> (x + y)) 2 3.

represents exactly the same function value that (plus 1) represents. The leading "\" is pronounced *lambda* and is a typographical approximation to the symbol λ used for the same purpose in mathematical texts. The notation may be read as "a function that produces, for any *y*, one plus *y*."

The following expression:

\x -> \y -> (x + y)

can be read as

the function that, for any *x*, produces

the function that, for any *y*, produces

$x + y$

Thus, this expression represents exactly the same function value that the identifier plus represents. Two visualizations of the application of this function to arguments 2 and 3 are shown in Figure 2.1.

Instead of getting buried in nested λs for multiargument functions, *pH* provides the following abbreviation for the previous expression:

\x y -> (x + y)

In general, a lambda abstraction has the form

$\backslash x_1 \ldots x_n \rightarrow$ *expression*

and represents a function with *n* formal parameters, and *expression* as its body. In fact, whenever we write a definition of the form

f $x_1 \ldots x_n$ = *expression*

this should always be seen as syntactic sugar for the "purer" form

f = $\backslash x_1 \ldots x_n \rightarrow$ *expression*

For example:

plus = \x y -> x + y

Why these two ways of doing things, when one could do? The answer is mostly historical and a matter of stylistic preferences. The λ form is the purer form and has a longer history. However, in the original definition of plus, the structure of the left-hand side, "plus x y", resembles the way the function is used in an application, "plus $e_1 \ e_2$", and so it is easier to see the definition directly as a rewrite rule. In practice, in *pH* programs, the λ form is not often used; one usually employs this form only for simple, one-off, in situ function definitions.

An important restriction is that the identifiers in the formal parameters of a lambda abstraction or function definition must be distinct. Thus, it is syntactically incorrect to write functions like these:

f ... x ... x ... = *e*

\ ... y ... y ... -> *e*

which repeat x and y, respectively. This restriction is also known in the literature as *left linearity*.

2.3   Data Types

We can gain a much deeper understanding of a function like plus by examining its *data type*, which is an abstract description of the function.

2.3.1   Every Expression Has a Type

First, we think of basic values as belonging to different types. For example, we think of 23 as a number, "Hello" as a character string, True and False as booleans, and so on. We use the following notation to express this idea:

```
23        ::  Int
23.0      ::  Float
"Hello"   ::  String
True      ::  Bool
```

Intuitively, one can think of a type as a set. A value that belongs to that set has that type. The "::" notation is part of *pH* syntax—it can be used to specify the type of any expression.

In addition to basic values, we can think of an expression that produces a basic value as belonging to the type of that value. For example,

```
(sqrt 529.0)            ::  Float
(substring "Hello" 0 3) ::  String   -- string with first three letters
(not False)             ::  Bool
```

A function expects an argument from a particular set and produces a result in a particular set, which may be a different set. We call these sets the domain and range of the function, respectively. For example, the square root function sqrt both expects and produces a floating-point number. We express this idea as follows:

```
sqrt  ::  Float -> Float
```

The boolean not function takes a boolean value and produces a boolean value:

```
not   ::  Bool -> Bool
```

The even function expects an integer and produces a boolean value indicating whether the argument was an even number or not:

```
even  ::  Int -> Bool
```

The type of a function is also known as its *type signature*.

Other functions that have type Float->Float include sin, cos, and log. Thus, we can think of "Float->Float" also as a set: the set of all functions that, given a floating-point number, produce a floating-point number. Each of the functions sqrt, sin, and so on are indeed members of this set.

The symbol "->" is read as an arrow. We call "->" a *type constructor* because, given two types t_1 and t_2, it builds a new type t_1->t_2. Again, thinking of types as sets, the type constructor "->" takes two sets represented by t_1 and t_2 and defines a new set named t_1->t_2 that contains all functions that, when given an argument in the set t_1, produce a result in the set t_2. Consider our function plus:

        plus   ::   Int -> (Int -> Int)

We can read this as saying: plus belongs to the set of functions that, when applied to an argument belonging to Int, produces a function in the set Int->Int, that is, the set that contains all functions that, when applied to an argument belonging to Int, produce a result belonging to Int. The infix arrow type operator associates to the right, so we can drop the parentheses above:

        plus   ::   Int -> Int -> Int

Exercise 2.5   Give an example of a function of type String->Int.   ■

Exercise 2.6   What is the type signature of the substring function that takes a string s, two integers i and n, and returns a string containing the characters $s_i, s_{i+1}, \ldots, s_{i+n-1}$?   ■

Exercise 2.7   Write down the type signature of a function that takes the x, y, and z coordinates of two points in three-dimensional space and returns the distance between these points.   ■

Exercise 2.8   Describe a function that has the following type signature:

        Float->Float->Float -> Float->Float->Float ->
                        Float->Float->Float -> Float

(*Hint:* The previous exercise described a property of two points; step it up one level.) Parenthesize the above type signature so that its structure is apparent.   ■

2.3.2   Type Correctness and Type Checking

Intuitively, we know that certain functions can only be applied to certain arguments. For example, it does not make sense to apply the square root function `sqrt` to a boolean value or to a string—it should only be applied to a number. Further, it does not make sense to use `sqrt`'s result in some context where a number is not expected, for example as an argument to the boolean negation function:

```
not (sqrt 3.5)
```

This idea can be expressed formally as a constraint on types. Suppose we have a function application (`f x`) and we annotate all subexpressions with subscripts representing their types:

$$(\ f_{(t1 \longrightarrow t2)} \quad x_{t3} \ )_{t4}$$

That is, the function has type ($t1 \longrightarrow t2$), the argument has type $t3$, and the result of the application has type $t4$. For this application to make sense, we must have the following constraints:

$$t1 \ = \ t3 \quad \text{and} \quad t2 \ = \ t4$$

This ensures that the expected type of the argument ($t1$) is indeed equal to the type of the actual argument ($t3$), and that the result type of the function ($t2$) is indeed equal to the type of the whole expression ($t4$).

For example, consider again the following expression:

```
plus 1 2
```

If we annotate all subexpressions with types as subscripts, we get

$$((\ plus_{(Int \ -> \ (Int \ -> \ Int))} \ 1_{Int}) \ _{(Int \ -> \ Int)} \ 2_{Int} \ )_{Int}$$

This is depicted pictorially in Figure 2.2.

Consider this function:

```
f x = plus x 10
```

Thinking of constraints on types, we can infer that `x` must be of type `Int` and, since the result of the function is an `Int`, we must have

```
f  :: Int -> Int
```

In a *pH* program, such constraints are always checked by the language implementation *statically* (i.e., before the program is actually compiled or executed). A program that does not successfully type check will not be compiled or executed. Unlike many other statically typed languages (like C, Pascal, Fortran, or Java), it is not necessary for the *pH* programmer

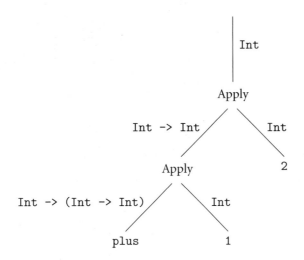

Figure 2.2 Expression "plus 1 2" fully annotated with types.

to declare the types explicitly for every variable; the type checker infers whatever it needs (in the way we inferred that the argument x above must be an Int). Nevertheless, it is considered good style explicitly to declare the types of every identifier defined at the top level. Typically, the type declaration is given just before the identifier's definition, like so:

```
f   :: Int -> Int
f x = plus x 10
```

with the "::" aligned with the "=". We will discuss types and type checking in more detail in the next chapter (Chapter 3).

2.4   Conditional Expressions

Programs do not really become interesting until they do some decision making. For this, we use conditional expressions. Here is a program to compute the maximum of two numbers:

```
max     :: Int -> Int -> Int
max x y = if x >= y then x
             else y
```

In words: if x is greater than or equal to y, return x, else return y. Thus, the expressions "max 3 5" and "max 5 3" both evaluate to 5.

In general, given a conditional expression

if e_1 **then** e_2 **else** e_3

e_1 is evaluated to a boolean value (i.e., True or False). Then, depending on this value, the conditional expression is replaced by either e_2 or e_3, whose value thus represents the value of the entire conditional expression.[1] Expressed as rewrite rules, we have

if True **then** e_2 **else** e_3 $\longrightarrow$ e_2

if False **then** e_2 **else** e_3 $\longrightarrow$ e_3

We refer to e_1 as the *predicate* of the conditional and the expressions e_2 and e_3 as the *arms* of the conditional. It is clear the e_1 should have type Bool, but what about e_2 and e_3? Since conditionals may be used for arbitrary computations, they can have arbitrary type. However, in order to preserve static type checking, we *do* constrain e_2's type to be the same as e_3's, and this type, in turn, is the type of the whole conditional expression. (We will see that this is not a limitation at all when we discuss *union* or *sum* types in Chapter 6.)

Note that one of the two arms e_2 and e_3 is always discarded. This raises two very interesting issues. The first issue is semantic: suppose e_2 or e_3 contains an error, for example, "5.0 / 0.0" or "sqrt (–3.0)". We must ensure that this error has no effect on the computation should this arm be discarded. The second issue is a matter of efficiency: reducing an arm of a conditional is wasted effort if it is subsequently discarded. This is to be avoided in a real machine because it takes up machine resources (such as processor time) that could be better utilized elsewhere. The first issue is addressed by the formal rewrite rules for *pH* (to be introduced in Chapter 4) that ensure that errors inside arms of conditionals do not affect anything outside the conditional, thus keeping such problems contained. The second issue is addressed by a practical rule in implementations of *pH* whereby no reductions are performed in either arm of a conditional expression. After the predicate e_1 is reduced, the entire conditional is replaced by one of its arms; at this point, it is no longer within the arm

---

1. For programmers familiar with Fortran or Pascal, it may take a little effort getting used to the idea that an **if–then–else** form is an *expression* that reduces to a value. In those languages, it is usually a *command* and does not represent a value at all. For those familiar with C, the analog to *pH*'s conditional is the conditional operator $e_1?e_2:e_3$.

of a conditional, so this rule no longer applies and we can begin reducing it.

Exercise 2.9   What is the value of

```
10 * (if 2*2 < 4 then (sqr 4) else (plus 2 3))
```

(Here, "$a < b$" checks if a is strictly less than b.)   ∎

There is a small syntactic ambiguity related to the **else** in a conditional expression, which we solve using a precedence rule. When we have

```
if ... else a + b
```

it means

```
if ... else (a + b)
```

rather than

```
(if ... else a) + b
```

because **else** has a weaker precedence than any of the operators.

2.5   Recursion

Let us now look at programs that perform repetitive computations. For example, Euclid's method to compute the greatest common divisor (GCD) of two positive integers a and b works as follows. If b is zero, then a is the answer. Otherwise, the answer is the GCD of b and r, where r is the remainder when a is divided by b. In other words, beginning with an initial pair of numbers a and b, we must continually replace them by b and $remainder(a, b)$, respectively, until the second number is zero, at which point the answer is the first number. For example,

```
gcd 60 36  ⟶  gcd 36 24  ⟶  gcd 24 12  ⟶  gcd 12 0  ⟶  12
```

This kind of repetition, or iteration, is expressed very naturally using recursion. Here it is in *pH*:

```
gcd      :: Int -> Int -> Int
gcd a b  = if b == 0 then a
                else gcd b (rem a b)
```

(Here, "v == w" checks if v is equal to w.) Let us observe the computation of "gcd 24 12".

```
         gcd 24 12
    ⟶   if 12 == 0 then 24 else gcd 12 (rem 24 12)    using gcd
    ⟶   if False then 24 else gcd 12 (rem 24 12)      operator ==
    ⟶   gcd 12 (rem 24 12)                            conditional
    ⟶   gcd 12 0                                      primitive rem
    ⟶   if 0 == 0 then 12 else gcd 0 (rem 12 0)       using gcd
    ⟶   if True then 12 else gcd 0 (rem 12 0)         operator ==
    ⟶   12                                            conditional
```

Magic? How can we meaningfully define gcd in terms of itself? The answer is that gcd is defined inductively; the definition is split into two parts—a simple "base case" that does not rely on gcd and an "inductive case" that relies on gcd, but with arguments that are in some sense closer to the base case. Thus, any call to gcd results in a chain of calls that progressively get simpler until, eventually, it "bottoms out" in the base case.

Note that while recursion gives us great expressive power, it also provides an opportunity to write programs that will not terminate. For example,

```
gcd a b = gcd b (rem a b)
```

is a legal *pH* program, but will not terminate, since there is no base case. The question of whether a program will terminate or not may not always be so obvious. Even if there is a conditional expression and a base case, it may not be obvious whether the reduction process will ever reach it. The reader is invited to try such an analysis on this program, called "McCarthy's 91 function":

```
mc91   :: Int -> Int
mc91 x =  if x > 100 then x - 10
          else mc91 (mc91 (x+11))
```

Before the reader gets too excited about trying to find a general method to predict whether a function will terminate, we hasten to point out that this "halting problem" is the most famous of the undecidable problems; it can be proved that there cannot be any such method of prediction. The proof is most ingenious and uses the same kind of diagonalization argument by which we show that the real numbers are uncountable. We refer the reader to any book on the theory of computation for this discussion.[2]

Let us look at another example, where we want to raise a number x to an integer power n, without using pH's exponentiation operator x^n. We can take advantage of the following facts:

$$x^0 = 1$$
$$x^n = (x^{n/2})^2 \qquad n > 0, \; n \text{ is even}$$
$$x^n = x \cdot x^{n-1} \qquad n > 0, \; n \text{ is odd}$$

We can express this directly in pH:

```
exp n x = if n == 0 then 1
              else if (even  n) then sqr (exp (div n 2) x)
              else x * exp (n–1) x
```

where even tests if a number is even, div performs integer division, and sqr squares a number.

Exercise 2.10   What is the type signature of exp?   ∎

Exercise 2.11   Write a pH function to compute the x^n using repeated multiplication, that is,

$$x^0 \quad = 1$$
$$x^{n+1} = x \cdot x^n$$

Compare the number of multiplications performed in your solution and in the exp function above.   ∎

2.5.1   Integrating a Function

Suppose we want to compute the definite integral of a function f over some interval (a, b). One way to approximate it is to sum the areas of a series of rectangles that approximate the area under the curve, that is, to compute

$$(f(a + \frac{dx}{2}) + f(a + \frac{3dx}{2}) + f(a + \frac{5dx}{2}) + \cdots) \times dx$$

for suitably small dx, as shown in Figure 2.3. Of course, the approximation improves with smaller dx, but it involves the summation of more terms.

----

2. The proof is so simple, so elegant and magical that it is difficult to avoid the temptation to believe that there must be *some* way around it! It can be safely said that you have not achieved wisdom until you have spent some time of your life trying to invent a perpetual motion machine or trying to solve the halting problem.

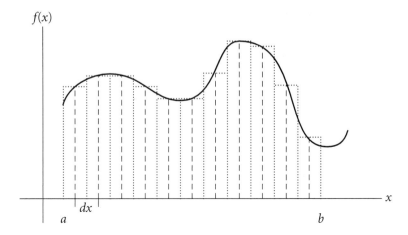

Figure 2.3 Computing the definite integral of a function.

We can express this in *pH*:

```
integrate          :: Float -> Float -> Float ->
                              (Float->Float) -> Float

integrate dx a b f = (accum dx b f (a + dx/2.0) 0.0) * dx

accum dx b f x tot = if x > b then tot
                         else accum dx b f (x+dx) (tot + f x)
```

Here, integrate calls accum to do the series addition beginning at $x = a + dx/2$ and initial total $= 0.0$ and multiplies the final total by dx. accum, in turn, iteratively adds dx to x and $f(x)$ to the total until $x > b$.

Now, for example, the expression

```
integrate  0.001  1.0  10.0  (exp 2)
```

computes the integral of the squaring function in the interval 1 to 10, with a "resolution" of 0.001.

Exercise 2.12   In the above application of integrate, how many times is the function accum called? Write down a general expression, in terms of dx, a, and b, that describes the number of times accum is called. ∎

Exercise 2.13   What happens if we call integrate with $a > b$? For example:

```
integrate  0.001  1.0  0.0  (exp 2)
```
∎

Exercise 2.14   Write down a type declaration for the function accum. ∎

Let us play around with `integrate` to get some practice with currying notation and higher-order functions. First, we define two integrators, one coarse, but fast, and the other fine, but slow:

```
coarse_integrate = integrate 0.01
```

```
fine_integrate = integrate 0.0001
```

Now, the expression

```
fine_integrate 5 10 sqr
```

gives us the fine-grained (more accurate) integral for the squaring function in the range 5 to 10.

We have used currying notation to specialize the general-purpose `inte-grate` function into a coarse-grained and a fine-grained integrator. Now let us specialize the fine-grained integrator further into a function that is a "fine-grained integrator in the range 1 to 10":

```
integrate_1_10 = fine_integrate 1 10
```

Alternatively, we could also have written this as

```
integrate_1_10 = integrate  0.0001  1  10
```

Exercise 2.15   Write down type declarations for `coarse_integrate`, `fine_integrate`, and `integrate_1_10`.   ■

Suppose we want to find the difference between the integrals of two functions f and g in the range 1 to 10. Referring to Figure 2.4, we want to find the area of the shaded region between the two curves $f(x)$ and $g(x)$. Here is one solution:

```
(integrate_1_10 f) - (integrate_1_10 g)
```

Specifically, if f and g were the cube and square functions, respectively, we would write

```
(integrate_1_10 (exp 3)) - (integrate_1_10 (exp 2))
```

Another solution is to define a general function that computes the difference of two other functions:

```
diff f g x = (f x) - (g x)
```

and then evaluate

```
integrate_1_10 (diff (exp 3) (exp 2))
```

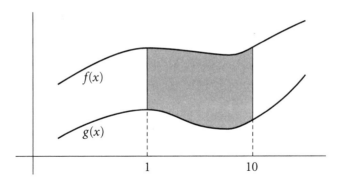

Figure 2.4   The difference between the integrals of two functions.

Exercise 2.16   How many additions and multiplications are performed by each of the two solutions above?   ■

Exercise 2.17   Write down a type declaration for `diff`.   ■

2.5.2   Higher-Order Computation Structures

Higher-order functions contribute greatly to the expressive power of *pH* because they enable us to capture the common computation structures of similar functions by abstracting away their differences into parameters. For example, in mathematics we can define addition, multiplication, and exponentiation starting with just the successor function $(+1)$, as follows:

$$a + b = a \overbrace{+ 1 + 1 \cdots + 1 + 1}^{b \text{ times}}$$
$$a \times b = 0 + a + a \cdots + a + a$$
$$a^b \quad = 1 \times a \times a \cdots \times a \times a$$

That is, the first line defines $+$ in terms of the successor function, the second line uses the definition of $+$ to define $\times$, and the third line uses the definition of $\times$ to define exponentiation.

All these computations share a common iterative structure. They differ in the initial value $(a, 0, \text{ or } 1)$ and in the function used to compute successive values $(+ 1, + a, \text{ or } \times a)$.

The common structure can be captured in the following *pH* function, which applies a function to a value n times:

```
apply_n  f  n  x = if n == 0 then x
                      else apply_n f (n–1) (f x)
```

Each of our specific functions can then be defined by supplying `apply_n` with the appropriate parameters.

```
succ x   = x + 1

plus a b = apply_n  succ  b  a

mult a b = apply_n  (plus a)  b  0

exp  a b = apply_n  (mult a)  b  1
```

2.5.3   Syntactic Spice: Infix Operators as Identifiers

Infix operators such as "+" have a dual role: they represent a binary function (here, the addition function), and they play a syntactic role whereby they appear between their arguments. By enclosing an infix operator in parentheses, we can treat the operator as if it were an ordinary identifier without any special syntactic role. In this form, it just represents a curried function. For example, we can declare

```
(+)  ::  Int -> Int -> Int
```

and we can use it as we would a curried function: the expression

```
(+) 10
```

represents a one-argument function that adds 10 to its argument. In particular,

```
x + y    ≡     (+) x y
```

Using this notation, our examples from the last section can be written even more succinctly:

```
plus a b = apply_n ((+) 1) b a

mult a b = apply_n ((+) a) b 0

exp  a b = apply_n ((*) a) b 1
```

This notation for converting infix operators into ordinary identifiers is one of the few exceptions to the general rule that parentheses are used only for grouping. Section 2.9 will discuss more issues and nuances concerning infix operators, including precedence and associativity, user-defined operators, and so on.

2.6   Blocks

Suppose we want to compute 2^4 (without using the `sqr` or `exp` functions). We could write "2*2*2*2" explicitly, which performs three multiplications. Another way would be first to compute $y = 2 \times 2$ and then compute $y \times y$, so that we perform only two multiplications. Basically, we need a way to name the intermediate result y so that it can be used more than once. We do this using a new construct called a block:

```
let
    y = 2 * 2
in
    y * y
```

A block is introduced by "**let**," followed by one or more definitions, the keyword "**in**," and a body, which is an expression. The body and the right-hand sides of the definitions may use identifiers defined by the definitions. In our example, there is only one definition, and it binds the identifier y to the value of the expression 2*2. The whole block is also an expression; that is, it represents a value—the value of the body. In our example, y represents the value 4 within the block, so the body of the block represents the value 16, and so the block as a whole represents the value 16. Clearly, the body expression's type is also the type of the block as a whole.

In general there may be many definitions in a block. However, each definition should define a distinct identifier—duplicate definitions would potentially be inconsistent. The order of these definitions in the block is not relevant; permuting the definitions does not change the semantics of the block. One should think of the definitions just as a declarative *specification* of the values that are bound to the identifiers. They do not imply any particular order of evaluation; indeed, they may be evaluated in parallel. In particular, one should never read the definitions in a block as a sequence of assignment statements—they are neither assignment statements nor are they textually sequenced!

2.6.1   The Function `integrate`, Revisited

In defining `integrate` in the previous section, we defined an auxiliary function `accum`, but there was a certain lack of modularity there. If one were to glance casually at a file of *pH* code containing these functions, one might wonder whether `accum` was used only by `integrate` or also by other functions elsewhere in the file. The only way to find out would be to scan the whole file. Instead, we can directly express the idea that `accum` is used only by `integrate` by localizing it in a block in the definition of `integrate`:

```
integrate dx a b f =
    let
        accum dx b f x tot = if x > b then tot
                             else accum dx b f (x+dx)
                                                (tot + f x)
    in
        dx * (accum dx b f (a + dx/2.0) 0.0)
```

In fact, since dx, b, and f are "visible" everywhere in `integrate`'s definition, and since they are not changed by `accum`, we do not have to pass them as parameters to `accum`—we can refer to them directly:

```
integrate dx a b f =
    let
        accum x tot = if x > b then tot
                      else accum (x+dx) (tot + f x)
    in
        dx * (accum (a + dx/2.0) 0.0)
```

We will explore more details about "visibility" in Section 2.7, which discusses static scoping.

2.6.2   Square Roots Using Newton's Method

Consider a function to compute the square root of a number using the Newton's method of successive approximations (this example is taken from [1]). We begin with a guess y_0 (say, 1) for the square root of the number x and continually improve it by averaging the current guess y with x/y. We stop and return the value of y when it is "good enough"—close enough to the actual square root. This test is performed by checking if y^2 is within a tolerance *epsilon* of x (for some constant *epsilon*). Here is the program, first written in a "flat" style:

```
is_good_enough x y = (abs (y*y - x) < epsilon)
improve          x y = (y + x/y) / 2.0
```

```
iter              x y = if is_good_enough x y then y
                           else iter x (improve x y)

sqrt              :: Float -> Float
sqrt x            = let
                        y0 = 1.0
                    in
                        iter x y0
```

Now, we rewrite it using a block to localize the auxiliary functions, and to exploit the visibility of x to avoid passing it as a parameter everywhere (since x does not change):

```
sqrt    :: Float -> Float
sqrt x = let
             y0                = 1.0
             is_good_enough y  = (abs (y*y - x) < epsilon)
             improve y         = (y + x/y) / 2.0
             iter y            = if is_good_enough y then y
                                      else iter (improve y)
         in
             iter y0
```

(Here, abs computes the absolute value of its argument.)

2.6.3   More Syntactic Spice: "Layout" and the "Offside Rule"

In the example above, one may note that there is no explicit punctuation between the definitions in the **let**-block (such as the semicolons that are popular in other languages). In *pH*, we use indentation and layout to separate the definitions. Each definition is allowed to extend to the right of ("east") and below ("southeast") the first letter of the definition. Each subsequent definition must begin directly below ("south") of the previous definition. For example, because the first letter "i" of the is_good_enough definition begins directly below the first letter "y" of the y0 definition, we know that it starts a new definition and that it is not an extension of the y0 definition. With this simple rule, there is no ambiguity about where one definition ends and the next one begins—being due south, the subsequent definition is "offsides" with respect to the legal region (east and southeast) for the first definition.

2.7   Static Scoping

Consider a function to compute the area of a circle:

```
circle_area r = pi * r * r
```

It seems quite intuitive that we could have written, equivalently,

```
circle_area radius = pi * radius * radius
```

That is, whether we choose to name the formal parameter r or radius may be important for readability, but has no semantic significance. However, we do not have *complete* freedom in choosing these names. For example, suppose we had chosen pi instead of radius:

```
circle_area pi = pi * pi * pi
```

This is a perfectly legal function, except that its meaning has changed: the name circle_area notwithstanding, it is really the cubing function $f(x) = x^3$!

This discussion brings out the important notions of *bound* and *free* variables. We start by distinguishing binding occurrences and use occurrences of variables. In a binding statement, the variable on the left-hand side that is being defined is a *binding occurrence*. The occurrence of circle_area on the left is such a binding occurrence. All formal parameter variables are also binding occurrences. In the example, r on the left-hand side is also a binding occurrence. Note that these definitions hold even if we had written

```
circle_area = \r -> pi * r * r
```

All other occurrences of variables are *use occurrences* or, simply, *uses*. Thus, the pi and two rs in the body of the function are all uses. Another practice example:

```
accum dx b f x tot = if x > b then tot
                          else accum dx b f (x+dx) (tot + f x)
```

Here, all identifiers to the left of the "=" are binding occurrences, and all identifiers to the right (including accum) are uses.

2.7.1   Scopes

The lexical structure of the text of a program defines a collection of nested *scopes*. For example, a λ-abstraction defines a new scope, and a **let**-block

defines a new scope. Scopes are always properly nested; they never overlap partially. In each scope (excluding any scopes nested inside), a particular identifier cannot have more than one binding (it can have any
number of uses, including zero). Consider the following program fragments:

```
\x -> ... x ... (\x -> ... x ...) ... x ...
```

and

```
x   = 23

f y = x + y

g x = f (x * x)

z   = g 5
```

The scopes in these programs are depicted as rectangles in Figure 2.5.
(The subscripts and superscripts are not part of the program syntax; we
have added them here just for convenience, so that we can discuss individual occurrences of identifiers separately.) The (unique) binding occurrence
corresponding to any particular use is the one in the nearest surrounding scope (rectangle). In Figure 2.5(a), x_2 and x_5 are uses, and x_1 is the
corresponding binding occurrence. Similarly, x_4 is a use, and x_3 is its corresponding binding. We also say that the binding occurrence x_3 *shadows*
the outer binding occurrence x_1 within the inner scope. In Figure 2.5(b),

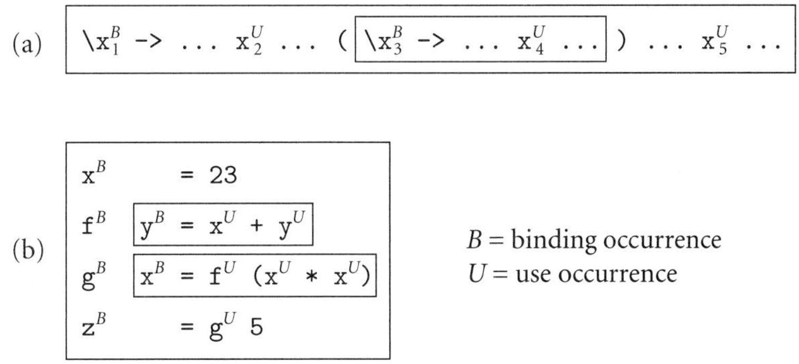

(a) $\boxed{\ \backslash x_1^B \ \text{->} \ \ldots \ x_2^U \ \ldots \ (\ \boxed{\backslash x_3^B \ \text{->} \ \ldots \ x_4^U \ \ldots} \ ) \ \ldots \ x_5^U \ \ldots\ }$

(b) $\boxed{\begin{array}{l} x^B \quad\ = 23 \\ f^B \ \boxed{y^B = x^U + y^U} \\ g^B \ \boxed{x^B = f^U \ (x^U * x^U)} \\ z^B \quad\ = g^U \ 5 \end{array}}$

B = binding occurrence
U = use occurrence

Figure 2.5 Static scoping and binding and use occurrences in (a) λ-terms and
(b) definition lists.

the use of x in f's definition corresponds to the outer-level binding of x to 23, whereas the use of x in g's definition corresponds to its formal parameter. This notion of scopes and binding is common to almost all modern programming languages and is called *lexical scoping* or *static scoping*.

2.7.2   Free Identifiers

An identifier x is *free* in a program region R if there is a use of x in R but R does not contain a corresponding binding occurrence of x. In our circle_area example (the lambda abstraction version):

- r is free in the expressions r and r * r.
- r and pi are both free in the function body (pi * r * r).
- r is not free in \r -> pi * r * r, but pi is free.

In Figure 2.5(a), the variable x is

- free in the expression ... x_4 ...
- not free in the expression \x_3 -> ... x_4 ...
- free in the expression ... x_2 ... (\x_3 -> ... x_4 ...) ... x_5 ... (because of x_2 and x_5)
- not free in the entire expression

2.7.3   Why Not Dynamic Scoping?

The program in Figure 2.5(b) can also be used to illustrate the alternative to static scoping, dynamic scoping: In the right-hand side of z, we call g, binding its formal parameter x to the actual argument 5. This, in turn, calls f, binding its formal parameter y to the square of x, that is, to 25. This is depicted pictorially in Figure 2.6. (In traditional programming language implementation parlance, the rectangles in the figure represent stack frames in the call tree.) In the f application (lowest rectangle), we add x to 25—but, which x do we mean? The two possibilities are depicted in the figure. If we look at the chain of computations, the "most recent" or "nearest" binding of x is to 5 (middle rectangle). The static scoping rule, however, states that the referend of x in the body of f is determined by the original text of the program and not on the particular chains of computations arising dynamically (i.e., it refers to 23).

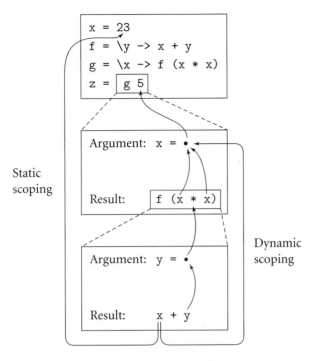

Figure 2.6 Static versus dynamic scoping.

The alternative, dynamic scoping, is very fragile. With dynamic scoping, x in f's computation refers to its nearest binding in the chain of computations (i.e., its binding to 5). Now, suppose we made the following apparently innocent change to g's definition:

```
g w = f (w * w)
```

and made corresponding changes to Figure 2.6. Suddenly, the nearest binding of x is the one binding it to 23! To appreciate the gravity of this unexpected change, consider that g's definition may be in a separate module written by some other programmer. We may not even be aware of what name that other programmer chose for g's formal parameter, but that decision crucially affects the meaning of our part of the program! It is to avoid this kind of unstable behavior that most modern programming languages, including *pH*, choose a static scope discipline. (Early versions of Lisp actually had dynamic scoping, but modern Common Lisp reverts to static scoping.)

2.7.4 α-Renaming

We can now be more precise about the freedom to rename variables. A binding occurrence of an identifier x and all its corresponding uses may together be renamed to y provided that there is no existing free variable y in the scope of x. The reason is obvious. In our original example:

```
\r -> pi * r * r
```

pi is free in the scope of r (it must be bound at some outer level). If we renamed r to pi, the existing pi gets *captured* by this binding. This systematic renaming of variables that avoids free variable capture is historically known as α-*renaming*.

2.7.5   Scoping in Blocks

In addition to being a mechanism for sharing computations, blocks are also a scoping mechanism. An entire block is a new scope nested within the scope where the block appears. All the identifiers defined in the definitions are binding occurrences, and their scope is the entire block, including all the right-hand sides of the definitions and the block's body. All the identifiers defined in the block are invisible outside the block.

Since blocks are expressions, they may appear within other blocks or within function bodies; they may contain other blocks or function bodies; and so on. The principle of lexical scoping continues to hold. For example:

```
let
    x = if b then
            let
                x = 23                    -- inner block
            in
                .
                .
                .

        else
            .
            .
            .

    f = \x -> ... x ...
in
    f (x+1)
```

In the outer block, including its body expression, x represents the value of the conditional expression. In the inner block, x represents the value 23. In the lambda abstraction, x represents any actual parameter to which f is applied.

The concept of free identifiers also makes sense with blocks. For example, in this block:

```
let
    y = x * x
in
    y * y
```

the identifier x is free, but the identifier y is not. α-renaming may also be applied to the identifiers bound in blocks. For example, we could have written this example like this:

```
let
    w = x * x
in
    w * w
```

with no change in meaning, but we could not have renamed y to x, because it would capture the free variable x.

2.8   Loops

In Section 2.5 we introduced recursion to express repetitive computations. A special case of recursion is "iteration," or "tail recursion." It is an important and frequent-enough structure to merit special syntactic treatment. In most programming languages, iteration is expressed using special syntactic constructs called *loops*. *pH* has notation for while and for loops, the latter being a further special case where the number of iterations is known before the loop begins execution.

Let us start by reexamining our original gcd program, which we repeat here for reference:

```
gcd     :: Int -> Int -> Int
gcd a b = if b == 0 then a
              else gcd b (rem a b)
```

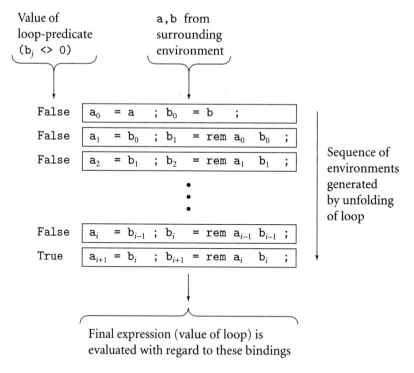

Figure 2.7 The structure of the gcd loop.

We can also write this in *pH* using a while-loop, as follows:

```
gcd a b = while b <> 0 do
              next a = b
              next b = (rem a b)
          finally a
```

The way to think about this loop is depicted in Figure 2.7.

Execution of the loop involves the generation of a sequence of bindings for a and b. The **next** bindings in the loop body (between **do** and **finally**) specify the relationship beween one set of bindings and the next. In the figure, we have subscripted the variables a and b to make this clear. In the first set of bindings, the values of a and b are simply the values extant in the surrounding environment (i.e., the values of the parameters of gcd). The last set of bindings to be generated is governed by the loop predicate (between **while** and **do**); it is evaluated with respect to each set of bindings, and a new set of bindings is generated as long as this value evaluates to

"True". The entire loop ultimately represents a value, which is the value of the final expression (after **finally**) evaluated with respect to the last set of bindings.

It is important to note that loops in *pH* are quite different from loops in other languages such as Fortran, Pascal, or Lisp. In those languages, variables like "a" and "b" correspond to memory locations that are repeatedly *updated* from one iteration to the next. A consequence of this is that no more than one iteration may be active at a time. In *pH* loops, on the other hand, one does not a priori impose any temporal ordering on the sequence of bindings—one thinks of all the sets of bindings as being evaluated concurrently, if possible. If there is any ordering, it is only because in a particular loop, one set of bindings may depend on previous bindings. This is the case in our gcd example, where the bindings of both a and b depend on previous bindings. However, in our next example, the dependencies are such that much more concurrency is possible. The `integrate` function is repeated here for reference:

```
integrate           :: Float -> Float -> Float -> Float -> Float
integrate dx a b f =
        let
            accum x tot = if x > b then tot
                             else accum (x+dx) (tot + f x)
        in
            dx * (accum (a + dx/2.0) 0.0)
```

Using loops, we can write

```
integrate dx a b f =
            let
                x   = a + dx/2
                tot = 0.0
            in
                while x <= b do
                    next x   = x + dx
                    next tot = tot + f x
                finally tot * dx
```

Here, the "unfolding" of the loop (i.e., the setting up of the sequence of environments that will contain bindings for x and tot) is controlled only by x, by repeated addition of dx until it exceeds b. One can imagine this happening very rapidly. Meanwhile, all the applications of "f" (to $x_0 = a + dx/2$,

$x_1 = a + 3 * dx/2, \ldots$, etc.) can execute concurrently. As these computations complete, the tot expressions gather their values up into the final sum. Thus, loops in *pH* have the same potential for concurrency as their recursive counterparts and should truly be viewed as just a different notation for iterative recursion.

In each of the recursive programs above that we converted into loops, the reader should notice that the recursive call itself represents the final value of the function; there is no further computation to be done with the result of the recursive call. This structure is called "tail recursion," and it is exactly the set of tail-recursive functions that can be expressed as loops. The following example illustrates the difference. Consider this function that computes *n!*, the factorial of *n:*

```
fact1   :: Int -> Int
fact1 n = if n == 1 then 1
          else n * fact1 (n-1)
```

This function is not tail-recursive because, after the recursive call, we still have to multiply the result by n. If we trace its reduction, we will see the following intermediate states:

```
      fact1 6
⟶ 6 * fact1 5
⟶ 6 * 5 * fact1 4
⟶ 6 * 5 * 4 * fact1 3
...
```

There is a series of pending multiplications stacked up waiting for the recursion to terminate. In general, the "size" of the term being reduced is proportional to the depth of the recursion, which is in turn proportional to the size of the original argument. Because it is not tail-recursive, the function cannot directly be translated into a loop.

On the other hand, here is a different way of computing *n!*:

```
fact2 n = fact2_aux n 1

fact2_aux n f = if n < 1 then f
                else fact2_aux (n-1) (f*n)
```

If we follow the reduction process, we see

```
      fact2 6
⟶ fact2_aux 6 1
```

```
⟶  fact2_aux 5 6
⟶  fact2_aux 4 30
⟶  fact2_aux 3 120
⟶  fact2_aux 2 360
⟶  fact2_aux 1 720
⟶  fact2_aux 0 720
⟶  720
```

Note that the size of the term being reduced remains constant, irrespective of the original argument to the function. This is the characteristic feature of tail recursion. Being tail-recursive, `fact2_aux` can be expressed as a loop:

```
fact2_aux n f = while n >= 1 do
                    next n = n−1
                    next f = f*n
                finally f
```

This conversion into tail-recursive form is not always possible. Observe that `fact1` computes $(6 \times (5 \times (4 \times \ldots \times 1)))$, whereas `fact2` computes $(((6 \times 5) \times 4) \ldots \times 1)$. Since multiplication is an *associative* operation, this did not change the answer. However, there are other functions where this transformation does change the answer, and in these cases a tail-recursive solution may not be possible.

Exercise 2.18 Write the function `iter` used in the `sqrt` function using a `while` loop instead of recursion. ∎

2.8.1   for Loops

In many applications, the unfolding of the loop is controlled by a simple arithmetic series. This is in fact the case for the `integrate` example above. To avoid the tedium of the bookkeeping for such loops—initializing the controlling variable, incrementing it, and testing it for completion—we provide a special **for** loop syntax:

```
integrate dx a b f =
              let
                  tot = 0
              in
                  for x <- [(a+dx/2), (a+dx+dx/2) .. b] do
                      next tot = tot + f x
                  finally tot * dx
```

The expression $[e_i \ldots e_f]$ represents the arithmetic sequence $e_i, e_i + 1,$ $e_i + 2, \ldots$ terminating at a value no greater than e_f. A nonunity increment can be specified explicitly using the notation $[e_i, e_d \ldots e_f]$, representing the sequence $e_i, e_i + \delta, e_i + 2\delta, \ldots$, where $\delta = e_d - e_1$.

Descending sequences can be given with the same notation, $[e_i, e_d \ldots e_f]$, where $e_d < e_i$; this represents the sequence $e_i, e_i - \delta, e_i - 2\delta, \ldots$, terminating at a value no smaller than e_f, where $\delta = e_i - e_d$.

Exercise 2.19   Write the function `apply_n` using a **for** loop.   ∎

A **for** loop can actually be controlled by an arbitrary list, and the above phrases are just special cases; we postpone the discussion of the general form until we discuss lists in Chapter 6.

2.9 ▾   More on Infix Operators

We have already seen that symbols like "+", "−", and "*" are infix operators; they represent binary (two-argument) functions and are written syntactically between their two arguments. We also saw that such symbols can be treated as ordinary identifiers by enclosing them in parentheses: "(+)", "(−)", and "(*)".

Conversely, it is also possible to use an identifier as an infix operator, by enclosing it in backquotes. Thus,

```
    x 'max' y      ≡      max x y
```

Sometimes, the infix form is more readable. For example, the expression

```
    item 'hasProperty' p
```

reads more smoothly than

```
    hasProperty item p
```

The programmer can define new infix operators. In general, an operator consists of sequence of symbols from the following set:

```
    ! # $ % & * + . / < = > ? @ \ ^ | - ~ :
```

except that the first symbol cannot be ":" (lexical terms beginning with ":" represent infix *data constructors*, which will be described in Chapter 6). In addition, certain lexical terms using these symbols are reserved. For example, "=" is used to separate left-hand sides from right-hand sides in definitions, "--" begins a comment, and so on.

For example, suppose, in an electronics program we want to express the idea of a signal voltage v "clamped" to a range $(-c, c)$. We could define an infix operator "|-|" for this, as follows:

```
(|-|)        :: Float -> Float -> Float

v  |-|  c  =  (-c) 'max' (v 'min' c)
```

In the first line (defining the type), it is not used in infix position and so we enclose it in parentheses. In the second line, we use it in infix position in the left-hand side of the definition.

We have already seen that with infix operators there is an issue of *precedence* and *associativity*. The expression

```
a + b * c
```

is considered equivalent to

```
a + (b * c)
```

because "*" has higher precedence than "+". In the expression

```
a - b - c
```

the two infix operators have the same precedence, but it is considered equivalent to

```
(a - b) - c
```

rather than the very different

```
a - (b - c)
```

because "-" is left-associative.

Some operators may be neither left- nor right-associative because they are not expected to be used in situations where associativity matters. Examples include the comparison operators "<" and ">". For example, we never use these operators in expressions like a<b<c where associativity would be needed to resolve the syntactic structure (if we did, the compiler will complain about ambiguous syntax).

The *pH* programmer can specify the precedence and associativity of operators defined in the program, including identifiers used as operators using backquotes, using *fixity* declarations. There are 10 precedence levels available, numbered from 0 (weakest) to 9 (strongest). Function application via juxtaposition, "f x", is considered to have precedence higher than 9. Thus, in any expression

f x *op* e   or   e *op* f x

the function application always binds more tightly:

(f x) *op* e   or   e *op* (f x)

Here are some examples of fixity declarations:

```
infixl  5  (|-|)
infix   5  'hasProperty'
```

The first line declares the operator "|-|" to have left-associativity (infixr is used to specify right-associativity) and precedence level 5, which is looser than "+", which has level 6, and is tighter than "<", which has level 4. The second line specifies that the identifier hasProperty, when used in infix form, has precedence level 5, but neither left- nor right-associativity.

One symbol, "-", is treated specially in *pH*. As is traditional in mathematics, it is used for two entirely different purposes—as the two-argument subtraction infix operator:

$$e_1 - e_2$$

and as the one-argument negation function:

$$- e$$

When enclosed in parentheses, "(-)", it represents the subtraction function.

2.10 ▾   Pragmatics: Inlining Function Calls

The *pH* programmer creates functions at the drop of a hat. Functions in *pH* are not luxury items—they are common, everyday consumer commodities. Breaking up a program into numerous small functions is also good from a software engineering standpoint. We frequently define functions that may be just a few lines long because each one expresses a simple, well-defined concept. We rarely write functions that are larger than a page or a screenfull, in order that they can be understood in isolation. By defining numerous functions with meaningful names, it becomes easier to read, understand, and maintain programs.

Unfortunately, a function call has some run-time cost (though the compiler works very hard to try and minimize it), and, in general, we are very interested in having our programs run as quickly as possible. For this reason the programmer may be tempted to eschew good software engineering practice and to write large, monolithic functions that involve as few function calls as possible. To resolve this tension, *pH* provides notation by which the programmer can advise the compiler to *inline* a function wherever possible, replacing a call to the function by the function body in situ, of course taking care of suitable renaming of identifiers (we will see in Chapter 4 that this is a static application of β-reduction rule). Such an advisory phrase is called a *pragma* because it addresses pragmatics, not semantics.

For example, consider these definitions presented earlier:

```
plus a b = apply_n ((+) 1) b a

mult a b = apply_n ((+) a) b 0

exp  a b = apply_n ((*) a) b 1
```

A performance-conscious programmer may choose not to make such apparently trivial definitions because of the overhead of a function call, choosing to write applications of apply_n directly; but, this makes the program harder to read. We can have our cake and eat it too by using the pragma

```
{-# inline  plus, mult, exp #-}
```

This advises the compiler to substitute these functions by their bodies wherever they are applied to all their arguments, avoiding the overhead.

There are some subtleties to consider with inlining. The first is to realize that the semantics of the *pH* program are not changed in the slightest. The substitution is completely transparent except for a change in efficiency. In fact, the compiler is free to ignore the pragma, with no change in the meaning of the program.

Second, whether or not the compiler chooses to follow the programmer's advice, the inlined functions are still available as function values. For example, we could write

```
integrate  dx  a  b  (plus 10)
```

This instance of `plus` cannot be inlined since it is not applied to two arguments.

Thus, inlining should not be confused with the "macro" facilities that are found in some programming languages. Macro facilities are purely a textual substitution device; a macro is not itself a function and has no role at run time. Further, because of textual substitutions, the concept of free and bound identifiers in macros can become very tricky.

What happens if the function to be inlined has a recursive definition? If we substitute the recursive call by the function body, the expanded body will again contain a recursive call. Clearly, the compiler cannot take the inlining advice too seriously because it would involve an infinite unfolding! Since a pragma is only a suggestion and is semantically transparent, the compiler is free to quit after a finite number of unfoldings (including zero unfoldings). Since inlining does not remove a function definition, the fact that the body still contains a recursive call is not a problem.

The compiler and programming environment also must deal with some subtleties relating to the order in which functions are compiled. For example, suppose we compile `f`, which contains a call to some function `g`, and then, while compiling some other module, the compiler encounters

```
g x = ...
{-# inline g #-}
```

The code previously produced for `f` contains an ordinary function call to `g`. The compiler may have to recompile the original module to benefit from inlining. Similarly, suppose the compiler has inlined `g` where it was called in `f`, and then the programmer changes the definition of `g`; the compiler would have to recompile `f` to keep it consistent. In short, inlining introduces another level of dependency between the definitions of `f` and `g` that the programming environment has to take into account.

Types and Type Checking

In **Chapter 2 we introduced** some aspects of types, which play a central role in *pH*. We saw that every expression has a type; that types represent sets of values; and that saying an expression has a type is an assertion that the value of the expression lies in the set of values denoted by the type. We saw basic types like integers, floating-point values, and booleans, and we saw function types representing sets of function values. We saw a notion of type correctness, whereby a function could only be applied to arguments of proper type. We said that the type correctness of a *pH* program is ascertained statically, before executing the program, via static type checking.

In this chapter, we explore types and type checking in greater detail, and then look at *polymorphism* and *overloading*, two devices that enhance expressive power significantly without compromising static type checkability.

The topics in this chapter are orthogonal to issues of parallelism, but are of central concern to the *pH* programmer.

3.1   Type Expressions

To write down an ordinary expression representing a value in *pH*, we start with primitive expressions—integer and other constants, and variable names—and then we build up more complex expressions by applying functions to arguments, using both ordinary application notation and infix operator notation.

Similarly, to write down a *type expression* representing a type, we start with primitive type expressions—Int, Bool, and so on—and then we build up more complex type expressions by applying *type constructors*, using both ordinary application notation and infix notation (and we will see shortly that there is also a notion of *type variable*). Thus, the type

```
Int -> Bool
```

consists of the primitive types Int and Bool, to which we have applied the infix "->" type constructor. In fact, we can regard primitive types like Int and Bool as 0-ary type constructors—type constructors with no arguments. In later chapters, we will see more examples of type constructors, such as

```
-- arrays with indices of type t₁ and elements of type t₂
Array  t₁  t₂
```

```
-- triples of values, with types t₁, t₂, and t₃, respectively
ThreeTuple  t₁  t₂  t₃
```

```
-- lists of values, each of type t
IList  t
```

As with ordinary computational expressions, we can use parentheses in type expressions to group terms, if necessary:

```
Int -> (Int -> Int)
(Int -> Int) -> Int
Array Int (ThreeTuple Char String (Float->Bool))
```

In general, a type constructor can be regarded as a function at a different level compared to ordinary functions; they are functions from types to types instead of from values to values.

In this book, all our type constructors will have alphanumeric names; such type constructors must begin with an initial uppercase (capital) letter. The only exceptions will be the infix "–>" and the special syntax used for tuple types (Chapter 5) and list types (Chapter 6). In *pH* the user can also define new infix type constructors, but we refer the reader to the manual for details.

Exercise 3.1   Define a function f that has the following type:

```
f     ::      (Int -> Int) -> Int                              ■
```

3.2   Static Type Checking and Type Inference

Type checking can be done statically (by examining the program, without executing it), dynamically (during program execution), some combination thereof, or even not at all. Languages without type checking (or with mininal type checking) include assembly languages and various "scripting" languages. Languages that have static type checking include C, C++, Fortran, Pascal, and Java. Languages that have dynamic type checking include Lisp, Scheme, Smalltalk, and APL. There is widespread consensus that type checking and type correctness is a Good Thing, whether it is done statically or dynamically. However, you can always start a good argument among language aficionados about the relative merits of static versus dynamic type checking.

In *pH*, type checking is static: if a *pH* program does not pass the type checker, it is not a valid *pH* program, and *pH* compilers and interpreters will not even attempt to compile or execute it. Experience with many programming languages has shown that a very large fraction of programming errors are type errors and that it is preferable to catch them early with static type checking rather than late, during program execution, with dynamic type checking. Further, when types are known statically, compilers are able to produce code that runs significantly faster (because they can omit all the dynamic type checks that would otherwise be present).

Static type checking sometimes has a reputation for excessive "bureaucracy," arising from several common limitations. First, in most statically typed languages, the programmer is required to declare the types of each and every identifier used in the program. Second, statically typed languages often do not allow *polymorphism* or *genericity*, whereby, for example, a single `length` function can be written to compute the length of all lists, whether lists of integers or lists of booleans or lists of whatever. Finally, static type systems often do not have sufficient *overloading* mechanisms, whereby, for example, one can extend the meaning of the operator symbol "*" to stand for the matrix multiplication function, in addition to its usual reference to the numeric multiplication function. In this section and those that follow, we discuss how *pH* overcomes these limitations.

pH's type checker uses *type inference* extensively to deduce the types of all expressions, based on the types of previously known identifiers and using type constraints such as the following: a function must be applied to proper arguments; the predicate of a conditional must have type `Bool`; the two arms of a conditional must have the same type; and so on. For example, consider the function:

```
fourth_root x = sqrt (sqrt x)
```

If we already know that the type of `sqrt` is (`Float->Float`), we can

- infer that x must have type `Float` from the inner application
- confirm that the outer application of `sqrt` is meaningful, since it expects a `Float` and is indeed supplied a `Float` from the inner application
- infer that the result of the whole function must have type `Float`, from the result type of the outer application

In fact, since `fourth_root`'s argument and result are both of type `Float`, we can infer its type as

```
fourth_root   ::   Float -> Float
```

We can then use this information to type check other parts of the program, wherever `fourth_root` is used, and so on.

Broadly speaking, the *pH* programmer need not declare the types of *any* identifiers at all. The type checker is capable of verifying type correctness entirely using type inferencing, starting with the known types of primitives and library functions.[1] Nevertheless, it is considered good programming style to supply at least the types of all top-level definitions. Typically, the type signature is given just before the function definition, like this:

```
plus      :: Int -> Int -> Int
plux x y = x + y
```

In general, any expression e can be annotated with a type t by writing $e::t$. Providing explicit top-level type declarations has several advantages:

- It greatly improves the readability of a program. When reading a program that someone else has written, or even reading your own program some days, months, or years after it was written, type declarations make it significantly easier to understand unfamiliar code.
- When explicit type declarations are given, the compiler can produce significantly better error diagnostics for programs that do have type errors.
- We will see, in Section 3.4, that some *overloaded* expressions have ambiguous types; explicit type declarations can resolve these ambiguities.

What follows are a series of type correctness rules that we, as *pH* programmers, must keep in mind as we write our programs and that the *pH* compiler uses in order to type check a program.

3.2.1   Type Rule for Functions

The type rule for functions is very natural. It says that if, assuming the argument x has a certain type,

$$x \ \ :: \ \ t_1$$

we find that the body expression e has a certain type,

$$e \ \ :: \ \ t_2$$

then the function with that argument and body has the following function type:

$$\backslash x\!\!-\!\!> e \ \ :: \ \ t_1\!\!-\!\!>t_2$$

---

1. This is not entirely true. The programmer is occasionally required to provide type declarations to allow the type checker to resolve certain cases of overloading, as discussed in Section 3.4.

3.2.2   Type Rule for Conditionals

In a conditional expression, it is clear that the predicate expression must have boolean type. But what about the type of the arms, and what about the type of the conditional expression itself? If the arms were of different types, then the type of the result would depend on which arm was selected, which is something we cannot decide statically. To avoid this problem, we insist that the two arms be of the same type, which, then, is also the type of the result. More formally, if

$$e_1 \ :: \ \texttt{Bool}$$
$$e_2 \ :: \ t$$
$$e_3 \ :: \ t$$

then

$$(\texttt{if } e_1 \texttt{ then } e_2 \texttt{ else } e_3) \ :: \ t$$

for any type t.

It is important to remember that these rules are applied statically at compile time. Consider the following definition:

```
f x = if False then x+5 else "Hello"
```

We may be tempted to think that this expression has type "`Int->String`", reasoning as follows: the argument must be an `Int` since we add 5 to it, and the result is obviously a `String` since the predicate is `False`. However, static type checking is blind to the actual values involved and the reductions they may imply and will reject this definition with a type error because it does not satisfy the typing rules for conditionals (the two arms of the conditional have different types here). We must take this position because otherwise we would be crossing into dangerous territory. Consider:

```
g y = False
```

```
f x = if g x then x+5 else "Hello"
```

Now we have to work a little harder before we realize that the result is always a string—and we could make this example even harder. There is no obvious place to draw the line. For this reason, static type checking blindly applies the type rules, without attempting to reason about what a particular expression may reduce to at run time.

3.2.3   Type Rule for Blocks

A block has a type—the type of the value it represents—and, since a block's value is the value of the body, the block's type is the same as the type of the block's body. More formally, if

$e :: t$

then

```
(let

    ⋮

 in
       e) :: t
```

Exercise 3.2   What is the value of

```
(if 3 < 4 then sqr else (plus 5)) 12
```

and what is the type of each subexpression?   ■

Exercise 3.3   Show the type of all occurrences of each identifier in

```
summap f n = if n < 0
                then 0
                else summap f (n-1) + f n
```
          ■

Exercise 3.4   Identify the type errors in the following terms:

```
f x = if x then x + 3 else x * 2

r g x y = if g x
             then g y
             else 2 + g y
```
          ■

3.3   Polymorphism

Let us look at a really fascinating function:

```
twice f x = f (f x)
```

twice takes a function f and a value x, applies f to x, and applies f again to the result. For example, the expression

```
twice sqr 4
```

should apply the squaring function twice to 4, that is, "`sqr (sqr 4)`", producing 256.

What about the following expression?

```
twice ((+) 3) 4
```

Recall that "`(+) 3`" represents a function of one argument that adds 3 to its argument. Thus, when applied twice to 4, we will add 3 to it twice, giving 10. Let us watch the reduction process:

```
    twice ((+) 3) 4
⟶  ((+) 3) (((+) 3) 4)       using the definition of twice
⟶  ((+) 3) 7                 using the built-in rules for (+)
⟶  10                        using the built-in rules for (+)
```

The type of `twice` as used in this example is very illuminating:

```
twice  ::  (Int->Int) -> Int -> Int
```

It takes two arguments, the first being a function from integers to integers, the second being an integer, and returns a result that is an integer.

Exercise 3.5   What does the following expression reduce to?

```
twice (twice sqr) 2
```

(*Hint:* The answer is the address space of the venerable old 8080 and 6502 microprocessors.)   ∎

If we examine the definition of `twice` carefully we see that, in fact, there is nothing to suggest that it is specific to numbers at all. For example, suppose we had a function that, given a character string, returned a string that was indented four spaces:

```
indent4  ::  String -> String
```

Now, it seems perfectly reasonable to define

```
indent8 s = twice  indent4  s
```

Let us try it out on an example:

```
    indent8 "Hi"
⟶  twice indent4 "Hi"          using the definition of indent8
⟶  indent4 (indent4 "Hi")      using the definition of twice
⟶  indent4 "␣␣␣␣Hi"            applying indent4
⟶  "␣␣␣␣␣␣␣␣Hi"                applying indent4 again
```

In this example,

```
twice  ::  (String->String) -> String -> String
```

Another example—the expression

```
twice  sqrt  16.0
```

produces the fourth root of 16.0 (i.e., 2.0). In this example:

```
twice  ::  (Float->Float) -> Float -> Float
```

This makes us wonder: how many types does twice have? Is there some general way of describing all its possible types? Let us infer the type of twice from its definition. We start by annotating it with types as subscripts, assuming that f has some type $(t1 \to t2)$ and x has some type $t3$:

$$\text{twice } f_{(t1 \to t2)} \; x_{t3} = (f_{(t1 \to t2)} \; (\; f_{(t1 \to t2)} \; x_{t3} \;)_{t4} \;)_{t5}$$

For x to be a sensible argument in the inner application, we must have

$$t3 = t1$$

The type of the result of the inner application of f is $t4$, so

$$t2 = t4$$

The result of the inner application is an argument to the outer f; for this to be sensible, we must have

$$t4 = t1$$

which implies that $t1 = t2$. And, similarly, we must have

$$t2 = t5$$

These constraints imply that if x has type $t3$, then the function f has type $(t3 \to t3)$ and the result of the function has type $t3$:

$$\text{twice } :: \; (t3 \to t3) \to t3 \to t3$$

In other words, if x has type Int, then f must have type (Int->Int), and the result has type Int. Similarly, if x has type String, then f must have type (String->String), and the result has type String.

Formally, we say that twice is a *polymorphic* function: it has (infinitely) many possible types. We indicate this using a *type variable:*

```
twice  ::  (a->a) -> a -> a
```

A type variable (here, a) is written just like an identifier (but there is no ambiguity because identifiers and type variables always occur in lexically distinct parts of a program). A type variable stands for *any* type, although multiple occurrences of a type variable in a type expression stand for the same (but unspecified) type. We also say that the above type is the *most general type* or *principal type* for twice because any particular type of twice can be obtained by substituting a specific type for the type variable; this process is called *instantiation*. When a type expression has no type variables in it, we refer to it as a *monomorphic* or *ground* type.

3.3.1   What Does a Polymorphic Type Mean?

Thinking of types as sets again, the polymorphic type

```
a -> a
```

represents the set of functions that, when given an argument of any particular type, return a result of the same type. A function in this set, given an Int argument, returns an Int result; given a String argument, returns a String result; given a (Float->Float) argument, returns a (Float->Float) result; and so on. Similarly, the polymorphic type

```
(a->a) -> a -> a
```

represents a set of functions. Each function that is a member of this set, when given Int->Int and Int arguments, returns an Int result; when given String->String and String arguments, returns a String result; when given (Float->Float)->(Float->Float) and Float->Float arguments, returns a Float->Float result; and so on.

It sometimes comes as a surprise to realize that the set of function values represented by the type

```
a -> a
```

is a *smaller* set than the set of function values represented by this monomorphic type:

```
Int -> Int
```

On closer reflection, the reason becomes clear: the polymorphic type is a *stronger constraint* on a function and so fewer function values satisfy it. A function f_i with the latter monomorphic type is merely constrained to return an Int if given an Int; it can do whatever it likes on floats or strings or booleans. A function f_p with the polymorphic type not only has to produce an Int when given an Int, but it must also produce a Bool if given a Bool, produce a String if given a String, and so on. This is a somewhat subtle philosophical position. If we think of a function as being implemented with code that operates blindly on the raw memory bits given to it as an argument, then a function with Int->Int type is only guaranteed to do the right thing on raw bits that actually represent integers; in the hypothetical case that we applied it to, say, a string representation, the code is free to misbehave arbitrarily. A function with a->a type, on the other hand, must not only produce output integer representations from input integer representations, but it must also produce string representations from string representations, and so on for booleans, floating-point numbers, and any other type. In fact, since a function with type a->a must accept *any* value at all, it cannot know anything about a specific argument. And, since it must return a result of the same type, there is nothing it can do except return this argument. Thus, there is exactly one function value with type a->a. (Even though we can write several different definitions in *pH* with this type, they all represent the same function value, which is the identity function that just returns its argument.) More insight into these observations may be found in [55, 73].

What does the type "a" represent, by itself? A value of this type must have all types. Any computation that has this type could not, for example, return an integer, nor a boolean, nor a function, because those values do not have all types. Thus, any computation with this type must either never return a value (e.g., it loops infinitely) or it must do something abnormal such as raise an error. Such behavior is typically formally lumped into a value called "bottom," written "$\perp$", representing "no information." More details may be found in [65, 59, 60, 64].

The set represented by the polymorphic type can be seen as an intersection of the sets represented by all its instances. A key point to remember is that a polymorphic function is not the union of several monomorphic function values; it is a *single* function value that has all the monomorphic types.

Exercise 3.6 What is the type of the following function?

```
loopy x = loopy x
```

3.3.2   Instantiating a Polymorphic Type

When a polymorphic identifier is used more than once, its polymorphic
type may be instantiated differently at each occurrence; however, in each
instantiation, each type variable must be instantiated uniformly. For example, in

```
let
    n =  twice  sqr  2
    s =  twice  indent4  "Hi"
in
    substring 0 n s
```

the two uses of `twice` are instantiated at different types. In one instance,
the type variable a is uniformly instantiated by Int, whereas in the other
case it is uniformly instantiated by String.

A polymorphic type may involve multiple type variables. Consider the
following function, just slightly different from `twice` (this function is predefined in *pH* in the form of the infix operator "."):

```
compose        :: (b->c) -> (a->b) -> a -> c
compose f g x = f (g x)
```

An example use of this function is in

```
compose  even  sqr  3
```

where its polymorphic type is instantiated as

```
(Int->Bool) -> (Int->Int) -> Int -> Bool
```

Here, the type variable a is uniformly instantiated by Int; the type variable b is uniformly instantiated by Int; and the type variable c is uniformly
instantiated by Bool. In this expression

```
compose  even  length  "Hello"
```

its polymorphic type is instantiated as

```
(Int->Bool) -> (String->Int) -> String -> Bool
```

with a, b, and c uniformly instantiated by String, Int, and Bool, respectively.

Exercise 3.7   In the following expression:

```
twice (twice sqr) 2
```

what are the types of each occurrence of `twice`? (*Hint*: Both occurrences have the same type.)   ■

Exercise 3.8   In the following expression:

```
twice twice sqr 2
```

what are the types of each occurrence of `twice`? (*Hint*: The two occurrences have different types.)   ■

Exercise 3.9   Prove the equivalence

```
twice (twice sqr)        =        twice twice sqr
```

(*Hint*: Apply each side to some unspecified argument x, perform some reductions, and show that both sides reduce to the same term.)   ■

3.3.3   Which Identifiers Are Polymorphic?

An intriguing aspect of *pH*'s type system is that not all identifiers are polymorphic—it depends on how the identifier is bound. We have seen that there are two kinds of binding occurrences of identifiers—identifiers defined by binding statements, and formal parameter identifiers. For example, in

```
f x y = ...
```

f is a binding occurrence of the first kind, whereas x and y are binding occurrences of the latter kind. Technically, we say that f is *let-bound*, whereas x and y are *lambda-bound*. In *pH*'s type system, *only let-bound identifiers can be polymorphic*. The reason, informally, is this. Within a function body, where a parameter (a lambda-bound identifier) is used, we have no information at all about the value to which the identifier will be bound. Indeed, it potentially has different values at each place where the function is applied and, moreover, because of higher-order functions, data structures, modules, and so on, we may not even be able to detect statically all the places where it is applied. Thus, we have no information about the parameter's principal type, and so we have no straightforward way to instantiate it differently at its different uses within the function body.

For example, consider the following two programs, which we would consider equivalent if we were to ignore types and type checking:

```
let
    g = \twice->
            (let
                    n = twice sqr 2
                    s = twice indent4 "Hi"
                in
                    substring 0 n s)
in
    g (\f->\x->f(f(x)))


let
    twice = (\f->\x->f(f(x)))
in
                (let
                    n = twice sqr 2
                    s = twice indent4 "Hi"
                in
                    substring 0 n s)
```

Unfortunately, the first program will not type check, while the second program will. The problem is that when type checking the binding for g, the identifier twice is lambda-bound and we have no information about its principal type. If we chose two different types for the two uses of twice, we have no way of expressing, within our type language, the constraint that those two types must be instances of a common (but unknown) principal type. Therefore, for a λ-bound identifier, the *pH* type checker conservatively tries to use the *same* type at all its uses; this will obviously fail in this example. In the second program, on the other hand, the identifier twice is let-bound. At its two uses, we know exactly what it is bound to, and this gives us its principal type, and so we can instantiate it at two different types at each of its two uses. (One might argue that a clever compiler could easily convert the first program into the second version and avoid this problem. This may be true for this example, but is not possible in general. In general, the application of g to its argument could be arbitrarily far away, hidden behind complicated higher-order functions and data structures, or even in another module.)

Polymorphism is one of the mechanisms in *pH* by which we gain expressive power without sacrificing static type checking. In later chapters, we will see various data structures such as lists and arrays. A list is just a linear collection of objects. We might use a list of integers to record the ages of players in a team, or a list of strings to represent their names, and so on. In fact, the `String` data type itself is just a shorthand for a list of characters. Whatever the contents of the list, we would like a single function that returns the length of the list (i.e., the number of items in the list), irrespective of whether those items are integers, strings, or characters. Polymorphism allows us to do this; without polymorphism, we would have to write separate functions to compute the length of lists of integers, lists of strings, lists of characters, and so on (this is actually the case in some statically typed languages like Pascal and C).

The particular flavor of polymorphism in *pH*'s type system (including the difference between let- and lambda-bound identifiers) is called Hindley-Milner polymorphism because it was developed independently by the logician Roger Hindley and the computer scientist Robin Milner. Milner developed this type system for a language called ML in the mid-1970s (ML is a predecessor of the modern SML programming language).

Exercise 3.10   In the definition

```
twice f x = f (f x)
```

can f be polymorphic and its two uses in the function body be instantiated at two different types? Explain.   ∎

Exercise 3.11   What is the type of the following function?

```
repeat n f x = if n == 0
                  then x
                  else repeat (n-1) f (f x)
```
∎

Exercise 3.12   Give examples of functions with the following types. Make sure your answers do not have more general types than the ones specified.

```
a -> Int

a -> b -> a

a -> b -> b

(a -> b -> c) -> b -> a -> c
```
∎

3.4   Type Classes and Overloading

In a mathematics textbook, we would have no trouble understanding an expression like "$x + 1$", whether x was an integer or real number. In fact, if it were a book on matrix algebra, we might even interpret this as matrix addition, with the symbol "1" representing the unit matrix. In other words, the context tells us how to interpret the symbols in the expression.

It is important to realize that this is not polymorphism as described in Section 3.3. There, a symbol like `twice` stands for *a single function value* that happens to work at infinitely many types; *any* instantiation of its type variables is acceptable. Instead, what we have here is known as *overloading*: a symbol (here, "+") stands for more than one function value—the integer addition function, the floating-point addition function, and perhaps other function values like complex number addition, matrix addition, and so on. "+" is an overloaded symbol. Each use of "+" represents just one of these function values, and in a statically type-checked language such as *pH*, it is the compiler's job to determine which one, based on the context. This process is known as *overloading resolution.*

It is easy to come up with some ad hoc rules for overloading resolution that solve the problem partially. An example rule might be the following: In an expression of the form $x + y$, if x is of floating-point type and y is of integer type, then replace the expression by

```
floating_point_add  x  (convert_Int_to_Float  y)
```

Here, we decided that the symbol "+" stands for the floating-point addition function, and we have also *coerced* the integer expression's value into a floating-point form.

Most programming languages (including Fortran, C, and Pascal) have such rules for overloading resolution and coercion. Unfortunately, such rules do not make overloading *extensible* to new functions that the user may write. For example, suppose we wrote this function:

```
sqr x = x * x
```

Most statically typed languages will insist that you declare types so that the overloading of "*" can be resolved locally; in other words, they will insist that you choose whether `sqr` is an integer squaring function, or a floating-point squaring function, and so on. If you want both integer and floating-point squaring functions, you would have to write two separate functions:

```
intSqr    :: Int -> Int
intSqr x = x * x

floatSqr    :: Float -> Float
floatSqr x = x * x
```

In other words, most languages will not let you say that the identifier sqr itself should be overloaded over integer and floating-point instantiations.

pH inherits, from Haskell, a *systematic* mechanism called *type classes* for expressing overloading. Rather than an ad hoc set of rules concerning a few built-in types and operators, it is a general mechanism that allows overloading and overloading resolution to be systematically extended to new types and functions. In particular, it allows us to let sqr itself be overloaded over all types over which "*" is overloaded.

Before going into details, we observe that in practice we often encounter collections of related functions that need a common overloading mechanism. For example, whatever mechanism we have for overloading "+", we'd like the same mechanism for "−", "*", and so on. Similarly, if we have a mechanism for overloading the "==" function (equality) over numbers and strings, we'd like the same mechanism also to work for overloading the "/=" function (inequality).

The notion of type class brings these two concepts together—a collection of related functions (such as "+", "−", and "*") and the collection of types over which we wish to overload all these functions. Each of these types (such as Int and Float) is called an *instance* of the class.

For example, the class Num (of numeric types) is declared like this in *pH*'s standard libraries:

```
class Num a where
    (==), (/=)        :: a -> a -> Bool        -- equality, inequality
    (+), (-), (*)     :: a -> a -> a           -- arithmetic
    negate            :: a -> a
    :
    :
```

This says that there is a class of types called the Num class. Corresponding to each type a that is a member of the Num class, there is a collection of functions: a function "==" with type a->a->Bool, a function "+" with type a->a->a, and so on.

Membership of a type in a class is not automatic; the class must be populated explicitly with instance types. For example, to declare that Int is a member of the Num class, we must provide specific functions, with appropriate types, that will subsequently be referred to using the overloaded names. In other words, for Int to be an instance of the type variable a, we must provide actual functions with type Int->Int->Bool for the equality and inequality symbols, actual functions with type Int->Int->Int for the arithmetic symbols, and so on. This is expressed as follows:

```
instance Num Int where
  x == y    = integer_eq x y
    .
    .
    .
  x + y     = integer_add x y
    .
    .
    .
```

Similarly, the type Float is declared as another instance of the Num class, with actual floating-point equality and addition functions associated with the names (==) and (+), and so on. On the other hand, the type Char is not declared as an instance of Num because we don't consider arithmetic to be meaningful on characters. The standard *pH* libraries declare standard classes, such as Num, and declare standard instances of these classes, such as (Num Int) and (Num Float). However, the *pH* programmer can declare new classes and can populate all classes (including Num) with new instances.

In general, the notation (Num *t*) is read as a predicate: "*t* is an instance of the class Num." The notation that types can be predicated by class membership is carried forward through user-defined lambda-abstractions. Thus,

```
sqr      :: (Num a) => a -> a
sqr x    = x * x
```

That is, sqr, in turn, has type a->a for those types a that are in the Num class. Even if the programmer did not write down the type declaration in the first line, *pH*'s type inference mechanism will infer this type automatically. In this manner, overloading is systematically propagated to user-defined functions.

Even primitive constants, and not just functions, need to be overloaded. Suppose we wrote

```
plus1  x   =   x + 1
```

What is the type of the symbol "1"? If we say that it is an integer, that would force "+" to be the integer addition function, which, in turn, would force plus1 to be a function on integers only. But, what if we wanted plus1 also to work on floating-point values? In fact, the situation is even more complex. In *pH*, Int is the type of limited-precision integers, such as those represented in a single machine word or machine register, typically 32 or 64 bits wide. The type Integer, on the other hand, is the type of unlimited-precision integers (bounded only by available memory in your machine). Float and Double are the types of single-precision and double-precision floating-point numbers, respectively. The constant "1" makes sense for each of these types and even for new types that we may want to throw into the mix (such as the unit matrix for matrix addition).

Thus, in *pH*, numeric literals like "1" are considered to be a shorthand for

    (fromInteger *the_Integer_1_value*)

where

    fromInteger :: (Num a) => Integer -> a

That is, fromInteger is an overloaded symbol in the Num class, predefined in *pH*, representing a family of actual functions that convert an actual integer value into an Int, an Integer, a Float, a Double, and so on. If we choose to declare matrices as an instance of the Num class, we must provide an actual function corresponding to fromInteger that produces a matrix from the Integer 1.

Thus, plus1 remains an overloaded function that can work on integers and floating-point numbers and any other instances of the Num class:

    plus1 :: (Num a) => a -> a

and the literal "1" converts the integer value 1 into a value of appropriate type for the "+" function.

It is important to remember that the collection of functions associated with a type class is arbitrary. For example, although our mathematical training may suggest that "+" and "−" are inverses of each other, there is absolutely nothing in the Num class definition that suggests or captures this. Indeed, when we declare a new instance *t* of the class Num, we can supply *any* actual functions of type *t->t->t* for the "+" and "−" symbols—they need have nothing to do with the mathematical concepts of addition and subtraction at all! (Of course, it may not be good style to misuse such well-known symbols in this manner, but that is a different matter.)

3.4.1   Some Useful Overloaded Functions

In *pH* programs, we frequently wish to read values from the keyboard or
a file, or write values to the screen or a file. For example, we may write a
small "temperature calculator" program that reads an integer in Fahrenheit
and prints the corresponding Celsius temperature (also an integer, say).
Or, we may write a "mortgage calculator" program that reads a principal
amount (integer dollars), a duration (integer years), and an interest rate
(floating-point) and prints out a monthly mortgage payment (floating-
point number).

The raw input from a keyboard/file and the raw output to the screen/file
are typically Strings (i.e., sequences of characters). To write our temperature calculator, we need a function that takes a keyboard string input such
as "83" and converts it to an integer (83). Once we have converted this
Fahrenheit value into a Celsius value (28), we need a function that takes
this integer value and converts it into a string ("28"), which can then be
output to the screen. Specifically, we need

```
read     :: String -> Int       -- for Fahrenheit temperature
show     :: Int -> String       -- for Celsius temperature
```

In our mortgage calculator, we need

```
read     :: String -> Int       -- for principal and duration
read     :: String -> Float     -- for rate
show     :: Float -> String     -- for monthly payment
```

This raises the question: Are read and show polymorphic functions with
the following types?

```
read     :: String -> a
show     :: a -> String
```

This does not really make sense. Conversion between strings and integers
and between strings and floating-point numbers are conceptually different
functions. This difference becomes even more dramatic in later chapters
when we talk about lists, arrays, and the like. Conversion between strings
and lists, or between strings and arrays, are even more different and unrelated actions. Further, for some types it does not even make sense to
convert to or from strings. For example, what does it mean to convert from
a string to a function value, or vice versa, since many functions are infinite objects—they can be applied to infinitely many different arguments,
producing infinitely many different results?

Thus, read and show are overloaded, not polymorphic functions. *pH* defines a type class Read of "readable" types and a type class Show of "showable" types. Each member type in these classes has corresponding actual read and show functions that know how to convert between strings and that particular type:

```
read    :: Read a => String -> a
show    :: Show a => a -> String
```

Resolving Ambiguity of Overloaded Functions
Consider the following function:

```
identity   :: String -> String
identity s = show (read s)
```

How should the overloading be resolved? The compiler could pick the read and show functions of type String->Int and Int->String, respectively. It could pick the read and show functions of type String->Float and Float->String, respectively. In fact, it could pick *any* matching pair of read and show functions with types String->*t* and *t*->String, respectively, and it would type check just fine (of course, the chosen read function may fail at run time because the contents of the string may not be syntactically correct for that version of read, but that is not something we can check statically).

This example demonstrates that some program fragments involving overloaded functions are inherently *ambiguous*—the program text does not provide sufficient context to resolve the overloading. Further, since identity is not a polymorphic function (its type String->String has no type variables), no usage of identity elsewhere in the program is going to provide any more contextual information. In this kind of situation, there is no alternative: the *pH* programmer has to supply type declarations that provide sufficient information to resolve the overloading. For example, we might say

```
identity   :: String -> String
identity s = show ((read s) :: Int)
```

This tells the compiler to choose the String->Int and Int->String instances of read and show, respectively.

Equality: The == Operator
Equality is another operation that is not polymorphic. For some types, equality is not even meaningful or practical. For example, checking if two

function values are equal implies checking that, for each possible argument, both functions produce equal arguments—this is not very practical for infinite domains! For other types, the notion of equality may be nonobvious. For example, in one scenario an array of items may be considered equal to another array of items if they contain the same items, in the same order. In another scenario, where an array is just considered to represent a *set* of items, the order of items in the array may be irrelevant; here, an equality check must be capable of ignoring the stored order.

Thus, equality is an overloaded operator; it needs to be defined separately for each type of interest. *pH* defines a type class Eq consisting of types for which equality makes sense; each such member type provides a specific "==" operator definition that specifies how to decide equality between two values of that type:

```
class    Eq a    where
  (==)    :: Eq a => a -> a -> Bool      -- Equality
  (/=)    :: Eq a => a -> a -> Bool      -- Inequality
```

Exercise 3.13   Infer the types of the following functions:

```
det a b c = (b * b) – 4 * a * c

h n f = if n == 0
        then 17
        else f (h (n–1) f)

alleq a b c = if a == b then a == c else False

f a b c = if a == b then a == c else c

g x y = if x == y then 5 else 2.7
```

3.4.2 ▼ Implementation Considerations of Overloading

Even though the overloading system that we have just described makes it possible to express overloaded types in a consistent fashion, the programmer who is concerned about language implementations is perhaps still not satisfied. What exactly *is* the code generated by a compiler for sqr? How can the same code do both integer and floating-point multiplication? The answer has two parts—a general part and a "specialization" part.

In general, the code generated for sqr is actually a function of *two* arguments, not one:

-- Warning: pseudocode here

internal_func_for_sqr =
```
            \class_instance  x -> (class_instance.(*)) x x
```

The first argument is an object representing the class instance, and the second argument is the real argument x. The class instance argument is a record containing the actual functions corresponding to the function names associated with this class. The body of the code extracts, from this record, the actual function for the multiplication operator and applies it to x and x. When sqr is applied to an Int argument, say, 23, the compiler converts this into

internal_func_for_sqr   IntClassInstance   23

When sqr is applied to a floating-point argument *e*, the compiler converts this into

internal_func_for_sqr   FloatClassInstance   23

The IntClassInstance object contains the integer multiplication function, whereas the FloatClassInstance object contains the floating-point multiplication function. Thus, the right multiplication function is applied to the argument x.

This of course raises the question of efficiency, since what looked like a simple multiplication (with the programmer's expectation, perhaps, of a single machine instruction) turns out to be a full-blown function call. In reality, *pH* and Haskell compilers attempt to create several specialized versions of sqr, one per instance of the Num class at which it is actually called. Now, when sqr is applied to an Int argument, the compiler can replace this with a direct call to the specialized integer version of sqr and similarly for floating-point arguments. In short, this is doing, automatically, what the programmer would have had to do manually if there had not been any overloading support—writing separate integer and floating-point versions of sqr.

3.5   Typeful Programming

Luca Cardelli has coined the term *typeful programming* for the process of programming in languages like *pH* (and its sibling languages like Haskell and SML). These languages are statically typed, and the programmer is constantly aware of, and consciously thinking about, the type signatures of identifiers and fragments of the program. Apart from the objective benefits of guaranteed type correctness and more efficient code, it is a great intellectual tool for the programmer, clarifying and structuring one's thinking about programs, often leading to cleaner, more perspicuous, and robust programs.

In a sense, static type checking is always a compromise on expressivity, despite features like type inference, polymorphism, and overloading. We saw that a type is a set of values; can just about *any* set be regarded as a type? For example, can we regard the set of even integers as a type? In a language with dynamic type checking, we can always perform this check on any particular value of interest, and so we can surely treat it as a type, just like any other. Unfortunately, there is no way in general to determine statically whether a given integer-valued expression will produce an even or an odd number, and so we cannot regard "the even numbers" as a type in a statically typed language. Thus, a static type system is always a delicately engineered balance that tries to maximize expressive power while maintaining static checkability. Extensive experience with languages like SML and Haskell has shown that the inference, polymorphism, and type class features of *pH*'s type system go a long way toward obtaining the best of both worlds—expressivity *and* type safety.

Exercise 3.14   What is the type signature of the div function (integer division)? The second argument to this function should not be zero. Does its *pH* type signature specify this? Why or why not?   ∎

Rewrite Rules, Reduction Strategies, and Parallelism

For a perfect sauce, follow the reduction rules.

—Advice in a French cookbook

The primary motivation for *pH* as a new programming language is parallelism. In Chapter 2 we mentioned parallelism informally in several places—the arguments of a function can be evaluated in parallel; the bindings in a **let**-block can be evaluated in parallel; nonstrictness allows a function call to be initiated while its argument is still being evaluated; and so on. In this chapter we describe formally what *can* be done in parallel and discuss strategies for choosing what is actually done in parallel.

A second goal in this chapter is to describe formally how computations are *shared* [4]. In particular, suppose identifier *x* is bound to an expression *e*, either in a **let**-block, or because *x* is the formal parameter of a function that is applied to *e*. Suppose *x* is used in multiple places in the program. We wish to describe precisely how the work of evaluating *e* is shared across all these uses. This is important not only for the pragmatic reason of avoiding replication of work, but also for the semantic reason that certain constructs in *pH* such as I-structures and M-structures do not make sense otherwise (these will be described in Chapters 9 and 10, respectively).

pH is a superset of the pure functional programming language Haskell. Can't we just extend an existing semantic description of Haskell in order to describe *pH*? Haskell and pure functional languages are usually described using *denotational semantics*, a technique whereby the meanings of program phrases are given in terms of abstract mathematical values and functions. Unfortunately, there are two reasons why this will not suit our purposes here. First, a key strength of denotational semantics is to abstract *away* from pragmatic details such as parallelism and sharing, the very details we are trying to describe here. Second, denotational semantics becomes messy when dealing with nonfunctional constructs such as I-structures and messier still when dealing with nonfunctional and nondeterministic constructs such as M-structures.

Our approach is to describe the semantics of *pH* programs using a formal *rewrite rule* system. This can be regarded as a high-level *operational semantics*. As informally suggested in Chapter 2, the system describes how the initial text of a *pH* program is transformed (or rewritten) by repeatedly replacing subterms with "simpler" subterms, eventually producing the result of the program (if the process terminates).

As is customary when describing the semantics of a real language (whether operationally or denotationally), we will focus on essentials. One aspect of this is to dispose of various aspects of the language that are present mostly for convenience reasons, by showing how they can be translated into a simpler *core* or *kernel* language that captures the semantic essence. For example, we have already shown how a definition like this:

```
f  x  y  z  = e
```

is really a more convenient way of expressing

```
f  =  \x -> \y -> \z -> e
```

We also keep the semantic description simple by assuming that the program has already been type checked.

We start by describing the *abstract syntax* of core *pH* programs and by showing how full *pH* programs can be "syntactically desugared" into this core. Next, we discuss the notion of "answers," which are the kinds of result terms we wish to compute in a *pH* program. In this connection, we will recognize certain special terms called Values, Simple Expressions, and Heap terms. Next, we describe certain *syntactic equivalences;* we do not want to worry about certain "trivial" differences between textually nonidentical terms (e.g., whether we chose to name a function's argument x or y). Then, we describe the rewrite rules themselves; central to *pH* are the rules on *instantiation* (substitution of identifiers by Values), which control sharing precisely.

Rewrite rules are local rules—they identify certain subterms and show how to replace them by other subterms. At any point in time, a program may have several candidate reductions available according to the rewrite rules. This raises a question of *determinacy*—whether different orders of application of rewrite rules can produce different answers. It also raises the question of *termination*—whether the repeated application of the rewrite rules eventually terminates and under what circumstances. These questions are discussed in general terms in Section 4.7.

It is customary to distinguish between rewrite rules themselves and a *reduction strategy*. Which candidates for reduction should be reduced, at each point in time? Often there are far more candidates than there are available computational resources. Section 4.8 discusses several popular strategies including lazy evaluation, call by value, and parallel strategies for *pH*.

The formal description below only covers the parts of *pH* discussed thus far. We will augment it in each of the following chapters as we introduce more and more features of *pH*. All the rewrite rules are collected for reference in Appendix B.

4.1   Syntax

We will show that the parts of *pH* presented thus far can be described using a core language having the following abstract syntax:

E	$::=$	x	Identifiers
	$\mid$	$\backslash x \; \rightarrow \; E$	Lambda-abstractions
	$\mid$	$E_1 \; E_2$	Applications
	$\mid$	**let** S **in** E	Let-blocks
	$\mid$	**Cond**$(E_p, \; E_t, \; E_f)$	Conditionals
	$\mid$	$\text{PF}_k(E_1, \cdots, E_k)$	Application of primitive functions
	$\mid$	CN_0	Constants
S	$::=$	ϵ	Empty statements
	$\mid$	$x \; = \; E$	Bindings
	$\mid$	$S \; ; \; S$	Parallel statement composition

PF_1	$::=$	negate | not | $\cdots$	Primitive functions of arity 1
PF_2	$::=$	+ | - | $\cdots$	Primitive functions of arity 2
CN_0	$::=$	*Integer* | *Boolean* | $\cdots$	

The notation in this table is called a *grammar*. Symbols not in monospaced font represent syntactic classes. For example, E represents the class of expressions, and S represents the class of statements. Symbols in monospaced and bold fonts represent literal program text. The symbols "$::=$" and "$|$" are part of the grammar's notation, not *pH* notation (for this reason, they are also known as metasymbols).

A grammar rule like "$P ::= Q_1|Q_2|\cdots$" is read as saying that a syntactic term of class P is a syntactic term from class Q_1, or a term from Q_2, and so on. The notation "$\backslash x\text{->}E$" represents the class of terms comprising a literal "$\backslash$" followed by an identifier followed by a literal "->" followed by an expression. The rules are recursive (e.g., subterms of expressions can themselves be expressions), and so they can describe an infinite number of programs. Collectively, the grammar describes all possible *pH* programs (for the subset of the language introduced so far).

We call this an *abstract* syntax because it clearly describes the structure of *pH* terms. When we write a term as linear text, however, there may be some ambiguity, which we will disambiguate using parentheses. For example, instead of

```
\x -> e1 e2
```

we will use parentheses to clarify which of the following two structures is the intended structure:

```
(\x -> e1) e2                versus                \x -> (e1 e2)
```

Thus, even though there is sometimes a textual ambiguity, we should always be clear about the intended underlying abstract structure.

4.2   Syntactic Desugaring: Translating into the Core

As described earlier, a function definition of the form

```
f   x   y   ...   =   e
```

does not conform to the core syntax. We translate this into

```
f   =   \x   y   ...   -> e
```

which, in turn, is translated into the following core term:

```
f  =  \x -> (\y -> (\ ... -> e))
```

In a λ-abstraction "$\backslash x \rightarrow e$", the identifier x is called its *bound variable* (x is also said to be λ-*bound*), and the expression e is called its *body*.

A **let**-block with multiple bindings, using indentation and layout,

let

$$x_1 = e_1$$
$$x_2 = e_2$$
$$x_3 = e_3$$
$$\vdots$$

in

$$e$$

is translated into the following explicit core form:

let

$$(\ x_1 = e_1\ ;$$
$$(\ x_2 = e_2\ ;$$
$$(\ x_3 = e_3\ ;$$
$$\ldots \qquad)\ )\ )$$

in

$$e$$

(We shall see shortly that the particular nesting of statements chosen is not important.) The final e is called the block's *body* or *return expression*. The semicolon here can be read as a parallel composition of statements (in contrast to the usual sequential reading of semicolons in imperative languages). The identifiers on the left-hand sides of all the bindings must be pairwise distinct. These variables are said to be *let-bound*. Any of these identifiers may be used in any of the right-hand sides e_j and in the body e. Thus, we say that the bindings are *simultaneous* and *recursive*.

The empty statement "ϵ" is a technical convenience. A *pH* program and its initial translation to the core will typically not have any instances of ϵ. However, in later chapters we will see various transformations on statements whose presentation becomes simpler with the device of an empty statement.

The conditional expression "**if** e_1 **then** e_2 **else** e_3" is translated into the more compact core form "**Cond** (e_1, e_2, e_3)". Primitive functions include things like not(e), negate(e), and so on. We will write some well-known primitives like "+" using infix notation.

A *pH* program consists of a collection of bindings

S_1

$\vdots$

S_n

One of the bindings must bind the identifier main. The entire program can then be translated into the core **let**-block:

```
let
    ( S₁ ; ( ... ; Sₙ ))
in
    main
```

(This special role of main has no deep semantic significance; it is just a pragmatic convention. In our discussions to follow we may not adhere to this rigidly.)

pH loops are also purely syntactic sugar—each loop can be translated into an equivalent program fragment in the core that just uses functions and recursion. The desugaring details will be described later, in Section 4.9.

4.3   Answers and Simple Expressions

A *pH* program is an expression, and the goal of executing it is to produce a *value* as an answer. In particular, in the outermost **let**-block corresponding to a program, we want to convert the block's body (main) into a value. A value is just a restricted form of expression. Some things are obviously values—any member of the syntax class CN_0 of constants, including numbers, booleans, floating-point numbers, and so on, is clearly a value. We will also refer to such values as *basic* values. But what about function values? Should we consider the following term to be a value?

```
\x -> x + (2 + 3)
```

Or, should we aim first to convert the expression into some kind of "standard" form, such as

```
\x -> x + 5
```

before we proclaim it to be a value? We argue that this distinction is not worth making. Ultimately, the only interesting thing about a function is its *observable behavior*—what happens when we apply it to an argument. When applied, does it produce a result (or does it loop forever)? What result does it produce, if it produces one? From this point of view, the two function terms above are identical.

In the presence of recursion, it is futile to attempt to reduce λ-values to any kind of "standard form." Consider the following program, which computes *n*!, the factorial of *n*:

```
let
    f = \n -> if n == 0 then 1
              else n * (f (n-1))
in
    f
```

If we substitute for f in the **let**-body, we get

```
let
    f = \n -> if n == 0 then 1
              else n * (f (n-1))
in
    \n -> if n == 0 then 1
          else n * (f (n-1))
```

But, this new **let**-body itself contains f, which we could substitute again, and again, ad infinitum. However, from a behavioral point of view, no new information has been gained beyond our original program. Thus, this program has an infinite number of unfoldings that are all observationally equivalent.

The following "odd-even" example is even more dramatic [5]. Consider the following fragment:

```
x = \f -> f 1 y
y = \g -> g 2 x
```

Suppose we substitute for y:

$$x = \text{\textbackslash}f \rightarrow f\ 1\ (\text{\textbackslash}g \rightarrow g\ 2\ x) \qquad (M_1)$$
$$y = \text{\textbackslash}g \rightarrow g\ 2\ x$$

Instead, suppose we had substituted for x:

$$x = \text{\textbackslash}f \rightarrow f\ 1\ y \qquad (M_2)$$
$$y = \text{\textbackslash}g \rightarrow g\ 2\ (\text{\textbackslash}f \rightarrow f\ 1\ y)$$

Now, no further reductions can *ever* reduce M_1 and M_2 to a common form. In M_1, if we substitute for x, then we get a four-deep λ-term containing another x. In M_2, if we substitute for y, then we get a three-deep λ-term containing another y. No matter how many times we repeat this, the λ-depth of terms derived from M_1 and M_2 will always be even and odd, respectively. But, again, there is no observational difference between all these versions.

Thus, even though the body expression of a λ-abstraction is of course important—it determines the behavior of the abstraction—there is really no point reducing inside λs in the hope that we might reach some canonical or "minimal" form for the body. This insight explains why we choose to treat a term of the form "\x->e" as a value, with *no restrictions* on the form of *e*, the λ-body—it can be any expression whatsoever.

Intuitively, a value is an expression in which there is no remaining "exposed" computation (any remaining computation can only be inside a λ-body). This notion is important not only for the final answer of a program, but also at intermediate points to control *sharing* of computations. Suppose we have a binding "x=e" and we wish to substitute for x at two or more of its uses (i.e., replace them by *e*). If we insist that this substitution is done only when *e* is a value, then we are assured that the substitution will not replicate any exposed computation. In other words, any exposed computation in *e* is effectively shared by all uses of x. It should also be intuitively obvious that for a trivial binding of one identifier to another, for example, x=y, there is no danger of replicating computation if we substitute y for uses of x.

Based on these observations, we identify two special subsets of terms called *Values* and *Simple Expressions*:

V	$::=$	CN_0	Constants
	$\|$	$\x \; -> \; E$	Lambda-abstractions
SE	$::=$	x	Identifiers
	$\|$	V	Values

The terms in V are also sometimes called *Weak Head Normal Forms* because they have no more pending computation at the outermost level (the "head" of the term) even though there may still be reductions possible inside λ-bodies. In later chapters we will extend V to include data structures (lists, trees, arrays, and so on). The extension will be recursive, to include lists of lists of numbers, arrays of trees of lists of booleans, and so on.

It will be useful to distinguish statements that bind names to actual values; we give them the name H, for *Heap* terms:

$$H \quad ::= \quad x = V \mid H \; ; \; H \qquad \text{Value bindings}$$

(Heap terms are so called because, in later chapters, data structures will fall into this syntactic class. In a real implementation, data structures are allocated in a memory area called the Heap.)

4.4 Syntactic Equivalences and Renaming

When writing *pH* programs, we make certain choices that are not fundamentally significant. For example, in a **let**-block, the ordering of statements is immaterial; they should be regarded as simultaneous recursive bindings. The following set of rules expresses this idea:

Equivalence properties of ";":

$$
\begin{aligned}
s_1 ; \; s_2 &\equiv s_2 ; \; s_1 \\
s_1 ; \; (s_2 ; \; s_3) &\equiv (s_1 ; \; s_2) ; \; s_3 \\
\epsilon ; \; s &\equiv s
\end{aligned}
$$

Another semantically insignificant choice that we make is in the particular names of variables. For example, there is no essential difference between the following three functions:

```
\x -> 1 + x
\y -> 1 + y
\the_argument -> 1 + the_argument
```

Our choice of x or y or the_argument is arbitrary. (We make these choices based on readability and other aesthetic or pragmatic considerations.) During the reduction of a program, we will need to exploit this fact. For example, suppose we have the following fragment:

```
z = 2
x = \y->(...z...)
g =   ...    (x 5)   ...
```

and we wish to substitute for x, to get

```
z = 2
x = \y->(...z...)
g =   ...      (\y->(...z...) 5)   ...
```

The key pitfall we have to avoid is called *free variable capture*. Suppose there was an intervening λ-binding of z in the original term, like this:

```
z = 2
x = \y->(...z...)
g =    ... \z->(.. z .. (x 5) ..)    ...
```

When we substitute for x, we get

```
z = 2
x = \y->(...z...)
g =    ... \z->(.. z .. (\y->(...z...) 5) ..)    ...
```

and the variable z in the substituted term, which previously referred to the outer binding to 2, now refers to the λ-binding; it has been erroneously *captured*. If, before substituting, we first renamed the λ-bound variable and all its uses:

```
z = 2
x = \y->(...z...)
g =    ... \z'->(.. z' .. (x 5) ..)    ...
```

then the substitution will not cause a capture problem. In general, when we substitute a term *a* for a free variable *x* in an expression *e*, we will usually want first to *rename* the expression *e* so that its internal bound variables don't accidentally capture any free variables of *a*.

Systematic renaming of an expression to avoid free variable capture is traditionally called α-renaming and is quite straightforward. We recursively descend into the expression, carrying along a data structure called an *environment*, which is an ordered sequence of mappings, which we write as

$$(x_n \rightarrow t_n) : \cdots : (x_0 \rightarrow t_0) : \phi$$

Each mapping $(x_j \rightarrow t_j)$ maps an existing bound variable x_j to a new identifier t_j. The sequence is read from left to right, so that if there are two mappings $(y \rightarrow t_i)$ and $(y \rightarrow t_j)$ for the same variable y, the left one takes precedence. We use the symbol ρ for environments and start the process with ϕ, the empty environment. As we recursively descend into the expression, whenever we go through a λ-abstraction or a **let**-block, we extend the environment from the left, giving new names to the bound variables of these constructs. When we finally reach an identifier, we rename it to its new name as specified in the current environment. If there is no entry for this identifier in the environment, then it must be a free variable of the expression (since we encountered no binding for it on the way down) and so it remains unchanged.

Here is the function to rename an identifier x according to a given environment ρ:

$$
\begin{aligned}
\text{RenId}[\![x]\!]\phi &= x \\
\text{RenId}[\![x]\!]((x \rightarrow x') : \rho_1) &= x' \\
\text{RenId}[\![x]\!]((y \rightarrow y') : \rho_1) &= \text{RenId}[\![x]\!]\rho_1 \qquad x \neq y
\end{aligned}
$$

(It is traditional, when describing functions over syntactic structures, to enclose syntax terms in "$[\![\ ]\!]$" brackets, which are also sometimes known as "syntax brackets." We think of the term between these brackets as a pattern to be matched against the syntax term that is being translated.) Now, here is the general function to rename all the bound variables in an arbitrary expression (we will always follow the convention that t represents a fresh identifier):

$$
\begin{aligned}
\text{Ren}[\![x]\!]\rho &= \text{RenId}[\![x]\!]\rho \\
\text{Ren}[\![\backslash x\!\!-\!\!>\!e]\!]\rho &= \backslash t\!\!-\!\!>(\text{Ren}[\![e]\!]\rho_1) \\
&\quad \text{where } \rho_1 = (x \rightarrow t) : \rho \\
\text{Ren}[\![e_1\ e_2]\!]\rho &= (\text{Ren}[\![e_1]\!]\rho)\ (\text{Ren}[\![e_2]\!]\rho) \\
\text{Ren}[\![\textbf{let}\ s\ \textbf{in}\ e]\!]\rho &= \textbf{let}\ \text{Ren}_S[\![s]\!]\rho_1\ \textbf{in}\ \text{Ren}[\![e]\!]\rho_1 \\
&\quad \text{where } \rho_1 = \text{ExtendEnv}_S[\![s]\!]\rho \\
\text{Ren}[\![\textbf{Cond}(e_p, e_t, e_f)]\!]\rho &= \textbf{Cond}(\text{Ren}[\![e_p]\!]\rho,\ \text{Ren}[\![e_t]\!]\rho,\ \text{Ren}[\![e_f]\!]\rho) \\
\text{Ren}[\![\text{PF}_k(e_1, \cdots, e_k)]\!]\rho &= \text{PF}_k(\text{Ren}[\![e_1]\!]\rho,\ \cdots,\ \text{Ren}[\![e_k]\!]\rho) \\
\text{Ren}[\![\text{CN}_0]\!]\rho &= \text{CN}_0
\end{aligned}
$$

For applications, conditionals, and primitive function applications, where no binding is taking place, we simply recursively rename the component expressions. Constants, of course, remain unchanged. For a $\backslash x\!\!-\!\!>\!e$ term, we wish to rename x to a fresh variable t. We extend the environment with a new entry mapping x to t and rename the body e using this new environment. Any x that is free in e corresponds to a use of this x and will be renamed to t. If, inside e, there is a nested $\backslash x\!\!-\!\!>\!e_1$, we will again extend the environment with a new entry mapping x to another new name t_1, and so any uses of x in e_1 will get renamed to t_1.

In a **let**-block, we first extend the environment with new names for all the bound variables of the block, using this function:

$$
\begin{aligned}
\text{ExtendEnv}_S[\![\epsilon]\!]\rho &= \rho \\
\text{ExtendEnv}_S[\![x = e]\!]\rho &= (x \rightarrow t) : \rho \\
\text{ExtendEnv}_S[\![s_1\ ;\ s_2]\!]\rho &= \text{ExtendEnv}_S[\![s_1]\!]\ (\text{ExtendEnv}_S[\![s_2]\!]\rho)
\end{aligned}
$$

Then, we rename the entire block in this new environment, using $\text{Ren}[\![\;]\!]$ to rename the block body and $\text{Ren}_S[\![\;]\!]$ to rename the statement. This latter function recursively descends to each statement and then renames both the left-hand side variable and the right-hand side expression, using $\text{Ren}[\![\;]\!]$:

$$
\begin{aligned}
\text{Ren}_S[\![\,\epsilon\,]\!]\rho \quad &= \epsilon \\
\text{Ren}_S[\![\; x \;=\; e \;]\!]\rho \quad &= \text{Ren}[\![x]\!]\rho \;=\; \text{Ren}[\![e]\!]\rho \\
\text{Ren}_S[\![\; s_1 \;;\; s_2\,]\!]\rho \quad &= \text{Ren}_S[\![s_1]\!]\rho \;;\; \text{Ren}_S[\![s_2]\!]\rho
\end{aligned}
$$

Exercise 4.1   Define a function $\text{FV}[\![e]\!]$ that computes the set of free variables in an expression. Define a function $\text{BV}[\![e]\!]$ that computes the set of bound variables in e (i.e., variables occurring in e that are not free).   ■

Now that we understand how to rename all the bound variables in an expression, we can present a syntactic equivalence rule:

α-renaming:
$\quad e \;\equiv\; \text{Ren}[\![e]\!]\phi$

which states, quite simply, that nothing essential changes when we systematically rename all bound variables in an expression. We will also say that two expressions are equal "up to α-renaming," or simply "up to renaming."

We adopt a uniform notational convention: e' and s' are renamed versions of e and s, respectively, in order to avoid name conflicts; t is always a fresh identifier that does not otherwise occur in the term. Another useful notation is "$e[t/x]$", which represents e with all free occurrences of x substituted by t. It can be defined as

$$
e[t/x] \;=\; \text{Ren}[\![e]\!] \;((x{\rightarrow}t):\phi)
$$

That is, we simply rename e in a new environment that binds x to the new variable t. Using this notation, our α-renaming equivalence rule can also be stated as follows:

α-renaming:
```
\x -> e                    ≡    \t -> e[t/x]
let x = e; s in e₀         ≡    let t = e[t/x]; s[t/x] in e₀[t/x]
```

4.5   Rewrite Rules

We are now ready to look at the reduction rules themselves. They can be divided into several groups:

1. Conditionals, constants, and primitives (δ rules)
2. Function application (or β-reduction)
3. Instantiation (or substitution)
4. Lifting and flattening

Each rewrite rule looks like "$e \longrightarrow e_1$", meaning that a subterm in the program that matches e can be replaced by e_1. Such a matching subterm is called a *redex*, for "reducible expression." In the discussions, we also use the same notation $e \longrightarrow e_1$ to indicate that e reduces to e_1 by a single application of some reduction rule to e or to one of its subterms, and we use $e \longrightarrow\!\!\!\!\rightarrow e_1$ to indicate that e reduces to e_1 by a finite sequence (zero or more) of such steps.

4.5.1   Constants, Conditionals, and δ Rules

There are no rewrite rules for constants (syntactic category CN_0); these are considered to be values already.

The rules for conditionals are obvious:

$$\textbf{Cond}(\texttt{True},\ e_1,\ e_2) \qquad \longrightarrow\ e_1 \qquad\qquad (\text{CondT})$$
$$\textbf{Cond}(\texttt{False},\ e_1,\ e_2) \qquad \longrightarrow\ e_2 \qquad\qquad (\text{CondF})$$

Traditionally, the rewrite rules for built-in primitive functions are called δ rules. For example, for "+", we have the following δ rule:

$$\underline{x}\ +\ \underline{y} \qquad\qquad\qquad \longrightarrow\ \underline{x + y} \qquad\qquad (+)$$

This single rule is meant to denote the infinite collection of rules:

$$
\begin{array}{ll}
0 + 0 & \longrightarrow\ 0 \\
0 + 1 & \longrightarrow\ 1 \\
1 + 0 & \longrightarrow\ 1 \\
0 + 2 & \longrightarrow\ 2 \\
2 + 0 & \longrightarrow\ 2 \\
\ldots & \longrightarrow\ \ldots
\end{array}
$$

The notation $\underline{x}$ denotes a *constant* (in this case, a numeral). Similarly, the notation $\underline{x + y}$ denotes the specific constant that is the sum of the constants $\underline{x}$ and $\underline{y}$; it does not represent an *expression* containing the "+" operator.

4.5.2   Function Application (β-Reduction)

A λ-abstraction can be applied to an argument:

$$(\backslash x\ \text{->}\ e_1)\ e_2 \qquad\qquad \longrightarrow\quad \textbf{let}\ t = e_2\ \textbf{in}\ e_1[t/x] \qquad (\beta)$$

Note that the argument e_2 can be any expression, not necessarily a Simple Expression or a Value. Thus, a *pH* function can be applied to its argument even before the argument has been reduced to a Value. This is quite unusual among programming languages (this property is called *nonstrictness*) and in fact gives us a degree of parallelism, whereby a function application can occur *while* its argument is being evaluated. In most programming languages, function application occurs only *after* the argument is evaluated.

An important point to note is that after the rewrite, there is still exactly one occurrence of the argument expression e_2; that is, we neither discard nor duplicate the argument, irrespective of how many uses of x there may be in e_1. Along with the restricted instantiation (substitution) rule to be presented next, it preserves *sharing*—all uses of x in e_1 share the computation e_2.

4.5.3   Instantiation (a.k.a. Substitution)

Substitution rules affect *sharing* crucially. Consider this example:

```
let y = (2*2) in (y * y)
```

If we replaced the uses of y by (2*2), we would get

```
let y = (2*2) in (2*2) * (2*2)
```

which replicates the computation. By insisting that the substitution occurs only after reducing (2*2) to the value 4, we can avoid this. This may look like a trivial saving, but instead of (2*2) we could have had an arbitrarily expensive computation (Section 4.6 will explore a more compelling example). For now, the issue of sharing is only an efficiency concern (i.e., to avoid unnecessary replication of work). Later, when we introduce nonfunctional constructs in Chapters 8, 9, and 10, we will see that sharing is a fundamental semantic issue.

There are two issues here: *what* can be substituted, and *where* it may be substituted. For the former, we insist that only Simple Expressions can be substituted. Simple Expressions, defined in Section 4.3, consist of identifiers and values (constants and λ-abstractions). These do not represent any further work and hence may be replicated freely.

To specify where a Simple Expression a may be substituted, we define the notion of an expression *context*, written $C[\,]$. This is an expression with a "hole" in it somewhere, depicted as "$[\,]$". The hole will contain a target identifier x that will get replaced by a Simple Expression a.

$$
\begin{array}{lll}
C[\,] & ::= & [\,] & \quad | \quad \backslash x \,\text{->}\, C[\,] \\
 & | & C[\,]\ E & \quad | \quad E\ C[\,] \\
 & | & \textbf{let}\ S\ \textbf{in}\ C[\,] & \quad | \quad \textbf{let}\ SC[\,]\ \textbf{in}\ E \\
 & | & \textbf{Cond}(C[\,],E_t,E_f) & \quad | \quad \textbf{Cond}(E_p,C[\,],E_f) \quad | \quad \textbf{Cond}(E_p,E_t,C[\,]) \\
 & | & \text{PF}_k(\cdots,\ C[\,],\cdots)
\end{array}
$$

In this definition, $SC[\,]$ is a *statement* context for an expression, that is, a statement with a hole in place of one of its subexpressions; it is defined as follows:

$$
SC[\,] \quad ::= \quad x = C[\,] \quad | \quad SC[\,]\ ;\ S
$$

Here (and henceforth) we omit the symmetric clause "$S\ ;\ SC[\,]$" because the semicolon is always symmetric.

The rewrite rules for instantiation are shown below. In all these rules, the x in $C[x]$ must be free in $C[x]$ and a must be a Simple Expression.

$$
\begin{array}{lll}
\textbf{let}\ x = a\ ;\ s\ \textbf{in}\ C[x] & \longrightarrow\ \textbf{let}\ x = a\ ;\ s\ \textbf{in}\ C'[a] & \text{(Inst1)} \\
x = a\ ;\ y = C[x] & \longrightarrow\ x = a\ ;\ y = C'[a] & \text{(Inst2)} \\[2ex]
x = C[x] & \longrightarrow\ x = C'[C[x]] & \text{(Inst3)}
\end{array}
$$

The right-hand sides of these rules have C', indicating that the contexts need to be α-renamed to avoid capturing free variables of the terms being substituted into the contexts. The third rule indicates that we can unfold a recursive value binding indefinitely.

Exercise 4.2   For each of the above three instantiation rules, give an example term where the substitution would be erroneous without renaming.   ■

The above definition of contexts, $C[\,]$, is not the only one possible. For example, we may wish to restrict instantiation so that it does not occur inside λ-abstractions, by omitting $\backslash x\text{->}C[\,]$ from the definition. This may be pragmatically useful because, if the λ-abstraction is never actually applied, work done in its body is wasted. Similarly, in an application $(E_1\ E_2)$, it is possible that the function represented by E_1 may not use its argument, and so we may choose to avoid doing any work in E_2 until really necessary by omitting $(E\ C[\ ])$ from the context definition. In fact, we could go further and treat these as restricted reduction contexts, preventing reduction and not merely instantiation in these locations. It is an interesting property of the system that nothing essential is thereby lost. Whatever could be computed with the full contexts can also be computed with the restricted contexts (although it may take more time, since restricting contexts postpones computations).

4.5.4   Block Flattening and Expression Lifting

Consider the following expression:

```
let
    f = let s₁ in (\x->e₁)                    -- (1)
    x = f a                                    -- (2)
in
    (let s₂ in \x->e₂)  e₃                     -- (3)
```

On line (2), we ultimately want to apply the β rule after somehow substituting $\x{-}{>}e_1$ for f. Similarly, on the last line, we ultimately want to apply the β rule to the application of $\x{-}{>}e_2$ to e_3. We can do so, using the following rules that "lift" expressions and massage the structure of blocks that are nested in certain ways. In order to avoid the possibility of infinite sequences of reductions (in which instantiation immediately cancels lifting), all these rules except the first two are inapplicable when e is a Simple Expression.

$$x = \textbf{let}\ s\ \textbf{in}\ e \quad \longrightarrow \quad x = e'\ ;\ s' \qquad\qquad \text{(Flat1)}$$
$$\textbf{let}\ \epsilon\ \textbf{in}\ e \quad \longrightarrow \quad e \qquad\qquad\qquad\qquad \text{(Flat2)}$$

In the lift rules below, $e \notin SE$:

$\textbf{let}\ s\ \textbf{in}\ e$	$\longrightarrow \quad \textbf{let}\ s\ ;\ t = e\ \textbf{in}\ t$	(LiftB)
$(e\ e_2)$	$\longrightarrow \quad \textbf{let}\ t = e\ \textbf{in}\ t\ e_2$	(LiftAp1)
$(e_1\ e)$	$\longrightarrow \quad \textbf{let}\ t = e\ \textbf{in}\ e_1\ t$	(LiftAp2)
$\textbf{Cond}(e,\ e_1,\ e_2)$	$\longrightarrow \quad \textbf{let}\ t = e\ \textbf{in}\ \textbf{Cond}(t,\ e_1,\ e_2)$	(LiftCond)
$\text{PF}_k(\cdots,\ e,\ \cdots)$	$\longrightarrow \quad \textbf{let}\ t = e\ \textbf{in}\ \text{PF}_k(\cdots,\ t,\ \cdots)$	(LiftPF)

(Recall that s' and e' represent α-renamings and t represents a fresh variable, in order to avoid free variable capture.)

Note that we do not lift the arms e_2 and e_3 from a conditional. This is for the usual reason that only one of these computations can finally be selected, and so we don't wish to expose these computations prematurely. The arm that is ultimately not selected may, for example, include an erroneous computation (e.g., a divide-by-zero), and keeping it unlifted has the effect of "containing" it safely where it does not matter.

Similarly, note that there is no lifting rule concerning λs; that is, we don't lift expressions out of λ-bodies. Again, there is no reason to do so—if the function is ever applied, the β rule will then expose the body, at which time it'll get reduced.

Exercise 4.3 Demonstrate the use of the rewrite rules of this section by applying them repeatedly to the example at the top of this section. ■

Exercise 4.4 Here is an entirely different set of lifting rules, following the approach of Z. Ariola:

let s_1 **in** (**let** s_2 **in** v)	$\longrightarrow$ **let** s_1 ; s_2' **in** v'	(LiftB')
(**let** s **in** v) e_2	$\longrightarrow$ **let** s' **in** (v' e_2)	(LiftAp1')
Cond((**let** s **in** v), e_1, e_2)	$\longrightarrow$ **let** s' **in** **Cond**(v', e_1, e_2)	(LiftCond')
$\text{PF}_k(\cdots, (\textbf{let } s \textbf{ in } e), \cdots)$	$\longrightarrow$ **let** s' **in** $\text{PF}_k(\cdots, v', \cdots)$	(LiftPF')

The flattening rules Flat1 and Flat2 remain unchanged, and there is no lift rule corresponding to LiftAp2. Demonstrate the use of these rewrite rules by applying them repeatedly to the example at the top of this section. ■

4.5.5 Canonical Form

In a sense, the block flattening and lifting rules don't do any "real" computation; they simply rearrange the expression to enable the other reduction rules, which do the real computation. In fact, a little analysis will reveal that if we try to apply just these rules repeatedly to any expression, the process will always terminate. The resulting terms conform to the following syntax:

E	::=	F	Flat expressions
	|	**let** S **in** SE	Let-blocks
F	::=	x	Identifiers
	|	$\backslash x$ -> E	Lambda-abstractions
	|	SE_1 SE_2	Applications
	|	**Cond**(SE_p, E_t, E_f)	Conditionals
	|	$\text{PF}_k(SE_1, \cdots, SE_k)$	Applications of primitive functions
	|	CN_0	Constants

$$
\begin{array}{llll}
S & ::= & \epsilon & \text{Empty statements} \\
  & | & x = F & \text{Bindings} \\
  & | & S ; S & \text{Parallel statement composition}
\end{array}
$$

We also say that such an expression is in *canonical* form, and that the expression has been canonicalized by repeated application of the flattening and lifting rules. In a canonical term, we can observe the following:

- Certain expressions will always be Simple (i.e., a variable or a value): the function and argument of an application; a block's body; the predicate of a conditional; all arguments of a primitive function application.
- We cannot have immediately nested blocks. Block bodies cannot be blocks (they're Simple Expressions, only), and the right-hand side of a binding cannot be a block (they're flattened expressions, only).
- The only subterms that are unrestricted expressions are bodies of λ-abstractions and the arms of conditionals.

Since canonicalization always terminates, it is safe to apply these rules statically, and compilers often do, because the resulting expressions are simpler to deal with.

We observe that if we perform any reduction on a canonical term (of course, it therefore cannot be a flattening or lifting reduction), the resulting term may deviate from canonical form in only one way—the right-hand side of a binding may now be a block. Specifically, if the right-hand side was a redex for the β, CondT, or CondF rules, it may be replaced by a block after the reduction. If we now apply the Flat1 rule once, the term is brought back into canonical form. Thus, if we start by applying all the flattening and lifting rules to the initial program to produce a canonical term, then for the rest of the execution we do not need those rules anymore, except for the Flat1 rule. Thus, we can consider the flattening and lifting rules as static preprocessing rules, with only Flat1 required dynamically.

4.6   Sharing and Nonstrictness

We now go through a series of examples to gain some practice with the rewrite rules and to illustrate in greater detail certain properties of *pH* execution that we have mentioned earlier.

4.6.1   Argument Sharing

Consider this *pH* program:

```
let
    sqr = \x -> x * x
in
    sqr (2 + 3)
```

We wish to ensure that the expression (2+3) is not duplicated, even though it is bound to x, which is used twice. In other words, we want the addition to be performed only once. Using a block transformation we get

```
let
    sqr = \x -> x * x
    t1  = sqr (2 + 3)
in
    t1
```

Using the β rule we get

```
let
    sqr = \x -> x * x
    t1  = let x1 = 2 + 3
          in
              x1 * x1
in
    t1
```

(Note that we have performed the application before evaluating the argument, an example of nonstrictness.) Using the Flat1 rule we get

```
let
    sqr = \x -> x * x
    t1  = x1 * x1
    x1  = 2 + 3
in
    t1
```

Note that our instantiation rule does not permit us to substitute the term (2+3) for x1, because (2+3) is not a Simple Expression. Once we perform the addition (using the δ rule for +), we get

```
let
    sqr = \x -> x * x
    t1  = x1 * x1
```

```
        x1  = 5
    in
        t1
```

Now, 5 is a Simple Expression, permitting x1 to be substituted, giving

```
let
    sqr = \x -> x * x
    t1  = 5 * 5
    x1  = 5
in
    t1
```

and, after a few more steps, the result:

```
let
    sqr = \x -> x * x
    t1  = 25
    x1  = 5
in
    25
```

4.6.2   Nonstrictness

A function is said to be *nonstrict* in some argument if it can sometimes return a result when the value of that argument is unknown. Suppose we have the following program:

```
let
    foo  = \x y -> if x then 0.0 else y

    sqrt = \x -> ...                          -- (details omitted)
in
    foo True (sqrt 18239.0)
```

Clearly, it is not necessary to know the value of "sqrt 18239.0" in order to produce the answer 0.0—the function foo is nonstrict in its second argument. Let us execute this program to demonstrate this.

Using the LiftB, LiftAp1, LiftAp2, Inst2, and β rules, we get

```
let
    foo  = \x y -> if x then 0.0 else y

    sqrt = \x -> ...                          -- (details omitted)
    x1   = True
```

```
        y1   = sqrt 18239.0
        t1   = if x1 then 0.0 else y1
    in
        t1
```

Substituting x1 using the Inst2 rule, we get

```
let
    foo  = \x y -> if x then 0.0 else y

    sqrt = \x -> ...                        -- (details omitted)
    x1   = True
    y1   = sqrt 18239.0
    t1   = if True then 0.0 else y1
in
    t1
```

The Cond rule can be applied immediately, giving

```
let
    foo  = \x y -> if x then 0.0 else y

    sqrt = \x -> ...                        -- (details omitted)
    x1   = True
    y1   = sqrt 18239.0
    t1   = 0.0
in
    t1
```

and, substituting t1 using the Inst1 rule gives us the answer 0.0. We did not have to evaluate the argument (sqrt 18239.0) at all!

Technically, the reduction of the whole program has not terminated since we still have a redex—the sqrt application. Is it ok to say that we have the answer and we can stop now? We will discuss this issue in Section 4.7.

Exercise 4.5   Perform the reductions for the following program:

```
let
    g    = \x ->
                let
                    a = x * x
                    f = \y -> x + y + a
                in
                    f
```

```
      g10 = g 10
  in
      (g10 20) + (g10 30)
```

(This will provide some practice with higher-order functions, α-renaming, and so on.) ∎

4.7   Reduction Strategies: Determinacy and Termination

The rewrite rules only describe what *can* be rewritten in a term, and, in general, there may be several redexes available. (It is not difficult to construct even simple example programs that exhibit hundreds, or even millions, of simultaneous candidate redexes.) However, any real computer has finite computational resources—typically from one to a small number of processors—and must therefore constantly make choices as to which of the candidate redexes it will actually pursue at each point in time. Formally, we need a *reduction strategy*, which is a procedure that we apply to the current term before each step and which identifies which redex(es) are to be reduced in that step. This immediately raises both semantic and pragmatic questions. Semantically: can we get different result terms from applying different strategies (the *determinacy* question)? Pragmatically: do different strategies result in different amounts of work in producing the same answer? Do different strategies result in different amounts of time in producing the same answer? And, the *termination* question is both semantic and pragmatic: Can one strategy lead us into an infinite sequence of reductions, while another strategy allows us to terminate successfully with an answer?

4.7.1   Determinacy

The determinacy question is of course the most serious. If we wrote a program to compute our monthly mortgage payment, we would likely be upset if the result depended on which implementation of *pH* we ran it on, since different implementations may have different reduction strategies, and even a single implementation may choose different strategies depending on machine configuration or load.

Some rewrite rule systems (including the λ calculus) have the famous *Church-Rosser property,* whereby if a term reduces to distinct terms t_1 and t_2

using two different reduction sequences, then we can always subsequently further reduce them to a common term t_3. An implication of this property is that answers are unique; that is, we cannot produce different answers using different reduction strategies. However, in a functional language with recursive terms (such as Haskell and *pH*), we lose this strong property. In Section 4.3 we showed a Church-Rosser counterexample—the "odd-even" example started with a common term and took two alternative steps, after which the resulting terms could never be brought back together again into a common term.

When discussing the determinacy properties of *pH*, we need to consider things in two stages. First, the purely functional subset of *pH* (which includes all that we have seen so far), and even the nonfunctional I-structure layer (Chapter 9), is determinate up to observational equivalence. As far as basic values like integers and floating-point numbers are concerned, we can be reassured that our mortgage payment calculation cannot give different answers on different implementations.

When we add the M-structure layer to *pH* (Chapter 10), we lose determinacy—a single program can produce different basic values depending on the reduction choices. But, this introduction of nondeterminism is deliberate, because while there are many programs that we want to be determinate (like our mortgage payment calculator), there are many others where certain kinds of nondeterminism are very useful. For example, in a program that is searching a map for *some* route shorter than 1 hour from city A to city B, we may wish to initiate multiple searches in parallel and accept the first available solution; this is an inherently nondeterministic computation. But exploiting nondeterminism is an advanced topic; for the next few chapters (through Chapter 9) we will only be dealing with determinate computations.

4.7.2   Termination

Consider the following program:

```
let
    loop = \x -> loop x
    y    = loop 1
    z    = 2 + 3
in
    z
```

Suppose we choose to reduce the redex "loop 1" using the β rule. After a few steps, we can reach this term:

```
let
    loop = \x -> loop x
    x1   = 1
    y    = loop x1
    z    = 2 + 3
in
    z
```

and then

```
let
    loop = \x -> loop x
    x1   = 1
    y    = loop 1
    z    = 2 + 3
in
    z
```

We could choose to reduce this new instance of "loop 1" again; and again, and so on, forever. Instead, if our strategy had directed us to focus on z, we could have quickly reached

```
let
    loop = \x -> loop x
    y    = loop 1
    z    = 5
in
    5
```

Based on our determinacy discussion above, we know that the value of this block must be 5, no matter how many more reductions we perform in the block bindings. So, the first important pragmatic point is that a good reduction strategy should somehow make progress on terms that contribute to the final answer of the program; it should not get stuck focusing on some irrelevant corner of the program.

The second important pragmatic question is, When can we safely stop? In the purely functional subset of pH, the answer is fairly clear. For results of basic types, such as the integer 5 in the above example, there is clearly nothing further to be gained by further reduction. But what if the block's result term was a λ-abstraction, since the body of the λ-abstraction may contain redexes? Again, keeping in mind that we are only interested in observational equivalence, we can stop as soon as the block's result term is a value, even if it is a λ-abstraction.

When we include the I-structure and M-structure layers of *pH*, however, the issue of termination is more complex. We will discuss this in more detail when we get to the relevant chapters, but with I- and M-structures we cannot stop reduction even if the result of the block body is manifestly a simple value such as the integer 5. The reason is that I- and M-structures introduce the possibility of certain run-time errors that can occur even after this point, so that a manifest result value such as 5 can only be regarded as tentative. Instead, we have to continue reduction until all block bindings become heap terms.

4.8   Specific Strategies

In general, the execution of a program can be modelled by the following process:

```
loop
    select redexes (mark them, e.g., by drawing a box around them)
    if there are selected redexes
        reduce them
    else
        terminate
```

If there is exactly one redex selected and reduced in each iteration, it is a sequential reduction strategy; otherwise it is a parallel strategy.

In the following sections, we will discuss some specific redex selection functions. We will first underline certain subterms, indicating that we *demand* their values. For example, we will initially demand the value of the outermost **let**-block's body, which is just the variable main. When we examine a demanded term *e*, there are three possibilities:

- ◆ It is already a value. We simply erase the underline.
- ◆ It is not already a value, but it is a redex. We erase the underline and draw a box around it, $\boxed{e}$, indicating that it is a selected redex.
- ◆ Otherwise, we erase the underline and *propagate* the demand to one or more other terms (by underlining them) that are necessary for this term to become a redex.

In order to consider fewer cases, we will only work with *canonical forms*, which were discussed in Section 4.5.5. Eventually, the program will have no remaining underlined terms and will have zero or more redexes identified by boxes around them. If there are zero redexes, execution will terminate. (Actually, the demand propagation rules given below may themselves loop, for example in bindings such as x=x, or x=y;y=x, or x=x+1. It is easy to detect this looping and to halt with an error message, but we omit the details in order to avoid cluttering the rules.)

Because of sharing of computations, when we propagate a demand, it is possible that the target term has already been underlined (demanded) or boxed (marked as a redex) from some other route. If so, we simply discard the current demand as being redundant. For example, if we have

```
x = 2 + 2
y = x * x
```

then we will propagate the demand to both arguments of the multiplication. Propagating any one of them will eventually mark 2+2 as a redex by boxing it; when we propagate the other we will encounter this marked redex and discard the demand. The net result will be, simply,

```
x = 2 + 2
y = x * x
```

Elimination of redundant demands is captured by the following rules:

$$\frac{\underline{e}}{\frac{x = e}{\boxed{e}}} \qquad\qquad \begin{array}{l}\longrightarrow \underline{e}\\ \longrightarrow \underline{x} = e \\ \longrightarrow \boxed{e}\end{array}$$

In the following, we assume this treatment of multiple simultaneous demands on a term, without showing it explicitly.

The resulting marked redexes will always be *disjoint*—the boxes will never be nested or overlap. Thus, reducing them in parallel is not a problem because they do not interfere with each other in any way.

4.8.1 Marking Redexes for Lazy Evaluation

Lazy evaluation is a popular strategy in many implementations of pure functional languages (including all the well-known implementations of Haskell). It is so called because we rewrite no redex until we are sure that the final answer depends on it.

How do we know whether a redex is needed? We work our way backwards from the outermost expression, identifying what is needed in order to convert it into a value. Initially, we demand the top-level block's body (the variable `main`) by underlining it. The following rules take such an expression and propagate the demand as necessary, eventually selecting zero or more redexes for reduction by drawing boxes around them.

The first three rules are given below. If the **let**-body is already a value, then we are done (we don't select any more redexes). If the block body is still the identifier `main` and `main` is now bound to a value, then the block body is itself the selected redex (it is eligible for the substitution rule). Otherwise, we simply propagate the demand to the variable's binding.

$$\textbf{let}\ s\ \textbf{in}\ \underline{v} \quad\longrightarrow\quad \textbf{let}\ s\ \textbf{in}\ v$$
$$\textbf{let}\ \texttt{main} = v;\ s\ \textbf{in}\ \underline{\texttt{main}} \quad\longrightarrow\quad \textbf{let}\ \texttt{main} = v;\ s\ \textbf{in}\ \boxed{\texttt{main}}$$
$$\textbf{let}\ \texttt{main} = e;\ s\ \textbf{in}\ \underline{\texttt{main}} \quad\longrightarrow\quad \textbf{let}\ \underline{\texttt{main} = e}\ ;\ s\ \textbf{in}\ \texttt{main} \qquad e \notin V$$

We underline the entire binding in order first to allow the Flat1 rule to do its work (block flattening):

$$\frac{x\ =\ \textbf{let}\ s\ \textbf{in}\ e}{x = f} \quad\longrightarrow\quad \frac{\boxed{x\ =\ \textbf{let}\ s\ \textbf{in}\ e}}{x = \underline{f}} \qquad f \in F$$

Otherwise, we propagate the demand to the right-hand side expression. What can this expression be? Since $e \notin V$, it can't be a λ or a constant, and we have just ruled out blocks. Thus, it can only be an identifier, an application, a conditional, or a primitive function application. Let us tackle the latter three cases first.

If it is an application, and the function part is a λ, then the application is a redex (eligible for the β rule), and we are done. Otherwise, our next task is to reduce the function part to a λ so that we can apply the β rule. So, we propagate the demand to the function part:

$$\frac{(\texttt{\\}x\texttt{->}e_1)\ e_2}{\underline{e_1}\ e_2} \quad\longrightarrow\quad \frac{\boxed{(\texttt{\\}x\texttt{->}e_1)\ e_2}}{\underline{e_1}\ e_2} \qquad e_1\ \text{is not a}\ \lambda$$

Note that we do not propagate demand to the argument because we do not yet know whether it is needed or not. If the function does not examine its argument, then reducing the argument is unnecessary.

If it is a conditional, and the predicate is a value (it can only be `True` or `False`, since the program has been type checked), the conditional itself is a redex (it is ready to be discharged), and we are done. Otherwise, our next task is to reduce the predicate to a value so that we can discharge the conditional, so we propagate the demand there:

$$\underline{\mathsf{Cond}(v,\; e_t,\; e_f)} \qquad\qquad \longrightarrow \quad \boxed{\mathsf{Cond}(v,\; e_t,\; e_f)}$$

$$\underline{\mathsf{Cond}(e_p,\; e_t,\; e_f)} \qquad\qquad \longrightarrow \quad \mathsf{Cond}(\underline{e_p},\; e_t,\; e_f) \qquad e_p \notin V$$

If it is a primitive function application, we need to use our knowledge of the particular primitive function in order to decide whether it is a redex and how to propagate demand. Here is an example set of rules for "+". If both arguments are values, then the "+" application itself is a redex (eligible for δ rule for "+"). Otherwise, our next task is to reduce the arguments to values, and so we propagate the demand to the arguments:

$$\underline{v_1 + v_2} \qquad\qquad\qquad \longrightarrow \quad \boxed{v_1 \;+\; v_2}$$

$$\underline{e_1 + e_2} \qquad\qquad\qquad \longrightarrow \quad \underline{e_1} \;+\; \underline{e_2} \qquad e_1 \notin V \text{ or } e_2 \notin V$$

The last rule introduces some parallelism, since we have propagated the demand simultaneously to both arguments. This is not the only choice. We could choose to propagate the demand to the right argument only if the left argument was a value, resulting in a left-to-right sequential evaluation, or vice versa. For some primitives, we may wish to examine one argument at a time. For example, the "&&" operator (logical conjunction) may return False if its first argument is False, without even examining the second argument.

In the last line above, one of the two arguments may already be a value. As discussed earlier, we simply discard demands on values:

$$\underline{v} \qquad\qquad\qquad\qquad \longrightarrow \quad v$$

So, if we didn't find a redex in the demanded right-hand side of a binding in the top-level **let**-block, then the right-hand side now contains a demanded identifier—either the right-hand side is itself a demanded identifier, or it is an application whose function part is a demanded identifier, or it is a conditional whose predicate is a demanded identifier, or it is a primitive function application whose function and/or argument are demanded identifiers. The following rules deal with all these cases. Either the demanded identifier y is bound elsewhere in the block to a value, in which case the demanded identifier $\underline{y}$ is a redex, or we propagate the demand to the binding of the identifier:

$$\begin{aligned}&\textbf{let } y = v;\; x = C[\underline{y}];\; s \quad \longrightarrow \quad \textbf{let } y = v;\; x = C[\boxed{\underline{y}}];\; s\\&\textbf{in } e \qquad\qquad\qquad\qquad\qquad\qquad \textbf{in } e\end{aligned}$$

$$\begin{array}{ll} \textbf{let}\ y\ =\ e_1;\ x\ =\ C[\underline{y}];\ s & \longrightarrow\ \textbf{let}\ \underline{y = e_1};\ x\ =\ C[y];\ s \quad e_1 \notin V \\ \textbf{in}\ e & \textbf{in}\ e \end{array}$$

$$\textbf{let}\ y\ =\ C[\underline{y}];\ s\ \textbf{in}\ e \qquad \longrightarrow\ \textbf{let}\ \underline{y = C[y]};\ s\ \textbf{in}\ e$$

In the second case, the binding is demanded, and we have already shown the rule to handle this. In the second and third cases, the demand propagation can loop forever (consider x=y;y=x̲ and x=x̲); a practical implementation may choose to terminate here with an error message.

In this manner, a lazy strategy selects one or more demanded redexes in each step of the evaluator. There is no *speculative* computation; at each stage we are assured that we are doing work that is critical for producing the answer. Notice also that we never reduce—not even using substitution— inside λ-abstractions and arms of conditionals.

Exercise 4.6   Suppose we had the following δ rules for multiplication:

$$\begin{array}{lll} 0\ *\ e & \longrightarrow\ 0 & \\ \underline{x}\ *\ \underline{y} & \longrightarrow\ x \times y & \underline{x} \neq 0 \end{array}$$

Give a set of lazy demand propagation rules for "*". (Of course, one could have a symmetric rule for a zero right-hand side argument.)   ■

Exercise 4.7   In the following rule:

$$\begin{array}{ll} \textbf{let}\ y\ =\ v;\ x\ =\ C[\underline{y}];\ s & \longrightarrow\ \textbf{let}\ y\ =\ v;\ x\ =\ C[\boxed{y}];\ s \\ \textbf{in}\ e & \textbf{in}\ e \end{array}$$

instead of "y=v" where $v \in V$, we could have said "y=a" where $a \in SE$. Demonstrate a program where this makes a difference. Is this a major difference?   ■

Strictness Information and Parallelism

The rules for propagating demand to primitive function arguments are the basic source of parallelism, but compiler analysis can improve this. For example, given a user-defined function

```
sqr = \x -> x * x
```

the compiler can infer, from the argument-need properties of "*", that sqr is going to need the value of its argument. Suppose the compiler then marks the λ with this information, using an s subscript to indicate that this function is *strict* in its argument. Then, we could have a new rule:

$$(\backslash_s x \text{->} e_1)\ e_2 \qquad\qquad \longrightarrow \qquad \boxed{(\backslash x \text{->} e_1)\ \underline{e_2}}$$

That is, in addition to marking the application as a redex, as before, we also demand the argument immediately, thereby permitting it to be evaluated even before the β rule has been applied. (This can potentially lead to a violation of our earlier claim that redexes will always be disjoint, for if e_2 is an identifier that is elsewhere bound to a value, then it, too, becomes a redex, and it is nested inside the β-redex. As it happens, this is the only kind of violation that can arise—an inner redex for instantiation; it is not serious and does not cause any technical problems.)

More sophisticated compiler analysis may be able to predict, even in an application where the function part has not yet evaluated to a λ, that all possible function values here will be strict in the argument, and so the argument can be demanded immediately:

$$\underline{e_1\ e_2} \qquad\qquad \longrightarrow \qquad \underline{e_1}\ \underline{e_2} \qquad\qquad \begin{array}{l} e_1 \text{ is not a } \lambda \text{, but is} \\ \text{known to be strict} \end{array}$$

Strictness analysis to produce this kind of information is very hard in the presence of higher-order functions and data structures. Therefore, many real implementations of Haskell have extensions by which the programmer can explicitly annotate λs and/or applications with this information. (In most Haskell implementations, strictness information is used not for parallelism but to eliminate overheads due to lazy evaluation.)

4.8.2   Marking Redexes for Call-by-Value Evaluation

Many functional languages such as SML and Scheme use call-by-value evaluation strategies. The key choices that implement call-by-value semantics are

$$\begin{array}{l} \underline{(\backslash x \text{->} e)\ v} \\ \underline{e_1\ e_2} \end{array} \qquad\qquad \begin{array}{l} \longrightarrow \quad \boxed{(\backslash x \text{->} e)\ \underline{v}} \\ \longrightarrow \quad \underline{e_1}\ \underline{e_2} \end{array} \qquad e_1 \notin V \text{ or } e_2 \notin V$$

(Compare them to the rules for applications in the lazy evaluator, given earlier.) The application becomes a β-redex only when the argument has been reduced to a value. Since we need both the function and the argument to be values, we also propagate demand to both of them eagerly.

Choosing to evaluate the function and the argument in parallel is an arbitrary choice; we could have done them sequentially. Similarly, for primitive function applications like "+", we could evaluate the arguments in parallel or sequentially. Scheme and SML in fact specify sequential evaluation, in order to give meaningful semantics to side effects and exception handling.

The function in an application could ignore its argument. In this case, reducing the argument is wasted work. The most extreme case of this is when the argument doesn't terminate. Suppose the application is of the form

```
y  =  (\x->23) (loop 1)
```

where loop is the perpetually looping function we have seen earlier. The function, if applied, ignores its argument and the application reduces to the value 23. However, by insisting that the argument should be a value before performing the application, we will get stuck in the loop.

We could use the same rules for **let**-blocks as we did for lazy evaluation. However, most call-by-value languages pursue a different approach. First, we note that although we have a single kind of block in *pH*, which we call a **let**-block, many call-by-value languages like Scheme and SML have two kinds of blocks: so-called **let**-blocks and **letrec**-blocks. The former is simply syntactic sugar for a λ-abstraction applied immediately to an argument and so is covered by the application rule already discussed. A **letrec**-block can have recursive bindings and is the analog of a *pH* block. In Scheme and SML, the approach is first to demand the values of the right-hand sides of *all* the bindings in a **letrec**-block and, after they have all been reduced to values, then to demand the value of the body of the block. In SML, this always terminates because, in a **letrec**-block, all right-hand sides must syntactically be λ-expressions, which are already values. In Scheme, the language specification is somewhat looser, but it effectively boils down to a restriction that any recursive definition in the block must be mediated by a λ. We will skip the rules for this demand propagation because they are similar to the rules described for *pH* in the next sections.

4.8.3   Marking Redexes for Parallel Evaluation of Functional *pH*

We have seen, in the last two sections, that there are opportunities for parallelism in lazy evaluation and in call-by-value evaluation. However, it is possible to be even more aggressive with respect to parallelism. First, consider the strategy for applications:

$$\frac{(\backslash x\text{->}e)\ e_2}{e_1\ e_2} \qquad \longrightarrow \quad \boxed{(\backslash x\text{->}e)\ \underline{e_2}}$$
$$\longrightarrow \quad \underline{e_1}\ \underline{e_2} \qquad e1 \notin V \text{ or } e2 \notin V$$

The first rule specifies that, like lazy evaluation and unlike call-by-value, the application becomes a redex as soon as the function is known to be a λ-abstraction. Thus, this strategy implements nonstrict functions just like lazy evaluation, which call-by-value does not. The two rules also specify that, like call-by-value and unlike lazy evaluation, we also immediately demand the argument, allowing it to be evaluated eagerly, speculatively, in parallel with the function evaluation (to a λ) and in parallel with the function application (β).

The next opportunity for more aggressive parallelism is in the way we propagate demand into the outermost block.

$$\texttt{let } s \texttt{ in } \underline{v} \quad \longrightarrow \quad \texttt{let } s \texttt{ in } v$$

$$\begin{array}{ll} \texttt{let main} = v; & \longrightarrow \quad \texttt{let main} = v; \\ \quad s & \qquad s \\ \texttt{in} & \texttt{in} \\ \quad \underline{\texttt{main}} & \quad \boxed{\texttt{main}} \end{array}$$

$$\begin{array}{llll} \texttt{let main} = e; & \longrightarrow \quad \texttt{let } \underline{\texttt{main} = e}; & \quad e \notin V \\ \quad \cdots & \qquad \cdots \\ \quad \texttt{x}_j = e_j; & \qquad \underline{\texttt{x}_j = e_j}; \\ \quad \cdots & \qquad \cdots \\ \texttt{in} & \texttt{in} \\ \quad \underline{\texttt{main}} & \quad \texttt{main} \end{array}$$

The first two rules are the same as in lazy evaluation. In the third rule, lazy evaluation only propagated demand to the binding of main, whereas here we immediately demand *all* right-hand sides of the block, allowing them to evaluate immediately. Consider the following program:

```
let
    f    = \ ...
    g    = \ ...
    x    = e_x
    y    = e_y
    main = f x + g y
in
    main
```

In a lazy evaluator, we first demand f x and g y. Eventually, they may demand x and y, at which point we will demand e_x and e_y. In the current strategy, we demand e_x and e_y immediately, so that the overall execution time of the program (in particular, its *critical path*) may be shorter.

An even more aggressive strategy might be to propagate demand into bodies of λ-abstractions and into arms of conditionals. *pH* does not go this far, but this is a heuristic choice, since we are already doing speculative evaluation by propagating demand to terms before we know whether we need them or not. We choose not to evaluate inside λs because λs are frequently recursive and this would result in infinite unfoldings. We choose not to evaluate inside conditionals because, again, the programmer usually employs conditionals precisely to control what should and should not be evaluated.

While no practical evaluator of functional languages evaluates inside λ-abstractions and arms of conditionals, many *compilers* do this statically as part of the compilation process. Program optimization, a central concern of any good compiler, is in fact nothing more than the static application of rewrite rules inside function bodies, conditionals, loops, and so on.

4.8.4   Marking Redexes for Parallel Evaluation of Full *pH*

In purely functional *pH*, when `main` has become a value, no further reduction in the body of the main **let**-block can have any further effect on this value. Thus, there was a well-defined notion of a "needed" computation, and we are justified in stopping when `main` becomes a value.

In full *pH*, however, adding nonfunctional constructs such as I-structures and M-structures (in Chapters 9 and 10, respectively), we can no longer terminate when `main` becomes a value; it is possible for certain run-time errors to occur after this point, causing the whole program to be in error. It is thus necessary to continue evaluation until all top-level bindings become value bindings. Thus, instead of starting by demanding just the outer **let**-block's body, we start by demanding everything in the block:

$$\textbf{let } \underline{x_1 = e_1}; \ \cdots; \ \underline{x_n = e_n} \textbf{ in } \underline{e}$$

So, we need only this one rule on the outer-level block to actually reduce `main` to a value:

$$\textbf{let } \cdots; \ \texttt{main} = v; \ \cdots \qquad \longrightarrow \qquad \textbf{let } \cdots; \ \texttt{main} = v; \ \cdots$$
$$\textbf{in } \underline{\texttt{main}} \qquad\qquad\qquad\qquad \textbf{in } \boxed{\texttt{main}}$$

When execution terminates, the only remaining redexes will be "unexposed" redexes (i.e., those inside a λ or arm of a conditional).

4.8.5   Reducing Marked Redexes

Let us turn our attention once again to the evaluation process presented at the top of this section:

```
loop
    select redexes (mark them, e.g., by drawing a box around them)
    if there are selected redexes
        reduce them
    else
        terminate
```

Note that we may terminate evaluation while there are still redexes in the program; it all depends on the redex selection algorithm. In the lazy evaluator, once main has become a value, we do not propagate demands anymore, and so we mark no more redexes.

Let us focus on the line "reduce them." Any real computer has finite computational resources (a certain maximum amount of processor parallelism, so that we can reduce at most p redexes at a time). What if, in the previous line, we have selected more than p redexes? We have several options for "reduce them":

1. Reduce all marked redexes, doing p at a time if necessary.
2. Reduce some p (or fewer) of the marked redexes, but be *fair* in the choice; that is, don't ignore a marked redex indefinitely.
3. Reduce some p (or fewer) of the marked redexes.

Strategies incorporating the first two options are *fair* strategies—they never ignore a marked redex indefinitely. It should be evident that, with these options, the purely functional parallel *pH* strategy will perform any redex that lazy evaluation would perform so that, if a lazy evaluator terminates with an answer, then so will the purely functional parallel *pH* strategy. Of course, it may do unnecessary work that a lazy evaluator would not do, and thereby take more time to produce the answer. On the other hand, it could also produce the answer *earlier* than a lazy evaluator because it gets started on some necessary work earlier than the lazy evaluator would.

The third option is potentially unfair and runs the risk of getting stuck in an irrelevant loop, if we always choose redexes in such a loop instead of making progress on other pending redexes. At first sight, it would appear that this is inferior to the other two strategies, and this may indeed be true for purely functional *pH*. However, for full *pH*, we can only terminate when all exposed redexes have been reduced. In this environment, lazy evaluation is not really an option and fairness is moot, since we need to evaluate all redexes anyway. Thus, *pH* uses the third option, which is simple to implement.

4.9 ▾   Semantics of Loops

pH loops are purely a syntactic convenience and are explained in terms of translation into equivalent loop-free *pH* programs. In general, a **while** loop has the form

> **while** *predicate* **do**
>   *loop-body statement*
>   .
>   .
>   .
>   *loop-body statement*
> **finally** *final-expression*

The predicate is an arbitrary boolean expression and the final-expression is an arbitrary expression representing the value of the whole loop. If the loop predicate evaluates to `False` the first time around, the loop body is never executed.

The loop-body statements are just like bindings in a block, except that binding occurrences of identifiers may also be qualified by the keyword "**next**". The value bound to "**next** x" in one iteration is available as "**next** x" in that iteration and as "x" in the next iteration. Such identifiers are called "nextified" or "circulating" variables, since their values generally vary from one iteration to the next.

Binding occurrences of identifiers that are *not* qualified by "**next**" are treated as ordinary identifier bindings (i.e., they are local to each iteration).

Free identifiers in the loop (which are not bound in any statement in the loop body, with or without "**next**") must be bound in the surrounding scope. Since their values do not change from one iteration to the next, such identifiers are also known as "loop constants."

A loop is translated into a term involving a recursive function, to which we can then apply the standard rewrite rules. It is important to remember that what we are presenting is a scheme for translating loops (i.e., each loop can be replaced in situ by a corresponding function that is unique for that loop); we are not describing a single function that is good for implementing all loops.

Without loss of generality, we assume that all the "**next** x = e" bindings precede all the ordinary bindings "y = e":

```
while e_p do
    next x1 = e_1
        .
        .
        .
    next xn = e_n
    y1 = e_{n+1}
        .
        .
        .
    ym = e_{n+m}
finally e_f
```

The loop is translated into the following *pH* expression:

```
let
    loop x1 ... xn =
        if e_p then
            let
                t1 = e_1[t1/next x1,...,tn/next xn]
                    .
                    .
                    .
                tn = e_n[t1/next x1,...,tn/next xn]
                y1 = e_{n+1}[t1/next x1,...,tn/next xn]
                    .
                    .
                    .
                ym = e_{n+m}[t1/next x1,...,tn/next xn]
            in
                loop t1 ... tn
        else
            e_f
in
    loop x1 ... xn
```

Here, the tjs are new variables and, in each e_i, we substitute the use of any nextified variable **next** xj by tj. (The notation "e[t1/**next** x1,..., tn/**next** xn]" is just an extension of our $e[t/x]$ notation, indicating several substitutions at once.)

Exercise 4.8   Write the recursive function that corresponds to the following loop expression:

```
another_gcd a b =
                while a <> b do
                    c = (a > b)
```

$$\textbf{next}\ a\ =\ \textbf{if}\ c\ \textbf{then}\ (a–b)$$
$$\textbf{else}\ a$$
$$\textbf{next}\ b\ =\ \textbf{if}\ c\ \textbf{then}\ b$$
$$\textbf{else}\ (b–a)$$
$$\textbf{finally}\ a \qquad ▪$$

for loops, in turn, are specified by a translation into **while** loops. For example:

```
for j <- [e₁ .. e₂] do
    s₁
    .
    .
    .
    sₙ
finally eₓ
```

is translated into

```
let
    j = e₁
    jLast = e₂
in
    while j <= jLast do
        s₁
        .
        .
        .
        sₙ
        next j = j + 1
    finally eₓ
```

Exercise 4.9   The above translation is for a **for** loop with an ascending sequence with increment 1. Write down a general translation that permits ascending and descending controlling sequences with arbitrary increments.   ▪

Tuples and Algebraic Product Types

So far, we have talked about scalars (such as numbers and booleans) and functions on them. However, we frequently wish to talk about composite objects. For example, a triangle may be regarded as a composite object comprising three points. To describe such objects, we need the notion of a *data structure*. *pH* has several kinds of data structures, such as tuples, arrays, lists, and others. In this chapter we examine tuples (and, more generally, product types), the simplest of *pH*'s data structures. Tuples are ubiquitous in functional programming and are used to hold "multiple values."

To make it interesting, we will base our discussion on the following scenario. Many of us are familiar with programs like MacDraw, the venerable drawing program for Apple Macintosh personal computers. In such a program, the user can draw various objects on the screen. For example, he may draw a horizontal rectangle by pointing and clicking the mouse at two

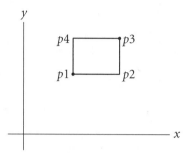

Figure 5.1   Specifying a horizontal rectangle by clicking on two points.

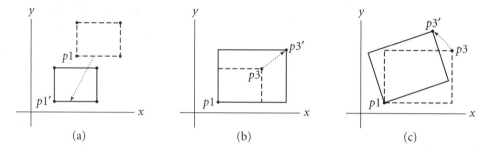

Figure 5.2   Transforming the rectangle in various ways: (a) translation, (b) scaling, and (c) rotation.

diagonally opposite points $p1$ and $p3$, as shown in Figure 5.1. Internally, the rectangle may be represented as a composite of the four points that comprise its corners.

Subsequently, the user may transform the rectangle in various ways. Figure 5.2 shows three such transformations. In Figure 5.2(a), the object is translated (i.e., moved uniformly) to a new position, by dragging point $p1$ to $p1'$. In Figure 5.2(b), it is scaled by keeping $p1$ fixed and dragging $p3$ to $p3'$; this specifies two things—a factor by which points should be scaled vertically away from the $p1$-$p2$ line, and a factor by which points should be scaled horizontally away from the $p1$-$p4$ line. In Figure 5.2(c), it is rotated by an angle of approximately 1 radian, keeping $p1$ fixed as a pivot and dragging the diagonal $p1$-$p3$ around it. In each case, the transformation of the entire object can be specified as a transformation of a single point, which is then applied to each of the vertex points of the object.

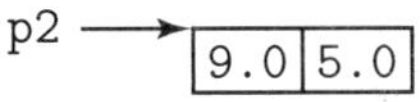

p2 ──────▶ | 9.0 | 5.0 |

Figure 5.3 A point in two-dimensional space, represented as a 2-tuple.

5.1   Tuple Construction

We can represent a point as a 2-tuple (i.e., a pair) by listing its x- and y-coordinates in parentheses and separated by commas.

```
p2 = (9.0, 5.0)
```

The value of the expression on the right-hand side is a 2-tuple whose components are the numbers 9 and 5, and the statement binds p2 to this composite object, as shown in Figure 5.3. The comma has lower precedence than most other operators. Thus, the expression "(f a, b)" stands for the 2-tuple "((f a), b)" and not "(f (a, b))". Tuples are first-class values, just like numbers or booleans or functions. For example, here is a function that takes a number x and returns the point on the x-axis with that x-coordinate:

```
x_point x = (x,0.0)
```

Exercise 5.1   The roots of a quadratic equation are given by the formulae

$$\frac{-b+\sqrt{b^2-4ac}}{2a} \qquad \text{and} \qquad \frac{-b-\sqrt{b^2-4ac}}{2a}$$

Write a function "quadroots a b c" that computes and returns both roots. Use a **let**-block to compute the discriminant $\sqrt{b^2 - 4ac}$ only once. ∎

5.2   Tuple Component Selection: Pattern Matching

To translate (move) a point p, we need to specify displacements dx and dy for its x- and y-coordinates:

```
translate dx dy p = ...
```

We have seen, in Chapter 2, that our notation for function definitions is really syntactic sugar for binding a value to a λ-expression:

```
translate = \dx -> \dy -> \p -> ...
```

The motivation for this syntactic sugar was to make the left-hand side be a "pattern" for a typical application:

```
translate  e_{dx}  e_{dy}  e_p
```

making it easier to visualize the correspondence between the formal parameters dx, dy, and p and the corresponding actual parameters e_{dx}, e_{dy}, and e_p, respectively. We now extend this idea of *pattern matching* to tuple arguments. We use a pattern both to indicate that a particular parameter is a tuple, as well as to name its components.

```
translate dx dy (x,y) = (x+dx, y+dy)
```

translate expects *three* arguments (not four). The first two arguments must be numbers and the third argument must be a 2-tuple. Given such a third argument, the names x and y are bound to the first and second components of the tuple, respectively. For example, a suitable actual parameter would be the point p2 described earlier, in which case x and y would be bound to the values 9.0 and 5.0, respectively. In other words, the formal parameter "(x,y)" is a pattern that matches the actual parameter and binds the identifiers in the pattern to the corresponding components in the actual parameter. With these bindings, the expression "(x+dx, y+dy)" is computed as the result of the function; that is, it returns a new 2-tuple with each coordinate value suitably displaced. Thus,

```
translate (–2.0) (–4.0) p2 ⟶ (7.0, 1.0)
```

Note that because commas have lower precedence than other operators, we do not need parentheses around x+dx or around y+dy in the body of translate.

To emphasize that translate takes only three parameters, and to show how tuple patterns can also be used in block bindings, we show another (equivalent) definition for the function:

```
translate dx dy p = let
                        (x,y) = p
                    in
                        (x+dx, y+dy)
```

The third formal parameter is p, a point. The tuple binding "(x,y) = p" *destructures* the tuple and binds x and y to its components. Similarly, tuple patterns can also be used as parameters of λ-expressions, as demonstrated in yet another definition for the function:

```
translate = \dx -> \dy -> \(x,y) -> (x+dx, y+dy)
```

Turning back to our drawing program, a scaling transformation is given two scaling factors s_x and s_y. All points are scaled away from the origin (the point $(0,0)$) horizontally by the scaling factor s_x and vertically by the scaling factor s_y.

```
scale sx sy (x,y) =  (sx * x, sy * y)
```

A rotation transformation is specified by an angle θ. When a point (x, y) is rotated about the origin (the point $(0,0)$) by θ, its new coordinates are given by

$$x' = x \cdot \cos \theta - y \cdot \sin \theta$$
$$y' = x \cdot \sin \theta + y \cdot \cos \theta$$

This is expressed directly in *pH* as follows:

```
rotate theta (x,y) =
        let
            costh = cos theta
            sinth = sin theta
            x'    = x * costh - y * sinth
            y'    = x * sinth + y * costh
        in
            (x',y')
```

Here, we have named several intermediate values, both to avoid duplication of computation as well as for readability.

5.3   Tuple Types

The type rules for tuples are very simple. Suppose we have n expressions with types

$$e_1 \ :: \ t_1$$
$$\vdots$$
$$e_n \ :: \ t_n$$

Recall that we think of the type t_j as a set of values to which the value of e_j belongs. Now, the n-tuple expression

$$(e_1, \ldots, e_n)$$

can be viewed as denoting a value that belongs to the *cross product* of those sets:

$$t_1 \times \cdots \times t_n$$

Since computer keyboards do not often include the $\times$ symbol, we write the tuple type in *pH* by mimicking the tuple expression notation (i.e., with parentheses and commas):

$$(e_1, \ldots, e_n) \quad :: \quad (t_1, \ldots, t_n)$$

Note that the components of a tuple may be of any type, including other tuples, scalars, functions, and so on. For example, `translate`'s type may be described as follows:

```
translate    ::    Float -> Float -> (Float,Float)
                                  -> (Float,Float)
```

It takes three arguments—a number, a number, and a 2-tuple of numbers—and produces a 2-tuple of numbers.

An *n*-tuple type can never be equal to an *m*-tuple type if $n \neq m$. For example, it is always incorrect to supply a 3-tuple or a 4-tuple for the third argument of `translate`. Similarly, a conditional expression that produces a 2-tuple in one arm and a 3-tuple in the other does not have a meaningful type; this is a type error. For example, any function that adds up the numbers in a tuple of numbers, such as

```
addup_3 (x,y,z) = x + y + z
```

will only work on tuples of a given size (here, 3); addup_3 cannot be applied to 2-tuples, to 4-tuples, and so on.

Two *n*-tuple types are equal if and only if the types of their corresponding components are equal. Thus, it is an error to supply a 2-tuple of strings or booleans for the third argument of `translate`. Similarly, it is impossible for a conditional expression to produce a 2-tuple of strings in one arm and a 2-tuple of numbers in the other.

5.3.1   Composition of Transformations

The `scale` and `rotate` functions are not by themselves adequate to describe the transformations in Figures 5.2(b) and 5.2(c). For example, in both the functions `scale` and `rotate`, the origin (i.e., the point with

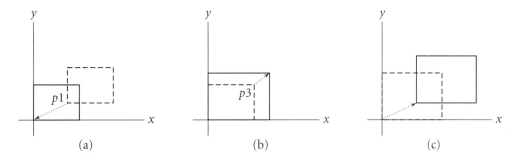

Figure 5.4 Scaling about an arbitrary fixed point: (a) translate, (b) scale, and (c) translate.

coordinates (0.0,0.0)) is the "fixed point" around which scaling and rotation takes place. If we directly applied scale or rotate to the rectangle in Figure 5.1, both points $p1$ and $p3$ would move away from the origin by the same scale, or both points would rotate around the origin by the same amount. In the figures, however, $p1$ stays fixed and the scaling and rotation are around $p1$, not the origin.

We can change the fixed point of a transformation by using a *composition* of transformations. For example, the transformation in Figure 5.2(b) can be expressed by first translating all four points so that $p1$ is at the origin, then scaling all four points (so $p1$ remains fixed), and then translating all four points so that $p1$ is restored to its original position. This is illustrated in Figure 5.4. Since $p1$ is the point (3.0,1.0), the first translation can be expressed by applying the following function to all four points:

```
t1 = translate (-3.0) (-1.0)
```

Observe that, by currying,

```
t1    ::    (Float,Float) -> (Float,Float)
```

and it transforms a point to another point. Similarly, the scaling can be expressed by applying the following function to all four points:

```
s = scale  1.5  1.33
```

(The scaling factors s_x and s_y are 1.5 and 1.33, respectively.) The final translation uses

```
t2 = translate 3.0 1.0
```

The composition of these transformations can be expressed using the following function:

```
compose f g x = f (g x)
```

(In mathematics, "compose f g" is usually written with an infix circle, "$f \circ g$". As mentioned in Section 3.3, the infix operator "." is predefined in pH's libraries for this purpose.) Using compose, if we compute

```
t = compose t2 (compose s t1)
```

then t is a function that represents the net transformation of Figure 5.2(b). In particular, when applied to point $p3$, it will produce the required point $p3'$.

Exercise 5.2   Use compose to describe the net transformation of Figure 5.2(c).   ∎

Exercise 5.3   Show that the composition of transformations is not commutative; that is, in general,

```
compose tA tB      ≠      compose tB tA
```
                                                                              ∎

Exercise 5.4   In some interactive drawing programs, the user can directly specify a composite transformation on an object by clicking on four points on the screen—call them a, b, a', and b'. As shown in Figure 5.5, a and a' specify a translation, and b and b' specify a scaling and rotation relative to a. This transformation is then applied to all the vertex points of the object in order to transform it. Write a function that, given the coordinates of the four points a, b, a', and b', computes the net point-transformation function.   ∎

Exercise 5.5   What is the type of compose as used in this section?   ∎

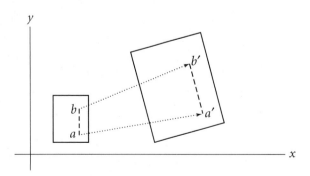

Figure 5.5   A general four-point transformation.

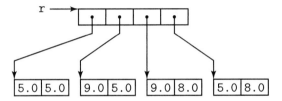

Figure 5.6 A rectangle, represented as a 4-tuple of points.

5.3.2   Nested Tuples

Our original goal was to represent and transform objects such as rectangles. Such objects can be described as a collection of the points that constitute their vertices. This idea can be expressed naturally in *pH* because tuples may be nested; that is, tuples may contain other tuples. Thus, a quadrilateral (four-sided shape) can be represented as a 4-tuple, each of whose components is a point, that is, a 2-tuple. Here is a statement that binds r to the rectangle of Figure 5.1.

```
r = ((5.0,5.0), (9.0,5.0), (9.0,8.0), (5.0,8.0))
```

The value bound to r may be visualized as shown in Figure 5.6. The parentheses are important—had we written

```
r = (5.0,5.0, 9.0,5.0, 9.0,8.0, 5.0,8.0)
```

we would be describing a flat 8-tuple instead.

We can now express our transformation of a rectangle. Here is a function that, given a general transformation *f* on points as developed in the previous section, applies the transformation to all four points of a quadrilateral, returning a new quadrilateral comprising the transformed points:

```
quad_xform f (p1,p2,p3,p4) = ((f p1), (f p2), (f p3), (f p4))
```

That is, we use a 4-tuple pattern as a formal parameter to access the four point components of the quadrilateral and build a new 4-tuple in the function body.

Tuples may also be used to represent other shapes: a triangle is a 3-tuple of points, a pentagon is a 5-tuple of points, and so on.

Patterns may also be nested, in order to access more deeply nested components directly. Here is a function to compute the point that is the centroid of a quadrilateral:

```
centroid ((x1,y1),(x2,y2),(x3,y3),(x4,y4)) =
                    ((x1+x2+x3+x4)/4.0, (y1+y2+y3+y4)/4.0)
```

The function takes a single argument, which is a 4-tuple of 2-tuples. The identifiers x1, y1, and so on are bound to the corresponding components of the argument. For example, x1 is bound to the first component of the 2-tuple, which is the first component of the 4-tuple argument.

5.3.3   Type Synonyms

We have already mentioned the type of translate:

```
translate :: Float -> Float -> (Float,Float) -> (Float,Float)
```

Unfortunately, this is not as descriptive as we would like. In particular, we have to remember that here (Float,Float) represents a point in two-dimensional space. Elsewhere, (Float,Float) may be used for some unrelated purpose, for example to represent an average and standard deviation. For this reason, *pH* provides *type synonyms* to provide existing types with more descriptive names. We can declare three type synonyms:

type Point = (Float,Float)

type X_displacement = Float

type Y_displacement = Float

so that we can write a more descriptive type for translate:

```
translate :: X_displacement -> Y_displacement -> Point
                                            -> Point
```

Similarly, if we define

type Quadrilateral = (Point, Point, Point, Point)

we then have

```
centroid :: Quadrilateral -> Point
```

Type synonyms do not have any semantic significance. They are simply convenient abbreviations for the type expressions to which they are equated.

5.3.4 More Higher-Order Computation Structures

With tuples, we can write more interesting higher-order functions. In Chapter 2, we saw three functions, sqrt, gcd, and integrate, that shared a common structure. In all cases, we computed a series of values

$$x_0, f\,x_0, f(f\,x_0), f(f(f\,x_0)), \ldots$$

until it satisfied a predicate p; that is, $p(f^i x_0)$ was true. In sqrt, we began with an initial guess and repeatedly improved it until it was good enough. In gcd, we began with the initial pair of numbers and repeatedly replaced them by the second number and the remainder of the first with respect to the second, until the second number was zero. In integrate, we began with $x = a + dx/2$ and an initial sum $s = 0$ and repeatedly replaced them by $x + dx$ and $s + f(x)$ until x was greater than b.

We can express this common structure using the following function:

```
until p f x = if p x then x else until p f (f x)
```

Our sqrt function can then be rewritten as follows:

```
sqrt x = until (is_good_enough x) (improve x) 1.0
```

The gcd function can be expressed as follows, in which the x argument of until is a 2-tuple, the p argument is a function from 2-tuples to Bool, and the f argument is a function from 2-tuples to 2-tuples:

```
gcd a b = let
              (an, bn) = until (\(ai,bi) -> (bi == 0))
                               (\(ai,bi) -> (bi,rem ai bi))
                               (a,b)
          in
              an
```

Here, the statement in the block binds an and bn to the components of the final 2-tuple result returned by the until function; an is then returned as the result of the block.

Exercise 5.6 Rewrite the integrate function using until. ∎

Exercise 5.7 The factorial of a positive nonzero integer n is given by

$$1 \times 2 \times 3 \times \ldots \times (n - 1) \times n$$

We can compute it as follows: Begin with $j = 1$ and $x = 1$ with the relation that $x = factorial(j)$. From this pair, we can compute the next pair in the relation: $j + 1$ and $j \times x$. We repeat this until $j = n$. Write this function in *pH* using the `until` function. ∎

Exercise 5.8   The Fibonacci numbers are

$$1, 1, 2, 3, 5, 8, 13, 21, \ldots$$

where, except for the first two numbers, each number is the sum of the previous two. The nth Fibonacci number can be computed as follows. Begin with $j = 1$, $a = 1$, and $b = 1$, with the relation that a and b are the jth and $(j + 1)$th Fibonacci numbers, respectively. From this triple we can compute the next triple in the relation: $j + 1$, b, and $a + b$. We repeat this until $j = n$. Write this function in *pH* using the `until` function. ∎

5.4   Algebraic Product Types

Tuples are, in fact, just one example of a more general facility in *pH* called *algebraic types*. Tuples are predefined in *pH*, but the user can define new (equally efficient) algebraic types. For example, instead of representing them as 2-tuples, we can define points in the two-dimensional plane as a *new* type:

```
data Point = Point Float Float
```

The keyword **data** indicates that this is a new algebraic type definition (which is different from a type synonym; we will discuss this difference shortly). The left-hand side introduces a new type, `Point`. The right-hand side introduces a new *constructor*, also called `Point`, containing two components, both of type `Float`. Despite the fact that the type and the constructor have the same name, there will never be any ambiguity because types and constructors always appear in different contexts.

A constructor plays two roles—it can be used as an ordinary function to create objects of the new type, and it can be used in pattern matching to access components of objects of the new type. Here are new versions of the point translation and scaling functions:

```
translate :: Float -> Float -> Point -> Point
translate dx dy (Point x y) = Point (x+dx) (y+dy)

scale      :: Float -> Float -> Point -> Point
scale      sx sy (Point x y) = Point (sx * x) (sy * y)
```

On the left-hand side of each function we have a pattern (Point x y) that will match any Point object and bind the identifiers x and y to the two floating-point components, respectively. On the right-hand side of each function, we use Point as a constructor function to create new Point objects with the appropriate components.

Here is a definition of a new type for quadrilaterals:

```
data Quad = Quad Point Point Point Point
```

and here is the centroid function:

```
centroid                      ::  Quad -> Point
centroid (Quad (Point x1 y1)
               (Point x2 y2)
               (Point x3 y3)
               (Point x4 y4)) = Point ((x1+x2+x3+x4)/4.0)
                                      ((y1+y2+y3+y4)/4.0)
```

5.4.1 Algebraic Types versus Type Synonyms

We discussed type synonyms in Section 5.3.3, where we defined Point to be a synonym for the type (Float,Float). As mentioned earlier, type synonyms are merely convenient abbreviations for existing types; they do not actually define any new type. While they can improve readability of our code, they do not offer much type safety; a function defined to take a Point argument can be applied to any 2-tuple of Floats, whether it represents a point or some other random pair of numbers.

Here, we defined Point to be a new algebraic type. An algebraic type definition always defines a brand-new type distinct from all other types. Thus, even though a Point contains two Float components, it is a distinct type from the type (Float,Float), which also contains two Float components. Static type checking will never allow tuples to masquerade as points.

In the next chapter we'll see that algebraic types are even more general, permitting the definition of *sum* types as well as products and permitting the definition of recursive types.

5.4.2 Polymorphism in Algebraic Types

Algebraic types can be polymorphic—the new type can be parameterized by type variables. Suppose that points, in addition to carrying x- and y-coordinates, also carried a label. We do not want to commit ourselves to the type of the label. In some graphs, labels may be strings, and in others they may be numbers, or something altogether more complex. We could define points to be polymorphic with respect to this third component:

```
data Point a = Point Float Float a
```

A point that had a string label would have type

```
Point String
```

whereas a point that had a numeric label would have type

```
Point Float
```

Using this notation, it is clear that we cannot confuse points with string labels and points with numeric labels. For example, if we wrote a function that took a point and added one to the label:

```
inc_label (Point x y lab) = Point x y (lab + 1.0)
```

then the function would have the type

```
inc_label    ::    (Point Float) -> (Point Float)
```

and so we could never apply it to a point with a string label.

The tuples that we studied at the beginning of this chapter are just predefined polymorphic algebraic types, but with some special syntax that uses parentheses and commas for the type and expression constructors. The predefined type declaration would look something like this:

```
data Two_tuple a b = Two_tuple_Cons a b
```

and, when we say

$$(e_1, e_2)   ::   (t_1, t_2)$$

this is just special syntax for

Two_tuple_Cons $e_1 e_2$ ::   Two_tuple $t_1 t_2$

Similarly, (x,y,z) and (x,y,z,w) and so on are just special syntax for Three_tuple, Four_tuple, and wider types. This also reinforces the idea that tuples of different widths are distinct types.

5.4.3   Syntax of Constructors and Variables

The observant reader may have noticed that all the constructors we introduced (via algebraic type definitions) begin with an uppercase letter. This is more than just a convention—it is required in *pH* syntax in order to distinguish constructors from ordinary identifiers. Consider the following two clauses:

```
let
     Point x y = e₁               -- (a)
     point x y = e₂               -- (b)
in
     ⋮
```

In (a), the left-hand side is a *pattern* built with the constructor `Point`. The right-hand side e_1 must evaluate to a point object; it is matched to the left-hand side, so that `x` and `y` are bound to the corresponding components. The binding (b), on the other hand, is an ordinary function definition, defining the ordinary variable `point`; that is, it is the same as

```
     ⋮

point = \x y -> e₂               -- (b)
     ⋮
```

We follow a similar rule for types: type variables (to express polymorphism) begin with a lowercase letter, and type constructors always begin with an uppercase letter (such as `Point`, `Quad`, and so on). The types `Int`, `Bool`, `Float`, and so on are just niladic type constructors. Thus, the type expression

```
Point String
```

is an instance of the polymorphic `Point a` type with the type variable a instantiated by the type `String`. However, in the type expression

```
Point string
```

`string` is just another type variable (i.e., this is just another way of writing the polymorphic type `Point a`).

5.4.4   Field Names in Algebraic Types

In the description of algebraic types thus far, all fields of an algebraic type were referenced *positionally*. Both in construction and in pattern matching, we use an expression like

Constructor t_1 ... t_n

where the term (expression or pattern) t_j refers to the jth field of the constructed value. Sometimes it is more convenient to have symbolic *field names* to refer to the fields of a constructed value, and *pH* provides a notation for this. For example, we could define our polymorphically labeled `Point` data type as follows:

```
data Point a = Point { x,y :: Float, label :: a }
```

Here, the right-hand side defines the `Point` constructor with three *named* fields: the first field has name x and type `Float`; the second field has name y and type `Float`; and the third field has name `label` and type a. To construct a value of this type, we can still say, as before,

```
Point  23.4  34.5  "last sighting"
```

but, equivalently, we can also say any of the following:

```
Point  { x = 23.4, y = 34.5, label = "last sighting" }
Point  { y = 34.5, x = 23.4, label = "last sighting" }
Point  { label = "last sighting", y = 34.5, x = 23.4 }
  .
  .
  .
```

In particular, note that when using the field name notation, the order in which the fields are specified is irrelevant. Thus, we do not have to remember the order in which the fields were declared in the algebraic data type definition.

Similarly, in pattern matching, where previously we might have used a pattern:

```
Point a b s
```

we can now say, equivalently,

```
Point { x = a, y = b, label = s }
Point { label = s, x = a, y = b }
  .
  .
  .
```

Again, when using field names in the patterns, the order in which they appear is irrelevant. We can omit field names entirely:

```
Point { y = b }
```

This just binds the y field value to the variable b and ignores the other fields (which is equivalent to binding them to the wildcard pattern "_"). This is especially convenient when the contructor has a large number of fields and we are interested in only one (or some small subset of fields); it allows us easily to ignore the fields that are not of interest.

In an expression, a field name can be used as a function directly to extract the corresponding component from a constructed value. For example, the expression

```
label  p
```

evaluates to the `label` field value of the `Point` value p. A field name may not be used in two different algebraic data type definitions that are in the same scope. With this restriction, each field name identifier, when used as a function, has an unambiguous type. For example, in the above expression the type of `label` is

```
label    ::    Point a -> a
```

Field names also enable a notation for "incremental update" of a constructed value. Suppose x represents a constructed value

$$Constructor \ \{ \ \cdots, \ f_j \ = \ v, \ \cdots \ \}$$

then the expression

$$x \ \{ \ f_j \ = \ w \ \}$$

represents the new value

$$Constructor \ \{ \ \cdots, \ f_j \ = \ w, \ \cdots \ \}$$

that is, a new constructed value with the same constructor and same field values as the old, except for field f_j which now has value w. For example:

```
p1  =  Point { x = 2.0, y = 3.0, label = "A" }
p2  =  p1 { label = "B" }
```

In the second line, p2 is a new `Point` that is incrementally different from p1: it has the same field values as p1 *except* that its `label` field has the string "B".

5.5   Tupled versus Curried Arguments

When a function requires more than one datum as input, we have a choice of two methods for passing arguments. We can curry it:

```
f x y = ...
```

or we can tuple the arguments:

```
g (x,y) = ...
```

Typically, currying is preferred when the structure of the problem is such that the partial application "f x" is a useful entity to name and manipulate. To partially apply g to some e_x, we would have to write

```
\y -> g (ex,y)
```

which is more verbose and inconvenient. On the other hand, tupling is useful when the function is often composed with other functions that return tuples as results. For example, suppose we had

```
h a = (e1,e2)
```

Then, we can directly write "g (h *e*)"; to do the same with f we would have to write

```
let
     (x,y) = h e
in
     f x y
```

The structure of the problem should dictate the choice between curried and tupled arguments.

Exercise 5.9   Suppose we have a function g that takes a 2-tuple (x,y) as argument, but we want to use it in a context where it will be applied in a curried manner to two arguments x and y. Write a function curry such that (curry g) is the curried version of g.   ∎

Exercise 5.10   (Inverse of previous problem.) Write a function uncurry such that (uncurry f) is a function on 2-tuples, where f is the corresponding curried function of two arguments.   ∎

5.6   Rewrite Rules for Algebraic Types

Algebraic types are mostly source level constructs, enabling the programmer to express and enforce a rich type structure. After type checking, they are statically desugared into a very simple common abstract syntax, with a single rewrite rule scheme.

5.6.1   Abstract Syntax

Algebraic type definitions (**data** statements) do not play any role at run time; they are merely used to support a static type discipline. After a program has been statically type checked, constructor functions and pattern matching are translated into more fundamental terms. The syntax of terms presented in Section 4.1 needs only the following simple extensions:

$$
\begin{array}{lll}
E & ::= & \cdots \qquad\qquad\qquad\qquad \cdots \\
  & | & \mathrm{CN}_k(SE_1, \cdots, SE_k) \qquad \text{Constructed terms}
\end{array}
$$

$$
\vdots
$$

$$
\begin{array}{lll}
\mathrm{PF}_1 & ::= & \cdots \qquad\qquad\qquad\qquad\qquad \text{Primitive functions of arity 1} \\
  & | & \mathrm{proj}_1 \mid \mathrm{proj}_2 \mid \cdots
\end{array}
$$

Constructed terms contain Simple Expressions (not arbitrary expressions). Each primitive function proj_j simply selects the jth Simple Expression from a constructed term.

We also extend the set of Values to include constructed terms:

$$
\begin{array}{lll}
V & ::= & \cdots \\
  & | & \mathrm{CN}_k(SE_1, \cdots, SE_k) \qquad \text{Constructed terms}
\end{array}
$$

5.6.2   Static Translation (Syntactic Desugaring)

After static type checking, each normal use of a constructor identifier CN_k in the original source program is replaced by

$$
\backslash \mathsf{x}_1 \cdots \mathsf{x}_k \; \text{->} \; \mathrm{CN}_k(\mathsf{x}_1, \cdots, \mathsf{x}_k)
$$

That is, it is a function of k arguments that produces a constructed term containing the k arguments. Note that, as a consequence of this, constructors can be viewed as curried functions and therefore can even be partially applied in *pH* source programs.

If a constructor pattern is used as an argument in a λ-abstraction:

$$
\backslash (\mathrm{CN}_k(p_1, \cdots, p_k)) \; \text{->} \; e
$$

we first convert it into a pattern binding (as usual, t is a fresh variable):

```
\t ->
    let
```

$$(\text{CN}_k(p_1, \cdots, p_k)) = t$$
$$\textbf{in}$$
$$e$$

Next, we destructure the pattern binding into

$$p_1 = \text{proj}_1 \ t$$
$$\vdots$$
$$p_k = \text{proj}_k \ t$$

Note that, because of nested patterns, p_j may itself be a pattern, so we simply repeat the process until we have only simple identifier bindings. For example, if we began with

```
f (x,(a,b,c)) = e
```

we first desugar to

```
f t2 = let  (x,(a,b,c)) = t2
        in
            e
```

and then to

```
f t2 = let  x       = proj₁ t2
            (a,b,c) = proj₂ t2
        in
            e
```

The second binding is itself a pattern binding, so we continue

```
f t2 = let  x       = proj₁ t2
            t3      = proj₂ t2

            a       = proj₁ t3
            b       = proj₂ t3
            c       = proj₃ t3
        in
            e
```

until we have only simple bindings.

5.6.3   Rewrite Rule

Since most of the work concerning algebraic types is done using static translation, all we need, dynamically, is a δ rule for each projection primitive:

$$\mathrm{proj}_j \; \mathrm{CN}_k(\cdots, e_j, \cdots) \qquad \longrightarrow \; e_j \tag{Proj}$$

Static type-checking and our static translation will ensure that $1 \le j \le k$; that is, we never have to check, at run time, that we are doing a "legal" projection of a component.

5.6.4   Nonstrictness

Algebraic type constructors are also nonstrict, just like ordinary functions. Suppose we have the following program:

```
let
     xCoord = \(x,y)->x
in
     xCoord (3.5, sqrt 18239.0)
```

Static translation and the lifting rules will convert it into something like this:

```
let
     xCoord = \t2-> proj₁(t2)
     a       = 3.5
     b       = sqrt 18239.0
     ab      = CN₂(a,b)
     r       = xCoord ab
in
     r
```

After some reductions, we can get

```
let
     xCoord = \t2-> proj₁(t2)
     a       = 3.5
     b       = sqrt 18239.0
     ab      = CNₖ(a,b)
     r       = proj₁(CNₖ(a,b))
in
     r
```

Applying the δ rule for proj_1 and doing a few more reductions, we get

```
let
     xCoord = \t2-> proj₁(t2)
     a       = 3.5
     b       = sqrt 18239.0
```

```
        ab      = CN_k(a,b)
        r       = 3.5
  in
        3.5
```

Note that we can produce the result even though the second component of the tuple is not yet ready (we have not even started the sqrt application), demonstrating the nonstrictness of tuples. In this manner, *all* data structures in *pH* are nonstrict; a data structure can be manipulated and treated as a value even though some or all of its components are still undefined.

5.7   Abstract Data Types

Type checking based on algebraic types gives us certain "structural" constraints on types. This is enormously useful, but there are often other constraints that cannot be expressed in this purely structural manner. For example, suppose we want to define a type for rational numbers. A rational number is expressed as a ratio of two integers; thus, a potential representation is a 2-tuple of integers. However, we would like the ratio always to be in "reduced" form; that is, after adding 3/32 and 7/32, we would like the result to be 5/16 instead of 10/32. Thus, the constructor for rational numbers, when given a pair of integers, shouldn't just package them into a 2-tuple; it should first reduce them until they have no common factors and then produce the 2-tuple. The type system described so far cannot enforce such a constraint; the 2-tuple constructor is a *free* constructor in that it can be applied to any two integers. What we need is a restricted constructor that will only make pairs of integers that are in reduced form.

pH has a mechanism called *modules* that allows us to express this idea. A module is a program fragment from which we can control the export of names (and also into which we can control the import of names). By this we mean that program fragments outside a module (*clients* of a module) can only "see" those names that have been exported from the module. We can define a new type inside the module (here, Ratio) and we can export the type, *but we can choose not to export its free constructors*. Instead, we can define a restricted constructor function inside the module and export it. The restricted constructor performs the reduction. Here is an example of such a module definition:

```
module RationalModule (Rational, rational, rationalParts)
where

data Rational = RatCons Int Int

rational      :: Int -> Int -> Rational
rational x y = let
                   d = gcd x y
              in
                   RatCons (x/d) (y/d)

rationalParts                :: Rational -> (Int, Int)
rationalParts  (RatCons x y) = (x,y)
```

In the module, we define a new type Rational that is simply a product type, containing two Ints. Within the module, the free constructor RatCons may be used to create objects of this type. We define a restricted constructor rational that produces such an object, but always in reduced form. We also define a function rationalParts that returns an ordinary 2-tuple containing the numerator and denominator of the rational number. The most interesting part of the module definition is the first line. It declares this program fragment to be a module called RationalModule, and the items in parentheses following the module name represent the *export list* of this module. This list specifies which of the names defined within the module are *visible* outside this module to clients of this module: the type Rational is visible; the restricted constructor rational is visible; and the "deconstructor" rationalParts is visible to clients. In particular, the free constructor RatCons is *not* visible to clients. Thus, the *only* way a client can produce a Rational value is by using the rational function, which performs the required reduction.

What does a client using this module look like? Let us say that it resides in another module M:

```
module M (...) where

import RationalModule

        ... let r1 = rational a b ...

            ... let (x,y) = rationalParts r2 ...
```

The **import** statement allows this module to use the entities (type names, identifiers, etc.) that were exported from RationalModule. Below that, the first code fragment creates a `Rational` object from two integers, and the second fragment deconstructs one into its two component integers. The key observation is that `RatCons` is *undefined* in this module, and so the client has no way of creating an "illegal" `Rational` point.

The structure just described is well known in computer science as an *abstract data type*. The type `Rational` is considered *abstract* to its clients because they cannot see the details of how it is implemented, that is, the fact that internally it is built using the `RatCons` constructor. Suppose we changed the code inside the module to

```
data Rational = AnotherCons (Int,Int)

rational      :: Int -> Int -> Rational
rational x y = let
                  d = gcd x y
               in
                  AnotherCons (x/d, y/d)

rationalParts                :: Rational -> (Int, Int)
rationalParts (AnotherCons xy) = xy
```

That is, we have changed the internal representation to use `AnotherCons`, a monadic constructor with a 2-tuple component, and we have changed the functions `rational` and `rationalParts` accordingly. These changes are completely invisible to external clients; not a line of code would have to be changed in any of the clients. This is the second positive feature of abstract types—not only does an abstract type allow us to impose arbitrary constraints on a data structure beyond what the type system is capable of expressing, but we can freely change its representation (perhaps for more efficiency) without affecting any client code.

The downside of the fact that an abstract type's representation is hidden from clients is that they can no longer use pattern matching to access its components. Pattern matching inherently exposes a certain aspect of data representation, which is exactly what we are trying to hide with data abstraction. This is the reason why we defined and exported the deconstructor `rationalParts`—without such a deconstructor or set of selector functions, a client would have no way of extracting the integers embedded in a `Rational` object! (A more general version of this, the module `Ratio`, is in fact a predefined abstract data type in the *pH* library. It is overloaded over all integral types, not just `Int`.)

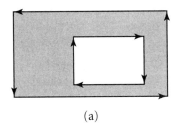
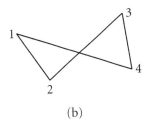

(a)   (b)

Figure 5.7   (a) Legal and (b) illegal quadrilaterals in a graphics package.

Exercise 5.11   In our `RationalModule`, the exported constructor function `rational` converted the fraction to a reduced form, and the `rationalParts` function simply returned those integers. Define, instead, a version in which `rational` simply holds its arguments in a `Rational` tuple, and `rationalParts` converts the integers to reduced form before returning the tuple. Can any client (code that uses this module) tell the difference between the two implementations? When might you use one implementation instead of the other?   ■

Another example: in a typical graphics package, quadrilaterals may be used to describe both objects, as well as holes in objects. Thus, the four points of a graphics quadrilateral have a definite order, with a convention such as "the object is on our left as we traverse the points in order." Figure 5.7(a) shows an example of a graphics "doughnut" object expressed with two such quadrilaterals. In this scenario, we can no longer collect just any sequence of four points into a graphics quadrilateral object. In order to prevent absurdities like that shown in Figure 5.7(b), the four points that make a graphics quadrilateral must also satisfy a "convexity" criterion that prevents the edges from crossing over each other. The solution is to define an abstract data type:

```
module GeomQuadModule (GeomQuad, geomQuad, geomQuadPoints)
where

import Point

data GeomQuad = GeomQuadCons Point Point Point Point

geomQuad :: Point->Point->Point->Point->GeomQuad
geomQuad p1 p2 p3 p4 =
```

```
    if okConvex  p1 p2 p3 p4 then
        GeomQuadCons  p1 p2 p3 p4
    else
        error "geomQuad: points are not convex"

okConvex :: Point->Point->Point->Point->Bool
okConvex p1 p2 p3 p4 = ...

geomQuadPoints :: GeomQuad->(Point,Point,Point,Point)
geomQuadPoints (GeomQuadCons p1 p2 p3 p4) = (p1,p2,p3,p4)
```

The restricted constructor geomQuad produces a GeomQuad type object
provided it meets the convexity criterion. We also define a function ge-
omQuadPoints that returns an ordinary 4-tuple containing the four points
of the quadrilateral. Only the restricted constructor, and not the free constructor, is exported. (Incidentally, the okConvex function is also not exported and is thus purely local to this module.) Thus, the *only* way a client
can produce a GeomQuad point is by using the geomQuad function, which
performs the required convexity check.

In summary, *pH*'s module system allows us to control the visibility of
names between program fragments. This control allows us to make a type
visible without making its free constructor(s) visible, thereby forcing all
clients to produce values of this type only by using the restricted constructor functions that we export. These restricted constructors can embed arbitrarily complicated computations, including dynamic validity checks and
transformations that are beyond the expressive power of the static type
system.

5.8   Modules and Large Programs

In addition to their role in defining abstract data types, modules in *pH* also
serve another purpose: keeping large programs manageable. When writing small programs (say, no more than a thousand lines or so), a single
programmer is often capable of keeping track of all the top-level names
in the program (function names, identifiers, type constructors, value constructors, field names, class names, etc.). This becomes more difficult when
writing larger programs, particularly when more than one programmer is
involved. For example, suppose a team of programmers is writing an air
traffic control program. One person may write a section to keep track of

the queue of planes currently waiting to land. Another person may write a section that manages a database of aircraft types (given an aircraft model number, it specifies properties like maximum gross weight and fuel capacity). A third person may be responsible for a section that assigns free gates to arriving and departing flights. Each of these people may wish to write functions called `insert` and `remove` that are particular to the collections in their task (queue of planes, table of aircraft, list of gates). They could of course sit down together in a conference and agree to use different names (e.g., `landingQueueInsert` versus `aircraftTableInsert`), but this is rather cumbersome when there are a large number of designers involved and when the design itself is evolving rapidly. The key issue is *control of names*, and this is exactly what modules are good for.

The *pH* module system provides two means to manage a large collection of names, which can be regarded as *avoiding conflicts* and *resolving conflicts*. Conflicts are avoided by restricting the visibility of names. We have already seen one example in the abstract data types in the previous section. A module can have an *export* list in which it selectively makes certain names defined in the module visible to clients. Names that are not in the export list are purely local to the module. In `GeomQuadModule`, we defined the `okConvex` function but did not export it. Some other part of the program may freely define another unrelated function called `okConvex` with no possibility of it referring to this one.

Visibility of names is further restricted by the fact that, within a module, the only nonlocal names that are visible are those from modules that are explicitly imported using an **import** statement (there is only one exception to this rule: all modules implicitly import a standard module called `Prelude` that defines basic *pH* types and primitives). A module typically imports only those modules that it needs to do its job, so that names from other modules are irrelevant and invisible.

By default, if a module contains an **import** M statement, then all names exported by M are available in this module as top-level names. We mention in passing that optional variations in the **import** statement permit an even finer degree of import control, by which we can selectively specify which of M's exported names are actually imported. We refer the reader to the Haskell manual for details.

While visibility control can avoid name conflicts, sometimes a name conflict is unavoidable and must be resolved in some other way. For example, suppose you went down to your friendly neighborhood module boutique and purchased two shiny new modules M1 and M2 to use in your program. The designers of those modules may both have independently chosen to export the name foo for functions that you need in your program. You cannot simply import both M1 and M2 into your module because the name foo would then be in conflict. It may be infeasible to ask the module designers to change the names they export. To resolve this, *pH* allows a variation on the **import** statement:

```
import qualified M1
import qualified M2

    ...    M1.foo    ...    M2.foo    ...
```

The **qualified** keyword specifies that the names imported from a module cannot be used directly—they must be used only in *qualified* form, that is, prefixed by the module name and a period. This disambiguates which foo you are referring to and resolves the conflict.

By convention, every *pH* program contains one module called Main, and this module must export an identifier called main. A *pH* implementation, by convention, executes a program by evaluating main and doing something with its value (e.g., printing it, or interpreting it as a command to the operating system). The module system has a number of other subtleties that are beyond the scope of this book, and we refer the reader to the Haskell manual and accompanying documents for details. In this book, our use of modules will simply be for expressing abstract data types.

Lists and Algebraic Sum Types

Prose about cons

—*Title of class notes on lists*

In the last chapter we discussed *product* types, with tuples being a specific example. The terminology came from set theory, where the cross product of two sets t_1 and t_2 is the set $t_1 \times t_2$, consisting of all ordered pairs (x_1, x_2) such that x_1 comes from the set t_1 and x_2 comes from the set t_2. Tuples and product types are essentially *pH*'s realization of this idea.

Another well-known operation in set theory is the *union*, or *sum* of two sets, written $t_1 \cup t_2$ or $t_1 + t_2$, consisting of all items x that come either from the set t_1 or from the set t_2. In this chapter we will see that types based on this idea, known as *sum types*, are also extremely useful in programming. We will see that sum types, when combined with product types, polymorphism, and recursion, allow us to define beautiful and powerful data structures such as lists and trees that can be arbitrarily large. We will see that sum types answer a question that may have been puzzling the reader—how can different types of objects be returned from the two arms of a conditional? And, we will see that some types (no pun intended!) that we have already encountered, such as booleans, characters, and integers, are in fact just sum types, with some of them enjoying special syntactic support.

6.1   Sums of Products

Suppose we wish to define a type for various geometric polygons, from two sides (lines) to five sides (pentagons). In other words, an object of this type is either a line, or a triangle, or a quadrilateral, or a pentagon. If it is a line, it is defined by two points; if it is a triangle, by three points, and so on. *pH*'s **data** declaration allows us to express this directly:

```
data Shape = Line           Point  Point
           | Triangle       Point  Point  Point
           | Quadrilateral  Point  Point  Point  Point
           | Pentagon       Point  Point  Point  Point  Point
```

This defines a new type Shape representing a sum with four summands (or disjuncts). The first summand is a product with constructor Line and two Point components. The second summand is a product with constructor Triangle and three Point components, and so on. Constructors may be used to construct new values, just as in Chapter 5. The following fragment constructs and returns either a line or a triangle object, depending on some condition b:

```
(if b
    then  Line      p1 p2
    else  Triangle q1 q2 q3)    ::      Shape
```

The type of each arm of the conditional, and the type of the conditional as a whole, is Shape.

6.1.1   Pattern Matching: Case Expressions

Suppose we want to write a function to compute the area of a Shape object. If the object is a line, its area is zero; if it is a triangle, we use a triangle area formula; if it is a quadrilateral, we use a quadrilateral area computation;

and, similarly, for a pentagon. Thus, our function needs to test which kind of a shape it is (i.e., which disjunct it belongs to); then, it needs to extract the components appropriate to that kind of shape and to apply the appropriate area computation. This can be expressed using pattern matching in a *case expression*:

```
area     :: Shape -> Float
area  s =
   case s of
      Line          p1 p2            -> 0.0
      Triangle      p1 p2 p3         -> triangle calculation
      Quadrilateral p1 p2 p3 p4      -> quadrilateral calculation
      Pentagon      p1 p2 p3 p4 p5 -> pentagon calculation
```

The case expression consists of a *discriminating* expression (s) and a series of clauses, each with a left-hand side pattern and a right-hand side expression body. It attempts to match the value of the discriminating expression against the patterns in each clause. If s is a quadrilateral, it will match the pattern in the third clause. In this case, p1, p2, p3, and p4 are bound to the four components, respectively; then, the quadrilateral area calculation is performed and the value returned as the value of the case expression (which is also the value of this function).

The Shape type is a sum of products. Each disjunct is a product. For example, the line disjunct is a cross product of two Points and the pentagon disjunct is a cross product of five Points. The Shape type is the union (or sum) of all these types. In fact, it is a special kind of union called a *disjoint union* or *separated sum*, because each Shape object retains some information that identifies which of the four summands it belongs to—line, triangle, quadrilateral, or pentagon. In the implementation, a triangle object not only contains the three component points, but also a *tag* that identifies it as a triangle (and not a line, quadrilateral, or pentagon). Since the case expression is the only way to analyze a Shape object, it is impossible, for example, for a line shape to masquerade as a triangle, quadrilateral, or pentagon. When the pattern matching in the above case expression binds p1, p2, and p3 to the components of a triangle object, we are assured that it really *is* a triangle object and these are meaningful bindings, and that we are not binding these identifiers to some garbage values because the object is really a line.[1]

Because we often write functions on sum types and immediately need to discriminate based on the summands, *pH* extends the syntactic sugar for function definitions so that they can be written directly with multiple clauses and pattern matching, avoiding the explicit use of a case expression. We would normally write the area function as follows, with the understanding that it desugars directly into the version presented earlier with a case expression:

```
area                                :: Shape -> Float
area (Line          p1 p2)          = 0.0
area (Triangle      p1 p2 p3)       = triangle calculation
area (Quadrilateral p1 p2 p3 p4)    = quadrilateral calculation
area (Pentagon      p1 p2 p3 p4 p5) = pentagon calculation
```

It is largely a matter of personal preference as to whether one uses case expressions or multiple-clause definitions. In practice, people seem to prefer the latter almost exclusively.

By analogy with conditional expressions, we can easily see the type rules for a case expression:

- The discriminating expression and the patterns must all be of the same type. For example the following case expression makes no sense:

```
case Line m n of
    .
    .
    .
(x,y) -> ...
    .
    .
    .
```

Since the discriminating expression has type Shape, it cannot possibly match with a tuple pattern.

---

1. In the programming language C, struct and union types are the realization of products and sums, respectively. Unions in C are ordinary unions, not disjoint unions; given an object of a union type, there is no language-specified way of telling which summand it came from. Thus, unions in C are unsafe—we can construct it as one summand and extract components as if were from another summand. C programmers therefore often embed a union within a struct, with the struct containing an integer tag field signaling which summand the union part comes from. This is essentially a programmer convention for encoding a disjoint union.

◆ All arms of the case expression must have the same type t, and t is the type of the entire case expression; that is, if

$$e_1 \quad :: \quad t$$
$$\vdots$$
$$e_n \quad :: \quad t$$

then

```
(case ... of
    pat₁ -> e₁
    :
    patₙ -> eₙ)     ::     t
```

Exercise 6.1 Define a type representing temperatures, allowing them to be either in Celsius or Fahrenheit. Write conversion functions to convert from one form to the other. (5 Celsius degrees span 9 Fahrenheit degrees, and 32°F is the same temperature as 0°C.) ∎

Exercise 6.2 Define a type representing weights, allowing them to be either in metric units (kilograms) or British units (pounds and ounces). Write conversion functions to convert from one form to the other. (1 kg is 2.2 lb, and 16 oz make 1 lb.) ∎

In Chapter 2, we said that both arms of a conditional expression (**if-then-else**) must have exactly the same type. This may have seemed overly restrictive, but sum types give us a way out. Suppose we want a conditional expression to either return an integer or a string (perhaps an error message). We could define an appropriate type and then write the conditional:

```
data I_or_S = I Int | S String

...     (if ... then I integer-expression
           else S string-expression)              :: I_or_S
```

6.1.2 The Maybe Type

As discussed in the previous chapter, data types can be polymorphic. The following polymorphic type is predefined in *pH* because it is extremely useful:

```
data Maybe a = Nothing | Just a
```

For example, suppose we want a function that returned the smallest prime number in a given range $m..n$, if any. What should the type of the returned value be? Suppose we say int. What should we return if there is no prime number in the given range? Since we must return an int, perhaps we could return a special "fake" result, say, $m - 1$, as an indication that there is no prime in the given range (this is often the practice in many other programming languages). In *pH*, we utilize the Maybe type:

```
f        ::  Int -> Int -> (Maybe Int)
f  m  n  =  if m > n then Nothing
            else if isPrime m then Just m
            else f (m+1) n
```

In general, the Maybe type is useful when we are searching for a number in a range, or looking up a particular item in a table, or searching for a word in a dictionary, and so on. In each case, there is the possibility that we do not find anything, in which case we return Nothing. If we do find an *x* that is acceptable, we return (Just x). Since the type of thing we are looking for varies from application to application, it is useful for the Maybe type to be polymorphic.

The result of such a search can be processed by code that looks like this:

```
case result of
   Nothing ->  ... handle search failure case . . .
   Just x  ->  ... handle search success case,
                   with x being the item found . . .
```

6.1.3   Subtleties in Pattern Matching

We now discuss some subtleties and nuances of pattern matching that do not arise in the simple examples seen so far. Sometimes we define a function that is only meaningful on a subset of the possible disjuncts of a type. For example, a lineLength function may be applied only to lines, and we may write

```
lineLength              :: Shape -> Float
lineLength (Line p1 p2) = distance(p1,p2)
```

What happens if such a function is applied to triangles? Such an application would be type correct and so may not be detected statically.

In other situations a function may be meaningful on all disjuncts, but may only be interesting on some of them. For example, while any two points make a line and any three points make a triangle, not all sequences of four and five points make meaningful quadrilaterals and pentagons, respectively. We need to ensure that when we trace the four or five points, we form a proper closed figure without the perimeter "crossing over" itself. We might write a function to check this:

```
okPoly                        :: Shape -> Bool
okPoly (Quadrilateral ...) = ...
okPoly (Pentagon      ...) = ...
okPoly        x            = True
```

In a multiple-clause definition (or, equivalently, in a case expression), pattern matching is attempted from the topmost clause down to the bottommost clause, in that order. As soon as a match is found, that clause is selected (even if a subsequent clause would also match). If none of the clauses match, a run-time error is generated. In our lineLength example, a run-time error will be generated if we ever apply it to a triangle, quadrilateral, or pentagon. Similarly, in our okPoly example, the last clause matches any argument. However, since the three clauses are tried in order, the first two clauses will pick off quadrilaterals and pentagons, respectively, and only lines and triangles will "fall through" to the third clause.

Technically, we say that pattern matching in *pH*

- is *sequential* (top to bottom, and left to right)
- may be *nonexhaustive* (all clauses may fail)
- may be *overlapping* (more than one clause may match a given argument)

Pattern Matching in Block Bindings

In Section 5.2 we introduced the idea of using pattern matching in **let**-block bindings to *destructure* a tuple value. For example:

```
let
    .
    .
    .
    (x,y) = p
    .
    .
    .
in
    .
    .
    .
```

Suppose the left-hand side pattern is from a sum type. For example:

```
let
      .
      .
      .
      (Triangle p1 p2 p3) = t
      .
      .
      .
in
      .
      .
      .
```

What happens if t evaluates to a disjunct that is not a Triangle, such as a Line or Quadrilateral?

When the left-hand side pattern is a pure tuple pattern (tuple constructor, with variables in all the tuple component positions), as in the first example above, there is no chance for the match to fail. Static type checking ensures that the right-hand side is a tuple of the correct width, and the binding can be seen as syntactic sugar for collection of primitive projection functions:

```
let
      .
      .
      .
      x = proj₁ p
      y = proj₂ p
      .
      .
      .
in
      .
      .
      .
```

All other kinds of left-hand patterns can be explained in terms of pure tuple pattern bindings by translation into a case expression:

```
let
      .
      .
      .
      (p1,p2,p3) = case t of
                      (Triangle p1 p2 p3) -> (p1,p2,p3)
      .
      .
      .
in
      .
      .
      .
```

In general, a statement of the form

$pat = e$

where *pat* is not a pure tuple pattern translates to

var-tuple = **case** *e* **of**
                pat -> *var-tuple*

where *var-tuple* is a pure tuple containing all the variables in *pat*. We can now see what happens if t evaluates to any Shape other than a Line: we get a pattern matching failure in the case expression, before any of the variables p1, p2, and p3 are bound.

Strictness and Sequentiality

Pattern matching can imply something about the evaluation of arguments and hence can imply something about the strictness of functions with pattern arguments. Consider this function:

```
isLine                    :: Shape -> Bool
isLine   (Line p1 p2) = True
isLine      _            = False
```

When applied to any argument, the argument must be evaluated at least until we can determine if it is a Line object or not (we do not need to know the values of p1 and p2). Thus, isLine is surely strict in its argument.
    Consider this function:

```
f   y (Line p1 p2) = 0
f   y     _           = y
```

The second argument must surely be evaluated in order to determine whether it is a Line or not (and hence which clause to select). However, the value of y is only needed in the second clause, and hence we conclude that the function is not strict in its first argument. This raises an interesting question: given a function definition with pattern matching and multiple clauses, is there some "minimum" amount of argument evaluation that can determine which clause is to be selected? The answer to this question is not trivial; consider the following definition:

```
f   x  0  0 = ...
f   0  y  1 = ...
f   1  1  z = ...
```

Suppose we evaluate the first argument, giving the value 0. The third clause is ruled out and so if we evaluate the third argument, it will choose between the first and second clauses. On the other hand, suppose we evaluate the second argument and find it is 1. The first clause is ruled out, and if we now evaluate the first argument, we can choose between the second and third clauses. In general, there is no procedure that guarantees to select a clause with "minimal" evaluation (i.e., no argument is evaluated unless it is needed for the decision).

It is partly to avoid these complexities that *pH* adopts a simple, sequential, top-to-bottom, left-to-right evaluation order for the patterns.

6.1.4   Enumerated Types (Simple Sums)

A special case of a sum of products is where the product in each summand is empty, that is, where each constructor is niladic. These are the simplest sum types and are also known as enumerated types (cf. the programming language Pascal). For example:

```
data Day = Sun | Mon | Tue | Wed | Thu | Fri | Sat
```

As with all algebraic types (beginning with the **data** keyword), this gives us a brand-new type and an associated set of constructors that cannot be confused with any other type or constructors, respectively. Each summand is a niladic constructor. A value of type Day can be either Sun, or Mon, or Tue, and so on.

In many other programming languages, the programmer has to encode the concept of "days" manually, for example using integers in the range 1 to 7. Unfortunately, this raises two problems. The program is less readable because we have to remember this encoding. Equally serious, we get no type safety; an integer that is supposed to represent, say, the population of a town, may accidentally be supplied as an argument to a function on days, without any complaint from the type checker. Enumerated types solve both these problems: the constructors are essentially new symbolic constants, and the type checker will prevent Day values from being confused with populations, integers, or the number of hours until the next millennium.

For example, to express the idea that we have a meeting every Monday and Wednesday except in certain exceptional cases when we meet on Tuesday and Thursday instead, we might say

```
nextWeekSchedule  :: (Day,Day)
nextWeekSchedule  = if ... then (Mon, Wed)
                       else (Tue, Thu)
```

We can use these constructors in patterns, as usual: for example, here is a predicate function that checks if a Day argument is a weekday or not:

```
isWeekday        :: Day -> Bool
isWeekday  Sun = False
isWeekday  Sat = False
isWeekday   _  = True
```

Here, we use a wildcard pattern in the last clause to map all other Day values to True.

The predefined boolean type in *pH* is itself just another simple sum:

```
data Bool = False | True
```

with the familiar constants False and True. In fact, the venerable old conditional expression:

```
if e_b then e_1 else e_2
```

is just syntactic sugar for the more fundamental (and general) case expression:

```
case e_b of
  True  -> e_1
  False -> e_2
```

Various other predefined types in *pH* can be seen as enumerated types with special syntax. For example, the predefined Char type's declaration would look like this:

```
data Char = ...
          | The_character_space
            .
            .
            .

          | The_character_A
          | The_character_B
            .
            .
            .

          | The_character_0
          | The_character_1
            .
            .
            .
```

```
           | The_character_question_mark
             .
             .
             .
```

with the special syntax `' '`, . . . , `'A'`, `'B'`, . . . , `'0'`, `'1'`, . . . , `'?'`, . . . , and so on for the above constants. Similarly, we can consider integers to be defined by an *enormous* enumerated type:

```
data Int = ...
           | The_number_minus_two
           | The_number_minus_one
           | The_number_zero
           | The_number_one
           | The_number_two
             .
             .
             .
```

with special syntax "–2", "–1", "0", "1", "2", . . . for these constants. These last few examples suggest (correctly) that we can use character and integer constants in patterns.

For example, the Fibonacci series is often found in nature in the arrangement of petals on flowers, the growth patterns of seashells, and so on. The series is 1, 1, 2, 3, 5, 8, . . . , obtained by starting with 1 as the zeroth and first elements and computing each successive element as the sum of its previous two elements. A function to compute the nth Fibonacci number is naturally expressed as follows:

```
fib     :: Int -> Int
fib  0  =  1
fib  1  =  1
fib  n  =  fib (n-1) + fib (n-2)
```

Another example: the function `gcd` to find the greatest common divisor of two integers was defined in Chapter 2:

```
gcd     :: Int -> Int -> Int
gcd a b = if b == 0 then a
               else gcd b (rem a b)
```

We can use multiple clauses and pattern matching to test if b is zero:

```
gcd a 0 = a
gcd a b = gcd b (rem a b)
```

Patterns, just like expressions, can be nested. Here is a function that takes a `Point` argument and decides whether it is at the origin or not:

```
at_origin  (0,0) = True
at_origin    _   = False
```

Due to static type checking, we know that in any application "at_origin
e", the argument *e* must be a 2-tuple. The pattern in the first clause matches
e if both its components are equal to 0. The pattern in the second clause will
match all remaining arguments.

Exercise 6.3   Rewrite the fib and gcd functions using case expressions.   ■

New sum types can be implemented with the same efficiency as predefined sums like Bool. New product types can be implemented with the same
efficiency as predefined product types such as tuples. Thus, the *pH* programmer should feel free to define new types in order to make programs
more readable and type safe.

So far, we've dealt with simple sums, products and sums of products,
and polymorphism. These are interesting and useful small steps for man;
the giant leap for mankind comes when we use these same mechanisms
and define recursive types. Certain recursive types such as lists and trees
are standard power tools on the programmer's toolbelt. From Section 6.2
onwards we will be focusing on these beautiful and fascinating types.

6.1.5   Field Names in Multiple Disjuncts

Field names were introduced in Section 5.4.4. Field names can be used even
when there are multiple disjuncts. For example:

```
data Shape = Line           {p1,p2          :: Point,
                             annot           :: String}
           | Triangle        {p1,p2,p3       :: Point,
                             annot           :: String}
           | Quadrilateral   {p1,p2,p3,p4    :: Point,
                             annot           :: String}
           | Pentagon        {p1,p2,p3,p4,p5 :: Point,
                             annot           :: String}
```

The Line disjunct is defined as having two fields named p1 and p2, both
of type Point, and one field named annot of type String. Notice that it is
all right to use the same field name in different disjuncts, provided that the
fields they name are all of the same type. Here, for example, the field name
p1 has the type Point in all the disjuncts, and the field name annot has the
type String in all the disjuncts. However, a field name may not be used in
two different algebraic data type definitions that are in the same scope.

As described in Section 5.4.4, the field names may be used during construction of a value to make the code more readable and to free us from
having to remember the order of the fields. For example, the following two
bindings to construct a triangle are equivalent:

```
s1 = Triangle  xy1  xy2  xy3  "Bermuda"
s1 = Triangle  { annot = "Bermuda",
                 p1 = xy1, p2 = xy2, p3 = xy3 }
```

As described in Section 5.4.4, the field names may also be used in
patterns:

```
case s of
   .
   .
   .
   Triangle  { annot=a, p1=m, p2=n, p3=o } ->
                                  ... use a, m, n, o ...
   .
   .
   .
```

and a field name can be used as a function to extract a component from an
object:

```
p4 s
```

This last expression is equivalent to

```
case s of
   Line            _ _        -> error ...
   Triangle        _ _ _      -> error ...
   Quadrilateral  { p4=m } -> m
   Pentagon       { p4=n } -> n
```

Note that our restriction that the field p4 must have the same type in all the
disjuncts where it is used assures us that this has an unambiguous type:

```
p4    ::    Shape -> Point
```

This again illustrates how field names can be quite advantageous—
"p4 s" is much more compact than the equivalent case expression. Field
names also enable a notation for "incremental update" of a constructed
value. Suppose x represents a constructed value

$$Constructor \; \{ \ldots, f_j \; = \; v, \ldots \}$$

then the expression

$$x \; \{ \; f_j \; = \; w \; \}$$

represents the new value

Constructor $\{ \ldots, \ f_j \ = \ w, \ldots \}$

that is, a new constructed value with the same constructor and same field values as the old, except for field f_j, which now has value w. For example, the expression

```
s1 = Triangle  xy1  xy2  xy3  "Bermuda"
s2 = s1 { annot = "MadRube" }
```

produces a new shape object s2 that is identical to the shape object s1 except that its string annotation is "MadRube" instead of "Bermuda"; their p1, p2, and p3 fields have the same values, respectively.

Exercise 6.4   Write down a case expression equivalent to the incremental update expression

```
s1 { annot = "MadRube" }
```

■

6.2   Lists: A Recursive Algebraic Type

Suppose we wanted a function that returns all prime numbers within a certain range, or all words from a file that begin with the letter *A*. In these problems, we do not know in advance how many items will be returned. None of the data structures we have seen so far are up to the job, because each one has a fixed size that is in fact known from its type. A 2-tuple has two components, a 3-tuple has three, a 2-tuple containing a 3-tuple has five, and so on. An object from a sum type is no larger than the largest of its disjuncts. We do not yet have any data structure that has n components, where n is determined dynamically, at run time.

The most commonly used data structure in functional languages for these purposes is the *list*. The list is an example of a *recursive* polymorphic algebraic data type:

```
data  List item  =  Nil  |  Cons item (List item)
```

This may be read as "a list of items is either empty (Nil), or it is a Cons structure containing an item and a list of items." The definition is recursive—the type being defined, List, is used within its own definition. It is also polymorphic because of the type variable item. Any particular list will be homogeneous—we can have lists of Ints, lists of Chars, lists of

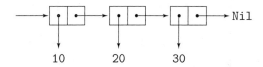

10   20   30

Figure 6.1 Box-and-pointer visualization of the list `Cons 10 (Cons 20 (Cons 30 Nil))`.

tuples, lists of lists of `Int`s, and so on—but this one type definition captures the type of all such lists.

In a constructed term (`Cons` x y), the objects x and y are also referred to as the "head" and "tail" of the list, or the "car" and "cdr" of the list, respectively.[2]

A list of three integers may be written

```
Cons 10 (Cons 20 (Cons 30 Nil))     ::     List Int
```

Let us dissect it a little to see the correspondence with our recursive type definition. The head of the list is 10, and the tail is the list

```
Cons 20 (Cons 30 Nil)
```

The head of this list, in turn, is 20, and its tail is the list

```
Cons 30 Nil
```

Finally, the head of this list is 30, and its tail is the list `Nil`.

Borrowing from Lisp culture, it is also customary to use the word "cons" as a verb, so that we say that our list is 10 *consed* onto the list `Cons 20 (Cons 30 Nil)`. It is useful to visualize the structure of lists using "box-and-pointer" diagrams, as shown in Figure 6.1. Each box is called a "cons cell" containing, in its two slots, the head and tail of the list.

6.2.1   Syntactic Sugar for Lists

Because lists are used so extensively in functional programming, *pH* provides a special syntax for lists that is more convenient than the notation above (in fact, in Haskell, this syntactic sugar is the *only* notation available

---

2. This latter terminology is borrowed from the programming language Lisp, where these names originally were acronyms. In a very early implementation of Lisp, they stood for "Contents of Address Register" and "Contents of Decrement Register," respectively.

for lists, and Cons and Nil are never used explicitly). In *pH*, our example list is written

    [10, 20, 30]

In general,

$$[e_1,\ e_2,\ \ldots,\ e_n] \quad\equiv\quad \text{Cons } e_1 \text{ (Cons } e_2 \text{ (}\ldots\text{(Cons } e_n \text{ Nil)}\ldots\text{))}$$

The empty list (Nil) is written []. The Cons constructor function is written using the infix operator ":" so that our example list can also be written

    10 : 20 : 30 : []

Square brackets are also used for the type notation:

    [item]   ≡   List item

Functions on lists are usually written using pattern matching, both to test whether a list is empty or a cons and, in the latter case, to bind identifiers to the head and tail of the cons. For example, *pH*'s standard Prelude module defines the following functions to extract the head and tail of a (nonempty) list:

```
head          :: [a] -> a
head (x:xs) = x
head []     = error "Prelude.head: empty list"

tail          :: [a] -> [a]
tail (x:xs) = xs
tail []     = error "Prelude.tail: empty list"
```

Exercise 6.5   One can test whether a given list xs is empty simply by writing "xs==[]". *pH*'s standard Prelude module defines a function null that, when applied to a list, performs this test. Write a function

    notNull   :: [a] -> Bool

that is the inverse of null, using pattern matching.   ∎

6.2.2   Arithmetic Sequences

pH has special syntax for constructing a list of numbers that form an arithmetic series. For example:

    [1 .. 5]   ≡   [1, 2, 3, 4, 5]

```
[0,2 .. 10]    ≡    [0, 2, 4, 6, 8, 10]
[5,4 ..  1]    ≡    [5, 4, 3, 2, 1]
```

This notation was introduced in Section 2.8.1, where it was used in the specific context of controlling the iterations of **for** loops. Here we see that this notation in fact represents a list of numbers and can be used as such in other contexts. In general, the notation

$$[e_i \;.. \; e_f]$$

represents a list containing the ascending sequence of numbers e_i, $e_i + 1, \ldots,$ until but not exceeding e_f. The notation

$$[e_i, \; e_2 \;.. \; e_f]$$

allows us to specify increments other than 1. If $e_i < e_2$, the expression represents a list containing the ascending sequence of numbers e_i, $e_i + d, \ldots,$ until but not more than e_f, where $d = e_2 - e_i$. If $e_i > e_2$, the expression represents a list containing the descending sequence of numbers $e_i, e_i - d, \ldots,$ until but not less than e_f, where $d = e_i - e_2$. If $e_i = e_2$ and $e_i \le e_f$, the expression represents an infinite list. If $e_i = e_2$ and $e_i > e_f$, the expression represents the empty list.

6.2.3   Recursive Functions on Lists

Lists are defined recursively; similarly, lists can be analyzed recursively. For example, suppose we want a function that computes the length of the list (i.e., how many items are there in a given list?). We analyze the given list recursively: either it is empty, in which case the answer is zero, or it is a cons, in which case we count one for the item in the head of the cons and add it to the length of the tail. This is expressed directly as follows:

```
length        :: [item] -> Int
length    []  = 0
length (x:xs) = 1 + length xs
```

The pattern in the first clause matches empty lists. The pattern in the second clause matches conses and binds x and xs to the head and tail components, respectively. (Pattern matching continues to work exactly as before; nothing changes in the presence of recursive types.) Let us watch the reduction process, in outline. Suppose we start with

```
length (10:(20:(30:[])))
```

The argument matches the second clause of the function, binding x to 10 and xs to (20:(30:[])). Rewriting to the clause body, we get

```
1 + length (20:(30:[]))
```

Again, the argument to length matches the second clause, binding x to 20 and xs to (30:[]), so that we get

```
1 + (1 + length (30:[]))
```

After one more step, we get

```
1 + (1 + (1 + length []))
```

Now, the function argument matches the first clause. Rewriting, we get

```
1 + (1 + (1 + 0))
```

which will reduce to 3, the length of the list.

Our example uses a cute notational convention that is common among functional programmers: the identifier "xs" used for the tail is the "plural" of the identifier "x" used for the head.

As seen in this example, the structure of a function on lists typically matches the recursive definition of lists. Usually, there is a clause for the empty case and a clause for the nonempty case. In the nonempty case, it recursively applies itself to the tail, which is itself a similar, but smaller list. Here is another example: a function to compute the sum of all the numbers in a list:

```
sum_list  []     = 0
sum_list (x:xs) = x + sum_list xs
```

As usual, patterns may be nested. For example, a function to retrieve the last element in a list:

```
last []        = error "Empty lists don't have last elements"
last (x:[])    = x
last (x:y:zs) = last (y:zs)
```

Note: Because patterns are tried in top-to-bottom order, the third clause of this function could have been simply written

```
last (x:ys)    = last ys
```

ys cannot be an empty list because such arguments match the second clause.

Exercise 6.6   Write new versions of `length`, `sum_list`, and `last` that use loops instead of recursion.   ∎

Now let us look at a program that not only traverses a list, but builds another list as its result. This function takes two lists and produces a new list that is their concatenation:

```
conc []     ys = ys
conc (x:xs) ys = x:(conc xs ys)
```

We can read this as follows. Concatenating an empty list onto any list `ys` is the same as `ys`. Concatenating a nonempty list (`x:xs`) onto a list `ys` is the same as concatenating `xs` onto `ys` and consing `x` in front of it. Let us watch the reduction process, giving it two arguments "`10:20:[]`" and "`30:[]`". We begin with

```
conc (10:20:[]) (30:[])
```

The arguments match the second clause, binding `x` to `10`, `xs` to (`20:[]`), and `ys` to (`30:[]`). Rewriting, using the body of the clause, we get

```
10:(conc (20:[]) (30:[]))
```

Again, the arguments match the second clause, binding `x` to `20`, `xs` to `[]`, and `ys` to (`30:[]`). Rewriting, we get

```
10:20:(conc [] (30:[]))
```

This time the arguments match the first clause, binding `ys` to (`30:[]`). Rewriting, we get

```
10:20:30:[]
```

which is indeed the answer we expect. Concatenation of lists is such a useful operation that in *pH* there is a predefined operator for it:

```
conc l1 l2    ≡    l1 ++ l2
```

Exercise 6.7   How many "`:`" operations are performed during the evaluation of the following expression?

```
l1 ++ l2
```

Does it depend on `l2`?   ∎

Exercise 6.8   Are the resulting lists produced by

```
l1 ++ (l2 ++ l3)
```

and

```
(l1 ++ l2) ++ l3
```

the same? How many ":" operations are performed in each case?   ∎

Exercise 6.9   Can conc be written as a loop? Why or why not?   ∎

6.2.4   Sparse Vectors

Ferdinand and Imelda are two young, upwardly mobile con artists. For both the financing and the proceeds of their cons, they share a bank account. Suppose we wish to keep a record of their daily deposits and withdrawals for the month of June. Ferdinand has deposits of 30, 16, and 14 on the 6th, 17th, and 21st of the month, respectively, and a withdrawal of 12 on the 12th of the month.[3] We can represent this activity as a list of 2-tuples:

```
[(6,30), (12,-12), (17,16), (21,14)]    ::    [(Int, Int)]
```

Such a list is sometimes called a *sparse vector* because, rather than keeping an entry for every day of the month, we keep an entry only for those days on which there was a net change in the account, with the implicit assumption that the net change was zero on all other dates. Had there been account activity on most days of June, it might have been more efficient to keep a list of 30 amounts, instead of a list of date-and-amount pairs, with the convention that the jth entry in the list is the activity for the date j. Such a representation would be called a *dense vector.*

Here is a sparse vector for Imelda's activities for June:

```
[(9,40), (12,2), (15,5), (17,-16), (29,1)]
```

Now, suppose we wish to find the net activity in the account due to both of them. Basically, if we think of the above vectors as representations of 30-element vectors, we wish to compute the vector sum of the corresponding 30-element vectors. The resulting sparse vector should be

```
[(6,30), (9,40), (12,-10), (15,5), (21,14), (29,1)]
```

---

3. The exact units of these numbers are not really known, but it is said that Ferdinand and Imelda had difficulty maintaining their accounts in the days of 16-bit machines.

Notice that there is no entry for the 17th because the deposit by Ferdinand on that date exactly matched the withdrawal made by Imelda, so that the net activity was zero. To compute this net activity, we feed the lists to the following function:

```
sparse_vector_sum                    []              das2  = das2
sparse_vector_sum              das1              []    = das1
sparse_vector_sum  ((d1,a1):das1) ((d2,a2):das2) =
          if d1 < d2 then
              (d1,a1):sparse_vector_sum das1 ((d2,a2):das2)
          else if d1 > d2 then
              (d2,a2):sparse_vector_sum ((d1,a1):das1) das2
          else                          -- i.e., d1 = d2
            let
                a   = (a1+a2)
                das = sparse_vector_sum das1 das2
            in
                if a == 0 then
                    das
                else
                    (d1,a):das
```

The first two clauses are the trivial ones where one or both of the input lists are empty. In the third clause, we check if the first elements of each list are for the same date. If not, then the earlier date entry is just passed through and we recursively work with the remaining entries. If they are for the same date, we compute the net amount (a1+a2) for that date and either keep it or drop it from the output depending on whether it is zero.

6.2.5   Sorting a List

Suppose we are given a list of numbers and we wish to produce a list that has the numbers in nondecreasing order. One approach that we may take is to split the list into two halves, sort each half separately, and then merge the sorted halves back into a sorted list. For example, given

```
[2, 6, 7, 4, 3, 0, 9, 1, 5, 8]
```

we can split it into

```
[2, 6, 7, 4, 3]          and          [0, 9, 1, 5, 8]
```

Sorting each half, we get

   [2, 3, 4, 6, 7]   and   [0, 1, 5, 8, 9]

How were the halves sorted? Let's defer that question for the moment and assume it happened, by magic.

The two sorted sublists can be merged by simultaneously scanning them from left to right, picking the smaller element from each list at each stage. For example, comparing the first two elements of each list (2 and 0) we pass the smaller one through to the output list (*i.e.*, 0), giving us

   0: (merge [2, 3, 4, 6, 7] [1, 5, 8, 9])

Again, comparing the first elements in each list, 2 and 1, we pass 1 through, giving

   0: 1: (merge [2, 3, 4, 6, 7] [5, 8, 9])

We repeat this process until we have exhausted one of the lists completely:

   0: 1: 2: 3: 4: 5: 6: 7: (merge [] [8, 9])

at which point we pass the remaining list through unchanged,

   [0, 1, 2, 3, 4, 5, 6, 7, 8, 9]

which is, indeed, the sorted list.

The structure of this merge closely resembles the function sparse_vector_sum we saw earlier:

```
merge    []      bs  = bs
merge    as      []  = as
merge (a:as) (b:bs) = if a <= b then
                          a:(merge as (b:bs))
                      else
                          b:(merge (a:as) bs)
```

The first two clauses handle the case when one or both of the lists is empty—we just return the other list as is. In the third clause, when both lists are nonempty, we compare the first elements of each, passing the smaller one into the output list and recursively merging the rest.

We still have to answer the question we deferred earlier—how are the two halves sorted? Well, since each half is itself a list of numbers, we can recursively apply the same sorting technique to them. Each of the halves, in turn, will split into quarters that are to be sorted. In this way, we try to sort smaller and smaller lists. Ultimately, we have to bottom out of this recursion by handling some trivial base case. This is easy—when the list is either empty or contains only one element, it is already sorted.

This method of sorting is called *mergesort* and is an example of divide-and-conquer algorithms, where, to solve a problem, we split it up into smaller problems, solve them independently, and then combine the results. Let us now write the program. Here is the top-level structure:

```
mergesort []  = []
mergesort [x] = [x]
mergesort xs  = let
                    (as,bs) = split xs
                    as'     = mergesort as
                    bs'     = mergesort bs
                in
                    merge as' bs'
```

The first two clauses handle the base cases—empty and singleton lists. The third clause splits the list into two lists as and bs, then merges them.

How should we split the list? In working through our example earlier, we split it into the front half and rear half of the list. However, this is not really necessary, since no matter how we split it, we are going to sort it anyway; that is, the correctness of the algorithm does not depend on how we split the list. Splitting a list into the front and rear halves is not easy to do efficiently because in order to do so, we need to know the length of the list, which itself would require a traversal of the list. Here is a more efficient way to split the list, in a single traversal:

```
split xs = let
               loop []     as bs = (as, bs)
               loop (x:xs) as bs = loop xs bs (x:as)
           in
               loop xs [] []
```

Here, we perform a single traversal of xs, carrying along two lists as and bs into which we will accumulate the members of xs. The accumulators are initially both []. At each step, we place the current x into as, but we swap the roles of as and bs before looping. Thus, we alternately place successive elements of xs first into one accumulated list, then into the other, so that each list gets half the elements of xs.

Exercise 6.10   What does "split [1,2,3,4,5]" evaluate to?   ∎

Exercise 6.11   Another method for splitting a list, sorting each half, and then combining the results is embodied in the *quicksort* method. Here, we split the list by picking one element *b* and collecting the remaining elements into *as* and *cs* such that every element in *as* is $\leq b$ and every element in *cs* is $> b$. After recursively sorting *as* into *as'* and *cs* into *cs'*, recombining is very easy—we simply form the list "*as'*++*b*:*cs'*" (recall that "++" is the built-in list concatenation operation). How should we pick *b*? Ideally, we would like a *b* that results in an exactly even split of the list into *as* and *cs*, but the only way to guarantee this is if we knew that the list was already sorted and we picked the middle element! However, if we assume that the list is a random permutation of numbers, picking *b* as the first element in the list is quite acceptable. Write a *pH* function `quicksort` that implements this sorting method.   ■

Exercise 6.12   What happens if `quicksort` is given an already sorted list?   ■

Exercise 6.13   Analyze the `quicksort` function to see how many ":" operations are performed due to the ++ operations. Much of this expense can be eliminated by reformulating the problem as follows. Instead of thinking of `quicksort` as taking a single argument `xs` (i.e., the list to be sorted), suppose it takes two arguments `xs` and `ys`, with the intention that it will sort `xs`, but it will build the sorted list in front of `ys`. Initially, we call it with `xs` as the initial input list and `ys` as `[]`. However, for the recursive calls, after splitting the input list around *b* into *as* and *cs*, instead of

    (quicksort *as*) ++ *b*:(quicksort *cs*)

we do

    quicksort *as* (*b*:(quicksort *cs* ys))

Complete this program and analyze it to see how many ":" operations it performs for a list of length *n*.   ■

6.2.6   A Lexical Analyzer

Suppose we have a file containing Lisp-like text, that is, a sequence of expressions built out of parentheses, words, and numbers separated by spaces and newlines. An example of an input text is

    (ab (xyz 23))

We can represent this text as a list of characters:

```
['(', 'a', 'b', ' ', ' ', '(',
 'x', 'y', 'z', ' ', '2', '3', ')', ')']
```

In *pH*, a character constant is written by enclosing the character in single quotes.

We wish to write a *lexical analyzer* for such text—a function that takes as input such a list of characters and returns a list of *lexical tokens* corresponding to the sequence of parentheses, words, and numbers in the text. A word is a sequence of alphabetic characters, and a number is a sequence of digit characters. The type of tokens is shown below:

```
data Token = Lparen
           | Rparen
           | Word [Char]
           | Int Int
           | End
           | Err Char
```

Given our sample input text, the lexical analyzer should produce

```
[Lparen, Word "ab", LParen,
 Word "xyz", Int 23, Rparen, Rparen, End]
```

The lexical analyzer will need a basic function that returns the first token from the input and the rest of the input:

```
lex           :: [Char] -> (Token, [Char])
```

The lexical analyzer will use this function repeatedly to produce all tokens from the input. Here is lex:

```
lex []        = (End, [])
lex (' ':cs) = lex cs
lex ('(':cs) = (Lparen, cs)
lex (')':cs) = (Rparen, cs)
lex ( c :cs) = if isDigit c then
                   lexInt  (digitToInt c)  cs
               else if isAlpha c then
                   lexWord  [c]  cs
               else
                   (Err c, cs)
```

The functions isDigit and isAlpha test if the character is a digit or alphabetic, respectively. The function digitToInt returns the number represented by a digit character. These functions are available in the standard *pH* library.

The first clause of the function applies when we reach the end of the input character list, when it returns the token End and an empty list of remaining characters. The second clause applies when the first character is a space, in which case it simply discards it and tries to lex a token from the remaining list. The third and fourth clauses apply when it encounters a parenthesis, where it does the obvious thing. The last, default, clause applies to all other characters. If it is a digit, we call lexInt to develop an integer token; if it is alphabetic, we call lexWord to develop a word token. Otherwise, it is an illegal character and we return the error token.

Here is the lexer for integers. The first argument j is the value of the number seen so far.

```
lexInt j []    = (Int j, [])
lexInt j (c:cs) = if isDigit c then
                      lexInt (j*10 + digitToInt c) cs
                  else
                      (Int j, c:cs)
```

On the empty list, we return a numeric token (Int j) containing the number, and the empty list. Otherwise, if the next character c is a digit character, we continue lexing this number from the remaining characters, updating the number seen so far by shifting it up one decimal place ($\times 10$) and adding the value of this digit. Finally, if the next character is not a digit character, then this is the end of the number, so we build a numeric token and return it along with the input list as is.

Here is the lexer for words. The first argument xs is the list of alphabetic characters seen so far.

```
lexWord xs []    = (makeWord xs, [])
lexWord xs (c:cs) = if isAlpha c then
                        lexWord (c:xs) cs
                    else
                        (makeWord xs, c:cs)
```

If the input list is empty, we simply make a word out of the word's characters (makeWord will be defined below) and return it with an empty list of remaining characters. Otherwise, if the first character is alphabetic, we continue to lex this word, adding c to the list of word characters. Otherwise, this signals the end of this word, so we make a word token out of the word characters and return it, along with the input list as is. It should be clear that the list of word characters xs contains the characters in reverse order. Accordingly,

```
makeWord xs = Word (reverse xs)
```

Exercise 6.14 Rewrite the Token type and the lexical analyzer so that it also accepts the tokens "<" and "<=". ∎

Exercise 6.15 Write the top-level lexical analyzer that uses lex repeatedly to convert a list of characters into a list of tokens. ∎

To see how the token type is used in pattern matching, let us write a function that, given a list of tokens, counts the number of tokens of each kind (returning a tuple of numbers). We assume that we do not have to count end tokens; that is, there is exactly one such token in the input list, and it is the last one.

```
count (End   : ts) counts       = counts
count (Lparen: ts) (l,r,w,n,e) = count ts (l+1,r  ,w  ,n  ,e  )
count (Rparen: ts) (l,r,w,n,e) = count ts (l  ,r+1,w  ,n  ,e  )
count (Word x: ts) (l,r,w,n,e) = count ts (l  ,r  ,w+1,n  ,e  )
count (Int j : ts) (l,r,w,n,e) = count ts (l  ,r  ,w  ,n+1,e  )
count (Err x : ts) (l,r,w,n,e) = count ts (l  ,r  ,w  ,n  ,e+1)
```

Here, (l,r,w,n,e) represents the counts for left and right parentheses, words, numbers, and errors, respectively.

Exercise 6.16 Write a function whose input is a list of tokens and that returns the first word containing the letter q. Since a given list of tokens may not contain such a word, use the following type (predefined in *pH*) to return the result:

```
data Maybe a = Nothing | Just a
```
∎

Exercise 6.17 Write a function called lookup with the following type:

```
lookup    ::    a -> [(a,b)] -> ((a,a)->Bool) -> Maybe b
```

In an application "lookup x' xys p", it traverses the list xys looking for a 2-tuple (x,y) such that the predicate p(x',x) is true, in which case it returns (Just y); if there is no such 2-tuple in the list, it returns Nothing. For example, x may be a name, xys may be a list of name-and-telephone-number pairs, and p may be a function that checks if two names are equal: lookup is then a function that looks up somebody's telephone number. ∎

6.3 Higher-Order Functions on Lists

There is a very large repertoire of functions on lists, but most of them have a structure that falls into a very small number of classes, which in turn can be expressed with higher-order functions. In this section we are going to look at a general way to synthesize lists and some general ways to analyze lists.

6.3.1 The Art of Folding Maps

The following function is a general method for generating a list:

```
gen       :: (a->Bool) -> (a->a) -> a -> [a]
gen p f x = if p x then x : gen p f (f x)
            else []
```

This function recursively computes x, $f(x)$, $f(f(x))$, and so on, and returns all such values as long as they satisfy the predicate p.

Here is a function for generating a list of integers in the range m to n:

```
range      :: Int -> Int -> [Int]
range m n = gen (leq n)   ((+) 1)   m
```

where leq n is a function that tests if its argument is less than or equal to n:

```
leq n x = (x <= n)
```

The range function could be a way of implementing pH's arithmetic series notation [m..n]. It conses m, then $1 + m$, then $1 + 1 + m$, and so on, as long as these numbers are $\leq n$, at which point it terminates the list with [].

Let us examine the functions sum_list and conc again:

```
sum_list []          = 0
sum_list (x:xs)      = x + sum_list xs

conc      []     ys = ys
conc      (x:xs) ys = x : (conc xs ys)
```

The two have a very similar structure. Both of them recursively traverse a list xs. At each step, they combine the head of the list with the result of the recursive call on the tail of the list. They differ only in the way they do this combination and in the value they return when they encounter the empty list. As we have become accustomed to doing, we can abstract out this common structure by relegating the differences between the two

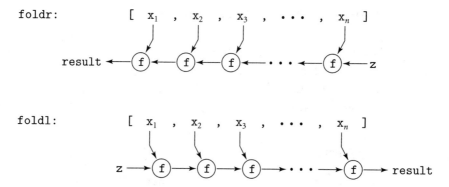

Figure 6.2   Visualization of (`foldr f z xs`) and (`foldl f z xs`) computations.

functions to parameters. This function is called `foldr` and is an example of a *reduction* operation on an aggregate data structure.

```
foldr f z []     = z
foldr f z (x:xs) = f x (foldr f z xs)
```

(The function `foldr` is predefined in *pH*.) Here, `f` is the combining function applied at each step, and `z` is the value returned for the empty list. The structure of a `foldr` computation is depicted pictorially in Figure 6.2. Thus, in general, what this function computes is

$$f\ x_1\ (f\ x_2 \ldots (f\ x_{n-1}\ (f\ x_n\ z)) \ldots)$$

which explains the "r" in the name `foldr`, because it is a *right*-associative expression (or, looking at the picture, it folds *from the right*). We can now reexpress the two functions as follows:

```
sum_list xs = foldr (+) 0 xs

conc l1 l2  = foldr (:) l2 l1
```

In `conc`, we supply the list construction operator "(`:`)" as the combining function, using the trick we described in Chapter 2 whereby we can treat an infix operator as an ordinary function by enclosing it in parentheses. Using `foldr`, we can now express other reductions as well. For example, a function to compute the product of the numbers in a list:

```
prod_list xs = foldr (*) 1 xs
```

Exercise 6.18   Write a function min_list using foldr that computes the minimum element in a list.   ■

Another very useful higher-order function on lists is map, which applies a function *f* to every member of a list and collects all the results into a list. For example,

```
map sqr [10,20,30]     → [100,400,900]
```

We can define it as follows:

```
map             :: (a->b) -> [a] -> [b]
map f []      = []
map f (x:xs) = (f x):(map f xs)
```

(The function map is predefined in *pH*.) If examined closely, we see that map also has the same recursive structure as sum_list and conc! Thus, here is an alternative definition of map in terms of foldr:

```
map f xs = foldr  (\x ys -> (f x):ys)  []  xs
```

The function filter takes a predicate function p and a list xs and returns a list containing only those elements x of xs such that "p x" is true. For example,

```
filter isPrime [2,3,4,5, ... ,18,19,20]
     → [2,3,5,7,11,13,17,19]
```

where isPrime tests if a number is a prime number. (The function filter is predefined in *pH*.) Here is a direct definition of filter:

```
filter  p  []    =  []
filter  p  (x:xs) =  let
                         ys = filter p xs
                     in
                         if p x then x:ys else ys
```

But, this, too has the same recursive structure as our previous examples. Here is a version using foldr:

```
filter  p  xs  =
        foldr  (\x ys -> if p x then x:ys else ys)  []  xs
```

Exercise 6.19   Consider:

```
map  (\x -> [1..x])  [1..4]
     → [[1], [1,2], [1,2,3], [1,2,3,4]]
```

The function `flatmap` is a variant of `map` that also "flattens" the output list to produce, instead,

```
[1, 1,2, 1,2,3, 1,2,3,4]
```

Write a definition of `flatmap` using `foldr`. (*Hint:* It differs from `map`'s definition in just one symbol.) ∎

Exercise 6.20   Write a definition of `filter` in terms of `flatmap`. (*Hint:* By concatenating either `[x]` or `[]` to another list we can either keep or discard `x`, respectively.) ∎

Combining functions like "+" and "∗" differ from combining functions like ":" in that they are commutative and associative:

$$a + b \qquad = b + a$$
$$a + (b + c) = (a + b) + c$$

(Actually, addition and multiplication are commutative and associative for integers but not for floating-point numbers.)

Thus, it is possible to reduce a collection of numbers using "+" in more than one way. An example is

$$f(f \ldots (f(f\ z\ x_1)\ x_2) \ldots x_{n-1})\ x_n$$

which is a left-associative expression. This kind of reduction may be expressed as follows:

```
foldl f z []     = z
foldl f z (x:xs) = foldl f (f z x) xs
```

(The function `foldl` is predefined in *pH*.) The structure of a `foldl` computation is depicted pictorially in Figure 6.2, which also clearly illustrates how it differs from `foldr`. Now, `sum_list` can also be defined as follows:

```
sum_list l = foldl (+) 0 l
```

which looks very similar to its definition using `foldr`. Which one is better? When we have a choice between the two folding functions (such as when using "+"), `foldl` is generally preferable because it is a *tail-recursive* function—the recursive call is not surrounded by any computation that needs to be done after it returns. Tail recursions are synonymous with loops and are generally implemented much more efficiently than function calls (see Section 2.8).

Exercise 6.21   What `f` and `z` arguments should be supplied to `foldl` so that it computes the length of a list? ∎

Exercise 6.22   What f and z arguments should be supplied to foldl so that, in a single traversal of a list of numbers, it computes both the sum as well as the length of the list? (*Hint:* Use 2-tuples.) Use this function to define a function that computes the average of a list of numbers.   ■

Exercise 6.23   What does the following function compute when applied to a list?

```
esrever xs = foldl (:) [] xs
```
■

Exercise 6.24   In our discussion of merge sorting in Section 6.2.5, we described a function split that takes a list xs and returns two lists as and bs, where as contains every other element of xs and bs contains the remaining elements (not necessarily in the original order). Write down a definition of split using foldl.   ■

Exercise 6.25   The following program is not a legal *pH* program because it is not type correct. However, it is interesting because it shows how data structures can be simulated by functions in a language with higher-order functions but without type checking. Therefore, ignoring types, trace its reduction:

```
let
    lispcons x y sel = if sel then x else y

    lispcar c = c True
    lispcdr c = c False

    a = lispcons 1 a
in
    lispcar a
```
■

As this section has amply demonstrated, foldr and foldl may be regarded as the "Dynamic Duo," the Two Great Functions on lists—almost any function we write on individual lists may be written using one of them. We have seen several examples of this already, such as length, sum_list, prod_list, conc, map, filter, and split. We find that, by thoroughly understanding Figure 6.2 and remembering it, one begins to use foldr and foldl routinely.

6.3.2   General Linear Recursion

Linear recursion refers to functions that make only one recursive call to themselves, either directly or indirectly. Most of the functions we have seen so far in this book have been linear recursive functions. The function fib computing Fibonacci numbers is not a linear recursive function because it contains two calls to itself. Similarly, we will see later that functions on *trees* are also typically not linear recursive. Lists, on the other hand, are linear structures (as is evident from Figure 6.1), and so most functions on lists, including `foldr` and `foldl`, are linear recursive.

There is a very general higher-order function that captures the structure of most linear recursive functions:

```
linrec                 :: (a -> Bool)    ->          -- p
                          (a -> a)       ->          -- f
                          a              ->          -- x
                          (a -> b -> b)  ->          -- g
                          (a -> b)                   -- h
                                         -> b        -- result
linrec p f x g h =
    let
        loop x = if p x then g x (loop (f x))
                 else h x
    in
        loop x
```

The structure of a `linrec` computation is shown pictorially in Figure 6.3. The function recursively computes x, $f(x)$, $f(f(x))$, and so on, applying the predicate p to each one in order to decide when to stop. As long as $p(f^j(x))$ is True, the recursion continues; eventually we reach a $p(f^{n+1}(x))$ that is False (for some n), and the recursion stops. When this happens, we return $h(f^{n+1}(x))$ as the value. As we return from the recursive calls, at each intermediate point we return $g(f^j(x), z)$, where z is the value returned by the recursive call.

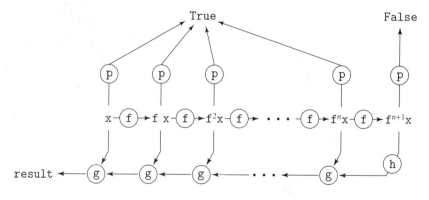

Figure 6.3   Visualization of a (`linrec p f x g h`) computation.

Notice, from the function text and from its type, that it has nothing to do with lists per se. To emphasize this, let us first use linrec to define the factorial function:

```
fact n = linrec (\x -> x <= n)                    -- p
                ((+) 1)                            -- f
                1                                  -- x
                (*)                                -- g
                (\x -> 1)                          -- h
```

Since f just increments its argument, the sequence $x, f(x), f(f(x)), \ldots$ is the sequence $1, 2, 3, \ldots$ The recursion stops at $n + 1$ because the predicate p checks that each number is $\leq n$. When the value is $n + 1$, we return $h(n + 1)$, which is just the constant value 1 (here, h ignores its argument and always returns 1). At each intermediate point during the returns from the recursive calls, where the number is j, we return $j * z$, where z is the value returned by the recursive call. In other words, we compute

$$1 \times (2 \times (3 \times \cdots \times (n \times 1)))$$

which is just $n!$, the factorial of n, as required.

Coming back to lists, both foldr and foldl can be defined in terms of linrec. foldr is the easier one:

```
foldr c z ys = linrec notNull                      -- p
                      tail                          -- f
                      ys                            -- x
                      (\ys z' -> c (head ys) z')    -- g
                      (\ys -> z)                    -- h
```

where notNull tests if a list is nonempty. Here, linrec recursively looks at ys, tail(ys), tail(tail(ys)), and so on (i.e., at successive suffixes of the list) until it reaches the empty list. At that point, it applies h to the empty list, which just returns z, the original second argument of foldr. At each intermediate point of the recursion, we have a suffix of the list. The function g extracts the head of this suffix and combines it with the result of the recursive call using the combining function c.

Exercise 6.26   Substitute the actual parameters to linrec (given above) into the definition of linrec and convince yourself that this really implements a foldr. ∎

At first sight, the structure of linrec looks fundamentally incompatible with the structure of foldl. linrec seems to use g to combine values as we return from the recursive calls, whereas `foldl` combines values going forward into the recursion. But, in fact, `linrec` can also combine values going forward, using its `f` argument. So, here is our strategy to implement `foldl` using `linrec`: the `x` argument of `linrec` will be a 2-tuple `(ys,z)`. As we move forward, the `ys` component will be successive suffixes of the input list, just as in `foldr`, and the recursion will stop when this becomes empty, also just as in `foldr`. The `z` component of the tuple will be the accumulated value thus far. When the recursion stops, this `z` will be the result we are looking for, and so we will implement *g* and *h* as trivial functions that simply pass this precious value all the way back, without touching a hair on its pretty little head:

```
foldl c z ys = linrec (\(ys,z) -> null ys)              -- p
                      (\(ys,z) -> (tail ys,              -- f
                                   c z (head ys)))
                      (ys,z)                             -- x
                      (\(ys,z) z' -> z')                 -- g
                      (\(ys,z)    -> z)                  -- h
```

The astute reader may observe that, although we have captured the semantics of `foldl` with this definition, there is still a pragmatic difference: `linrec` is not a tail-recursive function (and hence cannot be implemented with a loop), whereas the original, direct definition of `foldl` is tail-recursive.

Exercise 6.27 Substitute the actual parameters to `linrec` (given above) into the definition of `linrec` and convince yourself that this really implements a `foldl`.   ∎

The `linrec` function is a further demonstration of the fact that, in functional languages with higher-order functions, it is possible to abstract out common *control structures* from several specific cases. In most other programming languages, one is given a fixed repertoire of control structures: conditionals, **while** loops, **for** loops, and so on. Here, one can define one's own control structures, such as `linrec`, that are appropriate to the computations of interest in one's application. For example, we can define higher-order functions that capture the essence of traversing a tree data structure, or a graph data structure, and so on (we will see some examples later in this chapter).

6.3.3 Eliminating Intermediate Lists

Suppose we are asked to write a program that computes the sum of the squares of all prime numbers from 2 to 100. In traditional programming, we might roll up our sleeves and build the code from scratch: a loop to iterate from 2 to 100, a check to see if the current number is prime, and a running total to sum up the squares of all such numbers. A functional programmer, on the other hand, tends to reach for his toolbox of existing functions and may come up with the following "one-liner":

```
sum_list
    (map  sqr
         (filter  isPrime  [2..100]))
```

Note that the program as written produces, traverses, and discards three lists. This is a common paradigm in functional programming: we use lists as a common "glue" to communicate collections of data, and we use the available repertoire of powerful list-processing functions to manipulate and transform these collections. We build lists (e.g., using gen); we transform them (e.g., using map and filter); and we collapse them (e.g., using foldr or foldl).

This raises an efficiency question. Allocating, transforming, and consuming all these lists must constitute some overhead; is the functional programmer therefore trading expressive power for efficiency? It turns out that juxtapositions of these list-processing functions have interesting and useful properties (we also say that these functions obey certain *laws*), with the practical consequence that we can use them for eliminating intermediate lists. For example, for any functions f and g and any list xs,

```
map f (map g xs)      ≡      map (\x -> f (g x)) xs
```

If we utilize the "function composition" operator "." that we have seen before (and which is predefined in *pH*):

```
(f . g) x = f (g x)
```

then the above law can be expressed more succinctly:

```
(map f) . (map g)     ≡      map (f . g)
```

The truth of this law is easy to see. If we apply the left-hand side to a list containing $x_1 \ldots x_n$, then (map g) will first create a list containing

$g(x_1) \ldots g(x_n)$, and then (map f) will transform this into a list containing $f(g(x_1)) \ldots f(g(x_n))$. If we apply the right-hand side to the same original list, it directly produces a list containing $f(g(x_1)) \ldots f(g(x_n))$.

The interesting pragmatic consequence is that, whereas the left-hand side builds, traverses, and discards an intermediate list (containing $g(x_1) \ldots g(x_n)$), the right-hand side directly builds the final result list. Thus, using this law, a compiler (or the programmer) might transform a composition of map's into a single map that is presumably more efficient. Optimization operations that remove the construction and analysis of intermediate data structures like this are popularly known as *deforestations*, since analogous optimizations can also be performed on trees, which are more general data structures than lists [72].

Consider the following auxiliary function that simultaneously performs both a map and a filter:

```
mapfilt              ::  (a -> Maybe b) -> [a] -> [b]
mapfilt  pf  []      =  []
mapfilt  pf  (x:xs)  =  let
                           ys = mapfilt  pf  xs
                        in
                           case pf x of
                              Nothing -> ys
                              Just y  -> y:ys
```

It applies pf to each member x_i of the input list. Each such application returns either Nothing, indicating that this element is to be discarded, or Just y_i, indicating that y_i (which is presumably computed from x_i) is to be retained in the output list. It returns the list of all such y_i elements.

Using this function, a map juxtaposed with a filter can be collapsed into a single traversal, eliminating the intermediate list:

```
(map f) . (filter p) ≡ mapfilt
                         (\x -> if p x then Just (f x)
                                       else Nothing)
```

```
(filter p) . (map f) ≡ mapfilt
                         (\x -> if p (f x) then Just (f x)
                                          else Nothing)
```

Exercise 6.28   Write a definition of map in terms of mapfilt. Write a definition of filter in terms of mapfilt. ∎

Exercise 6.29   Prove the two laws regarding compositions of maps and filters. ∎

A `foldr` juxtaposed with a `mapfilt` can be collapsed into a single `foldr`:

```
(foldr g z) . (mapfilt pf)   ≡
              foldr (\x z' -> case pf x of
                                 Nothing -> z'
                                 Just y  -> g y z')
                    z
```

Similarly, a list generation using `gen` (defined at the beginning of Section 6.3.1) juxtaposed with a list collapsing using `foldr` can be collapsed into an application of `linrec`, the general linear recursive function described in the previous section:

```
foldr g z (gen p f x) ≡ linrec p            -- p
                               f            -- f
                               x            -- x
                               g            -- g
                               (\x' -> z)   -- h
```

Exercise 6.30   Prove that the above two laws hold.   ∎

Let us try to optimize the example from the beginning of this section:

```
sum_list
    (map  sqr
          (filter  isPrime  [2..100]))
```

Writing `sum_list` using `foldr` and the arithmetic sequence using `gen`, we have

```
foldr (+) 0
      (map sqr
           (filter isPrime
                   (gen leq100 inc 2)))
```

where `leq100` is an easy auxiliary function that tests if its argument is less than or equal to 100 and `inc` increments its argument. Collapsing the map and the `filter`, we get

```
foldr (+) 0
      (mapfilt (\x -> if isPrime x then Just (sqr x)
                                   else Nothing)
               (gen leq100 inc 2)))
```

Collapsing the `foldr` and the `mapfilt`, we have

```
foldr (\x z' -> case (\x' -> if isPrime x'
                                then Just (sqr x')
```

```
                                 else Nothing        )  x  of
                    Nothing -> z'
                    Just y  -> y + z')
        0
        (gen leq100 inc 2)
```

Reducing the β-redex in the discriminating expression in the case expression, we have

```
foldr (\x z' -> case (if isPrime x then Just (sqr x)
                                    else Nothing) of
                    Nothing -> z'
                    Just y  -> y + z')
        0
        (gen leq100 inc 2)
```

Now, we invoke a law about nested case expressions (remember that a conditional expression is just special syntax for a case expression on booleans):

```
case (case e of              ≡         case e of
         p1 -> e1                          p1 -> case e1 of
         pn -> en) of                               q1 -> f1
                                                    qn -> fn
      q1 -> f1                             pn -> case en of
      qn -> fn                                      q1 -> f1
                                                    qn -> fn
```

The nested case expression in our program thus becomes

```
case isPrime x of
   True  -> case Just (sqr x) of
               Nothing -> z'
               Just y  -> y + z'
   False -> case Nothing of
               Nothing -> z'
               Just y  -> y + z'
```

Then, we invoke the following law that eliminates a case expression by doing static pattern matching:

```
case C e1 ... eN of          ≡         let
   ...                                      x1=e1; ...;xN=eN
   C x1 ... xN -> e                     in
   ...                                      e
```

(assuming that the patterns in the earlier clauses can be shown to fail). With this transformation and doing some cleanup, our program becomes

```
foldr (\x z' -> if isPrime x then (sqr x) + z' else z')
      0
      (gen leq100 inc 2)
```

Collapsing the `foldr` juxtaposed with the `gen`, we have

```
linrec leq100
       inc
       2
       (\x z' -> if isPrime x then (sqr x) + z' else z')
       (\z -> 0)
```

If we create a specialized version of `linrec` that plugs in these functions and clean it up a bit, we get

```
let
    loop x = if x <= 100 then
                 let
                     z = loop (1 + x)
                 in
                     if isPrime x then (sqr x) + z else z
             else
                 0
in
    loop 2
```

et Voila! The final expression builds no lists at all! It directly generates the integers 2, 3, . . . , 100, tests each for primality, and collects the sum of the squares of the ones that pass the test.

Exercise 6.31   The `loop` function above does not build any intermediate lists, but it is still not tail-recursive. Use the associativity of "+" to transform it into a tail-recursive function.   ■

6.3.4   Nonstrictness and Pipeline Parallelism

Lists, like all *pH* data structures, are nonstrict; that is, it is possible to work with a list (e.g., embed it in another data structure) before any of its component items have been reduced to values. Similarly, it is possible to extract a component item of a list before other component items have been reduced to values.

Exercise 6.32 · The following expression is similar to the example in Section 5.6.4, which was based on tuples instead of lists:

```
head [3.5, sqrt 18239.0]
```

Show a reduction sequence that produces the answer (3.5) without doing a single reduction in the sqrt application. ∎

A particularly useful kind of parallelism associated with lists is called *pipeline* parallelism. Suppose we had the computation

```
map f (map g [x₁,..., xₙ])
```

If this structure is statically visible, the techniques of the previous section could collapse this statically into a single map, but let us say that this structure emerged dynamically because the pieces were in separately compiled modules or hidden behind complex higher-order functions.

Because of nonstrictness, the inner map can deliver the head of its result list to the outer list as soon as it is ready, even though it is still working on the rest of its input list. Conceptually, we have

```
map f ((g x₁):(map g [x₂,..., xₙ]))
```

The outer map can, in turn, immediately work on the first element of the intermediate list and even produce the first element of the final result. Conceptually:

```
(f (g x₁)):(map f (map g [x₂,..., xₙ]))
```

In this manner, the two computations can overlap in time, with the outer traversal chasing just behind the inner traversal. The mental image is of a pipeline through which the x_js are sent, being transformed in the process first by g and then by f. Suppose each of the two list transformations individually takes total time t (proportional to the length of the list). If the outer map had to wait for the entire inner map to complete, the total time for the program would be $2t$. However, because of pipelining, the total time for the program can still be t (plus some small amount because of the slight skew that must occur as the inner traversal hands items to the outer traversal; this amount is constant, not proportional to the size of the lists).

Similarly, it is not hard to see that the same kind of pipelining can occur in connections between gen, map, filter, foldl, and foldr, or any of their specializations.

Nonstrictness also allows us to express infinite and cyclic data structures, a topic we will begin exploring in Section 6.6.2.

6.4   List Comprehensions

A very powerful notation for constructing lists is the *list comprehension*.[4] It is best to learn this notation by looking at some examples. Consider a city with a grid of streets numbered according to their distance from city hall. The city of Philadelphia, for example, is laid out like this.[5] Thus, each street intersection is described by an (x, y) coordinate. Now, suppose we want a list of all the street intersections that lie within the northeast quadrant, within a five-block square, as shown in Figure 6.4(a). We can express this using list comprehensions as follows:

```
[ (x,y) | x <- [1..5], y <- [1..5] ]
```

A list comprehension is enclosed in square brackets (just like other list notation). The expression can be read as follows: "The list of all (x,y)s, for all xs drawn from the sequence 1 to 5 and all ys drawn from the sequence 1 to 5." The phrases to the right of the "|" are called *qualifiers* and are separated by commas (there can be any number of qualifiers). A qualifier of the form

identifier <- list-expression

4. List comprehension notation is derived from set expressions in mathematics. An early version of this notation existed in the language SETL by Jack Schwartz and was later adopted by John Darlington in the language NPL, which he designed with Rod Burstall at Edinburgh in the early to mid-1970s. It later became well known through the languages SASL and KRC, designed by David Turner, where he has variously referred to them as ZF-expressions, set expressions, and list expressions. The term "list comprehension" was apparently coined by Phil Wadler around 1983, by analogy with the existing mathematical term "set comprehension."
5. We understand that this plan was yet another product of the utterly ingenious and rational imagination of one of Philadelphia's most illustrious residents, Mr. Benjamin Franklin (cf. kites, keys, frogs' legs, Franklin stoves, and daylight saving time).

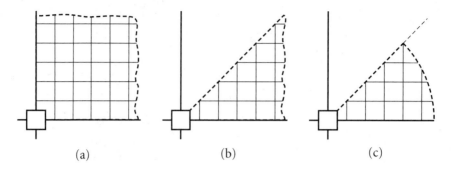

Figure 6.4 Street intersections (a) northeast, (b) east-northeast, and (c) within five blocks of City Hall.

is also called a *generator* and binds the identifier to each member of the list. Generators nest from left to right; that is, all the ys are repeatedly generated for each of the xs, so that the resulting list is

```
[ (1,1),(1,2),...,(1,5), (2,1),(2,2),...,(2,5), ... ,(5,5) ]
```

The left-to-right nesting also applies to the *scoping* of the identifiers bound in the generators; each binding in the first generator is available to compute the second generator list, each binding in the second generator is available to compute the third generator list, and so on. For example, suppose we want the list of all street intersections within the east-northeast octant as shown in Figure 6.4(b):

```
[ (x,y) | x <- [1..5], y <- [1..x] ]
```

Here, the second generator list ranges only from 1 to x. In other words, for each x, we generate all ys from 1 to x. Thus, the resulting list is

```
[ (1,1), (2,1),(2,2), (3,1),(3,2),(3,3), (4,1), ... ,(5,5) ]
```

A qualifier can also be a *guard*, which is a general boolean-valued expression, in order to allow only some of the bindings. For example, suppose we want the list of all street intersections within the east-northeast octant, within a radius of five blocks, as shown in Figure 6.4(c):

```
[ (x,y) | x <- [1..5], y <- [1..x], (sqr x + sqr y) <= 25 ]
```

The last qualifier is a guard that accepts only those xs and ys that satisfy the predicate $(x^2 + y^2 \le 25)$.

Exercise 6.33   Write a definition of `map` using a list comprehension.   ■

Exercise 6.34   Write a definition of `filter` using a list comprehension.   ■

6.4.1   List Comprehensions as a Database Query Language

In database systems there is a standard model called the *relational model*. Here, data is organized in a tabular form, each table being referred to as a relation. For example, in the foggy bottom of a garbage can in Georgetown we found a diskette containing a foreign relation, which shows the strongmen who have recently ruled the unstable government of the small island nation of Intrigua (Figure 6.5).

The third column indicates whether they were "our" puppet or "theirs." The fourth column specifies the number of Mercedes Benzes that each strongman accumulated during his tenure, and the fifth column is about treachery—it is the code name of the strongman he toppled. For example, Brigadier Barracuda (S4) toppled Captain Piranha (S10), who, in turn, briefly became president-for-life by toppling Admiral Weasel (S7). (Marechal Raccoon did not topple anyone—he was the one who started this whole sordid business, and Major Mantis—well, he consumed himself.)

Code	Name	Whose Side	MBs	Victim
S1	Maj. Bandicoot	Ours	6	S6
S2	Col. Salamander	Ours	12	S8
S3	Lt. Col. Gecko	Theirs	3	S4
S4	Brig. Barracuda	Ours	91	S10
S5	Maj. Mantis	Theirs	16	S5
S6	Maj. Gen. Shark	Theirs	25	S2
S7	Adm. Weasel	Ours	17	S9
S8	Col. Coyote	Theirs	7	S3
S9	Marechal Raccoon	Theirs	9	—
S10	Capt. Piranha	Ours	16	S7

Figure 6.5   The strongmen who have ruled Intrigua

Relations are queried using a language called SQL. For example, to find out the names of all strongmen on our side, one could use the following SQL expression:

```
SELECT s.Name
FROM Strongmen s
WHERE s.WhosSide = "Ours"
```

In words: for each strongman s such that s was on our side, list s's name.

In *pH*, we can first define a type to represent strongmen:

```
data Strongman = Strongman {
                     code, name, side,  :: String,
                     mbs                :: Int,
                     victim             :: String
            }
```

Then, we can represent the relation as a list of strongmen:

```
strongmen =
    [ Strongman "S1"    "Maj. Bandicoot"    "Ours"    6    "S6",
      Strongman "S2"    "Col. Salamander"   "Ours"    12   "S8",
            .
            .
            .
      Strongman "S9"    "Marechal Raccoon"  "Theirs"  9    "-",
      Strongman "S10"   "Capt. Piranha"     "Ours"    16   "S7" ]
```

Now, we can write our query using a list comprehension that looks very much like a simple reformulation of the SQL version:

```
[ name s | s <- strongmen, side s == "Ours" ]
```

Another SQL query: "List the names of all strongmen on our side who accumulated more Mercedes Benzes than their predecessors."

```
SELECT s1.Name
FROM Strongmen s1, Strongmen s2
WHERE s1.Victim   = s2.Code
AND   s1.WhosSide = "Ours"
AND   s1.MBs      > s2.MBs
```

In words: for each pair of strongmen s1 and s2, list s1's name, such that s1's victim was s2, s1 was on our side and s1 had more Mercedes Benzes than s2. The *pH* version:

```
[ name s1 | s1 <- strongmen,  s2 <- strongmen,
                              victim s1 == code s2,
                              side s1   == "Ours",
                              mbs s1     >  mbs s2 ]
```

List comprehensions are more expressive than SQL because (1) they allow arbitrary lists for generators (SQL allows only fixed database relations), (2) they allow arbitrary predicates for guards (SQL allows only a few that are built in), and (3) the returned values can be of arbitrary type and computed using arbitrary functions (in SQL they can only be scalar constants and fields of the input relations). Further, being embedded cleanly in a general programming language, we can perform arbitrary computations on the database in *pH*, whereas SQL allows only a small repertoire of built-in functions.[6]

Exercise 6.35 Write a query that finds the names of all strongmen who toppled someone of the other side.   ▪

Exercise 6.36 Write a function `predecessor` using list comprehensions that, given a strongman's codename, returns the codename of the strongman he toppled.

Use `predecessor` to write a function that, given a strongman's codename, finds out how many strongmen preceded him. (This example demonstrates that *pH* with list comprehensions is more expressive than so-called *relationally complete* languages since it is possible to express transitive closures.)   ▪

6.4.2 Syntax and Semantics of List Comprehensions

The syntax of list comprehensions can be specified as follows:

$list\_comprehension ::= [\ e\ |\ Q\ ]$

where qualifiers are specified by

$Q \quad ::= \quad \epsilon$ empty

---

6. So, should list comprehensions replace SQL? Not yet, because though SQL and relational databases have limited expressive power, there is an enormous body of knowledge on how to implement them efficiently, taking into account secondary storage, concurrent access, reliability, and so on. We are still a long way from achieving this with list comprehensions.

| | x <- e, Q | generator |
| | G, Q | guard |

where G is a boolean expression

The semantics of list comprehensions are specified using the following rewrite rules:

`[e	]`	$\rightarrow$ `[e]`	(ListCompEmpty)
`[e	x <- [], Q]`	$\rightarrow$ `[]`	(ListCompGenNil)
`[e	x <- `$e_x$`:`$e_{xs}$`, Q]`	$\rightarrow$ `(let x = `e_x` in [e	Q])`	(ListCompGenCons)
	`++`	
	`[e	x <- `$e_{xs}$`, Q]`	
`[e	False, Q]`	$\rightarrow$ `[]`	(ListCompGuardF)
`[e	True, Q]`	$\rightarrow$ `[e	Q]`	(ListCompGuardT)

Exercise 6.37   Apply the rewrite rules to

```
[ (x,y) | x <- [1..5], y <- [1..x], (sqr x + sqr y) <= 25 ]
```

and produce the answer.   ∎

6.4.3   The Expressive Power of List Comprehensions

While list comprehensions do not add any fundamental computational power to the language, they constitute a very elegant, concise, and powerful notation. To appreciate this, it is instructive to work out some examples without using list comprehensions. We begin with a simple list comprehension to establish the intuition that it expresses some form of `map`:

```
[ (x,x) | x <- [1..10] ]
```

It is clear that this is equivalent to

```
let
    segment x = (x,x)
in
    map segment [1..10]
```

that is, `segment` is a function that is used to produce each of the 10 segments of the output list; we simply map this function over the list "`[1..10]`".

Now, let us try an example with two generators:

```
[ (x,y) | x <- [1..10], y <- [1..5] ]
```

The result is a list of 50 pairs, but we can view it as comprising 10 segments, each of which comprises 5 segments, each of which is a primitive segment of the output list. Let us build this from the bottom up. We start with the constructor for primitive segments:

```
segment_2 x y = (x,y)
```

Segments at the next level up are obtained by mapping this over the generator for ys:

```
segment_1 x = map (segment_2 x) [1..5]
```

Segments at the next level up are obtained by mapping this over the generator for xs:

```
map segment_1 [1..10]
```

Unfortunately, this is not exactly what we want, because it has the wrong "shape": it produces a list of 10 segments, each of which is a list of 5 pairs; that is, it produces

```
[   [(1,1), (1,2), ... , (1,5)],
    [(2,1), (2,2), ... , (2,5)],
    .
    .
    .
    [(10,1), (10,2), ... , (10,5)]   ]
```

Instead, what we need is a "flat" list of 50 pairs. We can achieve this using the following function:

```
flatten_2     :: [[a]] -> [a]
flatten_2 xss = foldr (++) [] xss
```

which takes a two-level list (i.e., a list of lists of things) and flattens it out into a one-level list (i.e., a list of things). For example:

```
flatten_2 [ [x₁, x₂], [y₁, y₂, y₃] ]    → [ x₁, x₂, y₁, y₂, y₃ ]
```

A complete solution to our list comprehension translation, therefore, is

```
let
    segment_2 x y = (x,y)
    segment_1 x   = map (segment_2 x) [1..5]
in
    flatten_2 (map segment_1 [1..10])
```

While correct, this is still not entirely satisfactory. Consider the generalization to a list comprehension with more generators (we'll use three, to avoid being buried in ellipses):

```
[ e₍ₓ,ᵧ,z₎ | x <- xs,  y <- yz,  z <- zs ]
```

where $e_{(x,y,z)}$ is some expression in x, y, and z. This would be expressed as

```
let
    segment_3 x y z = e(x,y,z)
    segment_2 x y   = map (segment_3 x y) zs
    segment_1 x     = map (segment_2 x) ys
    segment_0       = map segment_1 xs
in
    flatten_3  segment_0
```

where `flatten_3` flattens a three-level list. But this is unsatisfactory because a four-generator list comprehension would need a `flatten_4`, a five-generator list comprehension would need a `flatten_5`, and so on. A more elegant solution is to flatten lists at each level; that is, each time we use `map` we assume we get a two-level list that we immediately flatten. As a base case, we assume that the primitive segments are one-level lists containing one element each:

```
let
    segment_3 x y z = [ e(x,y,z) ]
    segment_2 x y   = flatten_2 (map (segment_3 x y) zs)
    segment_1 x     = flatten_2 (map (segment_2 x) ys)
    segment_0       = flatten_2 (map segment_1 xs)
in
    segment_0
```

Now, the generalization to an arbitrary number of generators is obvious. But what about guards? Consider:

$$[\ e_{(x_1,...,x_n)} \ | \ x \ \text{<- xs}, \ p_x, \ y \ \text{<- ys}, \ p_y, \ z \ \text{<- zs}, \ p_z \ ]$$

A guard such as p_x is essentially a `filter` operation limiting the elements xs seen by the remaining generators and guards. This is easily incorporated into our translation of list comprehensions:

```
let
    segment_3 x y z = [ e(x,y,z) ]
    fpz       x y z = pz
    segment_2 x y   = flatten_2 (map (segment_3 x y)
                                     (filter (fpz x y) zs))
    fpy       x y   = py
    segment_1 x     = flatten_2 (map (segment_2 x)
                                     (filter (fpy x) ys))
```

```
fpx         x    = p_x
segment_0        = flatten_2 (map segment_1
                                  (filter fpx xs))
in
    segment_0
```

This translation illustrates the expressive power of list comprehension notation, which allows a much more compact and intuitive expression of the idea of nested loops and filters.

Exercise 6.38   How many appends (i.e., "++" operations) are performed by the translation of

```
[ (x,y) | x <- [1..2], y <- [1..2] ]
```

How many conses (i.e., ":" operations) does it perform?   ∎

6.4.4 ▼   Desugaring List Comprehensions

The translation of list comprehensions shown in the previous section is not very efficient. The maps, filters, and flattens create several intermediate lists that are subsequently discarded. We will now develop an alternative translation that is optimal in the sense that the only cons operations that it performs are those that are necessary for the elements in the final result list. What we want is a function

TE⟦ [e | Q] ⟧

that produces the translated code. Recall that, when showing syntactic translations, we enclose syntax terms in "⟦ ⟧" brackets. We introduced this notation in Section 4.4. Thus, TE⟦ ⟧ takes a *pH* syntactic term as input and produces a new *pH* syntactic term (the desugaring) as output.

It turns out that a simple change in viewpoint allows us to produce much more efficient code. Instead of translating the list comprehension directly, we translate the concatenation of the list comprehension onto a *continuation* list:

TQ⟦ [e | Q] ++ L ⟧

Given such a TQ, we can obviously implement TE using TQ, by simply passing it the expression "[]", representing the empty list, as the initial continuation list, since concatenating the list produced by the list comprehension with [] produces the list itself:

TE⟦ [e | Q] ⟧ = TQ⟦ [e | Q] ++ [] ⟧

The structure of TQ directly follows the structure of the rewrite rules for list comprehensions described in Section 6.4.2.

$$\text{TQ}[\![\ [e \ | \ ] \ \texttt{++} \ \texttt{L} \ ]\!] = \qquad e\texttt{:}L$$

$$\text{TQ}[\![\ [e \ | \ x \ \texttt{<-} \ e_{xs}, \ Q] \ \texttt{++} \ L]\!] =$$

```
let
    f []     = L
    f (x:xs) = TQ[ [e | Q] ++ (f xs)]
in
    f e_{xs}
```

$$\text{TQ}[\![\ [e \ | \ e_G, \ Q] \ \texttt{++} \ L]\!] =$$

```
if e_G then TQ[ [e | Q] ++ L ]
else L
```

Each right-hand side of these clauses should be read as the output syntactic term produced by the translation. For example, the second clause specifies that the $\text{TQ}[\![\cdots]\!]$ application on the left-hand side produces the syntactic term described on the right-hand side, which is a **let**-block containing a two-clause definition for a function "f" and a body containing an application of "f" (and "f" and "xs" are new identifiers). Note that "f" and "xs" are in the result term, but they are also fed in as part of the argument to TQ; that is, they also appear within the syntax brackets "$[\![\ ]\!]$". This is OK since TQ's argument and result are both *pH* syntax terms.

The key insight in the translation is that instead of constructing a list $a_1, \ldots, a_n$ ending in [] and then using "++" to append it to a list $[b_1, \ldots, b_n]$, we directly construct the list $a_1, \ldots, a_n$ to end in the list $[b_1, \ldots, b_n]$. Good compilers implement list comprehensions in this manner. (In Chapter 9 we will see another improvement whereby the recursions are replaced by loops.)

Exercise 6.39 Apply the translation to the list comprehension:

```
[ (x,y) | x <- [1..5], y <- [1..x], (sqr x + sqr y) <= 25 ]
```

and show the resulting code. ∎

6.5   More Recursive Algebraic Types

Let us look at some more recursive algebraic types.

6.5.1   Graphs

Suppose we wanted to represent the course catalog in a university. Each course listing contains a course name, the number of units/credits for the course, a description, and a list of prerequisites. We can express this in a *pH* type declaration:

```
data Course_type = Course String Int String [Course_type]
```

The type has a single disjunct with four components: a string (course name), an integer (units/credits), a string (course description), and a list of courses (prerequisites). For a course with no prerequisites, this list will be []. Note that a course may be the prerequisite for more than one course.

Here is a function that computes, for a course, the earliest term that it could possibly be taken, given that all its prerequisites must be completed first:

```
earliest                       :: Course_type -> Int
earliest (Course _ _ _ []) = 1
earliest (Course _ _ _ cs) = 1 + maximum (map earliest cs)
```

The first clause applies if the prerequisites are empty—the course can be taken in the first term. In the second, default, clause, which will be invoked knowing that cs is nonempty, we apply earliest recursively to each of the prerequisites using map, defined earlier. We use the predefined function maximum to find the maximum element of the list, which is the earliest term that all the prerequisites could be completed. This course can then be taken one term later.

Exercise 6.40   Write a type definition for an (inverted) family tree based on a single type person. A person is either unknown or has a name, which is a string, a year of birth, which is an integer, a mother, who is a person, and a father, who is a person.

Write a function num_ancestors that counts the number of known ancestors of a given person. First write it assuming that no person has an ancestor who can be reached by two different paths. Then write it assuming that this is possible.   ∎

In general, the types in the previous paragraphs and exercise are examples of the general notion of *graphs*. A graph consists of a set of *nodes* and *edges*. Each edge connects two nodes. In *directed* graphs, the edges are considered as having a direction; that is, they go *from* one node *to* another. In *undirected* graphs, the edges do not have a direction. An example of a directed graph is one where the nodes are cities and each edge represents a scheduled flight from one city to another. An example of an undirected graph is one where the nodes are cities and each edge represents the relation "are within 100 miles of each other." In both cases, it is possible for the graph to contain *cycles*—for there to be a nonempty path (a sequence of one or more connected edges) from a city to itself. A directed graph without cycles is known as a *directed acyclic graph* (DAG). The Course_type structure described above is intended to represent a DAG (a cycle would imply that a course is its own prerequisite), but the data type itself does not place any such restriction; the "DAGness" of any course structure we build has to be ensured by careful construction.

Graphs are actually quite problematic in pure functional languages. We will describe graphs and this issue in greater detail in Chapter 10.

6.5.2   Binary Trees

Binary trees are another example of a type that, like lists, uses algebraic types in their full generality (i.e., sums, products, recursion, and polymorphism). Here is the type definition:

```
data Bintree item = Leaf item
                  | Node (Bintree item) (Bintree item)
```

In words: a binary tree of items is either a leaf, in which case it contains an item, or it is a node, in which case it contains a left and a right subtree, each of which is itself a tree of items.[7] For example, the tree shown in Figure 6.6 may be constructed by the following expression:

```
Node (Node (Leaf 23)
           (Node (Leaf (–5))
                 (Leaf 96)))
     (Node (Node (Leaf 51)
                 (Node (Leaf 2)
                       (Leaf 37)))
           (Leaf 71))
```

---

7. Other formulations of binary trees are possible, such as one in which the leaf is empty and each node contains an item.

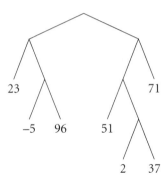

Figure 6.6   A binary tree.

Of course, one rarely constructs a binary tree by writing such a huge, manifest expression; trees are usually constructed algorithmically. This particular tree has type

```
Bintree Int
```

that is, it is a binary tree of integers, whereas the following tree:

```
Node (Node (Leaf "Beamon")
           (Leaf "Lewis"))
     (Leaf "Powell")
```

has type

```
Bintree String
```

Note that `Bintree`s have a homogeneous type, like lists. We cannot, for example, mix numbers and strings in the same tree; they would have to be packaged into a single type such as the `Token` type seen earlier.

Here is a function to compute the maximum depth of a binary tree:

```
depth (Leaf j)   = 0
depth (Node L R) = 1 + max (depth L) (depth R)
```

The depth of a leaf is 0 (by convention), and the depth of a nonempty tree is one more than the maximum depths of its left and right subtrees. The type of the function is

```
depth            :: (Bintree a) -> Int
```

that is, it works on binary trees whose components are of any type.

Here is a function to add up all the integers in a tree of integers:

```
sum_tree (Leaf j)   = j
sum_tree (Node L R) = (sum_tree L) + (sum_tree R)
```

The sum of a leaf is just the contents of the leaf, and the sum of a nonempty tree is the sum of its left subtree and its right subtree. The type of this function is

```
sum_tree              :: (Bintree Int) -> Int
```

Unlike `depth`, it works only on trees of integers.

But aha! The Higher-Order Detective should smell *similar structures* once again! Both `depth` and `sum_tree` do something simple at a leaf, and, at a node, they both recursively call themselves on the left and right subtrees and combine the results to produce a new result. This can be expressed as follows:

```
fold_tree f g (Leaf j)   = g j
fold_tree f g (Node L R) = f (fold_tree f g L)
                             (fold_tree f g R)
```

so that

```
depth t    = fold_tree (\a b -> 1 + max a b) (\x -> 0) t

sum_tree t = fold_tree (+) (\x -> x) t
```

Let us analyze the type of the function `fold_tree`. Suppose the type of the input tree is (`Bintree a`), and the type of the result of `fold_tree` is b. Then g must have type (a->b), since it applies to the contents of a leaf and returns a result of `fold_tree` in the first clause. Similarly, the output type of `f` must be b, since it returns a result of `fold_tree` in the second clause. It is applied to two arguments, each a result of `fold_tree`. Thus, it must be that

```
f    ::    (b -> b -> b)
```

Putting it all together, the type of `fold_tree` must be

```
fold_tree  ::   (b->b->b) -> (a->b) -> (Bintree a) -> b
```

Exercise 6.41   The function "`map_tree f t`" is also a very useful function. It returns a tree `t'` of the same shape as the input tree `t`, except the contents value of a leaf in `t'` is the result of applying `f` to the contents value of the corresponding leaf in `t`. For example:

```
map_tree sqr (Node (Node (Leaf 2)
                         (Leaf 3))
                   (Leaf 5))
 →
   (Node (Node (Leaf 4)
               (Leaf 9))
         (Leaf 25))
```

Write a definition for map_tree using fold_tree. ∎

Exercise 6.42 What is the most general type of the map_tree function in the previous exercise? ∎

6.6 Implications of Nonstrictness

All algebraic data types in *pH* are nonstrict, i.e., when a constructor is applied, the constructed value can be returned even if the component fields are still expressions that have not yet been reduced to values. This has a profound impact on parallelism (a nonstrict language allows more parallelism than a strict one) and expressiveness (a nonstrict language allows us to define cyclic and infinite data structures). We now examine these two points.

6.6.1 Nonstrictness and Parallelism

The following example vividly demonstrates the increased parallelism available due to nonstrictness. The *fringe* of a tree is defined as the list of the contents of the leaves, in a left-to-right order. For example, the fringe of the tree in Figure 6.6 is the list

```
[ 23, (-5), 96, 51, 2, 37, 71 ]
```

Here is a function to compute the fringe of the tree:

```
fringe t =
  let
      traverse (Leaf x)   xs = x:xs
      traverse (Node L R) xs = let  xs' = (traverse R xs)
                                in
                                    traverse L xs'
  in
      traverse t []
```

We use an auxiliary function "`traverse t xs`" that builds the fringe of the tree t onto the list xs. Initially, we call it with the input tree and an empty list. In the case of a leaf, we simply cons the contents onto the list. For nonempty trees, we build the fringe of the right subtree onto the list, giving a list xs', and then we build the fringe of the left subtree onto this list xs' to produce the output list.

Now, let us consider the issue of strictness. In a strict language, the computation of xs' must be completed before we could begin traversing the left subtree; that is, in the expression "`traverse L xs'`", the list xs' must be computed completely before we could perform the function call. Because of this, the traversal of the tree would end up as a sequential traversal from node to node, in a right-to-left order. The time taken for the whole computation is thus of the order of the number of nodes in the tree.

In a nonstrict language like *pH*, however, the traversal of the left subtree can begin immediately, even though the value of xs' is not yet available. Thus, both subtrees are traversed in parallel, and this parallelism grows exponentially as we go down the tree. The total time for the computation is thus only of the order of the depth of the tree. Thus, nonstrictness can increase the parallelism and speedup by an exponential factor.

6.6.2   Nonstrictness and Cyclic and Infinite Structures

Consider the following type that is intended to represent cities that are connected by direct flights:

```
data City = City  String  [City]
```

A City object has two fields: a string representing the city's name, and a list of other cities connected from this city by a direct flight. For example, suppose we had a small airline that operated shuttle flights between Boston and New York, and shuttle flights between New York and Washington. We can express the connectivity graph of its route map as follows:

```
let
    bos   = City  "Boston"         [ny]
    ny    = City  "New York"       [bos, washdc]
    washdc = City  "Washington DC"  [ny]
in
    [bos, ny, washdc]
```

Note that the three definitions are mutually recursive, directly expressing the idea that Boston is a destination from New York and vice versa, and that Washington is a destination from New York and vice versa. In most other programming languages that do not have nonstrictness, this idea is not directly expressible; instead, one would typically first construct three City objects with [] in their destinations field and, subsequently, using side effects, update the destinations field appropriately.

Cyclic data structures are closely related to, and sometimes indistinguishable from, "infinite" data structures. For example, the definition

```
let
    ones = 1 : ones
in
    ones
```

represents a cyclic list whose head contains 1 and whose tail is the list itself. When certain functions are applied to this list, they will not terminate, such as the length function, or (map sqr). On the other hand, taking the head of this list is perfectly fine, returning 1. In general, any function that only looks at a finite prefix of a list can safely be applied to this list.

Consider the following variation on the previous definition:

```
let
    f x = x : (f x)
in
    f 1
```

The result expression reduces to 1:(f 1), which in turn reduces to 1:1:(f 1), and so on. In other words, this, too, represents an infinite list of ones, but it is not a cyclic list like the previous example. If we apply the head function to this list to obtain the head of the list, the head application will indeed reduce to 1, as before. In a *pH* system, you might see the value "1" printed, but it will also indicate that the overall computation has not terminated because the infinite list continues to be computed, forever. In this behavior, *pH* diverges from Haskell. Haskell implementations employ lazy evaluation, which allows the computation to terminate as soon as it has printed "1". However, *pH* does not use lazy evaluation, both for additional parallelism as well as to accommodate side effects, described in Chapters 8, 9, and 10.

It might appear from the preceding discussion that infinite lists are not practically useful in *pH*. This is not entirely true. Infinite lists can be useful in particular to express I/O streams. Consider a program in a real-time system that is permanently monitoring readings from an external instrument, such as a seismograph. Such a program may have the type

```
monitor :: [Reading] -> [Warning]
```

It sits permanently in a loop analyzing the incoming stream for "interesting" readings and produces a warning each time it sees one. The structure of the program is

```
monitor  (r:rs)  state = let
                            state' = update state r
                            ws'    = monitor rs state'
                         in
                            if interesting r state
                            then (warning r state): ws'
                            else ws'
```

It recurses forever down the infinite list of readings, carrying a "state" along. When it sees an "interesting" reading with respect to the current state, it produces a warning on the output list. The rest of the output list is constructed by monitoring the remaining input readings, starting with a state that reflects the current reading.

Note that unlike all our previous list functions, this one does not have a clause testing for "[]", because the input stream is "infinite." The production of this infinite input list is presumably regulated by the availability of readings from some external instrument. *pH*'s parallelism and nonstrictness allow the monitor function to traverse and consume the partial prefix of the readings stream produced so far; at some point, it will hit a "tail" that is not yet manifest, and it will simply get stuck until it does become manifest.

Another example where infinite lists are useful is in modeling various mutual, interactive producer-consumer processes. For example, the structure

```
resps  =  processA  reqs
reqs   =  processB  resps
```

represents two processes A and B. Process A takes a stream of requests from process B and produces a stream of responses. Process B, in turn, takes the stream of responses and uses it to decide future requests. Again, even though streams are conceptually infinite objects, the interactivity of the processes can constrain them to move forward in lockstep, so that only finite portions of the streams are ever manifested at each point in time.

6.7   Semantics of Algebraic Sum Types and Case Expressions

Algebraic sum types do not require any new syntax in the core language, nor any new rewrite rules. They are handled completely by static translation (syntactic desugaring) into the existing core.

First, we assign a distinct integer *tag* to every constructor in every algebraic type definition in the program. (Actually, the tags need only be distinct among the constructors of a particular type definition. Constructors from different type definitions need not have distinct tags. Static type checking ensures that there is no chance for constructors from one type to be used where an object of another type is expected.) If the constructor is CN_k, we will represent its corresponding tag symbolically below by *TagForCN$_k$*.

For every use of CN_k as a constructor (i.e., not in patterns, but in expressions, to construct values), we replace CN_k by the core term:

$$\backslash t_1 \ \ldots \ \backslash t_k \ \text{->} \ CN_{(k+1)}(\textit{TagForCN}_k, t_1, \ldots, t_k)$$

That is, the k-ary constructor identifier represents a curried function of k arguments that produces a constructed term with $k + 1$ components: the tag and the k arguments. (This is only a suggested representation for the purpose of explaining semantics. Actual implementations are more sophisticated in how they encode tags. The only important point for the present discussion is that we can query the tag and project out the k components.)

Multiple-clause definitions are first desugared into the more fundamental case expressions. Then, a case expression of the form

    case e **of**
        p_1 -> e_1
        p_2 -> e_2
         .
         .
        p_n -> e_n

is translated into an expression like this:

    let
        $t = e$
    in
        Cond($[\![\text{match}(p_1, t)]\!]$,

               let $[\![\text{bind}(p_1, t)]\!]$ **in** e_1 ,

$$\textbf{Cond(}\; [\![\text{match}(p_2,t)]\!]\; ,$$

$$\textbf{let}\; [\![\text{bind}(p_2,t)]\!]\; \textbf{in}\; e_2\; ,$$

$$\vdots$$

$$\textbf{Cond(}\; [\![\text{match}(p_n,t)]\!]\; ,$$

$$\textbf{let}\; [\![\text{bind}(p_n,t)]\!]\; \textbf{in}\; e_n\; ,$$

$$\texttt{error "match failure") ...))}$$

Each $[\![\text{match}(p,t)]\!]$ represents the following translation into a boolean expression:

$$
\begin{array}{ll}
[\![\text{match}(x,t)]\!] & \Rightarrow\; \texttt{True} \\
[\![\text{match}(\text{CN}_0,t)]\!] & \Rightarrow\; (\text{CN}_0\; \texttt{==}\; t) \\
[\![\text{match}(\text{CN}_k(p_1,\ldots,p_k),t)]\!] & \Rightarrow\; \textbf{if}\; \text{proj}_1(t)\; \texttt{==}\; \textit{TagForCN}_k\; \textbf{then} \\
& \qquad ([\![\text{match}(p_1,\text{proj}_2(t))]\!] \\
& \qquad \texttt{\&\&} \\
& \qquad \vdots \\
& \qquad \texttt{\&\&} \\
& \qquad [\![\text{match}(p_k,\text{proj}_{k+1}(t))]\!]) \\
& \quad \textbf{else} \\
& \qquad \texttt{False}
\end{array}
$$

A variable pattern always matches an expression. A constant pattern (such as an integer literal) matches an expression if the value of the expression is the same as the constant. A constructor pattern matches an expression if the value of the expression is a constructed term with the correct tag and if each component subexpression matches the corresponding component subpattern.

Each $[\![\text{bind}(p,t)]\!]$ represents the following translation:

$$
\begin{array}{ll}
[\![\text{bind}(x,\; t)]\!] & \Rightarrow\; x\; \texttt{=}\; t \\
[\![\text{bind}(\text{CN}_0,t)]\!] & \Rightarrow\; \epsilon \\
[\![\text{bind}(\text{CN}_k(p_1,\ldots,p_k),t)]\!] & \Rightarrow\; [\![\text{bind}(p_1,\text{proj}_2(t))]\!]\; ; \\
& \qquad \vdots\; ; \\
& \qquad [\![\text{bind}(p_k,\text{proj}_{k+1}(t))]\!]
\end{array}
$$

A variable pattern yields a binding of the variable to the corresponding expression t. A constant pattern yields no binding (i.e., yields the empty statement). A constructor pattern yields a collection of simultaneous parallel bindings obtained by gathering the bindings yielded by considering each pattern component against the term $\text{proj}_j(t)$.

Note that all these translations depend only on the static structure of the patterns in the case expression. Also, the direct, naive translations given here are for illustrative purposes only; a real compiler would perform substantial optimizations on this basic idea. (For example, given an algebraic type with just one disjunct, such as pH's predefined 2-tuples, static type checking assures us that the tag never needs to be checked; in fact, therefore, the tag never even has to be stored in the constructed term.)

Arrays: Fast Indexed Data Structures

Folks, this is a glorious sight, what a splendid array of floats!

—TV commentator at a parade

Arrays are very important data structures in programming. An array is a mapping from *indexes* to *values*, with two additional properties: indexes are drawn from a finite, contiguous range of integers (or other type that has the notion of a finite enumerable contiguous range), and the values are homogeneous (i.e., all of the same type). These properties allow for efficient implementations, where the time to access an array element is constant (i.e., independent of the index value). In algorithmic terms, array access takes $O(1)$ time. An implementation can compute the memory address of an element directly from its index. This direct access to array elements also admits more parallelism, since accesses to the jth and kth elements, where $j \neq k$, are completely independent. Arrays are particularly important in scientific and technical computations (for many years, arrays were the *only* data structuring mechanism in the programming language Fortran, which has always been the predominant language for scientific and technical application programs).

Arrays do not add any fundamental expressive power. With sum and product types, polymorphism and recursive types, we already have a rich repertoire of tools for defining data structures. A mapping from indexes to values can be represented as a list of 2-tuples, with each 2-tuple containing an index and a value. Taking advantage of the fact that the indexes are drawn from a finite, contiguous range, we don't even need to keep the indexes in the list; we just need a list of values, with successive positions in the list representing successive indices. Using the technique of abstract data types described in Section 5.7, we could even hide all these representational details from clients who use arrays. However, with such a representation, accessing the jth element involves traversing the previous $j - 1$ cons cells; that is, access time is not constant—in algorithmic terms, access time is $O(n)$. Thus, the $O(1)$ access time of built-in arrays is the fundamental reason for their existence.

Arrays are a polymorphic type. We can have integer arrays, character arrays, arrays of arrays of floats, and so on. However, a particular array only has elements of a single type.

7.1   Arrays as Caches for Functions

Arrays can be regarded as a built-in abstract data type in *pH*. Simple one-dimensional integer-indexed arrays have the following abstract interface:

```
module ArrayI (ArrayI, mkArrayI, (!), bounds) where

infix  9  (!)

data ArrayI b

mkArrayI    ::    (Int,Int) -> (Int->b) -> (ArrayI b)
(!)         ::    (ArrayI b) -> Int -> b
bounds      ::    (ArrayI b) -> (Int,Int)
```

(The **module** and **infix** notations were discussed in Sections 5.7 and 2.9, respectively.) The module ArrayI exports the abstract type ArrayI to-

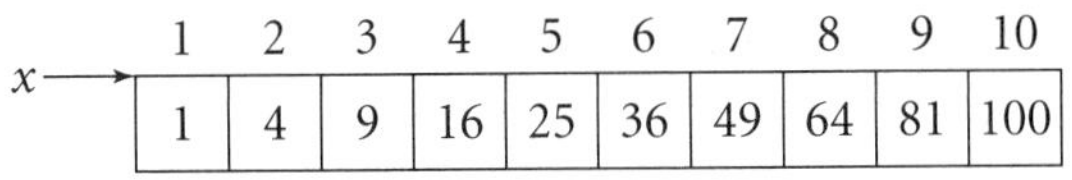

Figure 7.1   Result of `mkArrayI (1,10) sqr`.

gether with three functions `mkArrayI`, `(!)`, and `bounds`, the second of
which is an infix operator with precedence 9 (which is the highest available precedence level). The "`I`" suffix in some of these names indicates that
these are integer-indexed arrays; we shall see shortly that other index types
are also possible.

A useful way to think about an array is that it is a cache for a function
on integers, restricted to a contiguous subdomain of the function. The
endpoints of the contiguous subdomain are called the *index bounds* of the
array. For example, we can construct an array X with index bounds 1 to 10,
such that the jth element contains j^2, as follows:

    x = mkArrayI (1,10)   sqr

(Recall that `sqr` is the squaring function.) The array `x` can be visualized as
shown in Figure 7.1. We refer to `sqr` as the "filling" function because it is
used to specify what values are to be filled in the array elements.

We can access elements of the array by using "`!`", the infix array *subscripting* operator. For example, the expression

    x!4

represents the value of the fourth element and evaluates to 16. It is always
an error to attempt to select an element outside the index bounds of the
array. For example, the expression "`x!j`" for any $j < 1$ or $j > 10$ will raise
an error at run time (regardless of the fact that the filling function `sqr` is
perfectly well defined for such js).

Note that "`x!4`" has exactly the same value as "`sqr 4`"; selecting the jth
index of an array produces exactly the same value as applying the original
filling function to j. Thus, the main reason we use arrays at all, instead of
functions, is for efficiency. Selecting an element of an array is usually very
fast, whereas the computation performed by a function can be slow. Further, repeatedly selecting an array element does not cause the value to be

recomputed, whereas repeated application of a function will involve recomputation. It is for these reasons that we say that an array is a "cache" for a function; that is, it is a "memoization" of the function over a contiguous subdomain.[1]

In general the expression

```
mkArrayI   (l,u)   f
```

constructs an array whose indices are $l, l+1, \ldots, u$ and whose jth element contains the value of $f(j)$. Here, l and u may be arbitrary integer-valued expressions (so, the size of array may only be known dynamically). Normally, $l \leq u$, but if $l > u$, we simply get an empty array. The filling function f can be any function on integers, but its result does not have to be an integer. In other words, arrays can contain objects of any type. For example, suppose isPrime is a function that tests if an integer is prime. Then

```
mkArrayI   (2,10)   isPrime
```

produces an array of boolean values with True values at indices 2, 3, 5, and 7 and False everywhere else.

We can understand this more precisely by looking at types:

```
mkArrayI    ::    (Int,Int) -> (Int->b) -> (ArrayI b)
```

In other words, it takes two arguments. The first argument is a 2-tuple of integers (the index bounds). The second argument is an integer-to-something function (the filling function). The result is an array-of-somethings. A particular point to note is that arrays are homogeneous (i.e., all elements of an array must have the same type); one cannot build an array that contains both integers and booleans. Another point to note is that the *values* of the index bounds are not part of the type of the array. Thus, an array from 1 to 10 of strings has the same type as an array from 300 to 305 of strings: the type (ArrayI String).[2]

---

1. The term "memoization" (not "memorization"!) seems to be popular in the functional programming community to describe the trick of remembering a function's input-output behavior in a table, so that subsequent applications of the function can be accelerated by simply doing a table lookup instead [31].
2. In the language Pascal, the value of the index bounds are part of the type.

Exercise 7.1 Describe the arrays constructed by the following expressions, along with their types:

```
mkArrayI  (10,20)  (plus 10)

mkArrayI  (10,20)  plus

mkArrayI  (1,10)  (\ j -> 11 - j)
```

Exercise 7.2 Write a function that, given a value v, returns an array from 1 to 10 that contains v everywhere.

Since the values of the bounds of an array are not part of the type of an array, a function on arrays will not, in general, know the array bounds of an array given to it as an actual parameter. In order to confine selection to legal indices, pH provides a function by which one can query the index bounds of an array:

```
(l,u) = bounds x
```

The bounds function, when applied to an array, returns a 2-tuple containing its index bounds. Thus, in the statement above, the identifiers l and u will name these index bounds. For example, here is a function that sums up all the numbers in an array of floating-point numbers:

```
sumArray    :: ArrayI a -> Float
sumArray x = let
                  (l,u) = bounds x
                  s     = 0.0
             in
                  for j <- [l..u] do
                      next s = s + x!j
                  finally s
```

The type of bounds, as used here, is

```
bounds    ::    (ArrayI b) -> (Int,Int)
```

It takes an array with elements of any type and returns a 2-tuple of integers containing its lower and upper index bounds, respectively.

Let us now revisit the example we examined in Chapter 5. Suppose we want to move a shape S by a displacement d to a new shape S', as

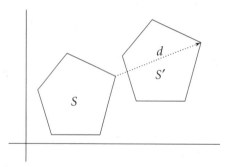

Figure 7.2 Moving a shape.

shown in Figure 7.2. In Chapter 5, we used 2-tuples to represent points on the xy-plane. Let us first generalize this so that we have points in some n-dimensional space. We will now represent a point as an array with indices from 1 to n, where the jth element is its coordinate in the jth dimension. For a two-dimensional space, we would use an array of two elements. Thus, instead of

```
(Float,Float)
```

a point now has type

```
(ArrayI Float)
```

To translate (i.e., move) a point, we can use the notion of vector addition (we use the term *vector* as a synonym for a one-dimensional array). We can think of a point p as representing a vector $\vec{p}$ from the origin to that point. A translation is specified by a vector $\vec{q}$ (i.e., it can be specified by a point q). To translate point p to p' by the vector specified by q, therefore, we simply perform the vector addition $\vec{p} + \vec{q}$, as depicted in Figure 7.3. Mathematically, to add two vectors, we simply add the coordinates pairwise. We can express this very simply in *pH:*

```
v_add p q = let
                f j = p!j + q!j
            in
                mkArrayI (bounds p) f
```

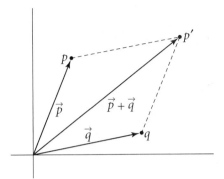

Figure 7.3 Vector addition.

That is, we make a new array with the same bounds as p, such that the jth element contains the sum of the jth elements of p and q. The type of the function is

```
v_add :: (ArrayI Float) -> (ArrayI Float) -> (ArrayI Float)
```

That is, it takes two arguments, each of which is an array of numbers and produces a result that is also an array of numbers.

Exercise 7.3   In v_add, we did not pay attention to the bounds of q, assuming instead that they were the same as the bounds of p. What would happen if the bounds were not the same?   ∎

Exercise 7.4   A scaling transformation in an n-dimensional space can also be represented as a vector. The vector $s_1 \ldots s_n$ specifies that a point with coordinates $x_1 \ldots x_n$ must move to the coordinates $s_1 \cdot x_1 \ldots s_n \cdot x_n$. Write a function v_scale s p that transforms a point p according to a scaling vector s.   ∎

We have successfully changed our representation of points from 2-tuples containing x- and y-coordinates to arrays of coordinates in n dimensions. Let us shift one level up and think about polygonal shapes, which are represented by the points that make up their vertices. In Chapter 5, we used 3-tuples of points to represent triangles, 4-tuples of points to represent quadrilaterals, and so on. There is a major problem with that representation: since a k-tuple and an l-tuple have different types when $k \neq l$, a function on triangles can never be used on other polygons such as lines, quadrilaterals, pentagons, and so on. Thus, we would have to write

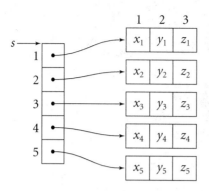

Figure 7.4 Representation of a pentagon in three-dimensional space.

separate, but very similar, functions for each k (e.g., a move_triangle, move_quadrilateral, move_pentagon, etc.). In this chapter, we will solve this problem by treating a k-sided shape as an array from 1 to k of points. Thus, whether a shape is a triangle, a quadrilateral, or whatever, it will always have the same type:

```
ArrayI (ArrayI Float)
```

that is, an array of points, each of which is itself an array of numbers. The pentagon shape in Figure 7.2 may be visualized as shown in Figure 7.4 (we assume the points are in a three-dimensional space).

With this representation, we can write a single function to transform an arbitrary shape s:

```
map f s = let
              fill j = f (s!j)
          in
              mkArrayI (bounds s) fill
```

This function creates a new array s' with the same index bounds as s such that the $s'!j = f s!j$. All we need to do is to supply a suitable point transformation function f. For example, to move a shape s by displacement d as shown in Figure 7.2, we can use the following function:

```
move_shape s d = map (v_add d) s
```

By currying, v_add d represents a function from points to points—given a point, it will add displacement d to it. This function is applied to each point in s, producing a new, displaced point. The resulting points are collected into the result array.

Exercise 7.5   What is the type of map as used in move_shape? What is its most general type?   ∎

Another very useful higher-order function on arrays is one that performs a *reduction* operation on its elements. For example, suppose we want to find the length of a k-dimensional vector x. Mathematically, this is given by

$$\sqrt{x_1^2 + x_2^2 + \cdots + x_k^2}$$

One part of this computation can be specified as follows:

```
map  sqr  x
```

which produces a new array containing the squares of each coordinate value. Next, we want to add them up, and this is a reduction operation. We can use the function sumArray that we saw earlier and repeat here for reference:

```
sumArray x = let
                (1,u) = bounds x
                s     = 0.0
            in
                for j <- [1..u] do
                    next s = s + x!j
                finally s
```

However, summing is only one of many possible reductions that we may wish to perform. For example, we may want to find the product of all the elements in an array. In sumArray, if we had used 1 instead of 0 in the block body and "*" instead of "+" in s+x!j, we would have computed this product. By now the reader should see where we are headed—we can abstract out these specific details into parameters in order to produce a more general reduction function:

```
foldl f s a = let
                (1,u) = bounds a
            in
                for j <- [1..u] do
                    next s = f s (a!j)
                finally s
```

Figure 7.5 The `foldl` array reduction operation.

Pictorially, this reduction can be visualized as shown in Figure 7.5. The reason for the letter "l" at the end of the name is because the function computes the term

```
f (...(f (f s (a!l)) (a!(l+1)))...) (a!u)
```

which is a left-associative form. Similarly, we could also define `foldr`, which computes the right-associative form. In fact, both these functions are part of the standard *pH* library, and they are just the array versions of list folding functions discussed in Section 6.3.1.

Now, each specific reduction may be written by supplying it suitable parameters:

```
sumArray  = foldl (+) 0.0

prodArray = foldl (*) 1.0

minArray  = foldl min maxfloat
```

(Here, `maxfloat` is the largest representable number and `min` computes the minimum of two numbers.)

We can now express our function to compute the length of a vector:

```
vector_length   :: ArrayI Float -> Float
vector_length x = sqrt (sumArray (map sqr x))
```

Exercise 7.6   The *inner product* of two vectors *U* and *V* is given by

$$\sum_{i=1}^{n} U_i \cdot V_i$$

Write a *pH* function that computes the inner product, using `sum_array` to perform the addition. ■

Exercise 7.7   Suppose we have an array a containing a permutation of its own indices:

a = | 3 | 1 | 4 | 2 |

and we want to compute an array b such that $b!(a!i) = i$:

$$b = \boxed{2\,|\,4\,|\,1\,|\,3}$$

Write a function that computes this for an array of n elements. (*Hint:* The filling function, when applied to i, would have to find that j such that $a!i=j$.) How many times does this function read an element of a (in terms of n)?   ∎

7.2   Arrays with Other Index Types: Overloading

So far, our arrays have been indexed by a contiguous range of integers. However, it often makes sense to have arrays indexed by other types that can also be regarded as having contiguous enumerable ranges. For example, if we were writing a function to compute the frequency of alphabetic letters in a text, it would make sense to have an array freq indexed by characters, with the value freq!'e' being an integer that describes how often the letter *e* was found. To describe such arrays, instead of ArrayI, there is a more general type constructor Array that takes two type parameters—the index type and the contents type. Thus, the array freq would have the following type:

```
freq    ::    Array  Char  Int
```

Another example: In Section 6.1.4 we introduced the following type:

```
data Day = Sun | Mon | Tue | Wed | Thu | Fri | Sat
```

Suppose we wanted to display a different message on each day of the week. We could store such messages in an array:

```
msgs    ::    Array  Day  String
```

with msgs!Thu being a string representing the message for Thursdays. We can now see that the integer-indexed arrays of the previous section are in fact a special case; the type ArrayI can be defined by a type synonym:

```
type  ArrayI b  =  Array Int b
```

What is an acceptable index type? The key feature of arrays is fast, constant-time access to array elements. Arrays are typically represented in a computer as a contiguous chunk of memory. When creating an array, given the lower and upper bounds, the system should be able to calculate how many elements there are in the array, from which it can calculate the size of the contiguous chunk of memory to be allocated for the array. When referring to an element of an array (during creation, or later, in an a!j expression), given an index the system should be able to decide whether the index is in bounds or not and to compute the position in the contiguous chunk of memory where that element lies, so that it can access it directly. These ideas are expressed by a type class Ix, the class of index types. Here is a minimal specification of this class (the *pH* standard library specification is a bit more complex):

```
class  Ix  a  where
     index   :: (a,a) -> a -> Int
     inRange :: (a,a) -> a -> Bool
```

The index function takes a lower-and-upper bound tuple and an index and returns an integer specifying the "position" of the index in the range of the bounds. Thus,

```
index  (1,10)     1    ⟶    0    (1 is item 0 in the range)
index  (1,10)    10    ⟶    9    (10 is item 9 in the range)
index  ('i','n')  'k'   ⟶    2    (k is item 2 in the range)
index  (Sun,Sat)  Wed   ⟶    3    (Wed is item 3 in the range)
```

The following expression can be used by the system during array allocation to find the number of items in the range (and, hence, the size of the array to be allocated):

```
1 + (index  (l,u)  u)
```

In summary, any type that is a member of the Ix class may be used as an index for an array. In Section 7.1, we said that arrays are a built-in abstract data type in *pH*, and we gave an abstract interface for integer-indexed arrays. We can now generalize that interface to arbitrary index types:

```
module Array (Array, mkArray, (!), bounds) where

infix  9  (!)

data (Ix a) => Array a b

mkArray   ::    (Ix a) => (a,a) -> (a->b) -> (Array a b)
(!)       ::    (Ix a) => (Array a b) -> a -> b
bounds    ::    (Ix a) => (Array a b) -> (a,a)
```

(The actual *pH* library specification is more detailed.) The type declaration specifies that for any type a in the class Ix, we have a corresponding type (Array a b) of arrays whose elements are indexed by values of type a and which contain values of type b. Similarly, the types of each of the three exported functions are now parameterized (polymorphic) over the index type a, which is restricted to those types belonging to the class Ix. For example,

```
mkArray  (Sun,Sat)  isWeekDay    :: Array Day Bool
```

produces an array with seven boolean elements indexed by Sun, Mon, . . . , Sat, containing False in the first and last elements and True everywhere else. The bounds function is also overloaded and has a more general type. For any index type a, given any array that uses that type for its index, bounds returns a 2-tuple of values of that type, representing the array's lower and upper bounds.

Exercise 7.8   Write down a definition for the function suggested in the first paragraph of Section 7.2:

```
charFreq  ::  String -> Array Char Int
```

that counts the number of occurrences of each alphabetic letter in the given string; that is, the result is an array indexed by alphabetic characters containing integer counts. Treat uppercase and lowercase alphabetic characters as equivalent. The string may contain nonalphabetic characters as well. Comment on the efficiency of your program. (The array here is called a *histogram*. We will examine histograms in more detail in Section 7.7.)   ■

Revisiting the sumArray function presented earlier, although we had started with the idea that it would have this type:

```
sumArray  ::  Array Int Float -> Float
```

we can now see that actually it has a much more general type:

```
sumArray  ::  (Ix a, Enum a, Fractional b) => Array a b -> b
```

The index type a must of course be in the Ix class of index types. Since we have an expression [1..u] in the function body where 1 and u are of type a, it must therefore also be in the Enum class—those types for which there is an enumeration function that can produce all the values in a range specified by two endpoints. Finally, since we use an initial value of 0.0 and the addition operation "+" to do the summation, the type b must be in the Fractional class, which includes the Float and Double types. In particular, this function will work on one-dimensional arrays, two-dimensional arrays, and so on.

One of the most useful and interesting benefits of overloading is that it allows us to use exactly the same array type and function notation for multidimensional arrays, which we discuss next.

7.3   Multidimensional Arrays

We have already seen that arrays may contain values of arbitrary type, including other arrays (a "shape" was an array containing "points," which were themselves arrays of floats). We could use this capability to represent a two-dimensional array (also called a matrix), for example. The matrix would be an array of rows, each row being an array of basic elements. To pick the (i, j)th element of a matrix m, therefore, we would write

```
(m!i)!j
```

This idea could be generalized so that an r-dimensional matrix is represented by an array, each of whose elements is an $(r - 1)$-dimensional matrix. Its type would be

$$\overbrace{\texttt{(ArrayI (ArrayI (\ldots (ArrayI } t\texttt{))))}}^{r}$$

Instead, in *pH* we can use r-tuples directly as an index type, to produce an array of the following type:

```
Array  (a₁,...,aᵣ)  b
```

We first look at some simple examples using 2-tuples of integers as indices. Consider:

```
m = let
        add (i,j) = i+j
    in
        mkArray  ((1,1),(5,10))  add
```

The two-dimensional matrix m can be visualized as in Figure 7.6. It is a matrix with index bounds 1 to 5 on its first index (i) and 1 to 10 on its

$$j$$

	1	2	3	4	5	6	7	8	9	10
1	2	3	4	5	6	7	8	9	10	11
2	3	4	5	6	7	8	9	10	11	12
3	4	5	6	7	8	9	10	11	12	13
4	5	6	7	8	9	10	11	12	13	14
5	6	7	8	9	10	11	12	13	14	15

(i labels the rows)

Figure 7.6 The result of `mkArray ((1,1),(5,10))` add.

second index (j). The (i, j)th location contains the value of add (i, j). To select an element of this matrix, say, the $(3, 6)$th element, we say

```
m!(3,6)
```

producing the value 9.

Another example: The *transpose* of an $m \times n$ matrix x is given by an $n \times m$ matrix x^T such that

$$x^T_{ij} = x_{ji}$$

Here it is, in *pH:*

```
transpose x = let
                ((l1,l2),(u1,u2)) = bounds x
                fill (i,j)        = x!(j,i)
              in
                mkArray  ((l2,l1),(u2,u1))  fill
```

Matrix multiplication is another extremely useful operation, particularly in computer graphics. Given an $m \times n$ matrix a and an $n \times l$ matrix b, their product $c = a \times b$ is an $m \times l$ matrix such that

$$c_{ij} = \sum_{k=1}^{n} a_{ik} \cdot b_{kj}$$

We can express this in *pH* as follows:

```
matmult a b =
    let
        ((1,1),(m,n))  = bounds a
        ((1,1),(n',l)) = bounds b
```

```
fill (i,j)      = let
                      s = 0.0
                  in
                      for k <- [1..n] do
                          next s = s + a!(i,k) * b!(k,j)
                      finally s
    in
        mkArray ((1,1),(m,1))  fill
```

The first two statements in the main block bind the relevant index bounds
m, n, and 1. Technically, we should also check that n = n′, but we have
omitted that for brevity. The fill function contains a loop that computes
the required sum.

The type of mkArray, as used in these examples, is

```
mkArray  :: ((Int,Int),(Int,Int)) ->
            ((Int,Int)->b) -> (Array (Int,Int) b)
```

The index bounds are again given by a 2-tuple (l, u) except that l and u are
now themselves 2-tuples. The filling function applies to an index, which
is itself a 2-tuple. It is easy to see that 2-tuples of integers are perfectly
good index types (i.e., members of the class Ix). Here are some definitions for the functions that are required for being a member of the Ix
class:

```
inRange ((li,lj),(ui,uj)) (i,j) = (li <= i)&& (i <= ui)&&
                                   (lj <= j)&& (j <= uj)

index   ((li,lj),(ui,uj)) (i,j) = let
                                      nJ = (uj - lj) + 1
                                  in
                                      (i-li)*nJ + j - lj
```

Looking at Figure 7.6, we see that this index function tells us which
slot an index corresponds to, if we count slots starting from 0 at the upper left, incrementing by one as we move right along the row, and then
wrapping around to the leftmost slot of the next row, and so on. Thus,
slots 0 through 9 refer to the topmost row, slots 10 through 19 to the
next row, and so on. For example, the index $(3, 6)$ corresponds to slot 25.
Thus, the implementation can lay out the conceptually two-dimensional
array into a linear chunk of memory and can directly compute the location
of any particular element, given its index. This particular linearization is
commonly known as *row-major* order. Another equally valid index function is

```
index    ((li,lj),(ui,uj))  (i,j)  = let
                                          nI = (ui – li) + 1
                                      in
                                          i – li + (j–lj)*nI
```

where slots are numbered 0 through 4 for the first column, 5 through 9 for the second column, and so on, with index $(3, 6)$ now occupying slot 27 in the linearization. This arrangement is commonly known as *column-major* order. The choice may differ from one *pH* implementation to another, but in *pH* it is impossible for the programmer to detect this choice.[3]

The most general type for arrays in pH is given by

data Ix a => Array a b

That is, for any type a in the Ix class, and for arbitrary types b, we have an Array type with indices of type a and contents of type b. If a is Int, we have traditional one-dimensional integer-indexed arrays; if a is (Int,Int), we have traditional two-dimensional integer-indexed arrays; and similarly for arrays of higher dimensions. It is perfectly possible to construct a three-dimensional array whose indices have the type (Int,Char,Day). The Array type is an interesting mix of overloading and polymorphism. It is completely polymorphic in b, the type of the array contents. It is overloaded across index types, but a particular index type may itself be polymorphic (such as 2-tuples). All the array functions (mkArray, (!), and bounds) are overloaded to work at any of the index types.

Let us look at the issue of efficiency more closely. If an r-dimensional array is represented as an r-deep nesting of one-dimensional arrays, then accessing a random element will take time proportional to r because the implementation will have to climb down to the target element, one level at a time. By implementing r-dimensional arrays directly, we can keep the access time constant, independent of r.[4] Now this may seem a minor advantage, since r is usually quite small. However, the difference is quite dramatic

---

3. In Fortran it is possible to detect the ordering, and column-major ordering is mandated by the language for portability reasons.

4. Actually, the cost of the arithmetic to calculate the offset for a particular index increases with r. However, in modern processors, arithmetic is cheap compared to memory references, and so we compare the relative costs of different array representations only in terms of the number of memory accesses for each element.

for the following reason. It is very rare that we are interested in just one random element of an array. Most applications involve a traversal of the whole array in some regular fashion. For example, in matrix multiplication, one array is traversed by row and the other is traversed by column. In various image-filtering codes, when we access any element we also examine its surrounding neighbors above, below, and to its left and right. In each such situation, it is usually a great advantage if, knowing the location of x!(i,j), we can efficiently and directly compute the locations of x!(i + k, j + 1) for some constants k and l. When this is possible, the compiler can generate extremely efficient code for accessing array elements during the traversal. This kind of optimization is difficult, if not impossible, to match when multidimensional arrays are represented as nested one-dimensional arrays.

Exercise 7.9 Modify your function charFreq from the earlier exercise that counted the frequencies of alphabetic characters in a string. Now, treat uppercase and lowercase alphabetic characters as distinct. Produce a two-dimensional array

```
data Case = Small | Cap

charFreq  ::  String -> Array (Case, Char) Int
```

such that (Small,'a') is a count of the lowercase as and (Cap,'a') is a count of the uppercase As, and so on.   ■

Exercise 7.10 Write a function that takes an $n \times n$ matrix A as input and returns a new $n \times n$ matrix B such that $B_{ij} = A_{ij}/A_{ii}$. In other words, each row i is scaled by the diagonal element in that row so that the resulting array diagonal elements are all unit-valued (1.0).   ■

Now we will consider the pragmatics of multidimensional arrays, and in particular, we will look at inlining and index names.

In an image-processing application, we may apply a filter function to a pixel array:

```
image_filter (x!(i,j))
             (x!(i-1,j))
             (x!(i+1,j))
             (x!(i,j-1))
             (x!(i,j+1))
```

A more readable rendition would be

```
image_filter (x!(i,j))
             (x!(above (i,j)))
             (x!(below (i,j)))
             (x!(left  (i,j)))
             (x!(right (i,j)))
```

with the following associated functions:

```
above (i,j) = (i-1,j)
below (i,j) = (i+1,j)
left  (i,j) = (i,j-1)
right (i,j) = (i,j+1)
```

However, despite the greater readability of this rendition, a performance-conscious programmer may avoid it because the overhead of a function call for each array-indexing operation is likely to be intolerable. Using the technique introduced in Section 2.10, the programmer can keep the readability and avoid the function call overhead by specifying that these functions should be expanded inline by the compiler:

```
{-# inline above, below, left, right #-}
```

Exercise 7.11   Extend the definition of the function above so that if we are in the top row of the matrix, it "wraps around" to the bottom row of the matrix.   ■

7.4   Nonstrictness of Arrays

Suppose we want to construct the $n \times n$ matrix x shown in Figure 7.7 containing 1s on its top and left borders and, for each interior point, the sum of its upper and left neighbors. In other words, the contents of the matrix are specified by a two-dimensional recurrence:

$$x[1, j] = 1 \qquad\qquad\qquad 1 \le j \le n$$
$$x[i, 1] = 1 \qquad\qquad\qquad 1 \le i \le n$$
$$x[i, j] = x[i, j - 1] + x[i - 1, j] \qquad 2 \le i \le n, 2 \le j \le n$$

This structure is known as Pascal's Triangle after the French mathematician Blaise Pascal (1623–1662) and is a way of generating binomial coefficients. As suggested in the figure, if we compute as many elements as we can

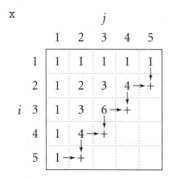

Figure 7.7   A matrix with a two-dimensional recurrence.

in parallel, the computation would sweep across the matrix in a diagonal "wave." We can express this in *pH* as follows:

```
pascal_triangle n =
          let
              fill (1,j) = 1
              fill (i,1) = 1
              fill (i,j) = x!(i,j-1) + x!(i-1,j)

              x           = mkArray ((1,1),(n,n))  fill
          in
              x
```

As expected, the recurrence is expressed in *pH* using recursion. The definition of the matrix x uses the function fill, while the definition of fill uses the matrix x. Let us pause to examine the implications of this. It is clear that in general mkArray must allocate storage for a matrix and must set up n^2 "filling" computations responsible for filling in the elements. However, in this program, most of the filling computations (all the interior ones) need to access the matrix itself, that is, the *result* of mkArray. Thus:

- We must be able to refer to a matrix (in general, any data structure) independently of whether its elements have been defined or not.
- mkArray must be able to return such a reference to the matrix as its result even though its n^2 subordinate computations are still at work filling in the elements.

♦ We have not specified that the n^2 filling computations initiated by mkArray should be scheduled in any particular order. Therefore, there must be some synchronization mechanism by which the computation for the (i, j)th element is automatically blocked (deferred) if it tries to read one of its neighbors before it has been filled in.

This kind of behavior of functions and data structures is called *non-strict* behavior. We have already seen nonstrict behavior in functions and algebraic types. In particular, the rewrite rules for functions in Chapter 2 showed how we can begin reducing the body of a function even before we know its argument values and, in fact, even return a value while some subcomputation of the function body is still in progress. It is this kind of behavior that allows mkArray to return a reference to the matrix while its filling computations are still at work.

Exercise 7.12 One way to compute the GCD (greatest common divisor) of two integers a and b is to use the following rule:

$$\begin{aligned}
\text{gcd } a\ b &= a & a &= b \\
\text{gcd } a\ b &= \text{gcd } (a - b)\ b & a &> b \\
\text{gcd } a\ b &= \text{gcd } a\ (b - a) & a &< b
\end{aligned}$$

Write a function that computes a *table* of GCDs in a 100×100 array (i.e., the (i, j)th element should contain gcd $i\ j$). The function should compute the GCD of any pair of integers exactly once. ∎

Arrays in *pH* are actually implemented using I-structure arrays, which are described in Chapter 9. (Arrays and I-structure arrays are different types and cannot be used interchangeably; but it is perfectly OK, after static type checking, to implement functional arrays in terms of I-structure arrays.) The rewrite rules for I-structure arrays will make it clear how nonstrictness works for arrays.

7.5 Generalizing Arrays Using Functions

We began this chapter by observing that an array can be viewed as a cache for a function. We will now develop this connection further to demonstrate the power of functional programming.

7.5.1   Arrays versus Functions

Earlier, we described matrix multiplication as follows. Given an $m \times n$ matrix A and an $n \times l$ matrix B, their product $C = A \times B$ is an $m \times l$ matrix such that

$$C_{ij} = \sum_{k=1}^{n} A_{ik} \cdot B_{kj}$$

A more elegant way of saying this is

$$C_{ij} = row_i(A) \cdot col_j(B)$$

That is, the *inner product* of the two vectors that are the ith row of A with the jth column of B.

We could express this in *pH* as follows. Here are the two functions to select rows and columns from a matrix:

```
row i x = let
             ((li,lj),(ui,uj)) = bounds x
             fill k            = x!(i,k)
          in
             mkArray  (lj,uj)  fill

col j x = let
             ((li,lj),(ui,uj)) = bounds x
             fill k            = x!(k,j)
          in
             mkArray  (li,ui)  fill
```

Note that each function returns a one-dimensional array. Here is a function to compute the inner product of two one-dimensional arrays with dimensions (k1,k2):

```
ip ar bc k1 k2 = let
                    s = 0.0
                 in
                    for k <- [k1..k2] do
                       next s = s + ar!k * bc!k
                    finally s
```

Finally, we can define matrix multiplication:

```
matmult a b = let
                 ((1,1),(m,n)) = bounds a
```

```
            ((1,1),(_,1)) = bounds b
            fill (i,j)    = ip (row i a) (col j b) 1 n
     in
       mkArray  ((1,1),(m,1))  fill
```

Unfortunately, this is not a very efficient program, because each use of row or column allocates a new vector and copies values into it from the original matrix.

Exercise 7.13   How much array storage does the above matmult program use? Assume that each location of an array counts as one cell. ∎

The problem is that the filling functions for row and column are trivial—they simply copy a value, doing no computation on it at all. We think of an array as a memoization of a function for the sake of efficiency, but these functions are not worth memoizing. With this observation, here is an alternative way of writing the row and column selectors:

```
row i x k = x!(i,k)

col j x k = x!(k,j)
```

We now have to modify the inner product program so that array elements are selected using function application rather than the usual array indexing syntax:

```
ip ar bc k1 k2 = let
                     s = 0.0
                 in
                     for k <- [k1..k2] do
                         next s = s + (ar k)*(bc k)
                     finally s
```

Here, as before, ar and bc represent a row and a column, respectively, obtained by the curried applications "row i a" and "col j b" in matmult. Each is thus a function of k, which is how they are used in ip. This program is much more efficient in terms of the array storage used!

Thus, while we began studying arrays as a more efficient way of representing functions, this example shows that sometimes the converse is true—functions may be more efficient than arrays.

7.5.2   Generalized Arrays

We can get the best of both worlds by generalizing our notion of arrays
so that we can choose exactly when we wish to memoize for efficiency.
Abstractly, the main features of a one-dimensional array are the following
(the generalization to multidimensional arrays is obvious):

- It has a selection operation defined on integers (the generalization to
  other index types is also obvious). When applied to an array and an
  integer, it returns the value associated with that integer. We can think
  of the notation a!i as syntactic sugar for select a i, where select
  is the selection function.
- It has index bounds; that is, it is an error to apply it to an integer
  outside these bounds. Moreover, one can query the array for these
  bounds.

Accordingly, we can pick the representation of a *generalized vector* (GV)
to have this type:

```
data GV b = GV (Int,Int) (Int->b)
```

that is, a pair, whose first component is a pair of integers (the index bounds)
and whose second component is a function from integers to something.
Then, we can define a selection function on GVs:

```
gv_sel              :: GV b -> Int -> b
gv_sel (GV (l,u) f) i =
              if (i < l) || (u < i) then error "Out of bounds"
              else f i
```

That is, we extract the index bounds and the function from the GV, check
the index against the bounds, and then apply the function to the index to
return the value. We note in passing that for technical reasons the type
of the error value is "compatible" with all types; thus any expression can
return an error value without violating the type discipline.

For example, here is a function that converts an ordinary vector into
a GV:

```
to_GV    :: Array Int b -> GV b
to_GV v  = let
                sel i = v!i
           in
                GV (bounds v) sel
```

Exercise 7.14   Write a function from_GV gv that converts a generalized vector back into an ordinary vector. ∎

Similarly, we can define a generalized two-dimensional matrix:

```
data GM b = GM  ((Int,Int),(Int,Int))  ((Int,Int) -> b)
```

Now, let us look at a function to project a row from a GM into a GV:

```
gm_row       :: Int -> GM b -> GV b
gm_row i gm =
    let
        GM ((i1,j1),(i2,j2)) m_sel = gm
        v_sel j                    = m_sel (i,j)
    in
        if (i < i1) || (i2 < i) then error "Out of bounds"
        else
            GV (j1,j2) v_sel
```

Exercise 7.15   Write a function similar to gm_row to project a column from a GM into a GV. ∎

Exercise 7.16   Write a function that projects the diagonal of an $n \times n$ GM into a GV. ∎

Exercise 7.17   Write a function that projects an $n \times n$ GM into an $(n-1) \times (n-1)$ GM′ such that GM′ is missing the first row and first column of GM. ∎

Let us continue limbering up with a function that computes the vector sum of two GVs:

```
gv_add           :: GV Float -> GV Float -> GV Float
gv_add gv1 gv2 = let
                     GV b  sel1 = gv1
                     GV b' sel2 = gv2
                     sel3 k     = (sel1 k) + (sel2 k)
                 in
                     GV b sel3
```

(We ought to check that $b = b'$, but we omit this for brevity.)

As a further warmup towards matrix multiplication, we can write an inner product function on GVs:

```
gv_ip           :: GV Float -> GV Float -> Float
gv_ip gv1 gv2 = let
                    GV (k1,k2)   sel1 = gv1
                    GV (k1',k2') sel2 = gv2
```

```
        s                           = 0.0
    in
        for k <- [k1..k2] do
            next s = s + (sel1 k)*(sel2 k)
        finally s
```

Our adrenaline now pumping, we attempt our matrix multiplication program on generalized matrices:

```
gm_matmult              :: GM Float -> GM Float -> GM Float
gm_matmult gm1 gm2 =
        let
            GM ((1,1),(m,n))  sel1 = gm1
            GM ((1,1),(n',1)) sel2 = gm2
            sel3 (i,j)             = gv_ip (gm_row i gm1)
                                          (gm_col j gm2)
        in
            GM ((1,1),(m,1)) sel3
```

Unfortunately, this is not enough, because if we set

```
c = gm_matmult a b
```

then each time we select the (i, j)th element of c, we will be recomputing the inner product of the ith row of A and the jth column of B. Thus, what we need is a function that is semantically the identity function on GMs; that is, it takes a GM and returns "the same" GM, except that it memoizes it in an ordinary matrix on the way:

```
gm_memoize     :: GM b -> GM b
gm_memoize gm = let
                    GM b sel   = gm
                    x          = mkArray b sel
                    sel' (i,j) = x!(i,j)
                in
                    GM b sel'
```

That is, the returned gm has the same bounds as the input gm, and the selection function sel' returns the same result as sel. However, sel' simply looks up its result in x, whereas sel may be very expensive.

Exercise 7.18   Write down the function gv_memoize gv that memoizes a generalized vector.

Finally, we can triumphantly write our matrix multiplication program so that it is also efficient, by changing only the last line so that it memoizes the result matrix:

```
gm_matmult            :: GM Float -> GM Float -> GM Float
gm_matmult gm1 gm2 =
    let
       GM ((1,1),(m,n))  sel1 = gm1
       GM ((1,1),(n',1)) sel2 = gm2
       sel3 (i,j)             = gv_ip (gm_row i gm1)
                                      (gm_col j gm2)
    in
       gm_memoize (GM ((1,1),(m,1)) sel3)
```

To sum up: We can write very elegant array manipulation programs using generalized arrays. We use memoization functions to "freeze" the values of a matrix whenever we produce one whose elements are likely to be accessed repeatedly.

Exercise 7.19   The GV and GM types have integer indices. Generalize GV to have an index from any type in the Ix class, and generalize GM to have a 2-tuple index type (a,b), where a and b are any types in the Ix class. Generalize all the functions in this section to work on these new types.   ∎

7.6   Array Comprehensions

While mkArray is an extremely powerful primitive, it has a limitation that makes its use inefficient in some applications. Let us look again at the Pascal_triangle function of Section 7.4. There, the filling function for mkArray was

```
fill (i,1) = 1
fill (1,j) = 1
fill (i,j) = m!(i,j-1) + m!(i-1,j)
```

Conceptually, there are three filling functions, corresponding to the three clauses, each appropriate for a particular region of the array. However, since we can only supply a single filling function for the entire array, we have to package them up into a single function that contains a conditional that tests, at each index, which region that index belongs to and then computes the appropriate filling expression for that region (here, the conditional test is in the pattern matching). This test is performed n^2 times (i.e., once for each location of the array).

Another example: Suppose we wanted to create an *identity* matrix—an $n \times n$ matrix that contains 1s on the main diagonal and 0s everywhere else. We could write

```
let
    fill (i,j) = if i==j then 1.0 else 0.0
in
    mkArray ((1,1),(n,n))  fill
```

Again, the conditional expression would be evaluated n^2 times, picking one of two filling expressions for each matrix element.

Both these examples have the following structure: the matrix is divided into several *regions*, each of which needs a different method to fill its elements. When using mkArray, we have to use a conditional expression to test which region we are in.

pH provides another function for constructing arrays based on list comprehensions. The array function takes two arguments: the index bounds of the desired array and an *association list* of index-and-value pairs specifying the contents of the array. To construct an identity matrix we would say

```
array ((1,1),(n,n))
       (  [ ((i,j), 0.0) | i <- [1..n-1], j <- [i+1..n] ]
       ++ [ ((i,j), 0.0) | i <- [2..n], j <- [1..(i-1)] ]
       ++ [ ((i,i), 1.0) | i <- [1..n] ] )
```

The three list comprehensions specify the values above, below, and on the diagonal, respectively.

This idiom is called an *array comprehension*. A *pH* compiler can usually compile array comprehensions into efficient code that directly constructs the resulting array without creating any of the lists implied by the list comprehensions and without any of the region-testing conditionals that we just discussed.

Here is the Pascal_triangle function written using an array comprehension:

```
pascal_triangle n =
    let
        m = array ((1,1),(n,n))
                   (  [((1,1), 1)]
                   ++ [((1,j),1)                    | j <- [2..n] ]
```

```
        ++  [((i,1),1)                    | i <- [2..n] ]
        ++  [((i,j), m!(i,j-1)
                        + m!(i-1,j)) | i <- [2..n],
                                       j <- [2..n] ] )
    in
        m
```

Here, we are using recursion again to specify the recurrence.

The ability to have computed indices in the list comprehensions is very useful. For example, suppose we had an array a that contained a permutation of its indices:

a = 3 1 4 2

and we wanted to compute an array b such that b!(a!i) = i:

b = 2 4 1 3

This transformation is sometimes called an *inverse permutation* because, if applied again to b, we would get back the array a. This can be expressed quite trivially and efficiently using an array comprehension:

```
inv_perm a n = array (1,n)
                 [ (a!i, i) | i <- [1..n] ]
```

Suppose we tried to write this function using only mkArray. What would the filling function be? When applied to an i, it would have to find that j such that a!i=j and return that j. This would involve a linear search of the array:

```
inv_perm a n = let
                 fill i = let
                            find j = if a!j == i then j
                                     else find (j+1)
                          in
                            find 1
               in
                 mkArray (1,n)  fill
```

Clearly this is a much more inefficient program because find is called $O(n^2)$ times.

The last example also shows that programs written using array comprehensions can sometimes be much clearer and more perspicuous than programs using mkArray. However, array comprehensions raise the possibility of a new kind of run-time error that was not possible with mkArray.

In particular, a run-time error will be raised if the region specifiers do not specify disjoint regions. If two region specifiers overlap, then it means that we have two separate specifications for the contents of some array element, and this is not permitted. This is a run-time error because, in general, it is not possible for a compiler to check for disjointness a priori.

In this respect, *pH* departs from Haskell semantics (this is one of the few places where the purely functional part of *pH* is not identical to Haskell). In Haskell array comprehensions, if an index is specified more than once, that element is considered to be in error, and it has no effect on other elements. If the program never attempts to read an erroneous element, it has no effect on the program. Further, if any index is out of bounds, the entire array (all elements) is considered to be in error. Again, if the program never attempts to read an erroneous element, it has no effect on the program. One implication of these semantics is that the `array` function is strict in all the index expressions in the array comprehension; it must evaluate and check all indices before returning the array.

pH does not impose this level of strictness. The array comprehension can return an array value as soon as it is allocated, and this only requires the evaluation of the bounds expression. The index and content expressions can be evaluated concurrently with any consumers of the array. Duplicate index values and out-of-bounds indices have the same effect—the entire program is considered to be in error.[5]

We will describe the above semantics of array comprehensions in more detail in Chapter 9, where we will see that array comprehensions are easy to understand in terms of a translation to I-structure arrays.

7.7   Accumulators

There is a class of array computations, which we call *accumulations*, that are inefficient both with `mkArray` and with array comprehensions. Consider the following problem: We are given the grades of students in a class of 200.

---

5. When Haskell was designed, it was expected that most implementations would use lazy evaluation. In such an implementation, an array comprehension must initialize all array slots with "closures" corresponding to their values before the array is returned. This in turn implies evaluation of all index expressions before the array is returned, and hence no strictness is lost by imposing Haskell's index error semantics. In *pH*, on the other hand, we use parallel evaluation instead of lazy evaluation, for which *pH*'s index error semantics makes more sense.

Each grade is an A, B, C, D, or F. The grades are stored in an array grades of size 200. We wish to build a histogram of the grades—an array h of size 5 such that h!A is the number of As, h!B is the number of Bs, and so on.

Here is an attempted solution:

```
data Grade = A | B | C | D | F
let
    count g grades = let
                        n = 0
                     in
                        for j <- [1..200] do
                            next n = if grades!j == g then n + 1
                                     else n
                        finally n
in
    array (A,F)
        [ (g, count g grades) | g <- [A..F] ]
```

The program makes five traversals over the grades array to count the number of As, the number of Bs, and so on, and this is clearly not very efficient. In many programs the situation is worse because both the size of the histogram array and the number of samples is much larger.

Suppose we wished to traverse the grades array only once. Here is another attempt:

```
let
    incr h g = array (A,F)
                    [ (j, if g == j   then
                              (h!j)+1
                          else
                              (h!j) ) | j <- [A..F] ]
    h         = array (A,F)
                    [ (j, 0) | j <- [A..F] ]
in
    for i <- [1..200] do
        next h = incr h grades[i]
    finally h
```

This program starts with a histogram initialized to zero in all five slots. It traverses grades once; at each step, it "increments" the appropriate slot, where incrementing means building a new array that differs from the old one only in the incremented slot. This is an enormous cost—200 copies of the histogram!

Another example of a histogram-like computation is building a hash table. Again, numerous samples are accumulated into a limited number of buckets.

To express such computations efficiently, *pH* provides another array construction primitive called `accumArray`. Our histogram program would be written

```
accumArray (+) 0 (A,F)
           [ (grades!i, 1) | i <- [1..200] ]
```

The first two arguments specify a reduction function and an initial value, respectively, for each slot of the array. The fourth and fifth arguments are just like the arguments for the `array` constructor: the bounds and an association list of index-and-value pairs. This first creates an array x with bounds (A,F) containing the initial value 0 everywhere. Then, for each index-and-value pair (j, v) in the list comprehension, it is accumulated into the array by performing the following replacement:

$$x!j \leftarrow x!j + v$$

The reader should convince himself that the accumulations can be performed in parallel—the final histogram produced does not depend on the order of accumulations.

Unlike array comprehensions, accumulators are *strict* expressions—no array is returned until all the accumulation operations have completed. This is because of determinacy; if we returned the array earlier, a consumer may read a slot of the array in some intermediate state, before all the accumulations on that slot have been completed. By making it strict, consumers can only see the final value of the accumulation.

There is still a determinacy loophole here, since we allow the programmer to specify any two-argument function "f" for the accumulation. If the function does not have the following property:

```
f (f x y) z = f (f x z) y
```

the accumulation will not be deterministic, since the *order* in which the accumulations at a particular index are done is not specified.

7.8   Parallel Blocked Matrix Multiplication

We have already seen several *pH* versions of matrix multiplication. In Section 1.7.1 we saw one using array comprehensions; in Section 7.3 we saw one using mkArray; and in Section 7.5 we saw one using generalized arrays. We repeat the array comprehension version here for reference:

```
matmult a b =
    array ((1,1), (n,n))
          [ ((i,j), ip a i b j) | i <- [1..n], j <- [1..n] ]

-- Inner product of the ith row with the jth column
ip a i b j =
    let
        s = a!(i,1) * b!(1,j)
    in
        for k <- [2..n] do
            next s = s + a!(i,k) * b!(k,j)
        finally s
```

All these versions implement the same algorithm, illustrated in Figure 1.1, namely, n^2 inner products that can all be computed in parallel.

In Section 1.9, we observed that architectural constraints can affect how we design algorithms. Most modern machines have a deep *memory hierarchy*. Even a uniprocessor has several levels of caches and paged virtual memory. In a multiprocessor, multicomputer, or cluster, main memory may also be partitioned so that some memory is "local" to a processor while the rest of memory is "remote," with a local access often an order of magnitude faster than a remote access.

Our matrix multiplication program above, although parallel, does not take into account *locality* issues arising from memory hierarchies. In this section, we examine *blocked* matrix multiplication, which can have substantially higher performance because it is better matched to deep memory hierarchies. (We discussed related algorithms in Chapter 1 in the context of HPF, High Performance Fortran, and message-passing.) In a sense this development goes against the goal of transparent, high-level parallel programming, but it is a useful exercise for several reasons. First, the code that we show is within the capability of automatic compiler optimization, and it is instructive to see what such optimizations do. Second, it is useful to see just how far one can go within *pH* itself to make a program more machine-friendly.

Suppose we are multiplying $n \times n$ matrices a and b, producing the result in c. Please refer to Figure 7.8(a). To compute $c_{i,j}$, the inner-product computation traverses, simultaneously, row $a_{i,*}$ from left to right and column $b_{*,j}$ from top to bottom (varying k). In a sequential implementation,

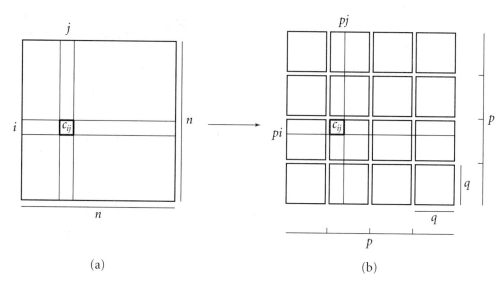

Figure 7.8 (a) A matrix and (b) its "blocked" view.

the elements of c are typically computed one after another, say left to right within each row and row by row from top to bottom. So, when we compute the next element $c_{i,\,j+1}$, we traverse row $a_{i,*}$ again from left to right and the next column $b_{*,\,j+1}$ from top to bottom. Later, in the next row, when we compute $c_{i+1,\,j}$, we traverse row $a_{i+1,*}$ from left to right and again traverse column $b_{*,\,j}$ from top to bottom.

Thus, between successive accesses to $a_{i,1}$, we traverse the rest of the entire row $a_{i,*}$. Between successive accesses to $b_{1,\,j}$, we traverse the rest of the b matrix in its entirety. Especially if the matrices are large, this lack of *temporal locality* is likely to result in these elements being displaced from "fast, near" memory (such as a cache) before they are reused. Successive accesses to each element, therefore, are likely to incur the full cost of fetching them from "remote, slow" memory. In other words, the access patterns of this program are not memory hierarchy friendly.

There are some observations about matrices and matrix multiplication that we can exploit to solve this problem. The first observation is that the definition of matrix multiplication is not limited to flat matrices of floating-point numbers. Looking at the code above, the only things indicating that the contents of the matrix are floating-point numbers are the "+" and "*" in the inner-product function (ip). In fact, the definition for matrix multiplication is valid for contents of any type that has meaningful addition and multiplication operations, not just floating-point numbers. In particular, the contents may themselves be matrices, provided that we interpret "+" and "*" as matrix addition and multiplication, respectively. This suggests the following recursive characterization: an h-deep matrix contains $(h - 1)$-deep matrices, and so on, with 0-deep matrices defined as being ordinary floating-point numbers. The code for matrix multiplication of h-deep matrices uses matrix addition and multiplication of $(h - 1)$-deep matrices, which, in turn, uses matrix addition and multiplication of $(h - 2)$-deep matrices, and so on. Eventually, we bottom out at 0-deep matrices, where we use ordinary floating-point addition and multiplication.

Using the power of overloading, we can fold all these levels into a single specification:

```
class Matclass a where
    ma    ::    a -> a -> a
    mm    ::    a -> a -> a
```

The members of the class Matclass will be floating-point numbers (0-deep matrices), 1-deep matrices, 2-deep matrices, and so on. We will use the functions ma and mm uniformly to add or multiply, respectively, at every type in this class.

Since floating-point numbers are 0-level matrices, we can define

```
instance Matclass Float where
    ma    =    (+)
    mm    =    (*)
```

For higher-level matrices, we define a new type and also make it an instance of Matclass:

```
data   Mat b = Mat (Array (Int,Int) b)

instance Matclass a => Matclass (Mat a) where
    ma    = madd
    mm    = mmult
```

where the functions madd and mmult, to be defined, deal with addition and mulitiplication at higher levels. Note the recursion: It says that if a is a type in Matclass, then (Mat a) is also in Matclass. Thus, Float, (Mat Float), (Mat (Mat Float)), and so on are all in Matclass.

Let us define the easier addition function for Mat first:

```
madd :: (Matclass b) => (Mat b) -> (Mat b) -> (Mat b)
madd (Mat a) (Mat b) =
```

```
let
    ((1,1),(n,n')) = bounds a
in
    Mat (array ((1,1),(n,n))
            [ ((i,j),
                (a!(i,j)) 'ma' (b!(i,j))) | i <- [1..n],
                                        j <- [1..n] ])
```

The (Matclass b) context, together with the use of ma to add components, overloads this addition function to work at all levels. Similarly, we can implement the multiplication function:

```
mmult :: (Matclass b) => Mat b -> Mat b -> Mat b
mmult (Mat a) (Mat b) =
    let
        ((1,1),(n,n')) = bounds a
    in
        Mat (array ((1,1),(n,n))
                [ ((i,j),
                    ip (Mat a) i (Mat b) j) | i <- [1..n],
                                            j <- [1..n] ])

ip :: (Matclass b) => Mat b -> Int -> Mat b -> Int -> b
ip (Mat a) i (Mat b) j =
    let
        ((1,1),(n,n')) = bounds a
        s              = ((a!(i,1)) 'mm' (b!(1,j)))
    in
        for k <- [2..n] do
            next s = (s 'ma' ((a!(i,k)) 'mm' (b!(k,j))))
        finally s
```

Now, given any h-level matrices a and b, for any h, we can multiply them using the expression:

```
a 'mm' b
```

Returning now to our goal of making matrix multiplication more suited to the memory hierarchies of modern computers, we make a second observation. Please refer to Figure 7.8(b). Suppose we view an $n \times n$ matrix of floating-point numbers as a two-level hierarchy. At the outer level it is a $p \times p$ matrix of blocks, and at the inner level each block is a $q \times q$ matrix of floating-point numbers (so, $pq = n$). Now, suppose we apply our hierarchical matrix multiplication to two such matrices. A little algebra will show that each element $c_{i,j}$ receives exactly the same value, whether we use the flat model or the hierarchical model (we leave this as an exercise to the reader). With this observation, we can see how to improve our matrix multiplication of two flat one-level matrices *a* and *b*: we convert them into two-level matrices, multiply them, and convert the resulting two-level matrix back into a flat one-level matrix. We call the one- to two-level conversion *blocking* and the reverse process *unblocking*. Here are two functions for this purpose:

```
block (Mat a) =
    Mat (array ((1,1),(p,p))
             [ ((pi,pj), mkblk a pi pj) | pi <- [1..p],
                                          pj <- [1..p] ])

mkblk a pi pj =
    Mat (array ((1,1),(q,q))
             [ ((qi,qj),
                a!((pi-1)*q+qi,(pj-1)*q+qj)) | qi <- [1..q],
                                               qj <- [1..q] ])

unblock (Mat a) =
    Mat (array ((1,1),(n,n))
             [ ((i,j),
                blk!(qi,qj)) | pi <- [1..p],
                               pj <- [1..p],
                               let Mat blk = a!(pi,pj),
                               qi <- [1..q],
                               qj <- [1..q],
                               let i = (pi-1)*q+qi,
                               let j = (pj-1)*q+qj
             ] )
```

Now, our flat matrix multiplication can be expressed as follows:

```
flatmm a b = unblock ((block a) 'mm' (block b))
```

The net result is that when computing the block that contains $c_{i,j}$, we perform a number of accesses to the block that contains $a_{i,1}$ and the block that contains $b_{1,j}$, thereby improving temporal locality of accesses to spatially proximate elements. Of course the exact choice of *p* (and therefore $q = n/p$) will depend on the architectural details of the machine on which the program is run.

Exercise 7.20 The development above takes a two-level view of a matrix—a matrix of blocks, where a block is a matrix of primitive elements (e.g., floating-point numbers). Instead, it is possible to think of it as a recursive decomposition:

mm: to multiply two $n \times n$ blocks,
    if n is below some threshold,
    then just do a simple matrix multiplication
    else
        treat it as a 2×2 matrix of $n/2 \times n/2$ blocks
        and do a blockwise matrix multiplication by recursively
            calling *mm*

Write the *pH* code that implements this algorithm.   ■

Our matrix multiplication program is still problematic. Although better suited to memory hierarchies, it introduces new inefficiencies. At the outer level we do p^2 inner products. Each of these performs p multiplications and additions of $q \times q$ blocks, and each of these operations allocates a q^2 array. Further, the functions `unblock` and `block` allocate more arrays and merely copy floating-point numbers. The original flat matrix multiplication, although poor in memory locality behavior, allocated no extra storage. It merely allocated the result matrix and directly computed each element of the result.

Is it possible to create a blocked multiplication that avoids all this extra storage allocation? At some cost in the clarity of the code, we can avoid blocking the input matrices and just use the original flat matrices. (This will involve carrying around extra indices for the current block and the index within the block and doing a suitable index calculation to fetch each component directly from the original *a* or *b* matrix.) Unfortunately, there is no way around creating a blocked result *c* matrix and then finally unblocking it. The problem is that for array comprehensions and `mkArray` we have an element-centric specification of the array; that is, for each $c_{i,j}$ we specify a single expression that represents its value. This structure matches the mathematical definition of matrix multiplication well. In a blocked matrix multiplication, on the other hand, we take a block-centric view, with the result that the computation of any single element $c_{i,j}$ is spread across multiple expressions. This does not match the structure of `mkArray` or array comprehensions, thereby forcing us to express it with several extra structures (blocks) to hold intermediate results.

Alternatively, we can observe that the computation of any particular $c_{i,j}$ is, ultimately, the sum of several floating-point products, and it does not matter in what order these values are summed. This is exactly the structure that is addressed by `accumArray` that was discussed in Section 7.7. Thus, we can also express our blocked matrix multiplication as follows:

```
matmult a b =
    accumArray (+)
              0.0
              ((1,1),(n,n))
              [ ((i,j), a!(i,k)*b!(k,j))
                 | -- iterate over blocks
                   pi <- [1..p],
                   pj <- [1..p],
                   pk <- [1..p],
                        -- iterate within blocks
                        qi <- [1..q], let i = (pi-1)*q + qi,
                        qj <- [1..q], let j = (pj-1)*q + qj,
                        qk <- [1..q], let k = (pk-1)*q + qk ]
```

This is a reasonably simple and straightforward specification, not much more complex than our original program. In any case, we emphasize again that modern compilers are capable of taking the original, simple program and producing the blocked version automatically, so that the extra complexity of blocking is not something the programmer need worry about. The purpose of this section has been to illustrate the issues involved in blocking and to gain some insight into how blocking can be expressed in a functional language.

(In the above discussion, we have assumed that n can be conveniently decomposed into factors p and q. In the recursive case, n would need even more factors. If n is not so factorizable, things can get very messy.)

7.9   LU Decomposition

LU decomposition is a classic problem in scientific computation. Suppose we have a system of n equations in n unknowns x_1 through x_n:

$$a_{1,1}x_1 \quad \cdots \quad + a_{1,j}x_j \quad \cdots \quad + a_{1,n}x_n \;\; = \;\; b_1$$
$$\vdots$$
$$a_{i,1}x_1 \quad \cdots \quad + a_{i,j}x_j \quad \cdots \quad + a_{i,n}x_n \;\; = \;\; b_i$$
$$\vdots$$
$$a_{n,1}x_1 \quad \cdots \quad + a_{n,j}x_j \quad \cdots \quad + a_{n,n}x_n \;\; = \;\; b_n$$

We are given the coefficients $a_{i,j}$ in a matrix **A** and b_i in a vector **b** and we are required to solve for the x_js (i.e., find x_js that satisfy the equations). In matrix algebra notation, the system is often written as follows:

$$Ax = b$$

where the boldface font indicates that A, x, and b are arrays, not scalars. Note that A is a square matrix.

Solving such a system of equations typically involves transforming A into one or more *triangular* matrices. An upper triangular matrix is one that has zeroes everywhere below the diagonal elements $a_{j,j}$. A lower triangular matrix has zeroes everywhere above the diagonal. In the next couple sections, we will look at two different ways to do this decomposition. The first one is called Gaussian elimination, and the second is called Crout's method. We will also use Crout's method to solve the problem for a class of sparse matrices called skyline matrices.

7.9.1   Gaussian Elimination

Gaussian elimination is a famous algorithm for solving linear equations. The basic step is to reduce the problem to a simpler problem: a system of $n - 1$ equations in x_2 through x_n, as depicted below (ignoring the first equation):

$$
\begin{array}{llllll}
a_{1,1}x_1 & + a_{1,2}x_2 & \cdots & + a_{1,j}x_j & \cdots & + a_{1,n}x_n & = b_1 \\
0 & + a'_{2,2}x_2 & \cdots & + a'_{2,j}x_j & \cdots & + a'_{2,n}x_n & = b'_2 \\
& & & \vdots & & & \\
0 & + a'_{i,2}x_2 & \cdots & + a'_{i,j}x_j & \cdots & + a'_{i,n}x_n & = b'_i \\
& & & \vdots & & & \\
0 & + a'_{n,2}x_2 & \cdots & + a'_{n,j}x_j & \cdots & + a'_{n,n}x_n & = b'_n
\end{array}
$$

This is called *eliminating* the first column (we will see how to do this shortly). By repeating this basic step, we end up with an upper triangular form:

$$
\begin{array}{llllll}
u_{1,1}x_1 & + u_{1,2}x_2 & + u_{1,3}x_3 & \cdots + u_{1,n-1}x_{n-1} & + u_{1,n}x_n & = c_1 \\
0 & + u_{2,2}x_2 & + u_{2,3}x_3 & \cdots + u_{2,n-1}x_{n-1} & + u_{2,n}x_n & = c_2 \\
0 & + 0 & + u_{3,3}x_3 & \cdots + u_{3,n-1}x_{n-1} & + u_{3,n}x_n & = c_3 \\
\vdots & & & \ddots & \vdots & = \vdots \\
0 & + 0 & + 0 & \cdots + u_{n-1,n-1}x_{n-1} & + u_{n-1,n}x_n & = c_{n-1} \\
0 & + 0 & + 0 & \cdots + 0 & + u_{n,n}x_n & = c_n
\end{array}
$$

The last equation is, of course, trivial to solve for x_n. Substituting x_n in the $(n - 1)$th equation, it becomes an equation in one unknown (x_{n-1}), which is again easy to solve. This *back substitution* proceeds until we have all the xs.

The elimination step is quite straightforward. Starting with the original set of equations, if we multiply the first equation by $\frac{a_{i,1}}{a_{1,1}}$ and subtract it from the ith equation, the ith equation then becomes

$$0 + a'_{i,2}x_2 \quad + \cdots \quad + a'_{i,j}x_j \quad + \cdots \quad + a'_{i,n}x_n \quad = \quad b'_i$$

where

$$a'_{i,j} = a_{i,j} - a_{1,j} \times \frac{a_{i,1}}{a_{1,1}}$$

$$b'_i \;=\; b_i - b_1 \times \frac{a_{i,1}}{a_{1,1}}$$

In general, after several steps, our focus is on a matrix whose top-left corner is $a_{k,k}$. The elimination step seeks to zero out all the coefficients directly below $a_{k,k}$. We do this by transforming each row below row k as follows:

$$a'_{i,j} = a_{i,j} - a_{k,j} \times \frac{a_{i,k}}{a_{k,k}}$$

$$b'_i \;=\; b_i - b_k \times \frac{a_{i,k}}{a_{k,k}}$$

The element $a_{k,k}$ is called the *pivot* element, and the term $\frac{a_{i,k}}{a_{k,k}}$ is called the *multiplier*.

It is often the case that we need repeatedly to solve several systems of equations that have the same left-hand sides (i.e., $a_{i,j}$s) but different right-hand sides (b_is). Thus, the problem is typically formulated as follows: Given a matrix **A** containing the initial coefficients $a_{i,j}$, compute two things:

- An upper triangular matrix **U**, containing the final coefficients $u_{i,j}$.
- A lower triangular matrix **L** in which we remember the multipliers used in computing **U** so that, when later given a vector **b** of b_is, we know how to scale them during back substitution. An element $l_{i,j}$ of **L** is determined in the jth step, when the **A** matrix has been reduced to a $(n - j) \times (n - j)$ matrix, and represents the multiplier used to transform the ith row at that step.

Now let us try translating these ideas into *pH*. The initial left-hand side coefficients ($a_{i,j}$s) are given in an $n \times n$ matrix called a. We will produce two matrices 1 and u. 1 is the lower triangular matrix containing the multipliers and is represented by a row (vector) of columns (vectors). u is the upper triangular matrix with the final coefficients, represented as a column (vector) of rows (vectors). This structure is depicted in Figure 7.9(a).

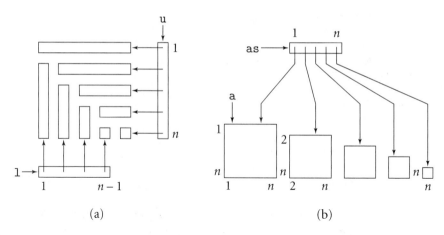

Figure 7.9   (a) Structure of l and u "matrices" and (b) the as matrices.

Let as be a series of n matrices. The first element is the original $n \times n$ a matrix, the second is an $(n - 1) \times (n - 1)$ matrix obtained after eliminating the first column of a, and so on; that is, the jth matrix is an $(n - j + 1) \times (n - j + 1)$ matrix obtained by eliminating the leftmost column of the $(j - 1)$th matrix. This structure is shown in Figure 7.9(b). It should be clear that the top rows of the matrices in as are the final coefficients of interest (i.e., they are to be copied into u).

The program for Gaussian elimination is shown in Figure 7.10. The program contains several mutually recursive definitions. Starting with as!1, which is the original a matrix, we compute the first column of multipliers (i.e., l!1). Then, using as!1 and l!1, we eliminate the first column to compute as!2, the reduced matrix. Using as!2, we compute the next column of multipliers (i.e., l!2), which allows us to compute as!3, and so on. The computation of u simply "skims" off the top row of each matrix in as.

While this solution is quite simple and elegant, it has some efficiency problems. One problem is the amount of storage taken by the as matrix. The first component (as!1) contains n^2 components, the second component contains $(n - 1)^2$ components, and so on. Thus, as contains on the order of n^3 components. This is quite wasteful because, at any stage, we are using only two components of as (i.e., reading from as!(j-1) and writing to as!j).

The second problem is the work done in producing the u matrix—it simply copies values from the as matrix into the u structure, without any "useful" computation along the way.

```
gauss_eliminate :: Array (Int,Int) Float ->
                                (Array Int (Array Int Float),
                                 Array Int (Array Int Float))
gauss_eliminate a =
  let
    ((_,_),(n,_)) = bounds a

    as = array (1,n)
         (  [ (1,a) ]
         ++ [ (k+1, eliminate (as!k) (l!k) k)
                        | k <- [1..n-1] ] )

    l  = array (1,n-1)
            [ (k, multipliers (as!k) k) | k <- [1..n-1] ]

    multipliers ak k =
        array (k+1,n)
           [ (i, ak!(i,k)/ak!(k,k)) | i <- [k+1..n] ]

    eliminate ak lk k =
        matrix  ((k+1,k+1), (n,n))
           [ ((i,j),  ak!(i,j) - ak!(k,j)*lk!(i))
                          | i <- [k+1..n],
                            j <- [k+1.. n] ]

    u  = array (1,n)
            [ (i, vector (i,n)
                    [ (j, as!(i)!(i,j))
                            | j <- [i..n] ] )
                        | i <- [1..n] ]
  in
      (l,u)
```

Figure 7.10 Gaussian elimination.

Exercise 7.21   Write a version of the above program that uses mkArray and mkMatrix and does not use array comprehensions. ■

7.9.2   Crout's Method

Crout's method is another way to do LU decomposition (our description is based on [54]). It is more amenable to an efficient solution in *pH*. Suppose we express **A** as the product of some **L** and **U**, which are lower and upper triangular matrices, respectively:

$$L \cdot U = A$$

By "product" here we mean matrix multiplication. For example (with $n = 4$):

$$
\begin{bmatrix}
l_{11} & 0 & 0 & 0 \\
l_{21} & l_{22} & 0 & 0 \\
l_{31} & l_{32} & l_{33} & 0 \\
l_{41} & l_{42} & l_{43} & l_{44}
\end{bmatrix}
\cdot
\begin{bmatrix}
u_{11} & u_{12} & u_{13} & u_{14} \\
0 & u_{22} & u_{23} & u_{24} \\
0 & 0 & u_{33} & u_{34} \\
0 & 0 & 0 & u_{44}
\end{bmatrix}
=
\begin{bmatrix}
a_{11} & a_{12} & a_{13} & a_{14} \\
a_{12} & a_{22} & a_{23} & a_{24} \\
a_{13} & a_{32} & a_{33} & a_{34} \\
a_{14} & a_{42} & a_{43} & a_{44}
\end{bmatrix}
$$

Then, it is clear that

$$A \cdot x = L \cdot U \cdot x = b$$

So, we can solve for **x** in two stages. In the *forward substitution* stage, we find **y** such that

$$L \cdot y = b$$

and then, in the *backward substitution* stage, we find **x** such that

$$U \cdot x = y$$

Each of the last two equations involves triangular matrices, and so the solution is easy. For forward substitution:

$$y_1 = \frac{b_1}{l_{11}}$$

$$y_i = \frac{1}{l_{ii}} \left[b_i - \sum_{j=1}^{i-1} l_{ij} y_j \right] \qquad 2 \le i \le n$$

and, for backward substitution:

$$x_n = \frac{y_n}{u_{nn}}$$

$$x_i = \frac{1}{u_{ii}} \left[y_i - \sum_{j=i+1}^{n} u_{ij} x_j \right] \qquad 1 \le i \le (n-1)$$

Let us consider how to decompose **A** into **L** and **U**. It is clear from the equation $L \cdot U = A$ that the ijth element of **A** is the inner product of the ith row of **L** and the jth column of **U**:

$$l_{i1}u_{1j} + l_{i2}u_{2j} + \cdots + l_{in}u_{nj} = a_{ij}$$

However, since l_{ij} is zero whenever $i < j$ and u_{ij} is zero whenever $i > j$, this equation can be separated into two cases (note the final term in each case):

$$i \leq j: \qquad l_{i1}u_{1j} + l_{i2}u_{2j} + \cdots + l_{ii}u_{ij} = a_{ij}$$
$$i > j: \qquad l_{i1}u_{1j} + l_{i2}u_{2j} + \cdots + l_{ij}u_{jj} = a_{ij}$$

Further, it is always possible to choose the diagonal elements of L (i.e., l_{ii}) to be 1. The last two equations can then be rearranged as follows:

$$u_{ij} = \qquad a_{ij} - \sum_{k=1}^{i-1} l_{ik}u_{kj} \qquad\qquad 1 \leq j \leq n, 1 \leq i \leq j$$

$$l_{ij} = \frac{1}{u_{jj}} \left(a_{ij} - \sum_{k=1}^{j-1} l_{ik}u_{kj} \right) \qquad 1 \leq j \leq n, j+1 \leq i \leq n$$

Since L's diagonal elements (l_{ii}) are assumed to be 1, we do not compute them, and we do not store them. When this diagonal of L is omitted, the remaining L and U elements have disjoint indices. Therefore, they can be stored in a single $n \times n$ matrix called LU. This structure, along with the computation of the L and U elements, is depicted in Figure 7.11.

The forward and backward substitution computations are depicted in Figures 7.12 and 7.13, respectively.

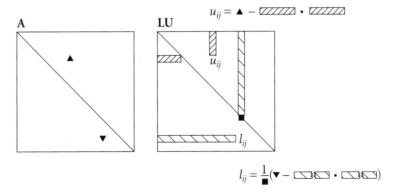

Figure 7.11   Computation of LU from A.

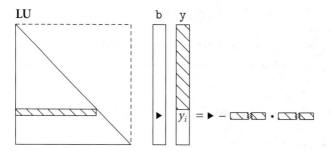

Figure 7.12   Solving $L \cdot y = b$ (forward substitution).

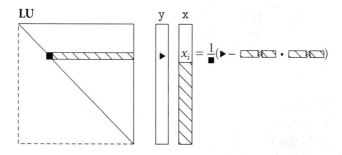

Figure 7.13   Solving $U \cdot x = y$ (backward substitution).

The *pH* code for LU decomposition of a dense matrix follows the equations given above exactly (Figure 7.11):

```
ludcmp_dense a =
  let
    ((_,_),(_,n)) = bounds a

    lu = array ((1,1),(n,n))
         -- upper
         ( [((i,j), ufn i j) | j <- [1..n], i <- [1..j] ]
         -- lower
         ++ [((i,j), lfn i j) | j <- [1..n], i <- [(j+1)..n] ] )
    -- upper
    ufn i j = sum_down 1 (i-1) (a!(i,j)) (term i j)

    -- lower
    lfn i j = (1.0/lu!(j,j)) * (sum_down 1
                                        (j-1)
                                        (a!(i,j))
                                        (term i j))
```

```
          term i j k = (lu!(i,k)) * (lu!(k,j))
  in
    lu
```

In the first line in the block, we find *n*, the dimension of the problem. The primitive function bounds returns the index bounds of a, represented as a pair of pairs. The pattern on the left-side of the binding shows this pair-of-pairs structure and ignores three of the components (using "_" for a "don't care" pattern) and binds n to the fourth. Here, we are assuming that a has bounds $((1,1),(n,n))$—it would be quite easy to bind all four components and verify that this is indeed so.

The second binding defines the actual LU matrix, using an array comprehension. It specifies the contents of the two-dimensional array in two regions corresponding to **U** and **L**, respectively, using the functions ufn and lfn. Each expression of the form (sum_down k_1 k_2 a f) computes

$$a - \sum_{k=k_1}^{k_2} f(k)$$

the *pH* code for which is

```
sum_down k1 k2 a f = for k <- [k1..k2] do
                       next a = a - (f k)
                     finally a
```

Here is the code for the forward and backward substitutions. Again, the code is self-evident, corresponding exactly to the equations and Figures 7.12 and 7.13.

```
lubksb_dense lu b =
  let
    (_,n) = bounds b

    y = array (1,n)
        (  [ (1, b!1) ]
        ++ [ (i, sum_down 1 (i-1) (b!i) (yfn i))
                                    | i <- [2..n] ] )

    yfn i j = lu!(i,j) * y!(j)

    x = array (1,n)
        (  [ (n, y!n/lu!(n,n)) ]
```

```
            ++ [ (i, (1.0/lu!(i,i)) *
                      (sum_down (i+1) n (y!i) (xfn i)))
                                         | i <- [(n-1),(n-2)..1] ])

        xfn i j = lu!(i,j) * x!j
    in
        x
```

7.9.3   LU Decomposition of Skyline Matrices

A skyline matrix is a square matrix. In each column j, it has nonzero elements in rows k through j, for some $1 \leq k \leq j$. In each row i, it has nonzero elements in columns k through i, for some $1 \leq k \leq i$. The first constraint defines the skyline above the diagonal, which is towards the top, and the second constraint defines the skyline below the diagonal, which is towards the left. The shape of a skyline matrix is depicted in Figure 7.14 (only the shaded region contains nonzeroes).

In Figure 7.11, in each inner product, note that the low index of each component vector is always 1. In a skyline matrix, on the other hand, the low index of the horizontal vector will be some $i1 \geq 1$ and the low index of the vertical vector will be some $j1 \geq 1$. Thus, the inner product can be "clipped" to begin at $max(i1, j1)$.

A second important observation is that it is clear from the equations that the LU matrix will always have exactly the same skyline shape as the original **A** matrix, so that the data structure for LU can be identical to the data structure for **A**.

The data structure that we choose for **A** (and **LU**) is shown in Figure 7.15. The subdiagonal elements of **A** are held in **AL**, which is an n-vector of vectors. The ith row is represented by a vector with dimensions $(j1, i-1)$, where $1 \leq j1 \leq i$ is the minimum index. When $j1 = i$, the lower index is greater than the upper index, representing an *empty* row vector. These are

Figure 7.14 The shape of a skyline matrix.

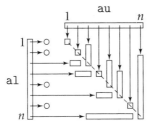

Figure 7.15 Data structure for **A** (LU is similar).

depicted by little circles "o" in the figure. The diagonal and superdiagonal elements of **A** are held in **AU**, which is also an n-vector of vectors. The jth row is represented by a vector with dimensions $(i1, j)$, where $1 \leq i1 \leq j$ is the minimum index. Note that none of the column vectors can be empty.

The code for the decomposition function is shown in Figure 7.16. In the definition of u, the jth column vector is specified as a vector with the same bounds as the jth column vector in au (from i1 to j). In calling ufn, we supply it i1 and j1, the lowest indices of the column vector and row vector of the inner product. In ufn, we clip the iteration to begin at $max(i1, j1)$. A similar strategy is used in the specification of l.

The code for forward and backward substitution is shown in Figure 7.17. Recall that in the dense version, yfn was defined as

```
yfn i j = (lu!(i,j)) * (y!j)
```

Now, however, the term lu!(i,j) must be replaced by l!i!j. However, l!i is fixed for each sum_down traversal, and so we optimize it by passing the entire row vector l!i to yfn, which then just indexes it with j.

In xfn, we run across the following problem: the inner product traverses a *row* of **U**. However, because of our representation of the skyline **U**, not all elements in a particular row may be present. So, our code first extracts the jth column vector and then extracts the index bounds of that vector. If i is outside the bounds, the term is 0; otherwise, we extract the normal $LU[i, j]$ (i.e., $U[j][i]$, which is uj!i).

Of course, this conditional is executed $O(n^2)$ times (once for every position in the upper triangle). We could trade time for space by first reformatting u into a full upper triangular matrix (filling in all the zeroes) and then indexing it as usual. We do not pursue this possibility here.

```
ludcmp_sky (al, au) =
    let
        (_,n) = bounds au

        u = array (1,n)
            [ (j, let
                       (i1,_) = bounds  (au!j)
                  in
                       array (i1,j)
                       [ (i, let
                                  (j1,_) = bounds  (al!i)
                             in
                                  ufn i1 j1 i j )
                         | i <- [i1..j] ] )
              | j <- [1..n] ]

        l = array (2,n)
            [ (i, let
                       (j1,_) = bounds  (al!i)
                  in
                       array (j1,i-1)
                       [ (j, let
                                  (i1,_) = bounds  (au!j)
                             in
                                  lfn i1 j1 i j )
                         | j <- [j1..(i-1)] ] )
              | i <- [2..n] ]

        ufn i1 j1 i j = sum_down  (max i1 j1)
                                  (i-1)
                                  (au!j!i)
                                  (term i j)

        lfn i1 j1 i j = (1.0/(u!j!j)) * (sum_down (max i1 j1)
                                                  (j-1)
                                                  (al!i!j)
                                                  (term i j))

        term i j k = (l!i!k) * (u!j!k)
    in
        (l,u)
```

Figure 7.16 LU decomposition for skyline matrices.

```
lubksb_sky (l,u) b =
  let
      (_,n) = bounds b

      y = array (1,n)
          ( [ (1, b!1) ]
         ++ [ (i, let
                      (j1,_) = bounds  (l!i)
                  in
                      sum_down j1 (i-1) (b!i) (yfn (l!i) i) )
              | i <- [2..n] ] )

      yfn li i j = (li!j) * (y!j)

      x = array (1,n)
          ( [ (n, y!n) / u!n!n ]
         ++ [ (i, (1.0/u!i!i) * (sum_down (i+1) n
                                          (y!i) (xfn i)))
              | i <- [(n-1),(n-2)..1] ] )

      xfn i j = let
                    uj = u!j
                    (i1,_) = bounds uj
                in
                    if i < i1 then
                        0.0
                    else
                        uj!i * x!j
  in
      x
```

Figure 7.17 Forward and backward substitution for skyline matrices.

Finally, the top-level function to solve a given set of equations is shown below, where we assume that a is a pair of skylines (al,au):

```
solve_sky (a,b) = lubksb_sky (ludcmp_sky a) b
```

7.10   The "Paraffins" Problem

The "Paraffins" problem is more "symbolic" in nature. It was posed and solved by David Turner [68]. Paraffins are molecules with chemical

Figure 7.18   (a) Methane (CH_4); (b) butane (C_4H_{10}); and (c) iso-butane (C_4H_{10}).

formula C_nH_{2n+2}, where C and H stand for carbon and hydrogen atoms, respectively, and $n > 0$. Carbon and hydrogen atoms have valence 4 and 1, respectively. Some examples of paraffins are given in Figure 7.18.

The butane example shows that for a given n, there can be many *isomers*, that is, distinct paraffins with the same formula C_nH_{2n+2}.

We can describe the structure of paraffin molecules in terms of *radicals*. Let us pick any carbon in a paraffin molecule, call it the *root*. Its four bonds are each attached to a radical, which is a molecule of valence 1, with formula C_nH_{2n+1}. The structure of a radical can be defined inductively as follows:

- A hydrogen atom is a radical.
- If $r1$, $r2$, and $r3$ are three radicals, then attaching them to three bonds of a carbon atom—(C $r1$ $r2$ $r3$)—also constitutes a radical.

Note that this description is not unique. First, the four bonds of a carbon atom are chemically indistinguishable, so that (C $r1$ $r2$ $r3$), (C $r2$ $r1$ $r3$), (C $r2$ $r3$ $r1$), and so on are all the same radical. Second, the choice of the root carbon in a paraffin is arbitrary, so that, for example, C attached to four radicals CH_3, CH_3, H, and H is the same paraffin as C attached to C_2H_5, H, H, and H.[6] Figure 7.19 shows some examples of different pictorial representations of the *same* molecule (by convention, we omit the hydrogen atoms, showing only the carbon "spine", and place an asterisk to the right of the chosen root). It may interest the reader to note that for this particular C_6H_{14} molecule, there are 108 equivalent representations.

---

6. Radicals are called *oriented* or *unordered trees*, and paraffins are called *free trees*; see [36] for a general discussion of these structures, including the equivalence issue.

```
    C                 C              C  C
C* C  C  C      C  C* C  C      C  C* C  C
    C                 C
```

Figure 7.19   Different representations of C_6H_{14}.

The specification of the programming problem is this:

"Generate all distinct paraffins containing up to *n* carbon atoms."

What makes this problem especially interesting is that we do not want the result to contain multiple representations of the same paraffin. A straight-forward solution would be first to pick a representation for paraffins and enumerate all possibilities containing up to *n* carbons. Then, we could group them according to the equivalences described above and pick just one member from each group. In fact, Turner's original solution was coded in this way.

In this section, we develop a solution that is more efficient in that it never generates any paraffin that does not belong in the final output. The basic idea is this. We define a "canonical" form for paraffins such that there is exactly one in each equivalence class. Then, our algorithm will only generate these canonical representatives.

7.10.1   Radicals, Orderings, and Canonical Forms

The inductive definition of radicals can be expressed directly in *pH:*

```
data Radical = H | C Radical Radical Radical
```

That is, objects of type `radical` are either the constant H, or a data structure (C r1 r2 r3), where the three components r1, r2, and r3 are themselves objects representing radicals.

Let us define a function `carbons` that counts the number of carbon atoms contained in a radical (we shall also speak of the number of carbons in a molecule as its *size*):

```
carbons H            = 0
carbons (C r1 r2 r3) = 1 + (carbons r1) + (carbons r2)
                                        + (carbons r3)
```

If the argument is just H, the count is 0; otherwise, it matches the pattern (C r1 r2 r3), and so the count is 1 (for the carbon) plus the sum of the carbons in r1, r2, and r3.

We can define a canonical form for radicals, assuming we had a total ordering on radicals:

◆ The radical H is in canonical form.
◆ A radical C r1 r2 r3 is in canonical form if and only if r1 ≤ r2 ≤ r3, *and* r1, r2, and r3 are themselves in canonical form.

How do we define this total ordering? First, a comparison of two radicals will result in r1 < r2, r1 = r2, or r1 > r2. We define a new algebraic type containing three constants to represent these outcomes:

```
data Ordering_outcome = Rad_lt | Rad_eq | Rad_gt
```

Here is a function called `ordering` that computes the relative ordering of any two radicals, based on the number of carbons they contain:

```
ordering  H                 H             = Rad_eq
ordering  H                 (C r21 r22 r23) = Rad_lt
ordering (C r11 r12 r13)   H             = Rad_gt
ordering (C r11 r12 r13)   (C r21 r22 r23) =
   let
       nc1 = carbons (C r11 r12 r13)
       nc2 = carbons (C r21 r22 r23)
   in
       if      nc1 < nc2 then Rad_lt
       else if nc1 > nc2 then Rad_gt
       else
          case ordering r11 r21 of
              Rad_lt -> Rad_lt
              Rad_gt -> Rad_gt
              Rad_eq -> case ordering r12 r22 of
                           Rad_lt -> Rad_lt
                           Rad_gt -> Rad_gt
                           Rad_eq -> (ordering r13 r23)
```

The first three clauses are straightforward: comparing a hydrogen with a hydrogen, a hydrogen with a nonhydrogen, and *vice versa*. The fourth clause compares two nonhydrogens. nc1 and nc2 are bound to the sizes of the given radicals, which are computed using the carbons function. In the body of the block, the first two lines of the conditional expression specify that if sizes are unequal, we immediately know the ordering. In the final else clause, the sizes are known to be equal. The outer case expression recursively determines the ordering of the corresponding component radicals r11 and r21. If Rad_lt or Rad_gt, the ordering is known. If equal, the nested case expression similarly tests the ordering of r12 and r21. If these, too, are equal, the ordering is determined by that of r13 and r23.

Here is a useful help function that uses ordering to check if one radical is less than or equal to another:

```
isLE r1 r2 = case ordering r1 r2 of
                Rad_lt -> True
                Rad_eq -> True
                Rad_gt -> False
```

7.10.2   More Efficient Representations

Unfortunately, the ordering computation described above is *very* inefficient! Consider supplying this function with two arguments that are equal, but deeply nested, radicals. The ordering function will traverse them both completely, calling carbons at every level. But carbons itself traverses the entire substructure. Thus, we will compute the carbons of an inner radical repeatedly, once for each carbon above it!

It seems unnecessary to construct a radical first and then to traverse it again to compute its number of carbons. As we build radicals, we can simultaneously count the carbons and "cache" the count at each level in the radical structure itself. To do this, we can change our type definition for radicals:

```
data Radical = H | CI Int Radical Radical Radical
```

Here, the nonhydrogen structure is augmented with an integer component in which the size of the radical will be cached. The carbons function is now trivial:

```
carbons H              = 0
carbons (CI nc r1 r2 r3) = nc
```

To construct a radical given its three components, we use the following function:

```
c r1 r2 r3 = let
                nc1 = carbons r1
                nc2 = carbons r2
                nc3 = carbons r3
            in
                CI (1+nc1+nc2+nc3) r1 r2 r3
```

Finally, we can rewrite our ordering function (it is identical to the earlier version except that we do not have to call `carbons` to compute the number of carbons in a radical):

```
ordering  H                         H                 = Rad_eq
ordering  H                         (CI nc2 r21 r22 r23) = Rad_lt
ordering (CI nc1 r11 r12 r13)  H                 = Rad_gt
ordering (CI nc1 r11 r12 r13)  (CI nc2 r21 r22 r23) =
           if      nc1 < nc2 then Rad_lt
           else if nc1 > nc2 then Rad_gt
           else
             case ordering r11 r21 of
                 Rad_lt -> Rad_lt
                 Rad_gt -> Rad_gt
                 Rad_eq -> case ordering r12 r22 of
                               Rad_lt -> Rad_lt
                               Rad_gt -> Rad_gt
                               Rad_eq -> (ordering r13 r23)
```

7.10.3   Generating Radicals

The first step in our program is to generate all radicals with n carbons, which we do inductively, following the definition of radicals. Assume that we have generated all radicals with less than n carbons. Then, for each triple r1, r2, and r3 such that r1 $\leq$ r2 $\leq$ r3 and (carbons r1) + (carbons r2) + (carbons r3) = (n–1), we construct the radical (C r1 r2 r3) with n carbons.

We will first develop a transparent but slightly inefficient version of the radical generator. Then, we will analyze this solution to identify the inefficiencies and produce an efficient solution.

Let us first concentrate on the subproblem of generating a list containing all canonical three-partitions nc1, nc2, nc3 of a number m; that is, nc1 $\leq$ nc2 $\leq$ nc3 and nc1 + nc2 + nc3 = m. We can do this easily using a list comprehension:

```
three_partitions m =
        [ (nc1,nc2,nc3) | nc1 <- [0..m],
                          nc2 <- [0..m],
                          nc3 <- [0..m],
                          nc1 <= nc2,
                          nc2 <= nc3,
                          nc1+nc2+nc3 == m ]
```

However, we are generating m^3 triples only to discard most of them using the predicates (actually, more than $\frac{5}{6}$ of them are discarded). A little algebra makes it obvious that under the conditions imposed, nc1 cannot be more than $\frac{m}{3}$, nc2 cannot be more than $\frac{m-nc1}{2}$, and that nc3 = m − (nc1+nc2). Here is a more efficient solution that directly generates the required numbers:

```
three_partitions m =
        [ (nc1,nc2,nc3) | nc1 <- [0..(div m 3)],
                          nc2 <- [nc1..(div (m-nc1) 2)],
                          let nc3  = m - (nc1 + nc2) ]
```

We use the integer division function div to truncate each division. The list comprehension qualifier in the last line is just a shorthand for "nc3 <- [m − (nc1 + nc2)]"; that is, it just binds the identifier nc3 to the value of m−(nc1+nc2).

7.10.4   First Attempt

Let us now look at the inductive step in generating radicals of size n. Let us first assume that we are given an array radicals such that at each index j < n, radicals!j contains the ordered list of radicals with j carbons. This is depicted pictorially in Figure 7.20, where the ⊥ symbols indicate that the array elements are as yet undefined beyond index 3.

Here is a function for the inductive step. It generates the ordered list of radicals with n carbons, assuming it is given radicals with fewer than n carbons:

```
rads_of_size_n radicals n =
    [ c r1 r2 r3 | (nc1,nc2,nc3) <- three_partitions (n-1),
                r1 <- radicals!nc1,
                r2 <- radicals!nc2, (isLE r1 r2),
                r3 <- radicals!nc3, (isLE r2 r3) ]
```

The first generator produces the canonical three-partitions of radical sizes totalling (n–1). The second generator produces all radicals r1 with nc1 carbons. The third and fourth generators produce all radicals r2 and r3 with nc2 and nc3 carbons, respectively, and we ensure canonical ordering using the predicates. Finally, we collect together all radicals of the form (c r1 r2 r3) into the result list.

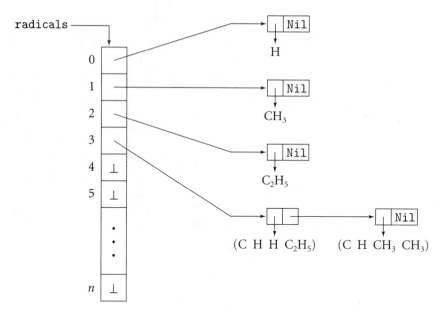

Figure 7.20   The radicals array.

All that remains is to package the base step and the inductive step to produce all radicals of size up to n. Here is a definition of the array radicals with indices 0 through n, such that the jth element is an ordered list of all radicals with j carbons:

```
radicals = array (0,n)
              ( [ (0, [H]) ]
              ++ [ (j, rads_of_size_n radicals j)
                                    | j <- [1..n] ] )
```

At index 0 (representing radicals with 0 carbons), the array contains a singleton list containing the radical H. At each index j in the range 1 through n, the array contains the list computed by (rads_of_size_n radicals j).

Note that the definition for the array radicals is recursive; that is, we are relying on *pH*'s non-strict semantics.

7.10.5   Critique of rads_of_size_n (Blind Carbon Copies)

Let us concentrate on that fragment of rads_of_size_n that produces radicals r1 and r2 in canonical order (with nc1 and nc2 carbons, respectively). When $nc1 < nc2$, we know that $r1 < r2$, by definition. It is only at the boundary condition when $nc1 = nc2$ that $r1$ and $r2$ may be in the wrong order. To protect against this, we used the filter "(isLE r1 r2)". The inefficiency is this: we are unnecessarily performing radical comparisons even when $nc1 < nc2$.

We can fix this immediately as follows:

```
rads_of_size_n radicals n =
    [ c r1 r2 r3 | (nc1,nc2,nc3) <- three_partitions (n-1),
             r1 <- radicals!nc1,
             r2 <- radicals!nc2, if nc1 == nc2 then
                                     (isLE r1 r2)
                                 else True,
             r3 <- radicals!nc3, if nc2 == nc3 then
                                     (isLE r2 r3)
                                 else True ]
```

so that the radical comparison is done only when $nc1 = nc2$. This may be worthwhile because the equality test on the numbers $nc1$ and $nc2$ is likely to be cheaper than the radical comparison.

Another possible fix is this:

```
rads_of_size_n radicals n =
    [ c r1 r2 r3 | (nc1,nc2,nc3) <- three_partitions (n-1),
             r1 <- radicals!nc1,
             r2 <- if nc1 == nc2 then
                       [ r2temp | r2temp <- radicals!nc2,
                                  (isLE r1 r2temp) ]
                   else
                       radicals!nc2,
             r3 <- if nc2 == nc3 then
                       [ r3temp | r3temp <- radicals!nc3
                                  (isLE r2 r3) ]
                   else
                       radicals!nc3 ]
```

which brings the equality test outside. When $nc1 \neq nc2$, we directly use the list radicals!nc2; otherwise we filter the list. But in this solution we generate many extra intermediate lists which may be difficult to optimize away.

In any case, there is still a lingering inefficiency. Even if the filtering is limited to the case when $nc1 = nc2$, we are still generating many $r1$, $r2$ pairs that are out of order, only to have them filtered out subsequently. For

example, let nc1 = nc2 = 3. r1 and r2 will be drawn from radicals!3.
Referring back to Figure 7.20, each will be bound, in turn, to the values
(C H H H C_2H_5) and (C H H CH_3 CH_3). But when r1 is (C H H CH_3 CH_3) and r2
is (C H H H C_2H_5), they are out of order. In general, we are generating n^2
pairs and rejecting half of them.

7.10.6   Second Attempt

The basic problem in rads_of_size_n is this: when picking a radical r1
from the list radicals!nc1, we do not keep track of the position in the list
that r1 was drawn from. Thus, when we pick radicals r2 from the same list
(i.e., when nc1 = nc2), we pick some radicals from earlier positions in the
list, so that r1 and r2 are not in canonical order.

To correct this, whenever we pick an r1 from the list radicals!nc1,
we will also keep the *remainder* of the list starting at that radical, so that
whenever nc1 = nc2, we will pick r2s from this remainder instead of the
full list radicals!nc2. In this way, we never pick any r2s that are earlier
than r1.

Similarly, whenever we pick an r2 from a list, we keep with it the remainder of the list starting at that radical, so that whenever we wish to pick r3s
with the same size, we pick it from this remainder instead of the full list
radicals!nc3.

For this purpose, we first define a help function called remainders that
takes a list of radicals:

$$r_a, r_b, r_c \ldots$$

and produces a list of remainders of this list (i.e., a list of lists of radicals):

$$(r_a, r_b, r_c, r_d, r_e, \ldots), (r_b, r_c, r_d, r_e \ldots), (r_c, r_d, r_e \ldots), \ldots$$

Then, we can pick r1s from the heads of these lists, to get $r_a, r_b, r_c, \ldots$,
but for each of them, we also have available the remainder of the list, from
which we can pick r2s, ensuring canonical order. For example, when we
pick r1 to be r_c, the first element of the third list, we can also pick r2s
from the third list, to get $r_c, r_d, r_e, \ldots$. Here is the code to generate the
remainders list:

```
remainders  []    = []
remainders (r:rs) = (r:rs) : (remainders rs)
```

Note that remainders is actually a polymorphic function—it will work on lists of anything, not just radicals. Here is the efficient version of rads_of_size_n:

```
rads_of_size_n radicals n =
    [ C r1 r2 r3
        | (nc1,nc2,nc3) <- three_partitions (n-1),
          r1:r1s <- remainders (radicals!nc1),
          r2:r2s <- remainders (if nc1 == nc2 then r1:r1s
                                              else radicals!nc2),
          r3     <- if nc2 == nc3 then r2:r2s
                    else radicals!nc3 ]
```

Note that in this version, we do no radical comparisons at all; the functions isLE and ordering, which were useful for expository purposes, are not really necessary (this is why we reverted back to the original C constructor, since we no longer need CI and its cached carbon count).

Finally, we abstract our definition of the array radicals into a function on n:

```
radical_generator n =
    let
        radicals = array (0,n)
                    (  [ (0, [H]) ]
                    ++ [ (j, rads_of_size_n radicals j)
                                    | j <- [1..n] ] )
    in
        radicals
```

7.10.7   Paraffins from Radicals (Molotov Cocktails)

We now turn our attention to assembling paraffin molecules from radicals.

Representation and Canonical Forms for Paraffins

Suppose we chose the following simple representation for paraffins:

```
data Paraffin = ROOT_CARBON Radical Radical Radical Radical
```

that is, a root carbon connected to four radicals. To avoid duplicates, we may impose the condition that the radicals in a paraffin ROOT_CARBON r1 r2 r3 r4 must be ordered (i.e., $r1 \leq r2 \leq r3 \leq r4$). Unfortunately, this is

not sufficient to guarantee uniqueness of representation, as shown by the
following example:

1. Attach radicals H, H, CH_3, and CH_3 to a carbon atom to get

    ROOT_CARBON H H (C H H H) (C H H H)

2. Attach radicals H, H, H, and C_2H_5 to a carbon atom to get

    ROOT_CARBON H H H (C H H (C H H H))

Despite satisfying the ordering constraint, both represent the same molecule.

The solution is straightforward[7]—rather than picking an arbitrary root
in a paraffin, we define a unique "center" such that it is "balanced" on all
sides. We define the *center* of a paraffin with n carbons to be either

- a *bond* with radicals of size $\frac{n}{2}$ on either side or
- a carbon atom connected to four radicals such that all of them have
  size strictly less than $\frac{n}{2}$.

In the former case, we call it a *bond-centered* paraffin (BCP) and, in the
latter, a *carbon-centered* paraffin (CCP). We leave it as an exercise to the
reader to prove that the definition is sound—that the center is uniquely
defined, and that every paraffin is either a BCP or a CCP, but not both.

We can express this in the representation of paraffins:

```
data Paraffin = BCP Radical Radical
              | CCP Radical Radical Radical Radical
```

Having defined unique centers, we can avoid duplicates as follows:

- In a bond-centered paraffin (BCP r1 r2), we require that r1 ≤ r2.
- In a carbon-centered paraffin (CCP r1 r2 r3 r4), we require that
  r1 ≤ r2 ≤ r3 ≤ r4.

---

7. That is, it is straightforward in retrospect. One of the developers of this program (Steve Heller)
discovered several possible definitions for the "center" of a paraffin, based on carbon counts, size
of longest carbon chains, and so on. We were also assisted in this direction by hints in some code
for this problem that we received from Olaf Lubeck and Vance Faber of Los Alamos National
Laboratories.

Finally, (sigh! need we be surprised?) we discovered that this problem has been discussed
extensively by Knuth [36]. It turns out that it is identical to the problem of finding a unique
center for what Knuth calls *free trees* (i.e., trees for which the root is unknown).

Generating Bond-Centered Paraffins

Here is a function to generate all bond-centered paraffins with j carbons, given that we have already computed the array `radicals` where `radicals!i` contains the list of canonical radicals with i carbons in canonical order:

```
bcp_generator radicals j =
  if isOdd j then []
  else
      [ BCP r1 r2 | r1:r1s <- remainders (radicals!(div j 2)),
                    r2 <- r1:r1s ]
```

From the definition, we can see that the size of a bond-centered paraffin must be even, so that if j is odd, the list of BCPs is empty. When j is even, the radicals on either side of the bond must have $\frac{j}{2}$ carbons. We need pairs of radicals `r1` and `r2` with this carbon count, but to avoid duplicates, we need them in canonical order. So, we use the same trick as before—when picking an `r1` from the list, we also keep with it the remainder of the list, so that we can pick `r2` from that remainder, thus guaranteeing canonical order.

Generating Carbon-Centered Paraffins

As before, let us first concentrate on the problem of generating all canonical four-partitions `nc1`, `nc2`, `nc3`, `nc4` of a number m, representing the sizes of the four radicals of a carbon-centered paraffin of size $m+1$. We know that

1. $nc1, nc2, nc3, nc4 < \frac{m}{2}$, by the definition of "center"
2. $nc1 + nc2 + nc3 + nc4 = m$
3. $nc1 \le nc2 \le nc3 \le nc4$, by our canonical ordering

Under these conditions, it is obvious that:

- `nc1` ranges from 0 to $\frac{m}{4}$
- `nc2` ranges from `nc1` to $\frac{m-nc1}{3}$
- normally, `nc3` ranges from `nc2` up to $\frac{m-nc1-nc2}{2}$
- `nc4 = m - nc1 - nc2 - nc3`

It is clear that `nc1`, `nc2`, and `nc3` satisfy condition 1, above. Unfortunately, when they are all small, `nc4` can become greater than $\frac{m}{2}$. We can avoid generating large `nc4`s by imposing an additional condition on `nc3` so that it is always large enough to keep nc4 $< \frac{m}{2}$. We ensure that nc3 must be at least $\frac{m}{2}$ – nc1 – nc2. Here is the code to generate the partitions:

```
four_partitions m =
        [ (nc1,nc2,nc3,nc4)
            | nc1 <- [0..(div m 4)],
              nc2 <- [nc1.. (div (m-nc1) 3)],
              nc3 <- [(max nc2 (ceiling (m/2.0-nc1-nc2)))
                      .. (div ((m-nc1-nc2) 2))],
            let nc4 =  m - nc1 - nc2 - nc3 ]
```

The ceiling function converts a fraction to the next integer.

Assume, again, that we are given the array radicals, where radicals!i contains the list of canonical radicals with i carbons in canonical order. Here is the function to generate all carbon-centered paraffins with j carbons:

```
ccp_generator radicals j =
        [ CCP r1 r2 r3 r4
            | (nc1,nc2,nc3,nc4) <- four_partitions (j-1),
              r1:r1s <- remainders (radicals!nc1),
              r2:r2s <- remainders (if nc1==nc2 then r1:r1s
                                        else radicals!nc2),
              r3:r3s <- remainders (if nc2==nc3 then r2:r2s
                                        else radicals!nc3),
            r4 <- if nc3==nc4 then r3:r3s
                    else radicals!nc4 ]
```

7.10.8 The Solution to the Paraffins Problem

Here, finally, is the solution to the paraffins problem:

```
paraffins_until n =
      let
          radicals = radical_generator (div n 2)
      in
          array (1,n)
          [ (j, ((bcp_generator radicals j),
                 (ccp_generator radicals j)) | j <- [1..n] ]
```

Because our paraffins are "centered," we need generate radicals only up to size $\frac{n}{2}$. The result is an array of pairs of lists. The jth index of the array contains all paraffins with j carbons, represented as a pair—a list

n	Number of paraffins with n carbons	Number of radicals with n carbons
0	—	1
1	1	1
2	1	1
3	1	2
4	2	4
5	3	8
6	5	17
7	9	39
8	18	89
9	35	211
10	75	507
11	159	1238
12	355	3057
13	802	7639
14	1858	19241
15	4347	48865
16	10359	124906
17	24894	321198

Table 7.1 The number of distinct paraffins and radicals of a given size

of bond-centered paraffins and a list of carbon-centered paraffins with j carbons.

Table 7.1 lists some interesting statistics concerning the size of the problem.

Sequencing, Input/Output, and Side Effects

> The moving Finger writes; and, having writ,
> Moves on: nor all thy Piety nor Wit
> Shall lure it back to cancel half a Line,
> Nor all thy Tears wash out a Word of it.

—The Rubaiyat of Omar Khayyam *(Fitzgerald translation)*

Conspicuously missing in our presentation of *pH* so far is any notion of *side effects*. There is no hidden action or effect during the evaluation of an expression. An expression merely represents the value that it finally produces, and it can always be replaced by any other expression that produces the same value. This property of functional *pH* is known as *referential transparency*. In a referentially transparent program, it is always legal to perform the following transformation:

```
(... (f x) + (f x) ...)        ⟶        let t = (f x)
                                        in
                                            (... t + t ...)
```

where t is a new variable. This is clearly a useful property for a programmer or a compiler to exploit because it replaces two executions of an expression by a single one (this optimization is called *common subexpression elimination*).

Two more properties of functional *pH* are

♦ *Implicit parallelism (or no explicit sequencing):* The order in which operations are performed is limited only by data dependencies.
♦ *Determinacy:* Each functional *pH* program produces a unique result. No matter which *pH* compiler we use, no matter which machine we run on, no matter what else is running on the machine at the same time, a particular *pH* program always produces a particular, unique result.[1]

These two properties are closely related—determinacy permits the language implementation to execute program fragments in any order, subject only to data dependencies.

All these properties—referential transparency, implicit parallelism, and determinacy—are lost when we introduce side effects. By "side effects" we mean any action performed during the evaluation of an expression that is visible externally or which can affect the evaluation of other expressions. The most common kind of side effect, ubiquitous in most programming languages, is the "assignment statement" by which, for example, the contents of a "variable" can be repeatedly changed during program execution. The assignment statement is so central to most programming languages that it is indeed quite remarkable that we have been able to come this far in *pH* programming without using it at all! Another common kind of side effect, impossible to live without, is input/output: reading a file, printing a string, sensing the mouse position, sending a network packet, and so on.

Suppose we had the following statement in a traditional language such as C or Pascal:

```
z := f(x)  +  g(y);
```

and suppose the programmer had placed `print` statements inside the functions f and g. Suppose the expression `f(x)` returned the value 16. In a

---

1. This is not to say that the result is right or wrong—one can always write incorrect programs; it just says that the result is unique.

referentially transparent language, we could replace this expression by the expression 16, or 20–4, or sqr(4). However, here it would be incorrect because those expressions do not print out the string that f(x) does; they do not duplicate the side effect of the original expression. Further, the order in which f(x) and g(y) are evaluated matters since it affects the order in which they print their strings. Note that this order is not constrained by any data dependencies; g(y) does not need any result of f(x) or vice versa. For this reason, some languages, such as Standard ML, pick an ordering explicitly (e.g., left argument of "+" before the right argument). Other languages, such as C and Scheme, leave the ordering unspecified to give language implementations the flexibility to choose an order based on other considerations, such as performance. In this case, the language is *nondeterministic*—the same program, compiled with two compilers that chose different orders, will produce different results. Therefore, in these languages the prudent programmer is advised to use explicit sequencing to force a particular order:

```
a := f(x);
b := g(y);
z := a + b;
```

(using the traditional programming language convention that these statements are executed sequentially).

These are all very good reasons why we have postponed the discussion of side effects up to this point. Simply put, side effects complicate the semantics of programs and can be dangerous. However, side effects are like fire—though dangerous, they can also be very useful. The danger that they introduce is also the source of their power.

First, side effects can increase the *modularity* of some programs: a procedure whose behavior is intended to depend on the history of its calls is usually more simply expressed using an encapsulated side effect than in pure functional style where the "history" must be passed in as an explicit argument and returned as an explicit result. Second, many programs can effectively exploit nondeterminism to *remove* constraints, which, in turn, leads to shorter, clearer, and more parallel programs. Finally, side effects can often result in better performance because they can reduce the algorithmic complexity of some programs.

In this chapter we will study sequencing, I/O, and side effects. We begin by looking at *monadic* I/O, which is an ingenious mechanism in Haskell (and hence also in *pH*) that retains referential transparency while still being able to express many kinds of I/O. It cleanly separates the actual side effects of I/O into a separate layer that is outside the language itself, so that the language remains purely functional. However, it has two drawbacks: (1) it is purely sequential, and (2) it has poor modularity in that introducing an I/O action into an existing functional fragment can result in significant restructuring of the program. Thus, we finally depart from pure functional programming in order to overcome these drawbacks. This, in turn, will necessitate explicit control over sequencing, and we discuss the ">>>" construct (the "barrier") for this purpose. A barrier is a heavy hammer, sometimes causing more things to be sequenced than just the I/O actions we wish to sequence, and so we study *threaded* I/O by which the programmer has fine-grained control on exactly what I/O is sequenced and what I/O is parallel.

Finally, we will look at how to incorporate the assignment statement into *pH*. The key difference from traditional assignment statements in other languages is *implicit synchronization*. This property makes assignment manageable in the presence of *pH*'s massive, implicit parallelism. In this chapter we will focus on the semantics of assignment in *pH* (in terms of rewrite rules); we will leave it to the following two chapters to see how this semantic concept is integrated into usable language-level constructs in *pH*.

8.1   Monadic I/O

At first glance, it seems impossible to mix pure functional languages, which are free of side effects, and I/O, which are quintessentially side effects. Indeed this tension has persisted for decades, and it was only in the mid-1990s that the technique of monadic I/O was fully developed, providing a resolution of the problem. It is called monadic I/O because it is built on a mathematical framework called *monads* [75], but it is not necessary to go into that background to understand it. It is also sometimes called "functional I/O," but we will eschew that terminology here because it is somewhat misleading.

8.1.1   Preliminaries: The "Unit" Data Type

As we explore the topic of side effects, we will come across various expressions for which the side effect is the important thing and the return value is uninteresting. For example, the main purpose of an expression may be to print a string; the "value" of this expression may be uninteresting.

Since every expression must return *some* value, we define a trivial data type for this purpose, containing a single value:

```
data () = ()
```

Both the type, and the single value in that type, are traditionally pronounced "Unit." (This use of parentheses is special syntax and is another exception to the usual use of parentheses for grouping.)

This data type has no primitive operations on it. The only things you can do with it are the usual polymorphic things—use it as a function argument or result, or as the contents of a data structure field, and so on.

8.1.2   The Basic Intuition

We will first discuss a simpler, limited, hypothetical I/O system to build up the intuition behind monadic I/O. Suppose that in our language we are interested only in a simple form of I/O—writing text strings to the screen. Suppose we introduced a primitive procedure:

```
printString :: String -> ()
```

which we might use as follows:

```
printString "Hello world!"
```

Unfortunately, as we discussed earlier, the language then loses referential transparency and implicit parallelism.

We can instead take an entirely different tack. Let us start by examining what it means to execute one of our functional programs. Every programming language has some convention. For example, in every C program, there must be one C function called main; to execute a C program means to execute this procedure (and all that it entails). In interactive systems like Basic and Lisp, we typically define the behavior of a "read-eval-print-loop" that reads syntactic terms, executes them, and prints out resulting values. These approaches are both possible for a functional language. We could say that a functional program must define an identifier called main and that executing the program means to evaluate main and print the value. Or, we could specify a read-eval-print-loop that reads expressions from some standard input port, evaluates them, and prints their values. Note that this part of the specification is outside the language itself. Rather, we will refer to this as a specification of the *program driver*, which is a collective term referring to the entire environment in which programs are executed (this includes the run-time system, the operating system, the computer system, and so on).

Now, to handle the issue of output commands to write strings to the screen, suppose we define our functional language with the following rule: each program must define the identifier `main` and its type must be a list of strings:

```
main :: [String]
```

The program driver is required to evaluate `main` and to ouput the resulting strings, in the order that they appear in the list. For example, a program in this language may be

```
main = ["Hello", " ", "world!"]
```

Under this regime, note that the following two programs are equivalent:

```
main =                                    main =
    let                    ≡                  let
        f x = "Hello"                             f x = "Hello"
        a   = f x                                 a   = f x
        b   = f x                                 b   = a
    in                                        in
        [a,b]                                     [a,b]
```

In both cases, we output two copies of "Hello". So, the program remains referentially transparent. Further, given the program

```
main =
    let
        a = "Hello"
        b = "world!"
    in
        [a,b]
```

the output is always "Hello" followed by "world!", irrespective of the order of evaluation in the block, because the program driver outputs the strings in the result list in order. So, we have retained implicit parallelism.

What we have done is to take the actual side effects out of the language and into the external environment in which the program is run (the program driver). The language itself remains purely functional. A program has no effects; instead, a program is a *specification* of intended effects that are actually performed by the program driver. Alternatively, the functional program produces, as its result, an imperative (nonfunctional) program that, when executed by a program driver, has the desired effects (the "imperative program" here is a very primitive one, the list of strings, which can be viewed as a sequence of commands to print strings).

Considering the issue of sequencing again, we have essentially finessed the problem of temporal sequencing by pushing it out into the program driver. We have converted it into a spatial sequencing problem—namely, the order in which items appear in the list—and relegated to the external program driver the requirement that it should print the strings in the order that they appear in the list.

We will not push this hypothetical language much further, because it gets messy if we try to extend it to handle outputs of different types and to handle inputs. Yet, it demonstrates the key insights in keeping the functional and nonfunctional worlds separate yet safely related.

8.1.3   Monadic I/O in Haskell and *pH*

If we were only interested in doing output actions, we could easily handle it by extending the hypothetical tack just taken. Instead of a list of strings, a program's `main` value would be a list of commands, and we could define a suitable type to represent all the kinds of output commands we might be interested in (screen bitmap updates, network packet-sends, disk block-writes, audio beeps, and so on). But of course we also want to perform input actions. An input action must produce some value within our functional world, on which we wish to operate, and which in turn may enable us to produce more output or input actions. The monadic I/O system is a way to stitch together this apparent interaction with the I/O world without actually doing the I/O.

In keeping with the insight presented in the last section, our program will only deal with specifications of actions (which we'll call "actionspecs"), not actions themselves. We no longer distinguish between input and output actionspecs. We will refer to them uniformly as "I/O actionspecs." Each I/O actionspec will have a type

```
IO a
```

which represents some action and the type "a" of the value it would return, when it is executed. For input actionspecs, this returned value corresponds to the actual entity that would be input; for output actionspecs the returned value is usually Unit.

As in our hypothetical tack, the special identifier `main` represents the overall actionspec of the program:

```
main :: IO ()
```

How do we construct an I/O actionspec of type "()"? We can start with a built-in function that produces such an actionspec:

```
putChar :: Char  ->  IO ()
```

So,

```
main = putChar 'a'
```

is an actionspec that indicates that the character "a" is to be output to some standard output device.

A primitive actionspec

```
getChar :: IO Char
```

represents the action that would return a character from some standard input device.

We can construct a composite actionspec by combining two other actionspecs using the following binary infix operator:

```
(>>=) :: IO a  ->  (a -> IO b)  ->  IO b
```

Suppose

```
f = \a -> x₂
y = x₁  >>=  f
```

The actionspec y represents an action that returns a value of type b. What is that action? It is the following:

- Perform the action represented by x_1, producing a value of type a.
- Apply f to that value, producing a new actionspec x_2 of type IO b.
- Perform the action represented by x_2, producing a value of type b.
- Return the value of type b.

For example:

```
getChar >>= putChar
```

represents an action that will simply echo an input character; it reads a character from the standard input device and writes it to the standard output device. The following program:

```
main =
    let
        islc  c = putChar (if ('a' <= c) && (c <= 'z')
                           then 'y'
                           else 'n')
    in
        getChar >>= islc
```

represents the action of inputting a character, testing whether it is a lower-case alphabet character, and outputting the character `'y'` or the character `'n'` accordingly.

Sometimes we wish to combine two actionspecs that are otherwise unrelated—the result of the first actionspec does not have to be fed into the second. In this situation we can use the simpler binary infix operator:

```
(>>) :: IO a  ->  IO b  ->  IO b
```

Suppose

$$y = x_1 \; >> \; x_2$$

The actionspec y represents the performance of the action represented by x_1 followed by the action represented by x_2. For example:

```
putStr "Hello"  >>  putStr " "  >>  putStr "world!"
```

represents the action of writing the string `"Hello"`, then writing a string with a blank character, and finally writing the string `"world!"`. The following expression:

```
getChar >> getChar
```

specifies an action that will read two characters from the input and return the second one (effectively skipping the first character).

Any value can be converted into the trivial actionspec that represents the null action (no effect) and that returns the given value, by applying the function `return` to the value:

```
return :: a  ->  IO a
```

For example, `getLine` is an actionspec for reading characters from the standard input device up to and including a newline character (written in *pH* as '\n'), and returning the characters (without the newline) as a string:

```
getLine :: IO String
getLine = getChar
          >>=
          \c -> if c == '\n' then
                   return ""
                else
                   getLine
                   >>=
                   \s -> (return c:s)
```

The program structure is based on the following recursive description of an input line: it is either empty (just the newline character) or it is a character followed by an input line. The outer >>= performs the action in its left argument, getChar, returning the next character from the input. Then, it applies its right argument, expressed as a λ-expression, to this character. This binds c to the character and executes the body of the λ-expression. If c is the newline character, we return the empty string "". Otherwise the inner ">>=" operator first performs its left argument, getLine, which returns the rest of the line. It then applies its right argument to this string. This binds the rest of the line to s, conses the current character c in front of it, and returns the line.

Exercise 8.1   What is the type of each instance of ">>=" in getLine?   ■

Deeply nested compositions of I/O actions can become quite messy, particularly because the second argument of >>= is a function that is usually written as a λ-expression. For this reason, *pH* provides some syntactic sugar: the **do** notation. A **do** expression contains a sequence of do statements. A do statement can be an action (an expression), or a binding of an identifier to the result of an action, or a let-binding of identifiers to expressions. The last do statement must be an expression. A **do** expression is itself an actionspec; its type is the type of the final actionspec in its sequence of do statements.

E	::=	· · ·	
	|	**do** *dostmts* *E*	
dostmts	::=	*dostmt* · · · *dostmt*	
dostmt	::=	*E*	action
	|	*pat* <- *E*	action binding result
	|	**let** *decl* · · · *decl*	intermediate bindings

This is purely syntactic sugar. A **do** expression can always be eliminated by translating it into an expression that uses the binary composition operators for actionspecs.

$$
\begin{array}{lll}
\textbf{do } e & \rightarrow & e \\
\textbf{do } (e) \ dostmts & \rightarrow & e \ \texttt{>>} \ \textbf{do } dostmts \\
\textbf{do } (p \ \texttt{<-} \ e) \ dostmts & \rightarrow & e \ \texttt{>>=} \ \backslash p \ \texttt{->} \ \textbf{do } dostmts \\
\textbf{do let } (p = e) \ dostmts & \rightarrow & \textbf{let } p = e \ \textbf{in do } dostmts
\end{array}
$$

For example, our `getLine` function can be written with **do** notation:

```
getLine :: IO String
getLine = do
            c <- getChar
            if c == '\n' then return ""
            else
                do
                    s <- getLine
                    return c:s
```

This notation looks remarkably similar to the notation in a traditional imperative language, but it is important to remember that "<–" is performing λ-binding, not assignment.

8.1.4   Counting Characters, Words, and Lines in a File

Suppose we want to count the number of characters, words, and lines in a file, where a "word" is defined as any contiguous sequence of nonwhitespace characters (this is just like the *wc* utility program that is available on most Unix machines).

We will need a number of utility functions that are available in *pH*'s standard libraries. The following types and function are useful for connecting to a file in the file system:

```
type  FilePath = String

data  IOMode = ReadMode | WriteMode | ...

data  Handle = ...  -- implemented as a built-in type

openFile :: FilePath  ->  IOMode  ->  IO Handle
```

The type `FilePath` is just a string that uses some operating-system-specific notation for naming files, such as `"/usr/rockford/files/data.text"`. The `IOMode` algebraic type just contains constants that allow us to specify the kind of connection to a file that we wish to establish, such as for reading or for writing. The Handle algebraic type is built in (just like Int and Float are built in). It is analogous to the "FILE *" type in C programs that represents a file and a "current position" within that file. Finally, the function openFile is analogous to the fopen() function in C: it opens the specified file in the specified mode and returns a handle that represents the starting position in that file. The function

```
hClose    ::  Handle -> IO ()
```

closes a connection to a file. The functions

```
hIsEOF   ::    Handle -> IO Bool
hGetChar ::    Handle -> IO Char
```

test if a handle is at the end of a file, and return the next character at the handle and advance the handle, respectively.

We first write an outer function wc:

```
wc              :: String  -> IO (Int,Int,Int)
wc  filename =
    do
        h <- openFile  filename  ReadMode
        (nc,nw,nl) <- wch  h  False  0  0  0
        hClose h
        return (nc,nw,nl)
```

wc takes a file name argument and returns an actionspec that will perform the requisite counting. The actions will open the file; perform the auxiliary actionspec wch (to be explained shortly) that will return the character, word, and line counts; close the file handle; and finally return the counts.

Our strategy to count words is to increment a counter every time we transition into a word as we scan the file. In other words, we increment the counter every time we see a whitespace character followed by a non-whitespace character. The auxiliary function wch takes five arguments: the file handle, a boolean inWord that is true whenever the previous character was not a whitespace character, and three integers for running counts of characters, words, and lines. It returns an actionspec that will return the three counts.

```
wch :: Handle->Bool->Int->Int->Int -> IO (Int,Int,Int)
wch h inWord nc nw nl =
```

```
do
    eof <- hIsEOF h
    if eof then return (nc,nw,nl)
    else
        do
            c <- hGetChar h
            if c == '\n' then
                (wch  h False (nc+1) nw (nl+1))
            else if isSpace c then
                (wch  h False (nc+1) nw nl)
            else if not inWord then
                (wch  h True (nc+1) (nw+1) nl)
            else
                (wch  h True (nc+1) nw nl)
```

wch is initially called with False (not in a word) and zero counts. It first
tests if we are at the end of the file; if so, it returns the counts. If not, it
gets the next character and this is bound to "c". It recursively calls wch with
arguments modified according to this character. In all cases, the character
count is incremented. If it is a newline, we increment the line count. If it is
not a space and we were previously not in a word, we increment the word
count. We can now package this up into a program, as follows:

```
main :: IO ()
main = do
            putStr "File name ? :"
            filename   <- getLine
            (nc,nw,nl) <- wc filename
            putStr "    "
            putStr (show nc)
            putStr "    "
            putStr (show nw)
            putStr "    "
            putStr (show nl)
            putStr "    "
            putStr filename
            putStr "\n"
```

The program prompts for a file name, reads the file name from the standard
input, performs the word count computation on the file, and finally prints
out the counts and the file name.

Exercise 8.2   Extend the word count program so that it also counts how many of the lines
in the file were blank.

Exercise 8.3   The standard libraries also provide an actionspec:

```
getArgs :: IO [String]
```

which returns a list of the command line arguments (excluding the command used to invoke the program itself). Modify main so that, instead of prompting for a file name, it performs and prints a word count on each command line argument interpreted as a file name.   ■

8.1.5   Limitations of Monadic I/O

There are two major limitations of the monadic I/O system: total sequentiality and lack of modularity. We discuss each in turn.

Total Sequentiality

The two composition operators for actionspecs, ">>=" and ">>", are sequencing operators. Any composite actionspec we build with these operators, therefore, results in a total sequential ordering of the component actions. Suppose we want to compute the combined word count on two files:

```
do
    (nc1,nw1,nl1) <- wc filename1
    (nc2,nw2,nl2) <- wc filename2
    return (nc1+nc2, nw1+nw2, nl1+nl2)
```

The two word counts will be performed one after the other. Thus, even though the two word counts are independent and could be performed in parallel, our composition operators do not give us any way to express this.

There are plenty of programs where we would like to perform I/O in parallel. When reading a file of data values to fill up a large matrix, we would like to start n parallel threads, each responsible for filling up $1/n$ of the matrix. Similarly, when writing out a large matrix that is the result of a program, we would like to write pieces of the matrix out to a file in parallel. Writing to a disk and writing to the screen are conceptually independent actions that need not be sequenced. "Parallel make" is popular with software developers because it allows the parallel execution of the steps involved in building a large software system (compilation of source files, generation of interface files, and so on).

The Modularity Problem

In Chapter 2 we saw a function to compute square roots using Newton's method:

```
sqrt    :: Float -> Float
sqrt x =
    let
          .
          .
          .
    in
          result
```

Suppose, as we develop the program, we are suspicious that the algorithm we have implemented is incorrect. A C programmer would think nothing of embedding a print statement inside the function to print out some key values that would help identify the problem. Suppose we try something analogous:

```
sqrt    :: Float -> Float
sqrt x =
    let
          .
          .
          .
          a = (writeString ...) :: IO String
    in
          result
```

Unfortunately, this does not achieve what we want. The binding that we have added does absolutely nothing at all! Recall that an expression of type (IO String) is not an action, it is only a specification for an action that can be performed by an external agent, the program driver. But here, since the actionspec has not been stitched into the top-level "IO ()" actionspec that is main (using ">>=" and ">>"), the actionspec is not visible to the program driver and so has no effect. It is the sound of a tree falling in an empty forest; nothing happens.

Can we fix this? Unfortunately we cannot do so without a wholesale change in the interface of sqrt. For this writeString to have an effect, it needs to be made part of the actionspec that is main. In order to do that, we have to transmit it out of the sqrt function, which implies changing its interface:

```
sqrt    :: Float -> (Float, IO String)
sqrt x =
```

```
let
    .
    .
    .
    a = (writeString ...) :: IO String
in
    (result, a)
```

This, in turn, implies changing all calls to the `sqrt` function, and perhaps to any function that calls `sqrt`, and so on. In general each such embedded I/O actionspec has to be "lifted" out, perhaps through several levels, in order to be incorporated into the `main` actionspec. This can result in a wholesale reorganization of the program.

This is but one example where it is useful to embed a side effect into a function. There are several other useful examples. For example, a pseudorandom number generator typically looks like a function:

```
random :: () -> Float

    ... random () ...
```

However, it returns a different (pseudorandom) number each time it is called. This can be achieved by embedding an *updatable* variable called a *seed* inside the function body that it can use to return fresh random numbers on each call. Other examples:

- In compilers we often want to generate new, unique names (e.g., for α-renaming, or during inlining). This is most conveniently expressed as a procedure:

    ```
    genNewName: () -> Name
    ```

    which returns a new, unique name each time it is called.
- In an operating system we want each new process to have a new, unique identifier.
- To analyze the performance of a program we sometimes want to count how many times a particular function is called. For example, if the `sqrt` function is called very many times, then it is a good candidate on which to focus our optimization efforts. So, we would like to embed, within the `sqrt` function, an update to a counter whose final value can be examined at the end of the program.

In each case, we need to embed some updatable state in the "function."
We will look at updatable state in more detail towards the end of this chapter, but all these examples have the same modularity issue that we have just
discussed above with respect to the embedding of `writeString`.

8.2   Parallel I/O

In order to overcome the above limitations, it is necessary to abandon the
idea of keeping the language purely functional. We can do this by simply
introducing one new primitive:

```
doIO :: IO a -> a
```

(This is also known as `unsafePerformIO` in some Haskell implementations.) This primitive does exactly what the program driver does: it takes
an actionspec and actually performs the actions specified therein; after performing the action, it returns the value produced by that action.

Now it is easy to express our word counting of two files in parallel:

```
let
    (nc1,nw1,nl1) = doIO (wc filename1)
    (nc2,nw2,nl2) = doIO (wc filename2)
in
    return (nc1+nc2, nw1+nw2, nl1+nl2)
```

Because the statements of a **let**-block can be evaluated in any order,
even in parallel, the two `doIO`s can execute in parallel, performing the
word counts in parallel. This can be useful even on a uniprocessor because
the disk waits encountered in one file traversal can be overlapped with
computation in the other, and vice versa.

We can also express our debugging print statement inside the `sqrt` function without changing its interface:

```
sqrt   :: Float -> Float
sqrt x =
    let
          :
          :
          a = doIO (writeString ...)
    in
          result
```

Exercise 8.4   Just as we had the sequential composition operator ">>" for actionspecs, we could have a parallel composition operator:

```
(||) :: IO a  ->  IO b  ->  (a,b)
```

with the meaning that the two argument actions will be executed in parallel, returning a pair with the two results. Define this operator in terms of doIO.   ■

At the start of Section 8.1.2 we discussed a hypothetical procedure called printString which had the side effect of printing its string argument. The introduction of doIO is equivalent, since we can now define that procedure:

```
printString    :: String -> ()
printString  s = doIO (writeString s)
```

We also discussed the fact that with such a side effecting construct, the language is no longer referentially transparent (i.e., no longer purely functional). And, we discussed the fact that with embedded side effects, it is now necessary to have some mechanism to control sequencing explicitly. We address this topic in the next section.

8.3   Explicit Sequencing

Consider the following program:

```
let
    .
    .
    .
    a = printString "Hello"
    b = printString " "
    c = printString "world!"
    .
    .
    .

in
    .
    .
    .
```

Unfortunately, since the statements in a **let**-block can be executed in any order, there is no guarantee that this will print the three strings in the right order. We need some way to sequence these actions explicitly. *pH* has a mechanism for this, a new syntactic form: a set of statements (in a **let**-block, **while** or **for** loop, etc.) can be separated by a "barrier":

```
let
    a = printString "Hello"
    >>>
    b = printString " "
    >>>
    c = printString "world!"
in
    .
    .
    .
```

The statements before a barrier are executed completely before any statement after the barrier begins execution. The phrase "executed completely" is important: it implies that it cannot have any further side effects. This is a nontrivial dynamic condition, since a statement's right-hand side may contain arbitrary function calls, conditional execution, and so on. We also say that the sequencing is *hyperstrict*.

For example, suppose we changed our example to

```
foo () = let
               a = printString "Hello"
           in
               23

let
    x = foo ()
    >>>
    b = printString " "
    >>>
    c = printString "world!"
in
    .
    .
    .
```

Due to nonstrictness the function foo can return 23 immediately, *before* it has printed "Hello". Thus, x could be bound to the value 23 before "Hello" has been written. If the sequencing waited only until x was bound to a value, we may again print the remaining strings too early. The requirement that the expression (foo ()) *and all its implicants* be executed completely ensures that all three strings are printed in the correct order.

8.3.1   Sequencing and Strictness

Sequencing can change the strictness properties of a program. Consider the following expression (which has no side effects):

```
let
    x = sqrt 6847.0
    >>>
    y = [1.0, 2.0, 3.0, x]
in
    y
```

Without sequencing, nonstrictness allows the list cells to be allocated and returned as a result even while the square root computation is going on. A consumer of y could even run down the first few elements of the list while the sqrt function is doing its work. With sequencing, on the other hand, the entire list can only be constructed *after* the square root computation is completed.

So far, the order in which statements appear in a block is immaterial; they can be freely permuted with no effect on the program. This is no longer true under sequencing. Suppose we exchanged the above two statements:

```
let
    y = [1.0, 2.0, 3.0, x]
    >>>
    x = sqrt 6847.0
in
    y
```

The square root computation cannot begin until all the list cells are allocated and all the head and tail values are stored. However, the value x cannot be stored until the square root computation is completed. Thus, we have a *deadlock* situation where computation cannot proceed.

Another surprising example:

```
    _ = y
    >>>
    x = e
```

The expression y has executed completely when y is bound to a value. Thus, the barrier has the effect of making the expression *e* strict in the variable y *even if it does not use variable y at all!*

8.3.2 Nested Sequential and Parallel Forms, and Scoping

Using parentheses, we can nest the sequential and parallel composition of statements in order to control more precisely exactly what gets sequenced. For example:

```
let
    s1
    (   s2
        >>>
        (   s3
            s4 ))
    s5
in
    e
```

The statements s1, s2, and s5 and the expression e are evaluated in parallel immediately. After s2 completes, s3 and s4 are evaluated in parallel (and may overlap with the evaluation of s1, s5, and e, if they are still executing). The block's return expression e always executes in parallel with the top-level statement(s) of the block.

The scope of identifiers is not affected by sequencing (i.e., scoping is entirely orthogonal). For example:

```
let
    s1
    (   x = ... y ...
        >>>
        (   s3
            s4 ))
    y = ... x ...
in
    e
```

The use of y inside the sequentialization, and the use of x outside, are both perfectly legal. Thus, sequencing structure can be completely ignored in order to decide scope issues.

8.3.3 Implicit versus Explicit Sequencing

Explicit sequencing using ">>>" may sequence more things than we want to sequence. For example:

```
let
    x = e₁ -- a large expression with a (printString s₁) deep inside
```

```
          >>>
          y = e₂ -- a large expression with a (printString s₂) deep inside
     in
          .
          .
          .
```

This sequences everything in e_1 before everything in e_2, even though we may only intend to sequence the two printStrings.

Two side effect actions can instead be sequenced specifically by *threading* them appropriately. Consider the following transformation of the code:

```
let
     (x,z') = let
                   .        .
                   .        .
                               z = printString s₁

                   .        .
                   .        .
              in
                  (result, z)

     y       = ...
                             let
                                 z'' = z'
                                 >>>
                                 printString s₂
                             in
                                 .
                                 .
                                 .

                   .
                   .
                   .
in
     .
     .
     .
```

We first capture the result of the first printString, for example by binding it to z. Then, we need to communicate this result to the vicinity of the second printString. This will typically involve restructuring e_1 appropriately so that it returns this z in addition to its original result x. It may also involve restructuring e_2 if, for example, the second printString is inside some function call; in this case, z will have to be passed down as an extra parameter. Finally, we replace the second printString using a sequentialization that first waits for the value z and then executes the printString. The outer barrier can now be eliminated.

Thus, at the cost of some program restructuring to introduce some "plumbing," we set up an artificial data dependency between the two sub-expressions that we want to sequence. The programmer therefore has a spectrum of choices for sequencing: he can use barriers as a simple but heavyweight hammer to sequence things, or he can make the sequencing as fine-grain and specific as he likes by constructing suitable data dependencies.

8.4   Rewrite Rules for Explicit Sequencing (Barriers)

Our rewrite rules for barriers use the syntactic category of Heap terms, defined in Section 4.3, which precisely capture the notion of "complete execution" of statements.

8.4.1   Syntax

We extend our formal syntax with the following:

$$E ::= \quad \cdots$$

$$
\begin{array}{lll}
S ::= & \cdots \\
 & | \quad S_1;\ S_2 & \text{Parallel statements} \\
 & | \quad S_1 >\!>\!> S_2 & \text{Sequential statements}
\end{array}
$$

In our formal syntax, the parallel and sequential statement-combining forms only work on pairs of statements. Any source code fragment that involves multiple statements can be converted into an equivalent set of nested combinations, each containing only two statements, as described in Section 8.3.2.

In a "$S_1 >\!>\!> S_2$" form, the statements S_1 and S_2 are known as the *pre-region* and the *postregion*, respectively.

8.4.2   Syntactic Equivalence Rules

In Section 4.3, we defined Heap terms as follows:

$$H ::= \quad x = V \quad | \quad H\ ;\ H \qquad \text{Value bindings}$$

It is clear that Heap terms are terminated terms (i.e., they do not contain any residual computation). Thus, a Heap term in the preregion of ">>>" does not contribute anything to sequencing. The following additional equivalence rule allows us to move Heap terms out of a preregion:

Equivalence properties of ";" (parallel statement composition):

$$(H ; S_1) \text{ >>> } S_2 \quad \equiv \quad H ; (S_1 \text{ >>> } S_2)$$

8.4.3   Rewrite Rules

We saw that Heap terms can escape out of the preregions of ">>>" terms. Eventually, the preregion becomes an empty statement. The following rules allow us to eliminate ">>>" forms because empty statements have no effect on sequencing:

$$\epsilon \text{ >>> } S \qquad \longrightarrow \quad S \qquad\qquad \text{(SEQ1)}$$
$$S \text{ >>> } \epsilon \qquad \longrightarrow \quad S \qquad\qquad \text{(SEQ2)}$$

8.4.4   Properties of Sequentialization

There are several interesting consequences of the rules for ">>>" forms. First, if the preregion consists entirely of Heap terms, we can convert the sequential composition into a parallel composition:

$$H \text{ >>> } S \qquad\qquad \longrightarrow \quad H ; S$$

Second, our rules are actually a little more liberal than our original explanation that the preregion must be executed completely before anything is executed in the postregion. In fact, we can freely perform reductions within the postregion; the rules ensure that postregion reductions cannot have any effect on the preregion or on the surrounding context. In other words, postregions are *opaque*, and it is always safe to postpone postregion reductions until the barrier is discharged. In fact, this is what we would do in any practical implementation, to avoid possibly wasted work. For this reason, the SEQ2 rule is there only for completeness.

Third, the ">>>" form is associative:

$$S_1 \text{ >>> } (S_2 \text{ >>> } S_3) \quad \equiv \quad (S_1 \text{ >>> } S_2) \text{ >>> } S_3$$

Fourth, the ">>>" form only constrains the set of results that can be achieved. In other words, if we replaced a ";" by a ">>>", no new results are thereby possible; only a subset of the original results are possible.

8.5   Updatable Cells

We now turn to updatable cells and assignment statements as the final topic of this chapter. Our focus here will only be on semantics using rewrite rules, and we will ignore questions about types and type checking. In the next two chapters we will consider how to build type-safe *pH* language constructs based on these semantics and how to use them in practical programming.

As mentioned earlier, the key difference between *pH*'s updatable cells and traditional "variables" in programming languages like C and Pascal is *implicit synchronization*. This is because ordinary variables are very tricky to use in any parallel language, let alone a language like *pH* with such abundant implicit parallelism. Let us briefly review why this is so. Suppose in a parallel Pascal program we have two parallel activities containing the following two statements:

```
  .                                   .
  .                                   .
  .                                   .
x := x + 1;                         x := x + 2;
  .                                   .
  .                                   .
  .                                   .
```

Suppose the variable x initially contained the value 0. The programmer may expect that after these two statements have executed, x will contain 3

Unfortunately, these statements are not *atomic*. In their compiled form, each consists of a sequence of actions:

```
  .                                   .
  .                                   .
  .                                   .
read₁ x                             read₂ x
compute x+1                         compute x+2
write₁ result to x                  write₂ result to x
  .                                   .
  .                                   .
  .                                   .
```

Although the actions in each thread are done in order, there is typically no guarantee about the relative timing of actions in different threads—it depends on the language's run-time system, the load on the machine, and many other factors. Thus, one possible schedule of these actions may be

```
read₁ ... read₂ ... write₂ ... write₁
```

which will leave the value 1 in x! Worse, another thread that happened to read the variable just after write₂ would read the value 2. Whereas the programmer may have expected x to have a steadily increasing value, a thread may observe x having the sequence of values 0, 2, 1, . . .

These kinds of *race* conditions make it very hard to program with ordinary variables and assignments in parallel programs. It is to avoid these kind of problems that *pH* has variables with implicit synchronization.

In traditional languages like C and Pascal, *every* variable can be assigned; its value can be changed—there is no such thing as a nonupdatable variable. In fact in such languages when we talk about the "value of a variable" what we really mean is the "value currently contained in the location bound to the variable." In *pH* we make this distinction explicit. As has been true throughout the book thus far, a *pH* variable never changes; it is uniquely bound to a value. Instead, to introduce updates and assignments into the language, we introduce a new type of value—an explicitly, dynamically allocated *cell*, with primitive operations to read from and write to the cell with implicit synchronization.

Cell allocation is performed by the procedure call `allocate()`, which returns a new, dynamically allocated cell:

```
x = allocate ()
```

Cells are first-class objects—we can bind identifiers to cells (like x above), pass cells as function arguments or return them as function results, build lists and arrays of cells, and so on. The `allocate()` procedure call is itself a kind of side effect because each invocation allocates and returns a brand-new cell. Consider the following two program fragments:

```
let                                      let
    x = allocate ()                          x = allocate ()
    y = allocate ()                          y = x
in                                       in
    (x,y)                                    (x,y)
```

The left fragment returns a 2-tuple each of whose components refers to a separate cell, whereas the right fragment returns a 2-tuple both of whose components refer to the same cell.

A cell cannot only contain a value, but it is also in one of two states *full* and *empty*. When allocated, the cell is intially empty. We can store a value into an empty cell, thereby making it full:

```
sStore   x   v
```

This is a new kind of *statement* in *pH* syntax and therefore appears in **let**-blocks and loop bodies just like value bindings and type declarations.

It is an error to attempt to `sStore` to a full cell. There are two operations to read a value from a full cell:

```
a = iFetch  x
```

and

```
b = mFetch  x
```

Both can only read from a full cell; they wait, if necessary, until the cell is full (due to an `sStore` in some other part of the program). The difference between the two is that an `iFetch` leaves the cell full (permitting further fetches), whereas an `mFetch` leaves the cell empty. It is this behavior with respect to the full and empty states of cells that we refer to as implicit synchronization.

In practice we will never mix `iFetch`es and `mFetch`es on the same cell. As we will see in the next two chapters, this will be enforced using types and type checking.

Suppose we have a *pH* program with the following parallel activities:

```
    :                    :                    :
    :                    :                    :
sStore x v           a = iFetch x         b = iFetch x
    :                    :                    :
    :                    :                    :
```

The synchronization semantics ensures that the latter two `iFetch` operations can execute only after the `sStore` has executed, even if they are attempted earlier. Similarly, consider the following parallel activities:

```
    :                    :
    :                    :
a = mFetch x         c = mFetch x
b = a + 1            d = c + 2
sStore x b           sStore x d
    :                    :
    :                    :
```

Suppose the left-hand `mFetch` executes first. This will leave the cell x empty, so that even if the right-hand `mFetch` is now attempted, it will have to wait until the left-hand `sStore` completes, making the cell full again. Thus, we do not encounter the kind of race condition problems that we outlined above with traditional assignment statements.

8.5.1   Random Number Generators, Unique Identifier Generators, and So On

In Section 8.1.5, we cited a random number generator as an example of a function where it is useful to embed a side effect. We now have the mechanisms to implement this. In programming languages we typically use so-called *pseudorandom number generators*. These are procedures that, each time they are called, return the next member of a sequence:

$$x, \quad f(x), \quad f(f(x)), \ldots$$

where f is chosen so that successive members of the sequence are "apparently" random. A popular choice for f is a function of the form

$$f(x) = (ax + b) \bmod c$$

for suitable choices of integers a, b, and c.

Why do programmers use such pseudorandom numbers instead of "truly" random numbers? There are two important reasons. First, it is actually quite hard to produce true, uniformly distributed random numbers in a computer, without actually sampling some physical phenomenon that has that property (such as electromagnetic noise) using a special I/O board in the computer. Second, we still often want *repeatability* in our programs (e.g., for debugging), which would not be possible with a truly random sequence.

Here, then, is the code for a pseudo-random number generator:

```
random :: () -> Float
random = let
            c = allocate ()
            sStore  c  initial_x
            g () = let
                      x  = mFetch c
                      x' = f  x
                      sStore  c  x'
                   in
                      x
         in
            g
```

We allocate a cell, store an initial value of x in the cell, and return the function g (which contains a reference to the cell) as the value of random. Each time random (i.e., g) is applied (to "()"), it returns the current contents of the cell and replaces the cell contents with $f(x)$. Thus, the cell is a "private" piece of state inside the function random that remembers something from the last time it was called.

Note also that even if random is called simultaneously from two or more parts of a parallel program, the implicit synchronization of mFetch and sStore will ensure that each update to the cell is done atomically.

Exactly the same structure can be used for a function that generates unique identifiers (uids). For example, in a compiler we may wish to finesse scoping problems by renaming all identifiers with unique names using α-renaming. We can represent the new names as integers. What we need, as we traverse the program text, is a function gen_uid() that returns a new, unique integer each time it is called. Here it is:

```
gen_uid :: () -> Int
gen_uid = let
              c = allocate ()
              sStore  c  0                  -- 0 is the initial uid
              g () = let
                        x  = mFetch c
                        sStore  c  (1 + x)
                     in
                        x
          in
              g
```

Note that the allocated cell is not a global variable. Our scope rules ensure that the only code that has access to it is the function g. In other words, the state has been "encapsulated" so that it is visible only to the code that actually uses it.

Let us push this idea a little further. Going back to our compiler example, the language being compiled may have multiple name spaces. For example, this is true when we are compiling *pH:* the name x in an ordinary expression, where it represents an ordinary variable, is unrelated to the name x in type expressions, where it represents a type variable. For this reason, our example compiler may need several uid generators, one per namespace. So, let us abstract our previous function up one level into a function that, when applied, returns a uid generator function:

```
make_gen_uid     :: () -> () -> Int
make_gen_uid () =
          let
                c = allocate ()
                sStore  c  0
                g () = let
                              x  = mFetch c
                              sStore   c   (1 + x)
                         in
                              x
          in
                g
```

Now consider the following uses:

```
typevar_gen = make_gen_uid()
ordvar_gen  = make_gen_uid()


    ... typevar_gen() ...
        ... typevar_gen() ...

    ... ordvar_gen() ...
        ... ordvar_gen() ...
```

In the first two lines, we produce two uid generator functions, binding them to typevar_gen and ordvar_gen. Each of these applications of make_gen_uid allocates and encapsulates its own cell. All subsequent applications of typevar_gen share the cell that was allocated by the first make_gen_uid () call. Similarly, all subsequent applications of ordvar_gen share the cell that was allocated by the second make_gen_uid () call. However, the typevar_gen and ordvar_gen calls have nothing in common—they use and update independent cells.

Exercise 8.5   Suppose we have written a program containing some definition

```
foo              ::      t
foo   x₁ ... xₙ = e
```

$$\text{foo} \quad :: \quad t$$
$$\text{foo} \quad x_1 \ldots x_n = e$$

Modify this definition so that it has the form

```
foo              :: t
report           :: () -> Int
(foo, report) = ...
```

The new foo should have exactly the same behavior as before. It should have exactly the same type t, and, when applied to any particular set of arguments, it should return exactly the same result as it would have before. Meanwhile, the call report() should return an integer corresponding to the number of times that foo has been called thus far.   ∎

Exercise 8.6 The gen_uid function can safely be called in parallel because of the implicit synchronization of mFetch and sStore. However, it can still be a performance bottleneck because many parallel calls may contend simultaneously for the single shared cell. Let us try to alleviate this bottleneck somewhat. Modify the gen_uid definition so that, instead, it defines a 2-tuple of functions gen_uid1 and gen_uid2, with two corresponding definitions f1 and f2 inside the **let**-block. Instead of a single encapsulated cell, it should have three encapsulated cells c, c1, and c2, initialized to the values 200, 0, and 100, respectively. The function f1 should normally use cell c1 for its uids, except when the value reaches a multiple of 100, it should get a fresh starting value from c, incrementing the value in c by 100. Similarly, the function f2 should normally use cell c2 for its uids, except when the value reaches a multiple of 100, it should get a fresh starting value from c, incrementing the value in c by 100. Thus, the two functions gen_uid1 and gen_uid2 can be called in parallel, mostly without any contention. Most of the time, they will work with their private cells c1 and c2, respectively. Every 100th uid, they will get a fresh value from c, during which they may contend with each other, but the probability of this is very low.

You can think of c as doling out a chunk of uids to be used by each uid generator. Each uid generator uses its own chunk; only when this chunk is exhausted does it go to c to get a new chunk. Since this occurs only once every 100 uids, it greatly reduces the pressure on c. Exactly this idea is used to avoid bottlenecks in parallel heap allocators, to dole out IP addresses on the Internet, to dole out UPC bar codes (universal bar codes) for supermarket products, and so on.   ∎

Exercise 8.7 Generalize the idea of the previous exercise to some arbitrary n (instead of 2). In particular, write a function

```
make_par_gen_uids    ::    Int -> Array Int (() -> Int)
```

When applied to an integer n, it returns an array with n slots, each containing a gen_uid function that behaves as in the previous exercise; that is, each gen_uid() works with its own updatable cell for 100 uids before going to a shared cell for a fresh chunk of 100 uids.   ∎

We will see many more examples of the usefulness of iFetch and mFetch in the next two chapters, respectively. For now, we will just study the formal semantics of cell operations.

8.5.2   Rewrite Rules for Updatable Cells

The rewrite rules use a notion of *cell identifiers* as an abstraction of the memory pointers that would be used in a concrete implementation.

Syntax
We extend our formal syntax with the following:

E	::=	$\cdots$	
	|	allocate()	Cell allocation
	|	iFetch(E)	I-structure fetch
	|	mFetch(E)	M-structure fetch
	|	0_j	Cell identifiers
S	::=	$\cdots$	
	|	sStore(E, E)	Synchronized store
	|	alloc_trig	Heap allocation trigger
	|	empty(0_j)	Empty cells
	|	error(0_j)	Error cells
	|	full(0_j, V)	Full cells

Cell identifiers, empty cells, error cells, and full cells arise only dynamically during the process of reduction (and so we call them "noninitial" terms). The heap allocation trigger alloc_trig is not part of *pH* source programs. A single occurrence of this term is introduced by the reduction system just prior to performing any reductions, as follows. Given an intial program *e*, we convert it to

```
let
    alloc_trig
in
    e
```

The purpose of the allocation trigger is to permit allocate() to execute only in the exposed areas of the program, that is, outside λ-expressions, conditionals, barrier postregions, and so on; how it does this will become apparent soon when we see the cell allocation rule.

Values and Heap Terms

We extend the class of Values and Heap terms as follows:

$$
\begin{array}{lll}
V & ::= & \cdots \\
  & | & 0_j & \text{Cell identifiers}
\end{array}
$$

$$
\begin{array}{lll}
H & ::= & \cdots \\
  & | & \texttt{alloc\_trig} & \text{Heap allocation trigger} \\
  & | & \texttt{empty}(0_j) & \text{Empty cells} \\
  & | & \texttt{error}(0_j) & \text{Error cells} \\
  & | & \texttt{full}(0_j,V) & \text{Full cells}
\end{array}
$$

Rewrite Rules for Cell Operations

Allocation creates a new memory cell, named by a brand-new cell identifier:

$$
\begin{array}{ll}
\begin{array}{l}
\texttt{alloc\_trig;} \\
x \texttt{ = allocate()}
\end{array}
& \longrightarrow
\begin{array}{l}
\texttt{alloc\_trig;} \\
\texttt{empty}(0_j); \\
x \texttt{ = } 0_j
\end{array}
& \text{(Alloc)}
\end{array}
$$

The `alloc_trig` term remains unchanged: it merely enables allocation. There are no rules that move `alloc_trig` into λ-bodies, conditionals, barrier postregions, and so on. Thus, no heap allocations can happen in those regions of a program; heap allocation can only happen in the parts of the program where computation has been "exposed" at the outermost level.

Since there are no rules that replicate the `alloc_trig` term, this rule also sequentializes—only one allocation can occur at a time. We can relax this to any fixed degree p of parallelism by introducing p `alloc_trig` terms instead of one in our initial step before reduction. We can even permit unbounded parallelism in heap allocation by adding a reduction rule to replicate the `alloc_trig` term:

$$
\texttt{alloc\_trig} \quad \longrightarrow \quad \texttt{alloc\_trig; alloc\_trig} \qquad \text{(ParHeap)}
$$

The assignment rules allow us to store a value into an empty cell, but generate an error if we try to store into a full cell:

$$
\begin{array}{ll}
\begin{array}{l}
\texttt{empty}(0_j); \\
\texttt{sStore}(0_j,\ v)
\end{array}
& \longrightarrow \quad \texttt{full}(0_j,v)
& \qquad \text{(SStore)}
\end{array}
$$

$$
\begin{array}{ll}
\begin{array}{l}
\texttt{full}(0_j,v); \\
\texttt{sStore}(0_j,\ w)
\end{array}
& \longrightarrow
\begin{array}{l}
\texttt{full}(0_j,v); \\
\texttt{error}(0_j)
\end{array}
& \qquad \text{(SStoreErr)}
\end{array}
$$

The introduction of the `error()` term "poisons" the whole program. Semantically, the presence of an `error()` term indicates that the whole program is in error. In a practical implementation, it is typically acceptable to stop program execution as soon as this term is created.

(In a variation of the SStoreErr rule, one could omit the $\text{full}(0_j, v)$ term on the right-hand side. By keeping the term, our version simply allows continued execution of iFetch operations against the cell.)

The following rule for iFetch ensures that it can only operate on a full cell:

$$\begin{array}{llr}
\text{full}(0_j, v); & \longrightarrow & \text{full}(0_j, v); & \text{(iFetch)} \\
x = \text{iFetch}(0_j) & & x = v
\end{array}$$

The cell remains unchanged, allowing more iFetches to occur on the cell. The following rule for mFetch ensures that it can only operate on a full cell:

$$\begin{array}{llr}
\text{full}(0_j, v); & \longrightarrow & \text{empty}(0_j); & \text{(mFetch)} \\
x = \text{mFetch}(0_j) & & x = v
\end{array}$$

Unlike iFetch, where the cell remained full with the value, an mFetch transitions the cell back into the empty state.

New Lifting Rules

As usual in lifting rules, t represents a variable that does not otherwise occur, and $e \notin SE$ (i.e., e is not a Simple Expression):

$$\begin{array}{llr}
\text{sStore}(e, e_2) & \longrightarrow & t = e; \ \text{sStore}(t, e_2) & \text{(LiftsStore1)} \\
\text{sStore}(e_1, e) & \longrightarrow & t = e; \ \text{sStore}(e_1, t) & \text{(LiftsStore2)}
\end{array}$$

I-structures

9

In the last chapter we introduced the basic semantic concepts underlying updatable cells with implicit synchronization. In this chapter and the next, we will see how to package those semantic concepts into type-safe, practical constructs in *pH*. There are two issues to consider.

First, we saw that there are two kinds of synchronized fetch operations: iFetch and mFetch. The difference is quite profound. In the presence of iFetches alone, it is impossible to read two different values from a cell. An mFetch, on the other hand, allows us to store a different value in the cell, allowing a subsequent fetch to read a different value. In other words, with iFetches alone, the language remains deterministic, whereas mFetches introduce nondeterminacy. For this reason, we use language constructs and type-checking rules to separate out their use—an updatable cell will either be an "I-cell," on which only iFetches are allowed, or it will be an "M-cell," on which only mFetches are allowed; we will never mix these operations.

We refer to the sStore/iFetch pair of operations as "I-structure semantics" and the sStore/mFetch pair of operations as "M-structure semantics." This chapter will consider the use of I-structure semantics, and the next chapter will consider M-structure updates.

Second, although individual updatable cells are technically expressive enough, from a language design point of view it makes more sense to incorporate updatable fields and elements directly into richer data structures. For example, if we want an array of updatable values, we could use a functional array, with each element referring to an updatable cell from the last chapter. However, this introduces an extra level of indirection that is both inconvenient for the programmer and inefficient to implement. The inefficiency arises not only because the implementation has to perform two memory references to access each element, but because the cells will have poorer cache behavior due to poorer locality of reference. Instead, we prefer to have a different kind of array, an "I-array," each of whose elements directly has I-structure semantics. A similar argument holds for algebraic types: although a normal field of an algebraic type could refer to a separate updatable cell, we prefer that the field directly have I-structure semantics; we will call such fields "I-fields."[1]

9.1   A Motivating Example

There are many problems for which it is difficult (perhaps impossible) to write an *efficient* pure functional program. Consider the following problem: we are given an array x containing n numbers:

$$x = \boxed{2\ 8\ -3\ 0\ 14\ 2\ 7\ -5}$$

We wish to produce an array y containing the same numbers, except that all negative numbers should precede all nonnegative numbers (the order within these two categories is immaterial):

$$y = \boxed{-3\ -5\ 7\ 2\ 14\ 0\ 8\ 2}$$

---

1. Historically, the name "I-structures" were only used to describe I-arrays. The name comes from *incremental structures* because they were originally proposed to solve the so-called incremental-update problem of functional languages, of which the program in the next section is an example.

Also, we would like to know the index where the nonnegative numbers begin. In the example, the first nonnegative number is 7, which is at index 3.

Here is a functional solution using an array comprehension:

```
let
    l   = 0
    r   = n+1
    jks = []
    (final_r,
     final_jks) = for j <- [1..n] do
                      (l',r',k) = if x!j >= 0 then (l,r-1,r-1)
                                              else          (l+1,r,l+1)
                      next jks  = (j,k):jks
                      next l    = l'
                      next r    = r'
                  finally (r, jks)

    y = array (1,n)
              [ (k, x!j) | (j,k) <- final_jks ]
in
    (y, final_r)
```

Conceptually, we scan the array x sequentially and, as we encounter each number, we want to "fill" it into array y either from the left or from the right, depending on whether it is negative or not. Since we cannot directly put these numbers into y, we first collect the old and new indexes of each number into a list. Then, in the array comprehension, we construct y using these old and new index pairs. The variables l and r may be regarded as cursors that point at the last filled locations from the left and right, respectively, during the scan. The final value of r is the index of the leftmost nonnegative number.

Exercise 9.1   How many times is each element of x read? Assuming that a cons cell takes two units of storage, how much storage is used by the list? Assuming that construction of a cons cell takes two writes and selection of each list element takes one read, how many reads and writes are performed on lists?   ∎

The crux of the problem is this: at the point where we know the old and the new indices j and k (inside the loop), there is no way of simply specifying that y!k should get the value of x!j. We have to remember the (j,k) pairs in a list and then separately use an array comprehension to construct y.

There does not appear to be any purely functional solution to this problem that is also efficient. With mkArray and array comprehensions, the computation for each y_i is specified independently, but in this problem there is no straightforward way of independently knowing which element of x should occupy the ith position of y.

9.2   I-fields: I-structure Fields in Algebraic Types

When we define an algebraic data type using a **data** declaration, we specify one or more disjuncts, each consisting of a constructor that may contain zero or more fields. In Sections 5.4.4 and 6.1.5 we introduced "field name" notation. *pH* leverages that notation, allowing us to specify that a particular field should have I-structure semantics.

The field name style of **data** declaration must be used. We cannot specify I-structure semantics for a field in a **data** declaration that uses ordinary positional notation for fields. This is because we need a notation for assigning a value to an I-structure field. This is awkward with positional notation and easy when we have field names.

We specify that a field has I-structure semantics by preceding its type with a "." in the data type definition. The simplest example has one constructor with one I-structure field:

```
data ICell a = ICell { contents :: . a }
```

As usual, this defines the polymorphic type ICell, with a constructor ICell and field contents. All the usual functional notations are still available. The constructor is a first-class function:

```
ICell   ::    a -> ICell a
```

We can construct a cell using ordinary application:

```
ICell  e
```

or using field name notation:

```
ICell { contents = e }
```

Given an I-cell ic, we can extract its contents using

```
contents  ic
```

or using positional pattern matching:

```
case ic of
    ICell x -> ... x ...
```

or using pattern matching with field names:

```
case ic of
    ICell { contents = x } -> ... x ...
```

However, because the field has I-structure semantics, we have some interesting new ways to use cells. We can create an I-cell with the field in the *empty* state:

```
ICell { }
```

Later, given an I-cell *ic* with an empty field, we can assign a value to the field using the following assignment statement:

```
contents ic := e
```

An assignment statement has the same syntactic status as a binding. It can appear in a sequence of bindings (e.g., in **let**-blocks and loop bodies). The notation can be understood as a definition of the value of the expression (contents *ic*).

I-cells can be viewed as a type-safe "dressing up" of the updatable cells whose semantics were described at the end of the last chapter. Allocating an I-cell with an empty field corresponds to the allocate semantic operation; assigning a value corresponds to an sStore semantic operation; and extracting the contents of the field (using any of the notations above) corresponds to the iFetch semantic operation.

The key difference between functional data structures and I-structures is the following. With functional data structures, we always specify a data structure *and its contents* together, in a single monolithic constructor application. With I-structures, on the other hand, we can separate these out. We can allocate a data structure leaving its I-fields empty, and, in a possibly distant part of the program, we can specify the contents of those fields. It is precisely this separation that gives I-structures their flexibility, often leading to more efficient programs.

Here is an attempt at a more efficient solution to our array rearrangement problem, using an array of I-cells:

```
let
    y       = array (1,n) [ (i, ic) | i <- [1..n],
                                let ic = ICell {} ]
```

```
(l,r)    = (0,n+1)
final_r = for j <- [1..n] do
             (l', r', k)     = if x!j >= 0
                               then (l,r-1,r-1)
                               else (l+1,r,l+1)
             contents (y!k) := x!j
             next l          = l'
             next r          = r'
          finally r
in
    (y, final_r)
```

In the first line, we create y, an array of empty I-cells. In the loop, we traverse the array x using the index j and we maintain, in l and r, the indices of the array y that we have filled up so far, from the left and right, respectively. We can think of l and r as "cursors" moving in from the left and right ends of the array y, respectively. The first binding in the loop computes the destination k where this jth element of x should land, and we advance l or r as appropriate. The second statement in the loop, an assignment statement, stores the jth element of x directly into the I-cell that is in the kth element of y.

Although this version is far more efficient than the functional version because it does not create any intermediate lists, it is still not quite satisfactory. The first problem is that the input and output arrays do not have the same type:

```
x    ::    Array  Int
y    ::    Array  (ICell Int)
```

The second problem is the one we mentioned earlier: the extra indirections due to the I-cells are a source of inefficiency (although not as bad as the inefficiency of the intermediate lists in the functional solution). We will solve both these problems in the following section on I-arrays.

An I-cell can also be viewed as a one-slot "mailbox." Consider the following general computation structure:

```
let
    ic = ICell { }
       .
       .
       .
    producer = ...
                    ... some big computation ...
```

```
                            containing . . .
                  let
                       contents ic := v
                  in

        .
        .
        .

consumer = ...
                       . . . some big computation . . .
                       containing . . .
                             ... (contents ic) ...

        .
        .
        .

in
        .
        .
        .
```

A "producer" computation can assign a value into an I-cell, and a "consumer" function can fetch the value. Because of the implicit synchronization of the underlying sStore and iFetch operations, it is safe to let the producer and consumer run in parallel; the consumer will simply wait, if necessary, to read the contents of the cell when it becomes full.

When used in this manner, I-cells are reminiscent of *logic variables* in logic programming languages and concurrent constraint programming languages, where they are often used exactly in this way.

And now for a few more details about I-field notation. We saw in Section 6.1.5 that a field name can be used repeatedly in multiple disjuncts of an algebraic type, provided that all these fields have the same type. The same is true for an I-structure field name as well, with the added proviso that the field must have I-structure semantics in all the disjuncts. With this proviso the I-structure assignment statement always makes sense, no matter which actual disjunct is encountered at run time.

A constructor can have both functional fields and I-structure fields (we will see an example soon with I-structure lists in Section 9.5). This is unlike arrays, where either the entire array is functional (Array type) or the entire array has I-structure elements (IArray type). The reason for this difference between algebraic types and arrays is type checking. Elements of arrays are specified by arbitrary index-valued expressions. Since we do not know these values statically, we insist that all elements must have the same type (functional or I-structure). On the other hand, field selection does not involve any computed selector—the selector is always a manifest field name and so it is easy for a static type checker to keep track of both functional and I-structure fields.

9.3   I-structure Arrays

I-arrays are arrays in which each element directly has I-structure semantics, eliminating the need for indirections via I-cells.

9.3.1   Basic I-array Operations

Operations on I-arrays include array creation, element assignment and selection, and bounds query. An I-array is created using an I-array comprehension that is just like the functional array comprehension of Section 7.6 except that we use the constructor function iArray instead of array:

    iArray   (l,u)   [... list of (index,value) pairs ...]

This denotes an I-array with index bounds l through u and initial contents given by the list of index-and-value pairs. Any index of the I-array that is not mentioned in the list is left undefined (we also say that such elements are initially *empty*). In particular, a "[]" argument would leave all elements empty.

The type of iArray is

    iArray ::   Ix a => (a,a) -> [(a,b)] -> IArray a b

That is, for any index type a (a type a in the Ix class), it takes a bounds 2-tuple and a list of index-and-value pairs and produces an I-array. The functional array subscripting notation also works for I-arrays, allowing us to read an element of an I-array:

$$e_a!e_i$$

so that the subscript operator is overloaded to also have the type

    (!)   ::   Ix a => (IArray a b) -> a -> b

As usual, e_i must be an index within the bounds of the array. Semantically, this is an iFetch operation, and so this expression reduces to a value only when the corresponding element is defined (i.e., the selection does not become a redex as long as the corresponding element is empty). An empty element of an I-array can later be defined using an I-array assignment statement:

$$e_a!e_i := e_v$$

Semantically, this is an sStore operation that defines the e_ith element of the I-array e_a to have value e_v. We can understand this notation as defining the value of the expression $e_a!e_i$. Here, e_i should evaluate to an index of suitable index type within the bounds of the array, and e_v is any value, including scalars, functions, arrays, and so on. We say that the element becomes *full* with the value of e_v. As usual with sStore operations, multiple definitions of a particular element are not allowed; if this occurs, the program is in error, and the error may only be detected at run time.

Like algebraic type I-field assignments, the I-array assignment statement can appear in binding lists, for example in **let**-blocks and loop bodies. It can be viewed as special syntax for a call to a built-in procedure:

```
iAStore   :: Ix a => (IArray a b) -> a -> b -> ()
_         = iAStore(e_a,e_i,e_v)
```

The bounds function is overloaded also to work on I-arrays; for example:

```
(1,u) = bounds a
```

is a pattern binding that extracts the index bounds of a as a 2-tuple and binds the lower and upper index bounds to 1 and u, respectively.

With these I-array operations, we can now return to our array partitioning problem. Here is a solution using I-arrays:

```
let
    y       = iArray (1,n) []
    (1,r)   = (0,n+1)
    final_r = for j <- [1..n] do
                   (1', r', k) = if x!j >= 0 then (1,r-1,r-1)
                                 else              (1+1,r,1+1)
                   y!k := x!j
                   next 1 = 1'
                   next r = r'
              finally r
in
    (y, final_r)
```

At the point where we know the old and new indexes j and k, we can directly define y!k := x!j. Not only is the program simpler and more perspicuous, but it also improves on our previous solution in that both input and output arrays are of the same type (IArray Int), and we no longer have I-cell indirections. We will soon see how we can use this solution to work even with functional input and output arrays.

Exercise 9.2   How many times is each element of x read?   ■

Exercise 9.3   In our solution above, the original order of the negative numbers is preserved, while the nonnegative elements are reversed. Devise a new solution that preserves both orders (without using any extra storage).   ■

As with functional arrays, I-arrays can also be multi-dimensional. An r-tuple may be used as the index type directly to produce an r-dimensional array, which is more efficient. The iArray comprehension, the I-array assignment, the I-array indexing operator, and the bounds function are all overloaded over index types so that they also work on multidimensional arrays.

9.3.2   Expressions as Statements

As we work more and more with I- and M-structures, we will encounter expressions that are executed purely for their side effect; the value of the expression is of no interest. Often, these expressions will have type "()" to indicate that the value is of no interest. Normally, we might use such expressions as follows, using a wildcard pattern to ignore its value:

```
let
     .
     .
     _ = e        -- an expression executed for its side effect
     .
     .
in
     .
     .
```

It is inconvenient to have to write "_ =" all the time just to discard unwanted values. For this reason, *pH* provides a shorthand where we can drop the "_ =" part. In a **let**-block, **while** loop, **for** loop, and so on, a statement that so far could only have been a binding or an assignment statement can also just be an expression:

```
let
    .
    .
    .
        e       -- an expression executed for its side effect
    .
    .
    .
in
    .
    .
    .
```

9.3.3   Run-Time Errors Due to Multiple Definitions

As we saw with sStore semantics in the last chapter, if an I-array element has multiple assignments, the program is in error. The intuitive reason is simple. If we had two assignments:

```
a!5 := 23
    .
    .
    .
a!5 := 34
```

then what should a corresponding selection expression a!5 reduce to? The multiple assignments are inconsistent.

We have seen a similar concept in Chapter 2: we do not allow multiple definitions of an identifier x in a block, nor multiple occurrences of an identifier x among the formal parameters of a function (we called this left linearity). Both cases may be regarded as constituting inconsistent definitions. However, there is a fundamental difference: multiple definitions of an identifier can be detected *statically* and rejected as syntactic errors, whereas multiple definitions of an I-structure element cannot, because they involve computed arrays and computed indices.

Multiple definitions are not possible with the functional array constructor mkArray. The definitions at each index are set up, not by the programmer, but by the system, at run time, and these are guaranteed by definition to be at distinct indices. However, multiple definitions are possible with array comprehensions, where the programmer has more freedom to specify computations at each index.

The run-time error due to multiple definitions of a data structure element is more serious than other run-time errors such as division by zero. For example, suppose we had the expression:

```
a!5 := (23.0 / 0.0)
```

We could simply store a special *floating-point error value* in a!5 and treat it as just another value. For example, it may turn out that the value is never selected out of the array. Even if it is selected, it may simply be copied elsewhere, for example,

```
b!10 := (a!5)
```

If it is actually used in an arithmetic computation:

```
f      = b!10 + 1.0
```

then the result of the "+" could be another error value that is bound to f, and so on. In other words, such errors can be propagated and even discarded.

However, consider multiple assignments of an I-array element and a corresponding selection:

```
let
      a!5  := 23
      a!e_i := 34
      .
      .
      .

in
      a!5
```

Suppose e_i has not yet been reduced to a value. The selection can be performed, giving

```
let
      a!5  := 23
      a!e_i := 34
      .
      .
      .

in
      23
```

Suppose that later, e_i reduces to 5. At that point we discover the multiple inconsistent definitions. But it is too late to convert a!5 into an error value, since we have already read the value 23 out of it. The value 23 may have been read out in many parts of the program, and these values may have propagated and affected many other parts of the program. Thus, we have no safe alternative except to proclaim (conservatively) that the entire program is in error. We also say that programs *blow up* on multiple definitions of I-structure elements.

9.3.4   Converting I-arrays into Functional Arrays

Consider the following function that mimics the built-in functional mkArray constructor, except that it produces an I-array:

```
mkIArray            :: Ix a => (a,a) -> (a->b) -> IArray a b
mkIArray   (l,u)  f = let
                          a = iArray (l,u) []
                          for j <- [l..u] do
                              a!j := f j
                          finally ()
                      in
                          a
```

Suppose we now have the binding

```
b = mkIArray  (1,10)  sqr
```

All elements of the I-array are full. Clearly, we cannot perform any assignments to b without raising a multiple-write error. Thus, the only operation we can perform on b is I-array selection. In other words, b behaves exactly like a functional array.

Unfortunately, because b has type (IArray Int Int) instead of (Array Int Int), we cannot manipulate it with any function that was written for functional arrays. We could not pass it as an argument to map, foldl, foldr, matrix multiplication, or any of the large number of useful library functions for functional arrays. We would need a separate version of each of these functions, with an I-array type instead of an array type.

To solve this problem we provide a conversion function:

```
cvt_IArray_to_Array :: Ix a => (IArray a b) -> (Array a b)
```

It is possible to write this conversion function explicitly:

```
cvt_IArray_to_Array ia = mkArray (bounds ia) (\j -> ia!j)
```

which simply copies the I-array into a functional array. We can then rewrite our binding as follows:

```
ib  = mkIArray  (1,10)  sqr
b   = cvt_IArray_to_Array  ib
```

Now, b has type (Array Int), so it can be manipulated as an ordinary functional array.

This brings up a very interesting and useful possibility. In a particular implementation of *pH*, if the internal representations of functional arrays and I-arrays are the same, then that implementation can supply cvt_IArray_to_Array as a primitive that *does absolutely nothing*. It is simply the identity function, directly returning its argument as its result! In particular, it does not copy the array. Let us convince ourselves that this is semantically safe. Suppose we had

```
b   = cvt_IArray_to_Array  ib
```

so that b and ib now refer to the same internal representation. Can b be safely treated as a functional array? It surely can, because the contents of the array cannot change. At any index j, the expression b!j is still uniquely defined; we cannot see different values at j depending on when we do the selection. It is possible that the program may later attempt a double assignment into ib!j, but the behavior of the program is identical whether we had copied the array during conversion or not—the program blows up with a multiple sStore error.

Since functional and I-arrays have the same notions of index bounds and subscripting, and since they both have the same notions of *full* and *empty* due to nonstrictness, there is in fact no reason to have separate internal representations for functional and I-arrays. Thus, a *pH* implementation can safely provide cvt_IArray_to_Array as a primitive that behaves as the identity function. In fact, cvt_IArray_to_Array is merely present for type checking purposes; after type checking, the compiler can simply eliminate it completely.

9.3.5   Desugaring Functional Arrays into I-arrays

Suppose we take things a step further and move the conversion into mkIArray. Since mkIArray performs all the assignments into the I-array that it allocates, there is no reason for it to return an I-array at all. So, we perform the conversion before returning the result (and we change the name of the function to reflect that):

```
mkArray  (1,u)  f = let
                        a = iArray (1,u) []
                        for j <- [1..u] do
                            a!j := f j
                        finally ()
                    in
                        cvt_IArray_to_Array a
```

Something very interesting has happened here. In Chapter 7 we presented mkArray as a built-in constructor of the array abstract data type, but here we have implemented it within the language itself! In fact, this is how it is implemented in the standard *pH* library; the module that implements the Array abstract data type is itself written in *pH*, using I-arrays. There are *many* functions that have this flavor, including the array partitioning problem presented earlier in this chapter and the Gaussian elimination example to be seen shortly. These functions allocate and fill an I-array completely, so that it can safely be converted into a functional array before returning it.

Another example: we can redo our array partitioning program so that both its input and its output arrays are functional arrays:

```
let
    y       = iArray (1,n) []
    (1,r)   = (0,n+1)
    final_r = for j <- [1..n] do
                  (1', r', k) = if x!j >= 0 then (1,r-1,r-1)
                                            else      (1+1,r,1+1)
                  y!k := x!j
                  next 1 = 1'
                  next r = r'
              finally r
in
    (cvt_IArray_to_Array y, final_r)
```

Conversion to a functional array can have performance benefits. First, for example, because of the conversion, the compiler can be assured that there can be no assignments to the array from elsewhere. This fact, combined with an analysis of the body of mkArray, guarantees that no multiple definitions can occur at all to this array. Therefore, the compiler can generate more efficient code that does not check for multiple definitions. Second, in a parallel machine, the system may choose to copy a functional array to bring it closer to a processor, whereas it is not allowed to make such copies with an I-array.

9.3.6   Implementing Array Comprehensions Using I-arrays

In Chapter 7 we discussed a "wavefront" computation using array comprehensions, which we repeat here:

```
pascal_triangle n =
  let
      m = array ((1,1),(n,n))
            (  [((1,1),  1)]
            ++ [((1,j),  1)                         | j <- [2..n]]
            ++ [((i,1),  1)                         | i <- [2..n]]
            ++ [((i,j),  m!(i,j-1) + m!(i-1,j)) | i <- [2..n],
                                                   j <- [2..n]])
  in
      m
```

Here is the corresponding version using I-arrays:

```
pascal_triangle n =
  let
      m = let
              a = iArray ((1,1),(n,n)) []
              A!(1,1) := 1

              for j <- [2..n] do
                  a!(1,j) := 1
              finally ()

              for i <- [2..n] do
                  a!(i,1) := 1
              finally ()

              for i <- [2..n] do
                  for j <- [2..n] do
                      a!(i,j) := (a!(i,j-1) + a!(i-1,j))
                  finally ()
              finally ()
          in
              cvt_IArray_to_Array a
  in
      m
```

This demonstrates that the translation from array comprehensions to the I-structure form is almost trivial. An array comprehension becomes a block (the inner block). Each of the appended list comprehensions in the original code becomes a statement in the block. The assignment statements are derived directly from the index-and-value expressions of the corresponding list comprehensions. Each assignment statement is enclosed in nested loops that are directly derived from the generators in the corresponding clause. The I-array is converted into a functional matrix before being returned.

Of course, in general the list of index-and-value pairs may be constructed elsewhere in the program, and in the worst case the compiler may not be able to see the structure of the bounds tuple or list constructions:

```
array b ivs
```

In this case its translation will have to revert to

```
let
    a = iArray b []
    for (i,v) <- ivs do
        a!i := v
    finally ()
in
    cvt_IArray_to_Array a
```

In practice, however, array comprehensions often have manifest bounds and region-specification expressions, permitting the more efficient direct translation.

9.3.7   map_foldl

Suppose we had an array xactions that showed Ferdinand's daily bank transactions (deposits and withdrawals) for the month of April. We wish to compute his daily balances and his final balance, given that his starting balance on April 1 was 100. We can use the following *pH* library function:

```
map_foldl   ::   Ix i => (s->a->(s,b)) ->
                         s                 ->
                         (Array i a)    -> (s, Array i b)
```

The structure of an application

```
map_foldl  f  s  a
```

can be seen in Figure 9.1, from which the reason for its name is obvious— it combines a mapping operation, which creates a new "image" array,

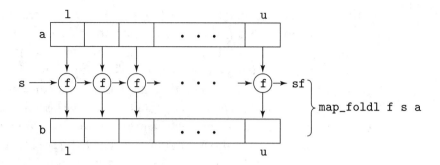

Figure 9.1 Structure of `map_foldl`.

with a folding (or reduction) operation, which returns a summary value. `map_foldl` is similar to the functions *scan* and *parallel prefix* that are well-known in the parallel programming literature. Using this function, Ferdinand's daily and final balances can then be expressed as follows:

```
(final_bal,daily_bals) = let  f s aj = ((s+aj),(s+aj))
                         in
                              map_foldl f 100 xactions
```

`map_foldl` can be implemented using I-arrays as follows:

```
map_foldl f s a = let
                      (1,u) = bounds a
                      b     = iArray (1,u) []
                      sf    = for j <- [1..u] do
                                  (next s, bj) = f s (a!j)
                                  b!j := bj
                              finally s
                  in
                      (sf, cvt_IArray_to_Array b)
```

In this manner, most of *pH*'s library functions for functional arrays can be implemented efficiently within the language itself, using I-arrays. Moreover, if we encounter a new functional array operation that is not available in the standard libraries, we can implement it efficiently within *pH* itself.

Exercise 9.4   Write a purely functional implementation of `map_foldl` and compare its efficiency with the I-array implementation. ∎

9.4   Gaussian Elimination

In Section 7.9.1, we showed a functional program for Gaussian elimination, a method for solving systems of linear equations. We now illustrate how I-arrays can give us a more succinct and efficient solution.

In designing a solution using I-arrays, we make use of the fact that the L and U matrices have complementary shapes; that is, they fit together exactly like jigsaw pieces to form an $n \times n$ matrix (this should be evident from Figure 7.9). Thus, our result will be a single $n \times n$ matrix called LU. We convert it from an I-matrix into a functional matrix before returning it, so that the external type of the function remains functional. The program is shown below:

```
gauss_eliminate :: Array (Int,Int) Float ->
                                    Array (Int,Int) Float
gauss_eliminate a =
  let
      ((_,_),(n,_)) = bounds a
      lu            = iArray ((1,1),(n,n)) []

      last_A =
          for k <- [1..(n-1)] do
              -- Compute multipliers in lu[*,k]
              for i <- [(k+1)..n] do
                  lu!(i,k) := (a!(i,k)/a!(k,k))
              finally ()

              -- Eliminate kth column, producing next a matrix
              next a = matrix ((k+1,k+1),(n,n))
                            [((i,j), a!(i,j) - a!(k,j)*lu!(i,k))
                            | i <- [k+1..n], j <- [k+1..n]]

              -- Copy final coeffs of kth eqn (top row of A) into LU
              for j <- [k..n] do
                  lu!(k,j) := (a!(k,j))
              finally ()
          finally a

      lu!(n,n) := (last_A!(n,n))
    in
      cvt_IArray_to_Array lu
```

The program itself is shorter and somewhat clearer than the previous one in Section 7.9.1. It also uses much less space. First, the lu representation is much more compact than the previous pair of triangular matrices. More importantly, in each iteration there are only two as in use—we read from the current one and construct a new one for the next iteration. Thus, this program uses $O(n^2)$ storage, where the previous functional solution used $O(n^3)$ storage for its "as" structure. The only remaining inefficiency is in the computationless copying of the $u_{i,j}$ elements in the final loop.

Exercise 9.5   The solution given above is inadequate in many applications because it does not take into account the accumulation and magnification of errors due to the representation of floating-point numbers with finite precision on most machines; round-off errors can accumulate and severely distort the resulting numbers. In particular, in the segment that computes the multipliers, the division by a!(k,k) is problematic if a!(k,k) is very small. We can improve the algorithm so that it uses *partial pivoting*. In each a matrix, we find the row that has the largest element in the left column and then exchange this row with the top row. Thus, at each step, we pick the largest pivot. Clearly, this does not change the overall solution. However, we have to remember the new permutation of the rows so that later, when given the right-hand sides for back-substitution, we know how to permute them accordingly.

Write a new version of the program with partial pivoting using array comprehensions. In addition to the L and U structures, you also need to return a structure specifying the permutation of the rows.   ∎

Exercise 9.6   Write a new version of the program with partial pivoting using I-arrays. In addition to the LU structure, you also need to return a structure specifying the permutation of the rows.   ∎

Exercise 9.7   The partial pivoting strategy described above is a little fragile, since we could make any coefficient arbitrarily large by multiplying that entire row by a large number. A better strategy is to compare scaled versions of the left column; we scale each row such that its largest coefficient becomes equal to 1. Modify the I-array solution from the previous exercise to take this into account.   ∎

9.5   I-structure Lists

We saw earlier that we can create an updatable array by constructing a functional array, each of whose elements is an empty I-cell. Similarly, we could create a "list with an updatable tail" using a type that is analogous to the list type, except that each cons cell's tail contains an I-cell that in turn refers to the rest of the list:

```
data UTList a = UTNil | UTCons a (ICell (UTList a))
```

We could then create a list with an empty tail using

```
utc = UTCons  x  ( ICell { } )
```

and the empty tail could later be updated with a list *xs* using

```
UTCons _ y  =  utc        -- pattern match to extract tail I-cell
contents  y := xs         -- update the I-cell
```

As with functional arrays of I-cells, this extra indirection is messy and inefficient. Instead, we will define the type of "I-structure lists" in which the tail field of a cons cell will directly have I-structure semantics, using the field name and "." notation introduced in Section 9.2 to designate I-structure fields:

```
data IList a = INil | ICons {head :: a, tail :: . (IList a)}
```

As usual, this **data** declaration defines the type `IList`, the constructors `INil` and `ICons`, the field names `head` and `tail`, and selector functions called `head` and `tail`. As before, an `ICons` term can be constructed by applying it to both arguments positionally:

```
x = ICons  3  INil
```

or using field notation:

```
x = ICons  { head = 3, tail = INil }
```

However, we can also leave the `tail` field empty, to be defined later in an I-structure assignment:

```
x = ICons { head = 3 }
```

Note: We could have also left the head field empty, but it would then remain empty forever, since we are not allowed to assign to functional fields.

We can later define the value of the empty `tail` field using an assignment statement:

```
tail x := xs
```

Semantically this is an sStore operation. The expression x must evaluate to an ICons object; it is a run-time error if it evaluates to INil.

Fields of an IList type can be accessed using positional pattern matching:

```
case x of
    INil      -> ...
    ICons h t -> ...
```

or field label pattern matching:

```
case x of
    INil                          -> ...
    ICons { head = h, tail = t } -> ...
```

or using selector functions:

```
head x
tail x
```

In each case, the fields are read with iFetch operations.

9.5.1 Tail-Recursive **map** (Tail Recursion Modulo Cons)

Since I-lists are so similar to functional lists, it is not surprising that we can write a function similar to the map function on lists:

```
imap                 :: (a -> b)  ->  IList a  ->  IList b
imap f INil          = INil
imap f (ICons x xs) = ICons  (f x)  (imap f xs)
```

This definition is recursive, just like the definition for functional map. It is not tail-recursive and so cannot directly be written as a loop. What is interesting is that, with I-lists, it is possible to transform this program into a loop form.

imap has a certain structure that is common to many functions on recursive data structures:

- The expressions that represent the function result are full-arity constructor applications (here, of INil and ICons).
- The recursive function call is a direct argument to a returned constructor (here, imap f xs).

D. H. D. Warren was the first to identify this structure and the associated optimization technique described below, during his construction of the seminal Edinburgh Prolog compiler. He referred to it as *tail recursion modulo cons* [76].

Using I-structures, we can turn this recursive-call-in-a-tail-recursive-constructor inside out. We pass the data structure to (a modified version of) the recursive call as an extra argument. The recursively called function, instead of returning a result, stores that result directly into the data structure that was passed down to it. The modified recursive function never returns anything; it simply terminates by storing its normal result into the data structure that is given to it.

Here is the new `imap`, which calls the modified procedure `imap'`:

```
imap                :: (a -> b)  ->  IList a  ->  IList b
imap f  INil       = INil
imap f (ICons x xs) = let
                          l = ICons {head = (f x)}
                          imap'  f  xs  l
                      in
                          l
```

It allocates an I-list cons cell filling the `head` field with the first value (`f x`) and leaving the tail empty. This is passed in to the procedure `imap'`. However, the cons cell is returned immediately. Meanwhile, `imap'` runs down the input list, simultaneously "growing" the output list. It looks like this:

```
imap' :: (a -> b)  ->  IList a  ->  Ilist b  -> ()
imap' f INil        l = let
                            tail l := INil
                        in
                            ()
imap' f (ICons x xs) l = let
                            l'      = ICons {head = (f x)}
                            tail l := l'
                        in
                            imap' f xs l'
```

It fills the tail of its argument `l`, either with `INil` or with the next cons cell, whose head contains the next element (`f x`) and whose tail is empty. In the latter case, this "incomplete" cons cell is passed down into the next recursive call.

This transformation retains all the nonstrictness properties of the original. imap can return the first cons cell as soon as it is allocated. A consumer function can then start running down the result I-list. It will simply follow behind the imap' loop, consuming the I-list as it is "grown" by the loop.

imap' is a tail-recursive function and can be translated into a loop. We first rewrite it as follows to make the transition clearer:

```
imap' f xs l =
   case xs of
      INil           -> let
                           tail l := INil
                         in
                           ()
      ICons x xs' -> let
                           tail l := l'
                           l'      =  ICons {head = (f x)}
                         in
                           imap' f xs' l'
```

and then straightforwardly convert it into a loop:

```
imap' f xs l = while not (xs == INil) do
                  (x: xs') =  xs
                  tail l    := l'
                  l'        =  ICons {head = (f x)}
                  next xs  =  xs'
                  next l   =  l'
               finally
                  let
                     tail l := INil
                  in
                     ()
```

In general, this method can be used to convert any function with tail recursion modulo any constructor into a loop.

Exercise 9.8   Exercise 6.41 requested that you write a function map_tree that performed a mapping function on binary trees analogous to the map function on lists. In your solution, map_tree should have had two recursive calls, for the left and right subtrees respectively. Both of these calls are tail-recursive modulo the tree constructor Node. Pick one of these, say the descent into the left subtree, and apply the above transformation to convert the traversal into a loop with respect to that call.

The resulting dynamic computation structure will involve a set of loops. At the outermost level, there will be a loop running down the left spine of the tree. At each node, it will have a call to the map_tree function, applied to the right child. Each of these calls, in turn, will initiate a loop running down the left spine of the corresponding subtree, and each of those loops, in turn, will contain calls to map_tree for each right child, and so on. ∎

9.5.2 Converting I-lists to Lists

Just as we could use I-arrays to implement functional array primitives with the help of a cvt_IArray_to_Array type-converter, we can also use I-list functions to implement functions on ordinary functional lists using a cvt_IList_to_List type converter to do the final type conversion back to lists. For example:

```
map          :: (a -> b)  ->  [a]  ->  [b]
map  f  xs  =  cvt_IArray_to_Array  (imap  f  xs)
```

Of course, this is still not quite type correct: imap's second argument here is a list, whereas it is expecting an I-list. This can easily be fixed by changing the types and the definitions of imap and imap' so that they expect lists in their second argument instead of I-lists.

Again, the type conversion function can trivially be written explicitly:

```
cvt_IList_to_List                :: IList a -> [a]
cvt_IList_to_List INil         = []
cvt_IList_to_List (ICons h t) = h:(cvt_IList_to_List t)
```

which just copies the I-list into a list.

As with the conversion of I-arrays to arrays, in a given implementation, if I-lists and lists have the same internal representation, then it is perfectly safe for that implementation to provide cvt_IList_to_List as a primitive that does nothing at all, such as being implemented as the identity function that simply returns its argument as its result. This opens the door for the *pH* programmer to implement new useful functions on functional lists with the efficiency of I-lists.

Exercise 9.9   Implement the standard list function take using I-lists and loops (take *n*, when applied to a list *l*, returns a list containing the first *n* elements of *l*). ∎

9.5.3   Implementing List Comprehensions with Open Lists

In Section 6.4.3 we showed that a list comprehension like this:

$$[\ e_{(x,y,z)} \ \ | \ x \ \text{<-} \ xs, \ y \ \text{<-} \ ys, \ z \ \text{<-} \ zs \ ]$$

can be translated into ordinary functions and function application like this:

```
let
    segment_3 x y z = [ e(x,y,z) ]
    segment_2 x y   = flatten_2 (map (segment_3 x y) zs)
    segment_1 x     = flatten_2 (map (segment_2 x) ys)
    segment_0       = flatten_2 (map segment_1 xs)
in
    segment_0
```

The combination of flatten_2 and map is often combined into a special function called flatmap:

```
flatmap          :: (a->[b]) -> [a] -> [b]
flatmap f  []    = []
flatmap f (a:as) = (f a) ++ (flatmap f as)
```

so that we have

```
let
    segment_3 x y z = [ e(x,y,z) ]
    segment_2 x y   = flatmap (segment_3 x y) zs
    segment_1 x     = flatmap (segment_2 x) ys
    segment_0       = flatmap segment_1 xs
in
    segment_0
```

We call this the *flatmap* translation. There are two problems with this. First, all the "++" operations result in a number of intermediate lists that are created and soon discarded. Second, it uses recursion instead of loops. In Section 6.4.4 we saw an alternative translation called TQ that solved the first problem optimally: it did exactly one cons operation for each element in the output list. However, it was still a recursive solution.

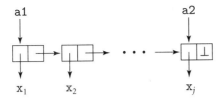

Figure 9.2 The structure of an open list.

Now, with I-structures, we can transform the flatmap solution into one that is not only optimal in the number of cons cells it uses, but is also based on loops. We use a powerful technique called *open lists.*[2]

An open list is represented by two references *a1* and *a2*, as shown in Figure 9.2.

Internally, we have a list structure in which the last tail is undefined (the symbol ⊥, pronounced "bottom," is used to denote this). *a1* points at the first cell and *a2* points at the last cell (these may in fact be the same cell). To represent an empty open list, *a1* and *a2* both have the value INil. Here is a definition for empty open lists and a procedure to make a singleton open list whose head is some value *x*:

```
nil_ol          = (INil,INil)

singleton_ol x = let
                     a1 = ICons { head = x }    -- tail is empty
                 in
                     (a1,a1)
```

The characteristic feature of open lists is that they are easy to append:

```
append_ol  as  (INil, _ ) = as
append_ol (a1,a2) (b1,b2) = case a1 of =
                              INil      -> (b1,b2)
                              ICons _ _ -> let
                                               tail a2 := b1
                                           in
                                               (a1,b2)
```

---

2. Open lists are closely related to *difference lists* in logic programming.

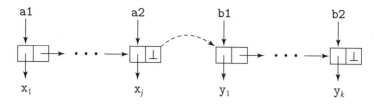

Figure 9.3 Appending open lists.

The operation is depicted in Figure 9.3. Thus, it is clear that appending open lists takes constant time; compare this with the "++" operation which takes $O(n)$ time, where n is the length of the first list. Attaching an element to the front of an open list is straightforward:

```
cons_ol x (a1,a2) = append_ol (singleton_ol x) (a1,a2)
```

When we have finished building an open list, we can *close* it, converting it into an ordinary list:

```
close_ol            :: IList a -> [a]
close_ol (a1,a2) = let
                       case a2 of
                          INil       -> ()
                          ICons _ _  -> let
                                            tail a2 := INil
                                        in
                                            ()
                   in
                       cvt_IList_to_list a1
```

That is, we "plug" the empty hole at the end.

The open list version of `flatmap` takes, as its first parameter, a function that produces an open list. And, `flatmap` itself returns an open list. Here it is:

```
flatmap_ol f xs =
       let
           (a1,a2) = nil_ol
       in
           for x <- xs do
               (next a1,next a2) = append_ol (a1, a2) (f x)
           finally (a1,a2)
```

Now, the translation of our list comprehension is quite straightforward:

```
let
    segment_3 x y z = singleton_ol e_(x,y,z)
    segment_2 x y   = flatmap_ol (segment_3 x y) zs
    segment_1 x     = flatmap_ol (segment_2 x) ys
    segment_0       = flatmap_ol segment_1 xs
in
    close_ol segment_0
```

Further Optimization

Our translation of the list comprehension into a program using open lists is optimal in the sense that it does only one "cons" per element in the output list. Further, it is expressed using loops instead of general recursion. However, it can still be quite inefficient, for the following reason: every time we call append_ol, we execute a conditional expression to test if the first argument is the empty open list. This is bad because we call append_ol very often—once in every iteration in every flatmap_ol loop.

As a first step, let us transform it so that append_ol is called only once for every element in the output list. The basic idea is to reformulate some of our procedures so that each one, instead of just returning a new open list, appends it to an existing open list that is supplied as an additional parameter. Here is the new version of flatmap_ol:

```
flatmap_ol' f' xs (a1,a2) =
        for x <- xs do
            (next a1,next a2) = f' x (a1,a2)
        finally (a1,a2)
```

where f' itself has been similarly modified (i.e., it also takes an open list as an additional parameter and appends to it). Here, then, is our new translation of the list comprehension:

```
let
    segment_3 x y z (a1,a2) =
        append_ol (a1,a2) (singleton_ol e_(x,y,z))
    segment_2 x y (a1,a2)   =
        flatmap_ol' (segment_3 x y) zs (a1,a2)
    segment_1 x (a1,a2)     =
        flatmap_ol' (segment_2 x) ys (a1,a2)
    segment_0               =
        flatmap_ol' segment_1 xs nil_ol
in
    close_ol segment_0
```

Using a Sentinel

Notice that in our latest solution, the open list is "threaded" through all the iterations of all the `flatmap_ol'` loops. Consequently, there is no more than one point at which it can change from an empty open list to a nonempty one. In other words, up to the first element in the output list, the test for emptiness within `append_ol` will always be true, and after that it will always be false. This kind of situation can always be optimized with the use of a "dummy" value known as a sentinel value. We can force the initial open list to be nonempty by giving it a dummy value that we will later discard. Then, we can use a version of `append_ol` that avoids the test for emptiness. Here it is:

```
fast_append_ol (a1,a2) (b1,b2) = let
                                        tail a2 := b1
                                 in
                                        (a1,b2)
```

so that our new solution is

```
let
    segment_3 x y z (a1,a2) =
        fast_append_ol (a1,a2) (singleton_ol e_(x,y,z))
    segment_2 x y (a1,a2)   =
        flatmap_ol' (segment_3 x y) zs (a1,a2)
    segment_1 x (a1,a2)     =
        flatmap_ol' (segment_2 x) ys (a1,a2)
    segment_0               =
        flatmap_ol' segment_1 xs (singleton_ol dummy_val)
    (_:ws)                  =
        close_ol segment_0
in
    ws
```

where `dummy_val` is an arbitrary value. We feed in a nonempty open list at the top containing this dummy value (in defining `segment_0`) and later discard it by selecting only the tail of the list `ws`. Thus, while we waste the cons cell containing the dummy value, we more than make up for it by avoiding completely any tests for the empty open list in `fast_append_ol`.

It should be clear that in our latest solution, the first reference of the open list *never* changes during its entire journey through all the `flatmap_ol'`s. With this observation, we can specialize our solution even further, so that we carry along only the reference to the last cons cell of the open list:

```
let
    special_append_ol a2 (b1,b2) = let
                                        tail a2 := b1
                                    in
                                        b2

    special_flatmap_ol f xs a2   = for x <- xs do
                                        next a2 = f x a2
                                    finally a2

    segment_3 x y z a2 =
        special_append_ol a2 (singleton_ol e(x,y,z))
    segment_2 x y a2   =
        special_flatmap_ol (segment_3 x y) zs a2
    segment_1 x a2     =
        special_flatmap_ol (segment_2 x) ys a2
    segment_0          =
        special_flatmap_ol segment_1 xs a2

    (a1,a2)                = (singleton_ol dummy_val)

    (_:ws)                 = (close_ol (a1,segment_0))
in
    ws
```

This is, in fact, how a good compiler would implement list comprehensions.

Exercise 9.10   Generalize the above implementation to also handle filters and let-bindings in the list comprehension's qualifier list.   ■

9.6   Semantics of I-structure Arrays, Functional Arrays, and I-fields

I-arrays are a simple generalization of the single cell whose semantics we saw in the last chapter.

9.6.1   Syntax

We extend our formal syntax with the following:

$$E \quad ::= \quad \cdots$$
$$| \quad \texttt{arrayAllocate}(E) \qquad \text{Array allocation}$$

	arrayIFetch(E, E)	I-structure array fetch
	arrayMFetch(E, E)	M-structure array fetch

$$S \quad ::= \quad \cdots$$

	arraySStore(E, E, E)	Synchronized array store
	arrayEmpty(O_j, V)	Empty array elements
	arrayError(O_j, V)	Error array elements
	arrayFull(O_j, V, V)	Full array elements

Instead of the single-cell `allocate()`, we have `arrayAllocate(n)`, which allocates n related cells (n is based on the index bounds specified for the array). An allocated array is represented by a heap identifier O_j, just like cells. Where `iFetch` and `mFetch` took a single cell as argument, `arrayIFetch` and `arrayMFetch` are new primitives that take an array and an integer index and select the indexed element of the array. The new statements are direct extensions of their cell counterparts, taking an array index as an additional argument.

9.6.2   Desugaring and Rewrite Rules

A functional array or an I-structure array can be represented as a sequence of adjacent cells in the heap containing the bounds tuple in the first cell and the array elements in subsequent cells.

Both array and I-array comprehensions of the form

```
array   b   jvs
iArray  b   jvs
```

are desugared into

```
let
    c =  ... Compute number of elements in array based on b ...
    a = arrayAllocate(c + 1)
    iAStore a 0 b
    for (j,v) <- jvs do
        j' = index b j;
        arraySStore(a,j'+1,v)
    finally ()
in
    a
```

If the array has c elements, we allocate $c + 1$ cells, with the zeroth cell containing the index bounds. We store the bounds tuple in the first cell. In the loop, we enumerate each index and value. We use the function `index` (available for any index type) to compute the integer offset j' of j in the range of index values represented by the bounds tuple b and store the value at the cell indexed by j'+1. The `index` function will raise an error if the index is not in bounds.

`arrayAllocate`(n) allocates a sequence of n empty cells:

$$
\begin{array}{ll}
\begin{aligned}
&\texttt{alloc\_trig;} \\
&x \texttt{ = arrayAllocate}(\underline{n})
\end{aligned}
\quad \longrightarrow \quad
\begin{aligned}
&\texttt{alloc\_trig;} \\
&x \texttt{ = } 0_a; \\
&\texttt{arrayEmpty}(0_a, \underline{0}); \\
&\cdots; \\
&\texttt{arrayEmpty}(0_a, \underline{n-1})
\end{aligned}
& \text{(ArrayAlloc)}
\end{array}
$$

The bounds query function

$$\texttt{bounds} \quad e_a$$

is desugared into

$$
\begin{aligned}
&\textbf{let} \\
&\quad \texttt{a = } e_a \\
&\textbf{in} \\
&\quad \texttt{arrayIFetch(a,0)}
\end{aligned}
$$

That is, it simply extracts the bounds tuple from the first cell of the array's representation.

An I-array assignment in the *pH* source of the form

$$e_a!e_j \texttt{ := } e_v$$

is translated into

$$
\begin{aligned}
\texttt{a} &\texttt{ = } e_a \\
\texttt{j} &\texttt{ = } e_j \\
\texttt{v} &\texttt{ = } e_v \\
\texttt{b} &\texttt{ = arrayIFetch(a,0)} \\
\texttt{j'} &\texttt{ = index b j} \\
&\texttt{arraySStore(a,j',v)}
\end{aligned}
$$

Here are the rules for I-array assignment:

$$
\begin{array}{ll}
\begin{aligned}
&\texttt{arrayEmpty}(0_a, j); \\
&\texttt{arraySStore}(0_a, j, v)
\end{aligned}
\quad \longrightarrow \quad
\texttt{arrayFull}(0_a, j, v)
& \text{(ArraySStore)}
\end{array}
$$

$$
\begin{array}{ll}
\begin{aligned}
&\texttt{arrayFull}(0_a, j, v); \\
&\texttt{arraySStore}(0_a, j, w)
\end{aligned}
\quad \longrightarrow \quad
\begin{aligned}
&\texttt{arrayFull}(0_a, j, v); \\
&\texttt{arrayError}(0_a, j)
\end{aligned}
& \text{(ArraySStoreErr)}
\end{array}
$$

An I-array selection in the *pH* source of the form

$$e_a!e_j$$

is translated into

```
let
    a  = e_a
    j  = e_j
    b  = arrayIFetch(a,0)
    j' = index b j
in
    arrayIFetch(a,j)
```

Here is the rule for fetching a value from a full I-array cell:

$$\begin{array}{ll} \text{arrayFull}(0_a,j,v); & \longrightarrow \quad \text{arrayFull}(0_a,j,v); \qquad \text{(ArrayIFetch)}\\ x=\text{arrayIFetch}(0_a,j) & x=v \end{array}$$

The cell remains unchanged, allowing more iFetches to occur on the cell. (arrayMFetch will be described in Section 10.10.)

The semantics of I-fields in algebraic types are even simpler than arrays. An n-ary constructed term (C _ $\cdots$ _) can be represented as an $n+1$ element array with the zeroth element containing a unique integer tag representing constructor C. The jth element of a term x is filled using

```
arraySStore(x, j, v)
```

and read using

```
arrayIFetch(x, j)
```

The value of j is always known statically (since it is always described manifestly as a field name and not with a computed value as in I-arrays or functional arrays) and so no bounds checking need be done.

9.7 Discussion

In purely functional languages a data structure is always constructed *mono-lithicly*—a single expression specifies both the desired data structure and its contents. For example, using the expression $(e_1:e_2)$, we indicate that we want a cons cell, and we also specify the contents of the cons cell. Using the expression (e_1,e_2,e_3), we indicate that we want a 3-tuple, and we also specify the contents of the 3-tuple. In a mkArray application and in array comprehensions, we indicate that we want an array with certain index bounds, and we also specify the entire contents of the array.

I-structures allow us to separate the specification of the data structure from the specification of its contents. The data structure can be constructed with empty elements, which can be defined elsewhere with I-structure assignment statements. So, in programs where complex control structures are necessary to specify the contents of a data structure, I-structures are typically much easier to use and result in much clearer programs. In functional counterparts of such programs, we often have to first execute the complex control structure and remember some information (say, index-and-value pairs) in a list, and later construct the data structure using this information. This can obscure the purpose of the program, and the intermediate lists are a source of inefficiency.

We repeat that I-structure assignments are not like the imperative assignment statements found in other programming languages like Fortran, C, or Pascal. With I-structure assignments, there is no notion of replacing an old value by a new one; I-structure assignments simply define a previously empty element. A concurrently executing selection of that element cannot read different values depending on when it is attempted. Formally, with I-structures we retain determinacy. As mentioned in Chapter 2, this is an invaluable property for parallel programs, since it guarantees that the outcome of a program does not depend on variations in scheduling due to different parallel machine configurations.

M-structures: Mutable Synchronized State

It's time for a change!

—Campaign slogan

In Chapter 8 we introduced the semantic concepts behind implicitly synchronized update by describing sStore, iFetch, and mFetch operations. In the last chapter we presented "I-structure" language constructs that only used the sStore and iFetch semantic operations, packaged up in suitable type-safe constructs. In this chapter we discuss "M-structures," which are type-safe updatable data structures based on the sStore and mFetch operations. The "M" in M-structures comes from "mutable." As discussed at the start of the last chapter, mFetch will for the first time introduce *nondeterminacy* into the language. A series of sStore and mFetch operations can place a sequence of different values in a cell. Thus, the value read by a particular mFetch operation depends on the time at which it attempts the operation; since it can read different values, the outcome of the entire program can be affected.

On any given updatable cell, it will only make sense to alternate mFetch and sStore operations. If we attempt two consecutive mFetch operations, the first one "wins" and leaves the cell empty. The second one can only wait until some other part of the program performs an intervening sStore to make it full again. If we attempt two consecutive sStore operations, the second one will be attempting an sStore on a full cell, which of course is an error. Most of the time, we will use natural data dependencies to ensure that we alternate mFetch and sStore operations. Sometimes, it will be necessary to use explicit sequencing (barriers) to force this alternation.

We can visualize an M-structure element of a data structure as a container or box that has room for one item. We can put an item into an empty container, but any attempt to put in more than one item is an error—there isn't room for it. We cannot take an item from an empty container—we must wait until somebody puts an item in. Taking out an item from a container removes it, leaving it empty again. Thus, if there are many simultaneous attempts to take out an item, only one attempt can succeed, and all the others will wait, finding the container empty. For this reason, in the context of M-structures, we sometimes refer to the mFetch and sStore operations as *take* and *put* operations, respectively.

As with I-structures, we have M-structure arrays (or M-arrays) and M-structure fields (or M-fields) in algebraic data types.

10.1   M-structure Algebraic Types

In Section 9.2 we introduced I-structure fields in constructed terms of algebraic types. Similarly, we can have M-structure fields in such terms. The simplest example is a polymorphic type with a single constructor with a single updatable field:[1]

```
data MCell a = MCell { contents :: & a }
```

As with I-fields, we must use field name notation, and not positional notation, if we want to specify M-fields. The "&" before the field type indicates that the field is an M-field. The constructor MCell is a polymorphic function, as usual:

```
MCell    ::    a -> MCell a
```

---

1. The notion of an updatable cell as a first-class value is also present in the language SML [42], where they are known as "ref" types and objects. However, SML being a sequential language, there is no notion of synchronization. Ref objects are read and written using the "raw" reads and writes of traditional programming languages.

We can construct an M-cell containing the value of expression *e* with the usual notations:

```
MCell  e                        -- constructor application
MCell { contents = e }          -- field name notation
```

but we can also allocate an empty M-cell using the following expression:

```
MCell { }
```

10.1.1   The mFetch and sStore Operations

We can `mFetch` the contents of an M-cell *mc* with the following expression:

```
contents & mc                   -- mFetch
```

Following `mFetch` semantics, this expression cannot be reduced until the cell *mc* is full; when it is finally reduced, the M-cell is left in the empty state, and the value that was in the cell is returned.

We can `sStore` the value of expression *e* into an M-cell *mc* with the following assignment statement:

```
contents  mc  := e              -- sStore
```

Following the semantics of `sStore` the cell must previously be in the empty state and the assignment leaves it in the full state. It is an error to attempt an assignment on a full cell.

The `MCell` type, together with these operations, can be viewed as a type-safe way to make visible in the language the semantic concepts of `allocate`, `sStore`, and `mFetch` discussed in Chapter 8.

10.1.2   The "Examine" and "Replace" Operations

It is frequently useful to query the value of an M-structure element without changing it. This can be accomplished using the following expression:

```
let
    v              =  contents & mc
    contents mc := v
in
    v
```

The first line waits, if necessary, until the cell is full and then takes the value out of the cell, leaving it empty. The second line puts it back, leaving it full again. Finally, we return the value just retrieved. This operation is called an *examine* operation and is sufficiently useful to warrant a special notation. We overload the normal field selection notation for this purpose:

```
contents  mc
```

The rationale for overloading this notation in this way is that it behaves exactly like normal functional field selection and I-field selection: it waits until the cell is full and then returns the value, leaving the cell intact.

A constructor with M-fields can also be used in pattern matching:

```
case e_mc of
    MCell x -> ... x ...
```

It is obviously undesirable to have any side effects during pattern matching. Consider the pattern:

```
case e_mc of
    (0, MCell 2) -> ...
    (x, MCell y) -> ...
```

The first pattern can fail, in two ways. It gets messy if, during a failed pattern match, we have also altered the object. For this reason, pattern matching only uses the examine operation, and not mFetch, to scrutinize M-fields.

It is also frequently useful to force an M-field to contain a particular value, overriding any value that it currently holds (e.g., when resetting a field to a known value). Nevertheless, since we are only allowed to store into empty cells, it is necessary first to take out (and discard) the old value. This can be accomplished using the following statements (the desired new value is the value of expression e):

```
v = e
(

    _                  = v
    >>>                                      -- (B1)
    _            = contents & mc
    >>>                                      -- (B2)
    contents  mc := v

)
```

First, we evaluate expression e. Then, we take out the old value from the cell and discard it. Finally, we put the new value v into the element. Note that there is no data dependency from the mFetch to the sStore operation. Thus, the explicit sequencing barrier B2 is used to ensure that the sStore is attempted only after the mFetch has completed, ensuring that the cell is empty and that it is legal to perform the sStore. Unlike B2, however, the barrier B1 is there for performance reasons and not for correctness reasons. Since the mFetch has no dependence on the value of *e*, it can be executed immediately, no matter how long it took to evaluate *e* (and even if *e* was stuck in a loop, never producing a value). This could leave the M-cell in the empty state for a long time, potentially holding up other computations that also want to update or replace the value therein. The barrier B1 ensures that we don't even attempt the mFetch until the replacement value has been computed, thus minimizing the interval for which the M-cell is left empty. This operation is called a *replace* operation and is sufficiently useful to warrant its own special notation:

contents & *mc* := *e*

In addition to the notational convenience, the examine and replace operations can also be implemented directly with greater efficiency, using a single round-trip to the specified memory location instead of two.

Exercise 10.1   The following alternative fragment is proposed to explain the semantics of a replace operation:

```
(
    v              =  e
    >>>
    _              =  contents & mc
    >>>
    contents mc := v
)
```

In what way, if any, is it different from the fragment given earlier?   ■

Our notations are carefully chosen so that the mFetch and replace operations, which are "dangerous" in that they open the door to nondeterminism, both use the new symbol "&". The relatively "benign" sStore and examine operations use the same notation as the corresponding functional and I-structure operations. In M-array notation, as well, the sStore and examine operations will reuse the corresponding functional and

I-structure notations, whereas notations for the `mFetch` and replace operations will involve the symbol "&". Any program with neither of the "&" operations will be deterministic.

10.2 A Shared Parallel Queue

Consider a program with multiple producers and consumers. For example, each producer may be a process that repeatedly receives an order from a customer window and appends it to the tail of shared queue. Each consumer may be a process that repeatedly picks up an order from the head of the shared queue and processes it. The overall structure of the program looks something like this:

```
q          = ... make a shared queue ...
           .
           .
           .
producer1 = while True do
                    x = get_customer_order()
                    enqueue x q
              finally ()
           .
           .
           .
producerN = ...
           .
           .
           .
consumer1 = while True do
                    x = dequeue q
                    process  x
              finally ()
           .
           .
           .
consumerM = ...
```

We can implement this shared parallel queue abstraction using M-cells and I-lists. The data structure that we will use to implement a queue is shown in Figure 10.1. The queue itself is a 2-tuple of M-cells corresponding to the head and tail of the queue, respectively (by convention we will draw M-fields with a dark fillet in the top left corner). The M-cells refer to the first and last `ICons` cells of an I-list, respectively. In the last `ICons` cell, the

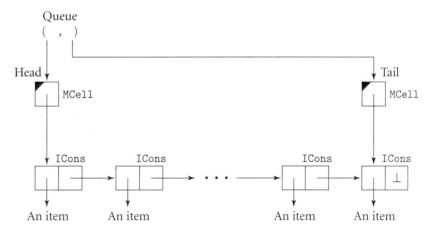

Figure 10.1   A shared, parallel queue.

tail field is empty, indicated in the figure by a "⊥" symbol. For example, we can create a queue with an initial item *i* by

```
type Queue a = (MCell (IList a), MCell (IList a))

q :: Queue item
q = let
        ic = ICons { head = i }
    in
        (MCell ic, MCell ic)
```

Here is the implementation of the enqueue operation, which appends a new item to the tail of the queue:

```
enqueue           :: item -> Queue item -> ()
enqueue  x  q  =
    let
        (_,tmc)  = q                               -- 1
        newtic   =  ICons { head = x }             -- 2
        (    tic         =  contents & tmc         -- 3
             >>>                                   -- B
             contents tmc := newtic    )           -- 4
        tail tic := newtic                         -- 5
    in
        ()
```

Statement 1 uses a pattern binding so that tmc refers to the tail M-cell of the queue. Statement 2 allocates an I-cell that will be the new tail of the queue; its head field contains the new item x and its tail field is empty. Statement 3 mFetches the contents of the tail M-cell, leaving the M-cell empty; tic now refers to the current tail I-cell, which also has an empty tail field. Statement 4 sStores a reference to the new tail I-cell into the tail M-cell, and statement 5 fills in the tail field of the old tail I-cell to point at the new tail I-cell. Referring to Figure 10.1, we have consistently *extended* the diagram to the right with a new I-cell at the tail. Note that the only explicit sequentialization that we needed was the barrier B; this is to ensure that the sStore of the new tail I-cell is not attempted before the mFetch of the old tail I-cell (since there is no dependency between these operations to sequence them otherwise).

The extension of the queue is *atomic*. Even if there are multiple producers simultaneously attempting enqueue operations, the implicit synchronizations in the mFetch and the sStore operations will ensure that they are properly sequentialized and that the data structure is updated correctly.

Here is the implementation of the dequeue operation, which removes an item from the head of the queue and returns it:

```
dequeue        :: Queue item -> item
dequeue   q  =
     let
          (hmc,_)                          =  q                    -- 1
          hic                              =  contents & hmc       -- 2
          ICons {head=x, tail=newhic} =  hic                       -- 3
          contents hmc                     :=  newhic              -- 4
     in
          x
```

Statement 1 uses a pattern binding so that hmc refers to the head M-cell of the queue. Statement 2 mFetches the contents, leaving the M-cell empty; hic now refers to the head I-cell. Statement 3 uses a pattern binding so that x refers to the item at the head of the queue, and newhic refers to the next I-cell of the queue. Statement 4 sStores the head M-cell to point at this new head I-cell. Referring to Figure 10.1, we have consistently eliminated the first I-cell at the left and returned the item that it contained.

Again, this operation is *atomic*. If there are multiple consumers attempting dequeue operations simultaneously, the implicit synchronization will

sequence them properly, distributing an item to each consumer and correctly updating the data structure to advance the head of the queue.

What happens if the consumers catch up with the producers? Eventually,
the queue will contain one I-cell whose head contains an item and whose
tail is empty. In the consumer that successfully dequeues this item, the
newhic binding in line 3 will wait until the tail field is made full by a
producer. In other words, the consumer will automatically wait until some
producer catches up. Meanwhile, if another consumer attempts a dequeue,
it will get stuck in the mFetch in statement 2, because the first consumer
has not yet done its sStore of line 4.

This example illustrates how the implicit synchronization of I- and M-
structures simplifies the complex atomic updates necessary in a shared parallel queue.

Exercise 10.2   From the previous paragraphs it should be evident that our queue must
always contain at least one item, and this may not be satisfactory in some
situations. Modify the Queue data structure so that it can also contain zero
items. (*Hint:* A possible encoding of an empty queue would be to have both
M-cells containing INil.)

For your new data structure, write a function

```
is_empty    ::    Queue item -> Bool
```

that tests if the queue is currently empty or not.   ■

Exercise 10.3   Ferdinand has produced a solution to the previous exercise. He tests the
code, and it usually works. Occasionally, however, the system seems to
freeze up and, after waiting until his patience has run out, he has to abort
the program. In desperation, he shows his code to Imelda who immediately
points out the following fragment as problematic:

```
(hmc,tmc) = q
hic       = contents & hmc
tic       = contents & tmc
if ((hic == INil) && (tic == INil)) ...
    .
    .

            contents hmc := ...
            contents tmc := ...
    .
    .
```

Explain what the problem might be, and propose a fix. (*Hint:* Consider concurrent executions of this fragment by different producers and consumers, and remember that these statements are unordered except for data dependencies.)   ∎

Exercise 10.4   Instead of a 2-tuple of M-cells, define a new Queue algebraic type that directly has two M-structure fields. Show the corresponding changes in the enqueue and dequeue functions.   ∎

10.3   M-structure Arrays

An M-structure array has the type

    MArray   a   b

where a is the index type and b is the type of the contents of the array. A one- or multi-dimensional M-array may be allocated using an M-array comprehension expression:

    mArray   (*l*,*u*)   [... *index-and-value pairs* ...]

which evaluates to a new M-array with lower and upper index bounds *l* and *u*, respectively, and initial contents specified by the list of index-and-value pairs.[2] Any index not mentioned in the initializing list is initialized to the empty state. If the initializing list has duplicated indices it will of course produce a multiple-store error.

An element of an M-array can be examined or mFetched using the expressions

    a ! j   -- examine
    a !& j   -- mFetch

A value v can be sStored into an empty element of an M-array using the statement

    a!j := v

An element of an M-array can be replaced by a new value using the statement

    a!&j := v

---

2. This can also be used to allocate M-arrays of higher dimensions, such as matrices.

For example, the assignment

```
a!j := (a !& j) + 1
```

reads, increments, and stores back the jth element of array a. The value
of implicit synchronization becomes apparent if we consider the following
program fragment:

```
let
   .
   .
   .
   a!j := (a !& j) + 1          -- (S1)
   .
   .
   .
   a!k := (a !& k) + 2          -- (S2)
   .
   .
   .
in
   .
   .
   .
```

Suppose j = k = 5, and suppose element 5 of a originally contained
the value 10. As usual in a *pH* block, the two statements may be executed in parallel. Suppose S1 performed its mFetch first. It reads the value
10, increments it, and sStores the value 11 back. S2 can then mFetch
this value, add 2 to it, and sStore the value 13 back. Thus, the sequence
of values in the array location is 10, 11, and 13. Alternatively, if S2
performed its mFetch first, the sequence of values would be 10, 12,
and 13.

Now, suppose for the moment that we did not have the implicit synchronization; that is, suppose S1 and S2 were like ordinary assignment
statements in traditional programming languages. The following sequence
of events would then be possible:

- (S1R) The value 10 is read in statement S1.
- (S2R) While S1 is performing its addition, S2 reads the element and
  also reads the value 10.
- (S1W) S1 writes its result back (the value 11).
- (S2W) S2 writes its result back (the value 12).

The final value in element 5 of a is 12, which is clearly not what was intended. In fact, the following sequences of events are possible with ordinary
reads and writes:

```
10,  11,  13        (S1R, S1W, S2R, S2W)
10,  12,  13        (S2R, S2W, S1R, S1W)
10,  11,  12        (S1R, S2R, S1W, S2W)
10,  11,  11        (S1R, S2R, S2W, S1W)
10,  12,  11        (S2R, S1R, S2W, S1W)
10,  11,  12        (S2R, S1R, S1W, S2W)
```

The implicit synchronization of mFetch and sStore ensures that only the first two sequences are possible. If S1 takes first, then S2 cannot take until S1 puts its result back, and vice versa. Thus, neither S2 nor any other statement in the program can "see" the value of element 5 of a while S1 is doing its work (for this reason, we also say that the increments are *atomic*). This ensures that the two increments are done correctly.

Notice also that the overall computation is determinate—the final value is 13. However, the array location goes through certain intermediate states that are not determinate (11 or 12). These intermediate states are *visible* to the rest of the program, in the sense that some other expression that executed a !& 5 may read 10, 11, 12, or 13, depending on when it tried to read it.

10.4   Parallel Histograms

Suppose we are given a tree t of numbers, where each number is in the range 1 to 5, and we wish to build a histogram of the numbers, that is, an array h from 1 to 5, such that h_i = the number of times i appears in the tree.

This problem statement is a highly abstracted account of MCNP, a real application program used by over 350 organizations in diverse industries such as oil exploration, medical imaging, and so on. The program models the diffusion of subatomic particles from a radioactive probe through the surrounding material, using Monte Carlo simulation. For each original particle, the program follows it through events in its lifetime, such as motion in some direction, collision with a material boundary or another particle, and so on. The tree structure arises because particles may split into two (and recursively, those particles may split again), after which the simulation follows each particle separately. Note that no data structure is required for the "tree"; it is simply represented by the call/return tree. When a particle finally dies, some of its properties are collected in various histograms (e.g., its final position, energy, etc.). This program is one that has eluded easy parallelization in all conventional programming models, but is "embarrassingly parallel," because the tree may have thousands of branches, and the events in a particle's life are decided purely locally, based on the toss of a coin.

Here is the type definition for the tree:

```
data Tree = Leaf Int | Node Tree Tree
```

A tree is either a leaf containing an integer, or a node with a left and right subtree.

10.4.1   A Solution Using M-structures

The solution is shown in the function hist below:

```
hist    :: Tree -> (MArray Int Int)
hist t = let
                h = mArray (1,5) [ (j,0) | j <- [1..5] ]
                traverse t h
                >>>
                h' = h
            in
                h'

traverse                :: tree -> (MArray Int Int) -> ()
traverse (Leaf i)    h = let
                                h!i := (h !& i + 1)
                            in ()
traverse (Node l r) h = let
                                traverse l h
                                traverse r h
                            in ()
```

hist creates an M-array and initializes it to contain zeroes everywhere. It also passes it into function traverse, which recursively passes it down to all leaves in parallel. At each leaf (containing i), traverse takes the ith count, increments it, and puts it back, thus guaranteeing that the increment is atomic. The barrier in hist ensures that the histogram array is not returned as a result until the traveral is complete.

The solution is quite clear. The only subtlety is the explicit sequencing barrier in hist, which is necessary because we do not want h to be returned until all the increments have completed. If we returned h before this, then some external computation may accidentally see some intermediate state of the array.

The solution is also very efficient and parallel. It constructs exactly one thing—the histogram array itself—and it performs the increments in parallel in some nondeterministic order. Despite this nondeterminism, note that the overall program is determinate; the resulting histogram depends only on the input tree and not on the order in which computations are performed.

Exercise 10.5   In the function hist, there is no barrier between the first statement (the M-array comprehension) and the next (the call to traverse). Why is it unnecessary? What would happen if a barrier were inserted there?   ∎

Exercise 10.6   What is the maximum number of increments that could occur in parallel on the histogram array?   ∎

Exercise 10.7   Suppose the argument t was not truly a tree, but a DAG (directed acyclic graph). In other words, some subtree is shared from at least two locations in t. Does this affect the behavior of the program? How many times will the leaves of a shared subtree be counted?   ∎

10.4.2   A Comparison with Functional Solutions

Let us look at some functional solutions for comparison, in order to better appreciate the benefits of M-structures.

Our first solution builds an initial array h0 containing 0 everywhere and then performs a right-to-left traversal of the tree. At each leaf, where i is the contents of the leaf, it "increments" the ith location of the array; that is, it builds a new array that is a copy of the old one except that the ith location is incremented.

```
hist      :: Tree -> (Array Int Int)
hist t = let
              h0 = array (1,5)
                         [ (j,0) | j <- [1..5] ]
          in
              traverse t h0

traverse :: Tree -> (Array Int Int) -> (Array Int Int)
traverse (Leaf i)   h = incr h i
traverse (Node l r) h = traverse l (traverse r h)

incr      :: (Array Int Int) -> Int -> (Array Int Int)
incr h i = array (1,5)
                      [ (j, if i == j then (h!j)+1
                            else h!j)            | j <- [1..5] ]
```

There are a couple problems with this solution. The first is threading. The array is carefully threaded through the arguments and results of `traverse`. Each invocation of `traverse` takes in one array and returns another. They are composed in such a way that conceptually there is one array that is passed all the way around the traversal. This kind of structure is also known as plumbing. This threading required by functional programming obscures the structure of the program.

Threading also penalizes parallelism. In principle, the increments can be done in any order, as shown in our M-array solution; however, the threading of the array in the functional solution picks a particular order for the accumulation, serializing it.

This kind of threading is even worse in the original MCNP problem. There, the tree is never constructed, but rather the results and arguments are passed between recursive calls.

The second problem is efficiency. The program builds n copies of the array, where n is the number of leaves in the tree. Further, it simply copies data from one array to the next.

Exercise 10.8   In the program, how many times is a number simply copied from one array to the next?   ■

In our second functional solution, we use an accumulator comprehension (described in Section 7.7). Each element of the accumulator array is initially zero. We call `traverse` on the tree to build a list of its leaves, and then we accumulate into the array using this list.

```
hist    :: Tree -> (Array Int Int)
hist t = accumArray (+) 0 (1,5)  [ (i, 1) | i <- traverse t ]

traverse   :: Tree -> [Int]
traverse t = aux t []

aux                 :: Tree -> [Int] -> [Int]
aux (Leaf i)    is = i:is
aux (Node l r) is = aux l (aux r is)
```

This solution also has a couple problems:

♦ *Threading:* The program picks an order in which to place the leaves into the intermediate list, even though this order is irrelevant to the solution.

◆ *Efficiency:* The construction of the intermediate list and its subsequent sequential traversal all cause this solution to be inefficient, as elaborated by the following exercises.

Exercise 10.9   How many list cells does the program allocate? How many list cells may be deallocated after the histogram is built? ▪

Exercise 10.10   How many reads and writes are performed on each list cell? ▪

Various other functional solutions are possible. In a third solution, the program recursively descends in parallel to every leaf. At a leaf containing, say, 2, it produces the array [0 1 0 0 0]. At each node, it adds the arrays from the two subtrees and returns the new array. Thus, the top node produces the sum for the whole tree.

```
hist (Leaf i)   = array (1,5)
                      [ (j, if i == j then 1
                                      else 0) | j <- [1..5] ]
hist (Node l r) = vsum (hist l) (hist r)

vsum h1 h2      = array (1,5)
                      [ (j, h1!j + h2!j) | j <- [1..5] ]
```

Although this gets rid of the threading in the previous two solutions, it doubles the storage use of the first solution (instead of just constructing a new array at each leaf, it also constructs a new array at each internal node).

In a fourth solution, the program performs five tree traversals in parallel. Each traversal itself traverses the tree in parallel, with the jth traversal counting the number of js at the leaves. Finally, we build the array containing the five sums.

```
hist t = array (1,5)
                  [ (j, traverse j t) | j <- [1..5] ]

traverse j (Leaf i)   = if i == j then 1 else 0
traverse j (Node l r) = (traverse j l) + (traverse j r)
```

Although this has excellent parallelism and does not use much storage, it is inefficient because of the number of independent traversals.

In two of our previous solutions, a large source of inefficiency was the creation of new arrays that differed only slightly from earlier ones, resulting in a lot of copying. Instead of using arrays, we could use balanced binary trees, so that the copying is proportional only to the log h, the number of elements in the histogram, instead of being proportional to h itself. Unfortunately, this would greatly constrain parallelism because all computations would now have to be funneled through the root of the binary tree.

10.5   M-lists

An M-list is a polymorphic list in which each tail field is updatable using M-structure semantics. Here is a type declaration for M-lists, with the updatable field indicated by "&":

data MList a = MNil | MCons {head :: a, tail :: & (MList a)}

As before, this **data** declaration defines the new type MList, the constructors MNil and MCons, the field names head and tail, and selector functions head and tail. When constructing an MCons object using positional notation or using field names

```
MCons   e_h   e_t
MCons   { head = e_h, tail = e_t }
```

the tail field is filled using an sStore operation. The tail field can also be left empty:

```
MCons   { head = e_h }
```

When selecting fields from an MCons term using pattern matching or the field selection functions

```
case mc of
    MNil         -> ...
    MCons h t -> ...

case mc of
    MNil                         -> ...
    MCons {head = h, tail = t} -> ...

head mc

tail mc
```

the tail field is extracted using an examine operation. To mFetch the tail field, we use the following notation:

```
tail & mc
```

To sStore and replace the value of the tail field, we use the following notations:

```
tail   mc  := v                    -- sStore
tail & mc  := v                    -- replace
```

M-fields are distinguished from other fields on the basis of type, and type checking ensures that M-fields and ordinary fields are accessed with the correct operations.

10.6   **Mutable Lists**

Consider the problem of inserting an integer x into a set ys, taking care not to insert duplicates. Representing the set as a list of integers, here is a purely functional solution using pattern matching:

```
insert_f             :: [Int] -> Int -> [Int]
insert_f []     x = [x]
insert_f (y:ys) x = if x == y then
                        y:ys
                    else
                        y:(insert_f ys x)
```

We use the "_f" suffix to remind us that this is a functional solution. Let us first familiarize ourselves with the behavior of this function. Consider the following call:

```
ys1 = insert_f ys xA
```

If ys already contains xA, then ys1 is essentially a copy of ys (until the list element that contains xA). In other words, the recursion descends the list ys until it finds xA and then constructs a copy of the prefix on the way back. If ys does not contain xA, then ys1 is a new list whose last element is xA and remaining elements are the same as in ys. The recursion descends all the way to the end, creates a new element for xA, and constructs a copy of the prefix (which is the whole list) on the way back. In other words, the function allocates $O(n)$ storage, where n is the length of the list, *whether or not* xA *is already in the list*.

Now, here is a solution using M-structures (with an "_m" suffix to indicate this):

```
insert_m :: (MList Int) -> Int -> (MList Int)
insert_m ys x =
   case ys of
      MNil          -> MCons x MNil
      MCons y ys' -> if x == y then
                          ys
                       else
                          let
                             tail ys := (insert_m  (tail & ys)   x)
                          in
                             ys
```

The empty-list case, and the case where the head of the list equals the new element to be inserted, are the same as in the functional version. In the remaining case, we mFetch the tail of the list, insert x into it and sStore it back, and we *return the original list*. Please note that we mFetch the tail of ys again even though ys' is the tail of the list because ys' was extracted using an examine operation and not an mFetch, due to the semantics of pattern matching.

First, let us check correctness. We start by convincing ourselves that the takes and puts are correctly ordered. Consider the statement in the block

```
tail ys := (insert_m (tail & ys)   x)
```

If, due to nonstrictness, the recursive call to insert_m returned a value early, before the argument expression (tail&ys) was evaluated, we could have an error because the sStore operation on the left could occur before the mFetch operation on the right. This cannot happen since insert_m is strict in its argument ys because it cannot return any value until it has tested (ys==MNil). Thus, in the recursive call, the expression (tail&ys) must be evaluated before a result is returned; thus, the mFetch must occur before the sStore, and they are properly ordered.

With this established, the rest of the proof of correctness is similar to the functional case—we use induction on the length of the list. Clearly the function is correct if the list ys is empty (length zero). Now, assuming that the solution is correct for lists of some given length n, we can show that it is also correct for lists of length $n + 1$. It follows, by induction, that it is correct for lists of any length. Suppose the first element of the list is equal to x; clearly the solution is correct. Suppose the first element of the list is not equal to x. In this case, x is inserted into the tail, which, by assumption, is done correctly (since it is a list of length $n - 1$), and put back, and so the overall insertion is done correctly.

Exercise 10.11   In `insert_m`, the pattern matching for the second clause of the case expression of course uses the examine operation to extract `ys'`, the tail of the list. Ferdinand proposes replacing the expression `(tail & ys)` by `ys'`. What would be the effect of this change?   ■

From an efficiency standpoint the advantage of `insert_m` over the functional version is that it takes a constant amount of heap store per insertion, instead of $O(n)$, where n is the length of the list. The function allocates no heap store if x is already present and exactly one cons cell otherwise.

The difference between the two solutions is illustrated by the following similar program fragments:

```
ys1 = insert_f ys xA        -- A
ys2 = insert_f ys xB        -- B
```

and

```
ys1 = insert_m ys xA        -- A
ys2 = insert_m ys xB        -- B
```

Suppose the initial list ys does not contain xA or xB. In the functional case, ys1 and ys2 are two entirely different lists, each prefixed with a copy of ys and whose last element is xA or xB, respectively. In the M-structures case, if ys is MNil, then the ys1 and ys2 are two separate, singleton lists containing xA and xB, respectively, exactly as in the functional case. On the other hand, if ys is not MNil, then ys1 and ys2 are exactly the same list, the last two elements of which are xA and xB.

Under nonstrict semantics, `insert_f` has the attractive property that in the last line the new cons cell can be returned even while we are inserting x into its tail. Thus, multiple insertions can be "pipelined"—a second insertion can run closely behind the first, automatically synchronizing on empty fields.

Note that `insert_m` has the same kind of "pipeline" parallelism as `insert_f`. In the last line, nonstrictness allows us to return ys immediately. If a second insertion is attempted immediately, it can run closely behind the first, blocking on empty fields (due to takes) in the same manner as `insert_f` blocks on empty fields.

However, in the presence of two concurrent insertions A and B, it is interesting to note that `insert_m` has an additional nondeterministic behavior not exhibited by `insert_f`. Suppose A and B are the following two statements:

```
ys1 = insert_m ys  xA       -- A
ys2 = insert_m ys1 xB       -- B
```

Suppose the list `ys` already has a number of cells but contains neither `xA` nor `xB`. Consider the first list cell `ys` given to A. Because of nonstrictness, not only can A return `ys` in the last line before attempting to traverse the tail of the list, but, having returned `ys` to B (as `ys1`), it is possible for B to take the tail of `ys` before A takes it. Thus, it is possible for B to overtake A and to reach the second list cell `ys'` earlier. Repeating this argument, B could return `ys'` before taking its tail, this gets put into the tail of `ys`, allowing A to now take it and to proceed to the second list cell `ys'`, whereupon A could take the tail of `ys'` before B does. In this manner, it is possible for A and B to continually leapfrog each other toward the end of the list. Depending on their relative speeds of execution, the final list `ys2` could be either of the following:

```
[..., xA , xB ]
[..., xB , xA ]
```

Exercise 10.12   Justify the claim that for the analogous functional program

```
ys1 = insert_f ys  xA       -- A
ys2 = insert_f ys1 xB       -- B
```

the final list `ys2` could only be

```
[..., xA , xB ]                                                    ■
```

Exercise 10.13   Add a sequencing barrier in the code for `insert_m` that eliminates its nondeterminism.   ■

Exercise 10.14   Write a variant of `insert_m` of type

```
insert_m      :: (MList Int) -> Int -> (Bool, (MList Int))
```

that returns not only the updated list but also a boolean flag indicating whether it found the element already in the list or not.   ■

10.7   Atomicity Issues: Mutable Association Lists

Consider the following problem: given a list of strings (e.g., the words in a textbook), we wish to count the number of occurrences of each distinct word. The basic idea for the solution is to maintain a *table* that associates words to their frequencies. The table is initially empty. For each word, we check if it is present in the table or not; if present, we simply increment its associated count, and if absent, we insert it in the table, initializing its frequency to 1.

We can structure the table as a list of entries:

```
data Entry = Entry { word :: String, freq :: & Int }
```

```
data Table = LTable { contents :: & (MList Entry) }
```

This is depicted in Figure 10.2. Such tables have historically been called "association lists" in the Lisp community (or just "alists," for short).

As a warmup exercise, let us write a function that does not perform any updates; given a string s and a table t, it simply returns the entry corresponding to s in table t. The function either returns Nothing, if the string is not in the table, or (Just e), where e is the corresponding entry for the string. Recall that Just and Nothing are the constructors of the very useful Maybe algebraic type, which is predefined in *pH* and is used by many functions that either "fail" or return a useful result:

```
data Maybe a = Nothing | Just a
```

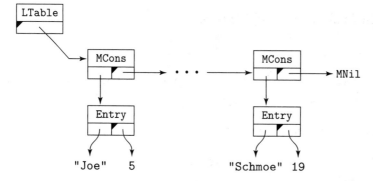

Figure 10.2 An association list (updatable fields are shown with a dark fillet in the top-left corner).

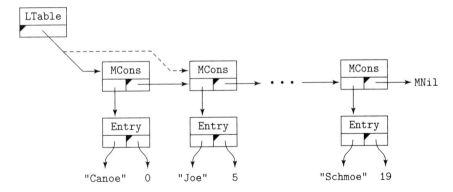

Figure 10.3 Operation of `table_insert`.

Here is the table lookup function:

```
table_lookup :: String -> Table -> (Maybe Entry)
table_lookup s t = list_lookup s (contents t)

list_lookup :: String -> (MList Entry) -> (Maybe Entry)
list_lookup  s  xjs =
  case xjs of
    MNil                                    -> Nothing
    MCons { head = xj, tail = xjs' } -> if s == (word xj) then
                                            Just xj
                                        else
                                            list_lookup s xjs'
```

The top-level function `table_lookup` calls the auxiliary function `list_lookup`, passing it the list which is in the `LTable` cell. This list is extracted from the `LTable` cell using the examine operator since we are not going to perform any updates. The `list_lookup` function recursively travels down the list of entries, at each stage comparing the given string s to the string in the current entry. If found, it returns the current entry, packaged under the constructor `Just`; if it runs off the end of the list, it returns `Nothing`. Again, note that the pattern matching uses the examine operator to bind `xjs'` to the tail of the list without modifying it.

Now let us try a simple update function, one that creates a new entry in the table, with an initial count of zero. It adds the new entry at the head of the original list of entries and returns the new entry. This is depicted pictorially in Figure 10.3. Here is our first attempt:

```
table_insert s t =
    let
        e              =  Entry s 0
        contents t := MCons e (contents & t)
    in
        e
```

Unfortunately, there is a bug in this function. Since MCons is nonstrict (as all constructors are), it may return a value before the take operation in its argument has occurred and, in turn, the put may be attempted before the take. Here is a possible fix, using sequencing to force the right order:

```
table_insert s t =
    let
        e              =  Entry s 0
        old_l          =  contents & t
        >>>
        contents t := MCons e old_l
    in
        e
```

This solution is correct, but it has oversequentialized things. In addition to sequentializing the take and the put, the MCons allocation cannot occur until the Entry construction and the take have completed, and no result can be returned until the take has completed. A more liberal, but more complex solution is this:

```
table_insert s t =
    let
        e    = Entry s 0
        new_l = MCons e old_l
        (
            old_l         =  contents & t
            >>>
            contents t :=  new_l
        )
    in
        e
```

Let us now examine the reason for having the LTable object that contains the list of Entry objects; why can't our table simply be the list of Entry objects? Consider two insertions into a single table t, and suppose they are performed in the order shown:

```
e1 = table_insert "Joe"    t        -- I1
e2 = table_insert "Schmoe" t        -- I2
```

Clearly, we expect the effect of I1 to be visible in I2; that is, the argument t in I2 should contain an entry for Joe. This means that t must originally have pointed to a sharable, updatable object *even if the table was empty*. When the table is empty, therefore, it does not suffice for t to be an "empty" value like MNil because it is not updatable. Since the list of entries is MNil when the table is empty, we need to package it into an updatable object; the LTable object is precisely this object.

Now, we return to the word frequency problem and attempt a solution:

```
word_frequencies        :: [String] -> Table
word_frequencies words =
    let
        t = LTable MNil
        for w <- words do
            y       = table_lookup w t
            e       = case y of
                         Nothing -> table_insert w t
                         Just e' -> e'
            freq e := (freq & e) + 1
        finally ()
        >>>
        t' = t
    in
        t'
```

First, the function creates an empty table. Then, for each word, it looks it up in the table; if not present, it inserts it. In either case, e is the entry for the word, and it increments the count in the entry. Finally, it returns the completed table. Again, as in the histogram example earlier, the barrier is present to ensure that the table is completely built before releasing it to the outside world.

There is a rather subtle bug in our program; in fact, this is another "atomicity" bug. As usual, the loop iterations may all run in parallel. Suppose two separate iterations are executing, at approximately the same moment, the following statement:

```
y = table_lookup  "Joe"  table
```

and suppose that the word "Joe" is not yet in the table. It is possible that both of them get Nothing for y; that is, both lookups complete before either one of them can insert an entry for "Joe" into the table. The net result will be that two entries for "Joe" will be inserted into the table, which is clearly erroneous.

We therefore observe that the table lookup and the insertion must be combined into a single atomic action. This is an example of a large class of atomic operations well known in the literature, called *test and set* operations. Lookups and insertions may not be arbitrarily interleaved. Once a lookup is performed, its corresponding insertion, if any, must be performed before any subsequent lookups can be performed. Here is a new function that combines the lookup and insert actions:

```
table_lookup_insert        :: String -> Table -> Entry
table_lookup_insert s t =
    let
        xjs        =   contents & t
        (e,xjs')   =   list_lookup_insert s xjs
        contents t := xjs'
    in
        e


list_lookup_insert          :: String -> (MList Entry)
                                       -> (Entry, (MList Entry))
list_lookup_insert s xjs =
    case  xjs  of
      MNil              -> let
                              e = Entry s 0
                           in
                              (e, MCons (Entry s 0) MNil)
      MCons xj xjs' -> if s == (word xj) then
                          (xj, xjs)
                       else
                         let
                           (e,xjs') = list_lookup_insert
                                               s (tail & xjs)
                           tail xjs := xjs'
                         in
                           (e,xjs)
```

The function `table_lookup_insert` takes the original list of entries `xjs` and passes it along with the string `s` to `list_lookup_insert`, which returns two things: the entry for `s` (possibly newly inserted) and the (possibly new) list of entries `xjs'`. The latter is put back into the table cell.

The function `list_lookup_insert` runs down the list looking for the string `s`. If it finds `s` at a particular list cell, it just returns the entry and returns the list as is. If it does not find `s` at a particular list cell, then it takes the tail, recursively looks up/inserts `s` in the tail, puts the updated list back in the tail, and returns the entry and the original list cell. If it falls off the end of the list, it creates a new entry for s and returns the new entry along with a nonempty list containing the entry.

Exercise 10.15   Prove that the lookup and insert operations are indeed atomic in the above `table_lookup_insert` function (i.e., that with two calls to `table_lookup_insert` in parallel with the same word argument, exactly one of them will actually insert an entry for that word if it did not already occur in the table). ∎

Exercise 10.16   Suppose the table has no entry for "Joe" and suppose computation *A* begins executing:

```
table_lookup_insert  "Joe"  t
```

and it has successfully evaluated the (contents & t) expression. Shortly thereafter, computation *B* also executes:

```
table_lookup_insert  "Joe"  t
```

Is it certain that computation *A* will be the one that creates the entry for "Joe"? (*Hint:* Watch out for nonstrictness!) ∎

Now, we can redo our solution to the word frequency problem:

```
word_frequencies         :: [String] -> Table
word_frequencies words =
    let
        table = LTable MNil
        for w <- words do
            e      = table_lookup_insert w table
            freq e := (freq & e) + 1
        finally ()
        >>>
        table' = table
    in
        table'
```

As before, we first create an empty table. Then, for each word, we look up/insert it into the table, obtaining its entry e, and increment its count. Finally, we return the completed table.

Exercise 10.17   Suppose the word "Joe" appears twice in the words list. Suppose `table_lookup_insert` is called with the first occurrence (call it "Joe$_1$") during which it creates the entry for "Joe" and later with the second occurrence (call it "Joe$_2$"). In what order do the freq increments happen? ∎

Exercise 10.18   Change the association list type and association list operations so that they are polymorphic in the information associated with each string (instead of being restricted to integers). ∎

Exercise 10.19   Can we simply change the association list type and type of the association list operations so that they are polymorphic in the search key (instead of being restricted to strings)? Explain why or why not. If not, can it be changed somewhat to achieve this? ∎

Exercise 10.20   Show how the association list type and the type of the association list operations can be generalized using overloading so that keys of different types may be used. ∎

10.8   Parallel Hash Tables

For many applications, the association list presented in the last section is quite inefficient, since we must perform a linear search of the list for each word. Each search takes $O(n)$ time, where n is the number of entries, so that the total cost is $O(mn)$, where m is the number of words.

A more efficient kind of table is a *hash table*, which is an array with indices ranging, say, from 0 to hmax. Each array element (also called a "bucket") is itself a table; we'll assume that each element contains an association list. The overall structure is depicted in Figure 10.4. When we encounter a word w, we compute an index j for w in the range 0 to hmax and we check only the association list at index j. If this index computation has the following properties:

- Index computation takes constant time and is fast.
- Index computation is a true *function* (i.e., when applied to the same argument it produces the same result).
- The words are scattered uniformly over the buckets of the array.

then each association list will be small (containing only n/hmax entries each, instead of n). If hmax is approximately equal to n, then each association list will contain only one entry, so that access to any entry will take constant time.

An index computation function that has the above properties is called a *hash function* (because it apparently randomly scatters words to different

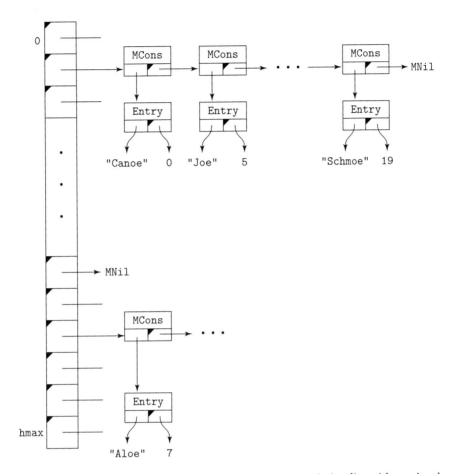

Figure 10.4   A hash table. Each element contains an association list with entries that hash to that index.

indexes of the table). Clearly, the following function is not a good hash function:

```
hash s = 0
```

Although it takes constant time and is very fast, it does not scatter the indexes uniformly over the array. All words would end up in a single list at index zero and all other indices would contain empty lists. Here is another bad hash function:

```
hash s = mod (time_of_day ()) hmax
```

Though it takes constant time and may nicely distribute strings across the buckets of the array, it is not repeatable, so that it will not be easy to look up a previously inserted string.

A simple and not unreasonable hash function is this:

```
hash s = let
              h  = 0 ;
              h' = for c <- s do
                        next h = h + char_code c
                    finally h
         in
              mod h' (hmax + 1)
```

We add up the ASCII codes of all the characters in the string and take the sum modulo the index range of interest. Strictly speaking, this is not a constant time function since it depends on the length of the string, but it is acceptable (it is fast and does not depend on the number of strings to be inserted in the table).

An empty hash table of size N (for some suitable constant N) is just an M-array containing MNil, the empty association list, in all locations.

```
mk_empty_table () = mArray (0,hmax)
                      [ (j, MNil) | j <- [0..hmax] ]
```

Here is a new version of table_lookup_insert that uses a hash table instead of an association list:

```
type Hash_table = MArray (MList Entry)

table_lookup_insert          :: String -> Hash_table -> Entry
table_lookup_insert  s  t =
  let
        j        = hash s
        es       = table !& j
        (e,es')  = list_lookup_insert es s
        table!j := es'
  in
        e
```

In the first line in the block we hash the given string s into an index j. Then, we take the alist at index j and use our function from the previous section to look up and possibly insert the string into that alist. We put back the (possibly) new alist into the array and return the entry for s.

Notice that the function can be applied to two strings s1 and s2 in parallel. If they hash to different indices, there is absolutely no interference between the two calls. Even if they hash to the same index, they may "pipeline" one behind the other, as discussed earlier.

Exercise 10.21   Write a new function

```
table_lookup  ::  String -> Hash_table -> (Maybe Entry)
```

that looks up a word in the hash table, returning its entry. If we initiate two lookups in parallel on words with different hash values, how (if at all) are they sequentialized? If we initiate two lookups in parallel on words that have the same hash value, how (if at all) are they sequentialized?   ■

10.9   Parallel Graph Manipulation

Suppose we are given a directed graph structure, such as the one shown in Figure 10.5, which has eight nodes connected by various edges. Each node contains a string as a unique identifier and some integer information. The problem is this: given a node N in such a graph, compute rsum(N), the sum of the integer information in all nodes reachable from N along the directed edges. For example, given node G, the reachable nodes are G and H, so that rsum(G) $= 9 + 19 = 28$. Given node A, the reachable nodes are A, B, C, and D, so that rsum(A) $= 2 + 5 + 9 + 1 = 17$. Note that the information in each node is only counted once, even though the node may be reachable along many paths. For example, node B is reachable directly from A, indirectly from C, indirectly from D via C, and so on; in fact, because of the cycle in the graph, it is reachable along infinitely many paths from A. Nevertheless, the information in B (i.e., 5) is counted only once.

We can represent graphs using the following type declaration:

```
data GNode = GNode { id     :: String,
                     info   :: Int,
                     neighbs :: [GNode] }
```

The first field contains a unique identifier for the node, the second field contains the integer information, and the third field contains a list of nodes (possibly empty) representing the neighbors, if any, of the current node. For

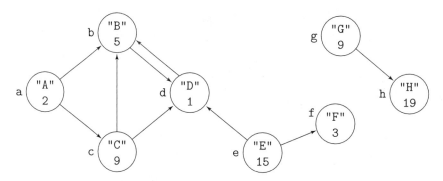

Figure 10.5   A directed graph. Each node contains a string as a unique identifier and
some integer information.

example, the graph of Figure 10.5 may be constructed using the following
set of declarations:

```
a = GNode  "A"   2   [b:c]
b = GNode  "B"   5   [d]
c = GNode  "C"   9   [b:d]
d = GNode  "D"   1   [b]
e = GNode  "E"   15  [d:f]
f = GNode  "F"   3   []
g = GNode  "G"   9   [h]
h = GNode  "H"   19  []
```

The mutually recursive definitions of b and d reflect the corresponding cycle
in the graph.

We will assume that each node has a unique string component, so that
the strings can be used as unique identifiers. In other words, given two
node-valued variables n1 and n2, we can test whether they refer to the same
node or not by testing if the strings in their referends are equal.

Graph traversals typically need some means of ensuring that they do not
repeatedly traverse shared subgraphs and cycles. Traditional graph traversal
algorithms rely on "marking" visited nodes to avoid repeated traversals (the
old storybook method of leaving a trail of bread crumbs to mark the spots
you have already visited). For familiarity with these traditional algorithms,
we begin with two M-structure programs that use imperative operations
to mark visited nodes. Later, we will examine the functional solution for
comparison.

10.9.1   A Simple M-structure Solution

The traditional imperative solution to this problem involves extending the node type to contain a *mark* field, which is used to avoid repeated traversals of shared subgraphs. We assume that the mark field is initially set to False. The following program expresses this solution:

```
data GNode = GNode { id      ::    String,
                     info    ::    Int,
                     neighbs ::    [GNode],
                     mark    :: & Bool }

rsum      :: GNode -> Int
rsum nd = if testAndSetMark nd then
              0
          else
              (info nd) + sum (map rsum (neighbs nd))

testAndSetMark      :: GNode -> Bool
testAndSetMark nd = let
                        -- take the mark field
                        m       =   mark & nd
                        >>>
                        -- put True in mark field
                        mark nd := True
                    in
                        m
```

(Note that in this solution, the unique id field is not used.)

The solution is very clear. The only subtle point is the atomicity of the testAndSetMark predicate. The value of the mark field is taken and returned and set to True regardless of its previous value. Since the mark field is set to True the first time the node is visited, the node will be counted only once. As described earlier, the serialization barrier between the take and put guarantee that they happen in the correct order.

While this solution corresponds to most textbook algorithms, it has two drawbacks:

◆ *Mark initialization:* We assumed that the marks in the graph were initialized to False before the traversal began. But don't we need a traversal of the graph to set all marks to False? In many applications, we also have some *independent* access to all the nodes, such as an array containing all the nodes. In this case, we can iterate through this array, resetting all marks to `False` before beginning the graph traversal. Note that resetting the marks cannot be overlapped with the traversal algorithm, and so this easily doubles the cost of the algorithm. Further, if the total number of nodes is large compared to the number of nodes actually reachable from the original node *A*, then resetting all marks may be a significant overhead for the graph traversal.

♦ *Multiple traversals:* Suppose we are given two nodes *A* and *B* and want to compute the reachable sum from each of them, in parallel. Our current program cannot be used for this, since the marks from the *A* and *B* traversals may interfere. Nodes marked by *A*'s traversal will not be counted by the traversal from *B*, and vice versa.

These drawbacks could be overcome by a simple extension of the "mark field" idea: suppose each traversal carries with it an additional parameter, a unique *traversal identifier*. Then, rather than marking nodes with a boolean, each node contains a list of traversal identifiers indicating which traversals have visited the node. The `testAndSetMark` predicate checks and updates this list.

This solution allows multiple traversals to occur in parallel, since they have distinct traversal IDs and will not interfere. Also, node marks do not have to be reset, since a brand-new traversal ID is used for each traversal. However, the performance of this solution degrades as more and more traversals are performed, creating unused IDs that slow the `testAndSetMark` predicate and occupy storage. Because of this weakness, we will not pursue this idea any further.

10.9.2   An M-structure Solution Allowing Multiple Concurrent Traversals

A better solution that allows multiple concurrent traversals uses a separate `visited` table to keep track of nodes already traversed. Rather than marking nodes directly, this table contains the unique IDs of visited nodes and is updated as each new node is encountered. The original definition of graph nodes (without a mark field) is used:

```
data GNode = GNode { id      :: String,
                     info    :: Int,
                     neighbs :: [GNode] }
```

Here is the code for the reachable sum:

```
rsum nd = let
              visited = mk_empty_table ()
```

```
              aux (GNode x i nbs) =
                  if isMember_and_insert visited x then
                      0
                  else
                      i + sum (map aux nbs)
        in
           aux  nd
```

The isMember_and_insert function is analogous to the testAndSetMark function in our first solution: as an atomic operation it returns a boolean indicating whether x is present in the visited table and inserts x in the table if it is not.

This solution is quite similar to our earlier one. There is no threading, and marking code is localized. The main difference between the programs is the modularity supplied by the visited table. It is shared by all calls to aux, but does not require threading or modification to the graphs.

We can implement the visited table in a number of ways; something along the lines of the parallel hash table in Section 10.8 is a good candidate (except that our problem here is a little simpler since we are only interested in the presence or absence of an entry in the table, and we do not need to actually retrieve the table entry).

Exercise 10.22   Implement the mk_empty_table and isMember_and_insert functions using the ideas presented in Section 10.8.   ∎

Exercise 10.23   The mk_empty_table and isMember_and_insert functions can be made very efficient if the unique identifiers in nodes are integers in some contiguous range, say, 1 to N. In this case, the visited table can be implemented as an M-array of booleans, all initialized to False. The element at index j is changed to True the first time that the node with unique identifier j is visited. Show an implementation of these functions that uses this strategy.   ∎

10.9.3   A Functional Solution

Since nodes cannot be imperatively marked, the functional solution also uses a visited table to keep track of nodes that have already been traversed. Further, since we cannot actually update the table (we can only insert an element in a table to produce a new table), the table operations need to be threaded through the traversal, as shown in the following program:

```
rsum nd = let
            visited = TEmpty

            aux (s,visited) (GNode x i nbs) =
                if isMember x visited then
                    (s,visited)
                else
                    let  visited' = insert visited x
                    in
                        foldl  aux  (s+i,visited')  nbs

            (s,visited') = aux (0,visited) nd
      in
            s
```

The function foldl was described in Chapter 6; it is similar to map, but passes partial results (the partial sum and visited table) to each successive call of aux:

```
foldl f z []     = z
foldl f z (x:xs) = foldl f (f z x) xs
```

The rsum program is obscured by the threading of the visited table through the traversal. Again, threading overspecifies the order in which the traversal is made; here, the order of insertions is determined by the function foldl. Conceptually, one imagines all outward edges from a node being explored in parallel, with a shared subnode being explored only by the first traversal that happens to arrive there (we don't care which one).[3]

Note that here, unlike the histogram example, sharing is critical to ensure a polynomial time algorithm. Therefore, threading is unavoidable in purely functional solutions. In more complex problems, the threading required by functional programming further complicates the solution, adding extra parameters and return values and imposing unnecessary serialization.

The visited table in the functional traversal can itself be implemented either purely functionally or with side effects. A purely functional imple-

---

3. Readers who are familiar with parallel graph reduction will recognize that this is exactly what happens in a parallel graph reducer—a shared node is evaluated by the first process that arrives there, which also marks it as "in progress," so that later-arriving processes will not duplicate the work.

mentation may represent the table as an ordered binary tree, with log n time for the isMember and insert functions, assuming the tree is balanced:

```
data Tree = TEmpty | TNode Int Tree Tree

isMember TEmpty        x = False
isMember (TNode y l r) x = if x == y then
                               True
                           else if x < y then
                               isMember l x
                           else
                               isMember r x

insert TEmpty          x = TNode x TEmpty TEmpty
insert (TNode y l r) x = if x == y then
                             (TNode y l r)
                         else if x < y then
                             (TNode y (insert l x) r)
                         else
                             (TNode y l (insert r x))
```

This functional implementation introduces a storage overhead. Each insert rebuilds the visited table along the path from the newly inserted leaf back to the root, allocating new tree nodes along the way. The total storage cost for the table over the complete graph traversal can therefore vary from $O(n \log n)$ to $O(n^2)$, depending on how well the tree is balanced. Including tree rebalancing operations introduces overhead that may be recouped over many operations.

10.9.4   Graphs That Change

In many real programs, graph structures are dynamic. For example, in an airline reservation system, a graph might represent current services, with nodes representing cities and edges representing flights. As services change (e.g., due to flight cancellations or closure of a city's airport), the graph needs to be changed accordingly. In a compiler, a graph may represent the current syntactic structure of the program, or the flow of data between different parts of the program. As the compiler optimizes the program, the graph structure is likely to change.

Without updatable data structures, operations to change graphs can be very expensive. Consider again the graph in Figure 10.5 and its purely functional definition:

```
a = GNode  "A"   2   [b:c]
b = GNode  "B"   5   [d]
c = GNode  "C"   9   [b:d]
d = GNode  "D"   1   [b]
e = GNode  "E"   15  [d:f]
f = GNode  "F"   3   []
g = GNode  "G"   9   [h]
h = GNode  "H"   19  []
```

Now, suppose that node D has to change: say, the integer information field changes from 1 to 3, or say that we need to add a new edge from node D to node H.

```
d' = GNode  "D"   3   [b, h]
```

However, since node B used to refer to d, we have to update it to refer to d':

```
b' = GNode  "B"   5   [d']
```

But, node d' still refers to b, whereas it should refer to b', so what we really need to do is to reconstruct both nodes simultaneously:

```
b' = GNode  "B"   5   [d']
d' = GNode  "D"   3   [b', h]
```

Similarly, we have to reconstruct node C to refer to b', node A to refer to b' and c', and node E to refer to d':

```
a' = GNode  "A"   2   [b':c']
b' = GNode  "B"   5   [d']
c' = GNode  "C"   9   [b':d']
d' = GNode  "D"   3   [b', h]
e' = GNode  "E"   15  [d':f]
```

In short, to reconstruct a single graph node, we have simultaneously to reconstruct any node that points to it, either directly or indirectly. In the worst case, if the graph is strongly connected (i.e., if any node is reachable from any other node), we have to reconstruct the entire graph from scratch every time we make any change at all.

With updatable fields, on the other hand, only the node that has a change needs to be changed. Given the type

```
data GNode = GNode { id       ::      String,
                     info    ::  & Int,
                     neighbs ::  & [GNode] }
```

and an original node construction

```
d = GNode   "D"   1    [b]
```

we can simply update it in situ, in constant space and constant time:

```
info d     :=   3
neighbs d :=   h : (neighbs & d)
```

One trade-off between these two approaches, again, is parallelism. In the purely functional version, the old graph is unchanged—we are simply constructing a new graph that may happen to share some nodes with the old graph. Any current or future computation on the old graph can proceed in parallel with any current or future computation on the new graph. For example, a computation that is writing out the old graph to a file for backup purposes can continue its work while we construct and start operating on the new graph. In the M-structure version, on the other hand, we have to sequence things carefully: we have first to ensure that there is no longer any computation in progress on the old graph (e.g., wait for the backup process to finish); we can then update the graph; and we can then enable future computations on the new graph.

Exercise 10.24   Identify the sequencing bug in the line of code shown above:

```
neighbs d :=   h : (neighbs & d)
```

and show a version of the code that fixes it.   ■

10.10   Rewrite Rules for M-structures

The rewrite rules for M-arrays and M-fields are exactly like those for I-structures shown in Section 9.6, except using mFetch operations in place of iFetch operations. In particular the only rule that is different is

$$
\begin{aligned}
\text{arrayFull}(0_a, j, v); &\quad\longrightarrow\quad \text{arrayEmpty}(0_a, j); \quad \text{(ArrayMFetch)} \\
x = \text{arrayMFetch}(0_a, j) &\qquad\qquad x = v
\end{aligned}
$$

Conclusion

> The ending's better in a parallel universe
>
> —*Last chapter quote in a contemporary book*

Changing the way people think about parallelism is what *pH* is about. The world around us seems naturally parallel. As computer hardware becomes cheaper and parallel machines become the norm, in programming, too, we would like parallelism to be the default and sequentialization to be the explicit special case, instead of the other way around. In implicitly parallel programming, there are no artificial sequencing constraints—parallelism is constrained only by the essential data and control dependencies of an algorithm. Such an approach seems eminently natural; deliberately expressing an algorithm sequentially seems almost like it would need extra effort, as if it must be an artificial exercise. We can imagine that an implicitly parallel language like *pH* is routinely taught as the first programming language for high school students and university freshmen (using more elementary books than this one), with sequential programming left as an advanced topic for those who want better to fine-tune and optimize their programs through a deeper understanding of the trade-offs between parallelism and resource control. And yet, the opposite is true today: most programming languages are still primarily sequential, with parallelism often introduced as an afterthought. The *pH* research effort has attempted to elevate the level of parallel programming to the point where parallelism is no longer difficult, no longer threatening—where parallelism is indeed second nature to the programmer.

In this final chapter, we close with two topics of discussion. First, we once again put *pH* in context, situating it among the various approaches to parallel programming. Second, we examine what remains in order to take *pH* (or at least its ideas) from a research language into a production language, covering topics such as efficient implementations, interoperability, and evangelism. These final comments will round out the discussions begun in Chapter 1.

11.1   *pH* in Context

There are many, many approaches to parallel programming, with a rich terminology that can often be quite confusing. One often encounters three terms to describe parallelism: *parallel*, *concurrent*, and *distributed*.

11.1.1   Parallel, Concurrent, and Distributed Languages

Originally (in the 1950s and 1960s), parallelism was introduced into programming languages for two reasons. The first reason was for *speed*. This occurred primarily in the High Performance Technical Computing (HPTC) community. The initial goal was "vectorization"—to take an existing scientific or engineering code, usually written in Fortran, and automatically produce machine code to exploit the "vector units" of contemporary supercomputers. Later, the scope expanded to include loop parallelization for symmetric multiprocessors (SMPs) and then even to clusters of SMPs. Fortran, Fortran 90, HPF, OpenMP annotations, and so on are all examples of this class.

An important characteristic of this class is that programs are expected to be deterministic. Usually, a program has a sequential reading, and all parallelizations of that program are expected to produce the same results as the sequential version, only faster.

The term "parallel" is more often used to describe this class of languages. The principal reason for parallelism is speed.

The second reason parallelism was introduced into programming languages was *simplified structure*. This occurred primarily in operating systems. Such programs consist of a collection of relatively independent tasks (scheduler, disk manager, terminal controller, network manager, etc.), and they are often "reactive" in nature—a task runs in response to some external event, such as disk activity or a network packet arrival.

These programs are more naturally structured as parallel programs, consisting of a number of processes or threads, each of which reacts to an event by doing some computation, communicating with other threads, or modifying some shared data structure, and then going to sleep waiting for the next relevant event.

More recently (since the late 1980s), even individual application programs have begun to take on this reactive structure: for example, a program that displays a directory structure (as in Windows Explorer) must monitor for mouse actions, keyboard input, as well as notifications from the file server (because some other user may be modifying the currently visible directory and the display needs to be updated to reflect those changes). An email client or shared calendar program must monitor for user input, for arrival of new messages, and for modifications to the shared view by other concurrent clients.

An important characteristic of this class is that programs are expected to be nondeterministic—program behavior depends on the relative timing of events to which it reacts.

The term "concurrent" is more often used to describe this class of languages. The principal reason for parallelism is clean program structure, leading to more robust programs. These programs are usually regarded as a collection of sequential programs that communicate and/or share data.

The term "distributed" introduced yet another dimension of parallelism in the late 1970s and early 1980s, along with the development of local-area networks such as Ethernet. A distributed program has an explicit notion of "sites"—machines or hosts where different parts of the program are located and executed. Locality with respect to such sites is a first-order concern to the programmer because the cost of communication between sites is usually orders of magnitude larger than the cost of accessing local data. Thus, distributed programs are typically structured explicitly to take sites and locality into account.

An additional issue in distributed systems is that different sites may be under different administrative control, and this may also impose certain program structures. For example, a file server, or a Web server, is usually under the control of their system administrators, and client programs cannot interact with them in arbitrary ways. Remote procedure calls (RPCs) are the primary way to structure such interactions, and authentication and security become additional concerns.

The distinctions between parallel, concurrent, and distributed programming are not precise. For example, in the 1990s, as workstations began approaching supercomputer speeds and local-area networks improved in latency and bandwidth, many researchers investigated the use of networks of workstations to implement parallel HPTC codes. The goal was speed, and the implementation was distributed. Many High Performance Fortran (HPF) implementations have this flavor, as do languages such as Split-C, Cid, Olden, Linda, and so on.

11.1.2   Where Does *pH* Sit in This Space?

pH sits in the traditional space of "parallel" and "concurrent" languages. The original motivation for, and the principal focus of, *pH* research has certainly been parallelism for speed, just like traditional parallel programming languages. However, the implicit parallelism in *pH* also subsumes the concurrency in many concurrent programming languages, and *pH* may thus be quite suitable for writing concurrent, nondeterministic, reactive programs as well.

pH does not address issues of distribution. The closest that any *pH* research has come to addressing distribution is in implementations of *pH* for multicomputers and networks of workstations [58, 23], but this is still a relatively unexplored area. In applications with a client-server architecture, *pH* could of course be used to code either or both sides of the interaction, but it is no different from other languages in this regard. See [22] for examples of how this has been done with Haskell.

There are two aspects of *pH* that remain fairly unique. First, *pH* has no explicit "processes" or "threads" to introduce parallelism; in principle, everything executes in parallel except as modulated by data and control dependencies (conditionals). Since *pH*'s model clearly subsumes a model with explicit threads, what are the advantages of explicit threads? The issues revolve around efficiency of implementation, which we will discuss in Section 11.2.1.

Second, *pH*'s fine-grain, implicit synchronization on data access, as seen in I-structures and M-structures, is quite unusual. The concept of monitors, introduced by Hoare in 1974 [30] and reproduced in several more recent languages including Java (synchronized classes), is an example of implicit data synchronization—synchronization is associated with a piece of data and happens automatically on procedure (method) entry and exit. However, the programmer still chooses which data should be protected in this manner, and the granularity is often very large. In *pH*, on the other hand the fine-grain implicit synchronization of I-structures and M-structures enables the effortless exploitation of producer-consumer parallelism in all its forms.

The only class of languages that are similar to *pH* in its implicit parallelism is the class of parallel logic programming languages [69] and their more recent descendants, concurrent constraint languages [62]. These languages are *relational* in nature, unlike *pH*'s more familiar functional basis. Many of these languages also have parallelism without explicit processes and threads, and they also have implicit, fine-grained data synchronization with logic variables (similar to I-structures). Like *pH*, these languages are also still research languages.

Finally, we reemphasize that there are many issues in programming languages that are orthogonal to implicit parallelism, which *pH* does not address. We have already mentioned issues connected with distributed systems—sites, authentication, security, and so on. The advent of the World Wide Web has surfaced new research issues such as "mobile" programs ("bots") and security and information flow.

11.2   What Remains for *pH* to Become a Production Language?

pH is based on over a decade of research in language design for implicit parallelism. During this period, the "look and feel" of the language has evolved significantly as we have increased our understanding of the expressivity issues surrounding topics such as functional arrays, I-structures, M-structures, and sequencing. The most recent visual change was the adoption of Haskell notation for the functional core, which forms the major part of the language. This change was made both to broaden the appeal of the language to those already familiar with the standard functional language Haskell and to enable leveraging of existing Haskell compiler infrastructures. The Haskell programmer should find it very easy to program in *pH*. There are a few traditional Haskell idioms that cannot be used in *pH*, but in practice we have found these differences to be very minor. (An example is the practice in Haskell to generate an "infinite" data structure and examine only a finite part of it. This works in a lazy evaluator for a pure functional language but, as described in Chapter 4, results in an infinite computation in *pH*.)

Throughout this period, we have had several research implementations of *pH* and Id, its predecessor. The current *pH* implementation is about the third or fourth complete rewrite of the compiler. Earlier implementations were focused on special hardware architectures known as *dataflow* machines [11], whereas the more recent implementations have focused on stock hardware—first uniprocessors and now SMPs.

Nevertheless, there is always a substantial gap between a research language implementation and a production implementation. There are several bridges to cross before *pH* can become a widely used production language:

- ◆ Efficient implementations. This is mostly a technical question. Most of the issues concerning efficient implementation of *pH* are shared with many other high-level programming languages, including Java, and well-known techniques can be applied. A few issues are fairly unique to *pH* and a few other languages, mostly arising out of the non-strictness of *pH*.
- ◆ Interoperability with other languages and systems. This is partly a technical issue, but it is also a social process because it involves standards, interaction models, and the involvement of many constituencies of programmers.
- ◆ And last, but not least, is evangelism and market forces. The history of programming languages is replete with examples of languages that did not succeed on technical merits alone.

The rest of this section discusses these issues in some more detail, rounding out our initial discussion in Chapter 1.

Efficient Implementation of *pH*

Ultimately, all applications programmers are concerned with efficiency. This has two major dimensions. First, there is programmer productivity—the speed at which we humans can create, debug, maintain, and evolve our programs. And, second, there is the space and time cost of program execution—how fast it runs and how much memory it takes. The history of programming languages, the trend towards higher-level languages, has precisely been the effort to improve programmer productivity without major sacrifices in program execution efficiency.

As computer systems have become faster and compilers have improved, program efficiency has decreased as a first-order concern. Today, many applications are written in "scripting" languages like Perl or Tcl/Tk and in high-level languages like Java. These programs perhaps would run much faster if written in C or Fortran, and probably even faster if written in assembler (with huge effort), but the premium on programmer productivity is gradually beginning to dominate the equation. In addition, scripting languages and high-level languages make programming accessible to a much larger community. For example, there are many Web site designers who know scripting languages but no other traditional language.

pH continues this trend of aiming towards higher and higher levels of programming. Nevertheless, there will always be applications where program execution efficiency is paramount, where the programmer would like to extract the absolute maximum performance that a machine is capable of delivering. At this "bleeding edge" of performance, very precise control of resources is necessary. C and Fortran, and even assembler, are typically the languages of choice in this regime because their computational model is quite close to the raw machine model, and hence the programmer is able to control resources quite precisely. (But even in this milieu, the recent architectural complexities of out-of-order execution, cache hierarchies, and nonuniform memory access make the resource/performance model quite complex even for the expert programmer.)

The higher the level of the language, the more difficult it is for the programmer to have a mental model of resource usage, and the more difficult it is to compile it to efficient code. This trend began in the 1960s with Lisp, and continues today with Java. Haskell makes resource management even more complex, and *pH*, with its implicit parallelism, makes it even more so (although *pH* does better than Haskell in that it specifies sharing precisely and permits shared updatable storage). The following features make it more and more difficult to implement a language efficiently:

- ◆ Automatic storage management
- ◆ Efficient implementation of polymorphism and overloading
- ◆ Implicit parallelism (no explicit threads)
- ◆ Nonstrictness and fine-grain implicit data synchronization

The first issue is shared with many other programming languages including Lisp, Scheme, Haskell, ML, and Java. The latter two issues are shared with a few other programming languages such as Haskell and concurrent constraint languages.

Automatic Storage Management

In modern high-level languages, data is typically allocated in an area of memory called the *heap*. As the program executes, more and more of the heap is used up. Eventually, when the heap is full, the run-time system engages in an activity called *garbage collection* (GC). GC identifies which data are still accessible to the program and which data are not, and then recycles the memory occupied by inaccessible data to be available once again for allocation as the program resumes execution. The run-time system typically needs to maintain some extra bookkeeping information with data so that it can identify objects in the heap and determine whether they are accessible by the program or not. This bookkeeping activity, known as "tagging," together with the reclamation process itself, constitutes an overhead for such languages.

A second way in which automatic storage management can slow the program down is in its interaction with the memory hierarchy. In modern computers, because of multiple levels of caches and virtual memory, achieving maximum speed of execution is crucially dependent on "locality of reference" (i.e., the program must try to maintain as small an active memory "footprint" as possible). Allocating data on a heap is usually antithetical to this objective, and the GC activity itself explores large memory areas without any locality structure.

The problem of efficient implementation of automatic storage management is not unique to *pH;* it also exists in Java, scripting languages, Lisp, ML, Haskell, and other functional and logic programming languages. There is a vast body of literature describing solutions to these problems [34, 52, 39,

50, 13, 70, 71, 74]. Dynamic techniques include clever representations of heap objects that reduce or eliminate tagging overhead; techniques to pack heap objects to reduce their memory footprint; "generational" garbage collectors that focus on short-lifetime data, thereby reducing the number of times that all of memory needs to be scanned for potential garbage; and so on. Static techniques include *escape analysis*, which attempts to identify data whose lifetime coincides with the call and return of some procedure. That data can then be allocated within the procedure's stack frame instead of on the heap, and thus the run-time system pays no extra overhead for allocation and deallocation. *Lifetime analysis* is more general than escape analysis in attempting to identify exactly when data is allocated and consumed. It can result in optimizations that pass arguments and results in registers instead of the heap; that avoid building tuples for multiple arguments and multiple results; and that aggregate heap allocation of multiple objects into a single allocation. *Linear types* allow the programmer to ensure that a particular data structure is passed from operation to operation in a single-threaded fashion (i.e., that it is never shared). This allows the compiler to implement functional updates to the data structure, which conceptually copies the data structure, with imperative in-place updates that do no copying.

Polymorphism and Overloading

The efficiency issues due to polymorphism and overloading are similar. Polymorphism often forces a uniform representation of data. A polymorphic procedure on arrays should work on arrays of booleans as well as on arrays of floats, and this naturally leads to representations where a float and a boolean occupy the same storage space, resulting in wastage in the latter case.

For an overloaded procedure that works on arrays of booleans and on arrays of floats, the overloading is typically accomplished by passing in a table of methods—a table of float methods if the array contains floats and a table of boolean methods if the array contains booleans. The overloaded procedure then invokes the appropriate method from the table. Unfortunately, this can add the overhead of a procedure call for something as simple as an addition operation, which would normally be a single machine instruction in the nonoverloaded case.

Type analysis is a compiler technique that attempts to detect more precisely the types of certain program fragments to eliminate polymorphism

and overloading. In the best case, identification of precise types can eliminate uniform representations in favor of natural machine representations
(this is often called "unboxing" [52, 39]).

Finally, we should note that many of the optimizations described above
make it harder to implement a good debugger for the language. For example, consider a debugger in which we wish to examine the data passed into
a polymorphic list-sorting function. In order to display the objects in the
input list, the debugger will need a way to reconstruct the type of those
objects. However, since the function is polymorphic, the debugger needs to
examine the caller of the function, and perhaps its caller, and so on, in order
to find out the actual type of the input list. This task is made more difficult
if optimizations have stripped away tags and other type-identifying information. This problem has been well-studied and solutions are described in
[25] and [2].

Implementing Implicit Parallelism

In Section 1.5, we described the explicit **fork** statement of some parallel
languages (such as C with P-Threads, or Java). The **fork** statement allows a
programmer to specify the creation of a new, parallel thread of control.

The fundamental problem with explicit forks is that it can be very difficult for the programmer to choose the placement of **fork** calls. Standard
implementations of **fork** have a high overhead (it is often hundreds or
thousands of times more expensive than a procedure call). Further, the cost
of multiplexing the computer's processors among threads is typically very
high. Thus, it is necessary to find just the right balance—too many threads
will result in too much forking and thread-switching overhead, whereas too
few threads will leave processors idle. Having too few threads can also introduce *deadlock*. For example, suppose in a call **fork** f(), the parent thread is
supposed to produce data for the child thread. Omitting the **fork** (thereby
converting f() into an ordinary procedure call) will deadlock the program:
the procedure f() will wait for its data, but since it has not returned, the
"parent" cannot produce it.

This problem, of choosing where to fork, is faced by programmers of
explicitly parallel languages and by compilers of implicitly parallel languages like *pH*. In principle, a *pH* program can be compiled into a sequential programming language with explicit **fork**s liberally sprinkled at
every point where there is potential parallelism according to *pH* semantics.
Unfortunately, the right number of threads is generally not syntactically
obvious—it depends on the program structure and the run-time synchro-

nization and data dependencies. Further, it can depend on program inputs; that is, there may be no single "correct" identification of fork points in the program.

A first and simple step towards solving this problem is to treat **fork**s as hints rather than imperatives. When encountering a **fork** call, the run-time system actually forks a thread only if there are idle processors available; otherwise, it simply calls the specified function using a normal function call. Thus, the programmer or the compiler can freely introduce **fork**s that may *potentially* specify hundreds or thousands of threads, confident that the run-time system will in fact create just enough threads to keep the processors of the computer busy. The language Cid is an example of a parallel language that explored this technique [45]. Unfortunately, this solution is not a complete solution. Most importantly, it does not solve the deadlock problem described above because once a **fork** is treated as a procedure call, there is no going back. Another problem, less serious, is that the decision whether or not to fork is taken at the time when the **fork** is encountered, based on the number of idle processors at that time. If the situation changes later, there is no way to revisit the decision (e.g., the system decides not to fork because all processors are busy, but processors become free shortly after the decision is taken).

A more sophisticated approach is called *lazy task creation* (or LTC). It was originally pioneered in the language Multilisp [28] with an efficient implementation by Marc Feeley [20] but has been further developed in Lazy Threads [26], StackThreads [66], and in the language Cilk from MIT [15]. Under LTC a **fork** statement is *always* treated as an ordinary function call, but the run-time system performs just a little additional bookkeeping, leaving a small record with enough information to revoke this decision if necessary. If a processor becomes idle, it is able to examine the run-time data structures, and if it finds such a record, it can retroactively convert the procedure call into a fork point, and execute the pending work. The processor that created the record may not be the same as the processor that exploits such a record; in this case, the second processor is said to "steal" the parent from the first. The key to making this work well is to minimize the overhead of the initial bookkeeping, even if it makes stealing expensive. The rationale is that, while there may be thousands or millions of potential fork points encountered during execution (it depends on the program structure and the data), the actual number of thread creation events (stealing) will be much lower, sometimes as low as the number of processors, which is typically a much smaller number.

Implementing Nonstrictness and Fine-Grain Data Synchronization

The final complication in implementing *pH* efficiently is in the cost of nonstrictness and implicit data synchronization (I-structures and M-structures). In these features, a thread of the program attempts to read a value, but it may have to wait because the value may not be available yet ("empty" in the case of I- and M-structures). That thread can spin and wait, or it can suspend itself, which means enqueuing some state related to the thread on the empty slot. Later, when some other thread writes data into the empty slot, it must reenable one or more of the threads waiting on that slot. This is a central activity in any *pH* implementation and is called thread switching or context switching.

Because of implicit parallelism, nonstrictness, and fine-grain data synchronization in *pH*, this activity is extremely frequent and is necessary even in a uniprocessor implementation. Consequently, it has to be extremely efficient, barely more expensive than a procedure call. Contrast this with conventional thread switching in POSIX threads (pthreads) [33], or modern operating systems, where the cost is typically two or more orders of magnitude higher than the cost of a procedure call. Implementations of *pH* must thus pay great attention to optimizing this operation, and the code sequences to accomplish this must usually be carefully hand-crafted. These implementation issues are considered in great detail in [51, 44, 58, 9].

A final point to note is that this particular efficiency issue is shared by all implementations of Haskell and other lazy functional languages, even though they may be sequential implementations. The requirement arises from non-strictness and fine-grain data synchronization, which are orthogonal to parallelism.

11.2.2   Interoperability and Application Domains

This book focuses on fundamentals of implicit parallelism, and as such, the programming examples and exercises illustrate classical algorithmic problems. Today, the world of programming is much more diverse, encompassing varied domains such as Web-based client-server programming, user interfaces, graphics, distributed computing, and so on. It is almost impossible for a single programming language to encompass such a rich diversity of application domains; instead, over the last few years we have seen the development and growth of several mechanisms for *interoperability*. For example a Web browser may be written in one language, but it may interact with a "plug-in" that is written in another language. Or, a spreadsheet may be written in one language while it accesses data from a database management system (possibly on a remote server) that is written in another language.

Ultimately, the success of a programming language depends not only on its core technical advantages, but also on the facilities it provides for interoperability with the vast existing base of software (screen, keyboard, and mouse control; file system access; database access; network access; and so on).

Many interoperability mechanisms are quite ad hoc (such as calls to compiled code from many "scripting" languages), but some have been designed with more principles and care. Two such standards are CORBA from the Object Management Group and COM from Microsoft Corporation. In these standards, the programmer specifies the interaction between two "components," possibly implemented with different programming languages, using a common, language-neutral specification language called an Interface Definition Language (IDL). For each component implementation language of interest, an "IDL Compiler" compiles this specification into stubs for each side of the interaction. These stubs can then be linked in with the actual code of the participant in the interaction.

Researchers in the Haskell community have done much research into interfacing Haskell to COM and CORBA [21, 22]. These Haskell solutions should carry over directly to *pH*. In fact, it is an open question whether *pH*'s implicit parallelism will improve the structure of interoperating programs because many of them are reactive in nature, which fits naturally into *pH*'s concurrent, data-driven behavior.

11.3 The Final Word

pH represents a radically different way of thinking about parallel programming. We believe that it is increasingly in tune with developments in computer hardware, where symmetric multiprocessors are becoming the norm due to the continually decreasing prices of semiconductor components. This vision is not a foolish dream. It is deployable now, with the right level of engineering effort. We hope that the vision presented in this book will excite researchers, students, and software engineers to form a critical mass that can make this vision a reality.

An Introduction to the λ-Calculus

Anything you can do, I can do β.

—*MIT T-shirt, circa 1985*

The pure mathematical notion of a function is simply a set of ordered pairs (d, r) where the first elements d are unique; that is, for any two members of the set (d_1, r_1) and (d_2, r_2), $d_1 \neq d_2$. Intuitively, each "argument" d is associated with a corresponding "result" r. We also says that the function "maps" d to r or "returns" r for argument d. The uniqueness constraint just implies that each distinct argument is uniquely mapped to a particular result. Because of this set-based view, we can talk about *the* "incrementing" function; it is simply the set with all pairs (x, y) where x and y are numbers and $x + 1 = y$. The sets can be infinite, as is indeed the case for the incrementing function.

With computers, however, we are generally more interested in *how* a function is computed—a process, or a method, or an algorithm for producing a result when given an argument. Many notations exist for this purpose.

The λ-calculus is one such notation, as are Turing machines and partial recursive functions. In particular, these notations are "universal" notations in that each notation is capable of expressing *all* computable functions. (There are indeed such things as "uncomputable" functions—functions for which we can define the set of argument-result pairs, but for which we cannot define any process to compute them.)

The λ-calculus was developed by Alonzo Church in the 1930s as a notation and calculus to express all computable functions [16, 17], well before the advent of digital computers and programming languages. Nevertheless, it has served as a central tool for the study of programming languages and their semantics (see, for example, [65, 37, 38, 59, 60, 61, 64]). The λ-calculus is itself a language. It can seem quite far removed from, say, Fortran or C or Java. Nevertheless, it is invaluable in understanding the fundamental computational mechanisms in these languages. Concepts as diverse as procedure calls, gotos, loops, exceptions, inheritance, and so on can all be expressed in terms of the basic functional mechanisms of the λ-calculus. The λ-calculus, in turn, has inspired the design of functional programming languages and is indeed the philosophical underpinning behind Lisp, Scheme, ML, and Haskell. The "semantic gap" between the λ-calculus and these languages is generally much smaller than the gap to more traditional imperative languages such as C and Fortran. Indeed, for pure functional languages such as Haskell, such languages can be seen as a thin veneer of syntactic sugar on top of the λ-calculus itself.

Recognizing the proximity of Haskell and *pH* to the λ-calculus, and the general importance of the λ-calculus in the study of programming languages, this appendix provides a brief overview of the λ-calculus and its expressive power. The book by Barendregt [12] is considered the definitive reference on the λ-calculus.

A.1   λ-Notation

The notions of *value* and *binding* are often not separated in many programming languages. For example, in C, one may write

```
int increment (int x)
{
    return x + 1;
}
```

There are actually two things going on here—the definition of an integer-incrementing procedure, as well as the binding of that procedure to the name `increment`. In the λ-calculus, these two activities are explicitly separated. Indeed, this is one reason why the λ-calculus is so useful in studying programming languages, because it helps separate out fundamentally orthogonal concepts such as value computation and name binding that may happen to be tightly intertwined in a particular language construct.

In order to do this it is necessary to think of a function or procedure as a *value* in its own right. What name we bind the function to is an entirely separate matter. Thus, the integer-incrementing function would be written with λ-notation as

$$\lambda x . x + 1$$

which can be read as "the function that, for any x, returns $x + 1$." (Of course, this begs the questions of what are "+" and "1", but we postpone that for now.)

Just as we can think of numbers as abstract values (for example, "four", "4", and "IV" are all notations for one such value), similarly we can think of functions—sets of ordered (argument, result) pairs—themselves as values. And, just as a function can take a value such as the one represented by "4" as an argument, or can return such a value as a result, similarly it makes perfect sense for one function to take another function as an argument or to return another function as a result. For example, consider a function that, given a function f as argument, returns a new function that, given an argument x, applies f to x and then applies f again to the result. We write it as follows, corresponding almost directly to the English description in the previous sentence:

$$\lambda f . (\lambda x . f (f (x)))$$

Another example: consider the difference between the following:

$$2$$

$$\lambda x . 2$$

The former represents the number two. We would consider it silly (more precisely, a type error) to apply it to the number five. On the other hand, the latter is a function that, when applied to any argument, returns the number two. It makes perfect sense to apply it to the number five—the result of the application is the number two. We can think of it as "the function-that-always-returns-two."

The action of sticking a "λx." in front of an expression and thereby converting it into a function is called λ-*abstraction*, or just *abstraction* for short. The expression $(x + 1)$ represents a value that is greater by 1 than some unknown x. The meaning of the expression (its value) crucially depends on what x is. However, the expression λx.$(x + 1)$ represents the increment-by-one function. It has "universalized" the name x—for *any* x, it returns its increment. In particular, the expression λy.$(y + 1)$ represents exactly the same function, as does λz.$(z + 1)$. The particular choice of name does not affect the meaning of the expression.

A.1.1   Syntax of the Pure λ-Calculus

The syntax of the pure λ-calculus is amazingly simple:

$$
\begin{array}{lll}
E & ::= \quad x & \text{Variables} \\
  & | \quad λx.E & \text{Abstraction} \\
  & | \quad E\ E & \text{Application}
\end{array}
$$

In an abstraction λx.E, we call x the *bound variable*, the *formal parameter*, or *argument*, and we call E the *body* or the result. In an application $(E_1\ E_2)$, we call E_1 the function and E_2 the *actual parameter* or the *argument*.

We can use parentheses freely to resolve any ambiguities in the notation, for example to distinguish

$$(λx.E_1)\ E_2 \qquad \text{from} \qquad λx.(E_1\ E_2)$$

and

$$E_1\ (E_2\ E_3) \qquad \text{from} \qquad (E_1\ E_2)\ E_3$$

However, to reduce the number of parentheses, we treat the "dot" in abstractions as extending as far to the right as possible:

$$λx.E_1\ E_2 \qquad \text{is equivalent to} \qquad λx.(E_1\ E_2)$$

and we treat application as left-associative:

$$E_1\ E_2\ E_3\ E_4 \quad \text{is equivalent to} \qquad ((E_1\ E_2)\ E_3)\ E_4$$

A.1.2   Free and Bound Variables

Central to the λ-calculus is the notion of *substituting* various occurrences of a variable by an expression. But before we describe that (in the next section), we need the defintions of *free* and *bound* variables, which allow us to specify which variables need to be substituted.

The set of free variables FV(E) of an expression E is defined recursively as follows:

$$
\begin{aligned}
\text{FV}(x) &= x \\
\text{FV}(E_1\ E_2) &= \text{FV}(E_1) \cup \text{FV}(E_2) \\
\text{FV}(\lambda x.E) &= \text{FV}(E) - \{x\}
\end{aligned}
$$

All other variables of E are said to be *bound variables* in E. Intuitively, a variable x is free if it is not "captured" by a surrounding "λx". A λ-expression that has no free variables is also called a *closed* expression or a *combinator*. For example, "$\lambda f.(\lambda x.f(f(x)))$" is a combinator.

Note that a variable can have both free and bound occurrences in an expression. For example, in this expression:

$$x(\lambda x.x)$$

the first occurrence of x is free, whereas the occurrence of x after the dot is bound.

A.2   β-Substitution

β-substitution is the key operation in the λ-calculus. It is what enables "computation" to occur. β-substitution is described by a single rewrite rule that describes what happens when a λ-expression is *applied* to an argument expression:

$$(\lambda x.E)E_a \quad = \quad E[E_a/x]$$

That is, the result is the body of the λ-expression (E) where all its *free* occurrences of x have been substituted by the argument expression (E_a). The substitution operation "$E[E_a/x]$" is defined recursively by case on the structure of E. When E is

- the variable x:

$$x[E_a/x] \quad = \quad E_a$$

- a variable y other than x:

$$y[E_a/x] \quad = \quad y$$

- an application:

$$(E_1 E_2)[E_a/x] \quad = \quad (E_1[E_a/x])(E_2[E_a/x])$$

- an abstraction on variable x:

$$(\lambda x.E_1)[E_a/x] \quad = \quad \lambda x.E_1$$

- an abstraction on a variable y other than x:

$$(\lambda y.E_1)[E_a/x] \quad = \quad \lambda z.((E_1[z/y])[E_a/x])$$
$$\text{where } z \notin \text{FV}(E_1) \cup \text{FV}(E_a) \cup \{x\}$$

The rules for variables and applications are straightforward. The first rule for λ-expressions expresses the idea that in an expression $\lambda x.E_1$, there can be no free occurrences of x in E_1 (since it is captured by this outermost λ-binding), and hence we are done.

The second rule for λ-expressions is the most tricky. The particular problem it addresses is the possibility that E_a may contain some *free* occurrences of y. If we blindly substituted xs in E_1 by E_a, then these previously free ys will inadvertently get captured by the λy. By first renaming the bound ys to a fresh variable z, we avoid this problem.

Let us look at an example of β-substitution:

$$(\lambda p.p(p\ q))\ [(a\ p\ b)\ /\ q]$$
$$\longrightarrow \quad (\lambda z.z\ (z\ q))\ [(a\ p\ b)\ /\ q] \qquad \text{(substituting the bound } p \text{ by } z)$$
$$\longrightarrow \quad \lambda z.(z\ (z\ (a\ p\ b)))$$

Note that p is the bound variable in the term into which we are substituting, and it is also free in the term being substituted, $(a\ p\ b)$. If we had omitted the renaming in the second line and substituted q by $(a\ p\ b)$ blindly, the result would have been

$$\lambda p.(p\ (p\ (a\ p\ b)))$$

which is incorrect. In the correct result, there is one occurrence of p and it is free, whereas in the incorrect result, there are three occurrences of p and all of them are bound by the λ-abstraction.

A.3   The λ-Calculus as a Reduction System

Computation using the λ-calculus can be formalized into a reduction system. The syntax is specified in Section A.1.1. The reduction rules are

◆ The α rule:

$$\lambda x.E \quad\longrightarrow\quad \lambda y.(E[y/x]) \qquad \text{if } y \notin \text{FV}(E)$$

◆ The β rule:

$$(\lambda x.E)E_a \quad\longrightarrow\quad E[E_a/x]$$

◆ The η rule:

$$(\lambda x.E \ \ x) \quad\longrightarrow\quad E \qquad \text{if } x \notin \text{FV}(E)$$

The α rule allows us to avoid inadvertent free-variable capture, express-ing the idea that the bound variable in a λ-abstraction can be changed with-out changing the meaning of the expression. Since it doesn't fundamentally "advance" the computation, some authors do not elevate this to the status of a full-blown rewrite rule. The β rule is the central computation rule, and the form $((\lambda x.E) \ E_a)$ on its left-hand side is traditionally called a *redex*, a convenient contraction of the phrase "reducible expression." The η rule is mainly a convenience.

Exercise A.1 Reduce the following expression:

$$\lambda z.((\lambda x.\lambda z.z \ \ (x \ \ z)) \ \ (\lambda f.z \ \ f)) \ \ (\lambda x.x) \qquad\qquad \blacksquare$$

Exercise A.2 Given the following terms:

$$
\begin{aligned}
C &\equiv \lambda x.\lambda y.\lambda f.f \ \ x \ \ y \\
H &\equiv \lambda f.f \,(\lambda x.\lambda y.x) \\
T &\equiv \lambda f.f \,(\lambda x.\lambda y.y)
\end{aligned}
$$

show that the terms on the left-hand side below reduce to the correspond-ing right-hand sides:

$$
\begin{aligned}
H \ \ (C \ \ a \ \ b) &\longrightarrow\!\!\!\!\!\longrightarrow \quad a \\
T \ \ (C \ \ a \ \ b) &\longrightarrow\!\!\!\!\!\longrightarrow \quad b
\end{aligned}
\qquad\qquad \blacksquare
$$

A.4 The Expressive Power of the λ-Calculus

In the exercise at the end of the last section, suppose we had used the names "head", "tail", and "Cons" instead of H, T, and C, respectively. Consider the reductions demonstrated in the exercise:

$$
\begin{aligned}
\text{head} \ (\text{Cons} \ a \ b) &\longrightarrow\!\!\!\!\!\longrightarrow \quad a \\
\text{tail} \ (\text{Cons} \ a \ b) &\longrightarrow\!\!\!\!\!\longrightarrow \quad b
\end{aligned}
$$

But this is exactly the behavior of lists described in Chapter 6! There is something remarkable going on here. The λ-calculus has the ability to simulate our basic list operations. Can it do more? Can the λ-calculus simulate the function `foldr`, which we saw in Chapter 6 was one of the most powerful and useful functions on lists? Indeed it can! In order to define `foldr` within the λ-calculus, we need to show how it can simulate empty lists, the test for empty lists versus conses, conditionals, and recursion.

A.4.1   Booleans and Conditionals

Here are some λ-encodings for the boolean constants `True` and `False`:

`True`	$\equiv$	$\lambda x.\lambda y.x$
`False`	$\equiv$	$\lambda x.\lambda y.y$

Here is a λ-encoding for a conditional. It takes three arguments. Depending on whether the first argument, a boolean, is `True` or `False`, it returns either the second or the third argument, respectively:

`cond`	$\equiv$	$\lambda b.\lambda x.\lambda y.b \; x \; y$

Let us verify its behavior:

$$
\begin{aligned}
& \texttt{cond True}\ E_1\ E_2 \\
\longrightarrow\ & (\lambda b.\lambda x.\lambda y.b\ x\ y)\ \texttt{True}\ E_1\ E_2 \\
\longrightarrow\ & \texttt{True}\ E_1\ E_2 \\
\longrightarrow\ & (\lambda x.\lambda y.x)\ E_1\ E_2 \\
\longrightarrow\ & E_1
\end{aligned}
$$

Similarly, we can verify that (`cond False` $E_1\ E_2$) reduces to E_2.

Exercise A.3   Write λ-terms corresponding to the boolean "and", "nor", and "not" functions.   ■

A.4.2   The Empty List and Testing for It

Here is an encoding for the empty list and for the test for an empty list versus a nonempty list (a cons):

`Nil`	$\equiv$	$\lambda f.\lambda g.\texttt{True}$
`null`	$\equiv$	$\lambda l.((l\ \lambda a.\lambda b.\lambda c.c)\ \texttt{False})$

Let us verify their behavior again. The application (`null Nil`) should reduce to `True`:

```
     null Nil
⟶  (λl.((l  λa.λb.λc.c) False)) Nil
⟶  (Nil λa.λb.λc.c) False
⟶  ((λf.λg.True) λa.λb.λc.c) False
⟶  (λg.True) False
⟶  True
```

and, the application (null (Cons *X Y*)) should reduce to False:

```
     null (Cons  X  Y)
⟶  (λl.((l  λa.λb.λc.c) False))(Cons  X  Y)
⟶  ((Cons  X  Y)  λa.λb.λc.c) False
⟶  (((λx.λy.λf.f  x  y)  X  Y)  λa.λb.λc.c) False
⟶  ((λf.(f  X  Y))  λa.λb.λc.c) False
⟶  (λa.λb.λc.c)  X  Y  False
⟶  False
```

A.4.3   Recursion

Recursion is all about infinite unfoldings. Consider the map function from Chapter 6, which applies a function f to every member of a list and returns a list of the results. Here we repeat the definition, mixing it a bit with λ-notation:

```
map = λf.λx.if null xs then Nil else
            Cons (f (head xs))
                 (map f (tail xs))
```

If we expand the inner application of map using map's own definition, we get

```
map = λf.λx.if null xs then Nil else
            Cons (f (head xs))
                 (if null (tail xs) then Nil else
                  Cons (f (head (tail xs)))
                       (map f (tail (tail xs))))
```

We could expand the new inner application of map again, and so on, producing an infinite unfolding of map.

In the definition of map, the occurrence of map on the right-hand side is deeply embedded—it is inside an application that is inside a Cons that is inside a conditional. Let us "surface" it to the top level using λ-abstraction:

```
map = (λm.λf.λx.if null xs then Nil else
                 Cons (f (head xs))
                      (m f (tail xs)))
       map
```

That is, we have λ-abstracted map from the original right-hand side, using the formal parameter m, and immediately applied it to map. Let us give the name H to the main term in parentheses on the right-hand side:

```
H = (λm.λf.λx.if null xs then Nil else
               Cons (f (head xs))
                    (m f (tail xs)))
```

This term is a pure λ-term, with no recursion or anything unusual. The recursion is now limited to the following:

```
map = H map                    (†)
```

This general form—an equation, with a variable occurring in both the left-hand and right-hand sides—is familiar in mathematics. We say that map is a *solution* to this equation. In fact, we would say that such a solution is a *fixed point* or *fixpoint* of H because H "takes map back to itself." If we had a general tool (a function Y) that, given a function f, found the fixpoint of f, we could solve the above equation (i.e., write a nonrecursive expression for map) as follows:

```
map = Y H
```

The first question we should ask ourselves is, Does the whole concept even make sense? Some equations have no solution (e.g., the traditional algebra equation $x = x^2 + 10$ has no solution in the real plane). Some equations have multiple solutions (e.g., the traditional algebra equation $x = x^2$ has two solutions at $x = 0.0$ and $x = 1.0$). Can we expect the equation (†) to have a unique solution?

The second question we should ask ourselves is, Even if a unique solution exists, does such a general tool like Y exist that can find the solution?

It turns out that there is an affirmative answer to both questions. An equation like (†) does indeed have multiple solutions, but the solutions have a certain ordering where it makes sense to talk about the *unique* "least" solution. Further, there is indeed a certain Y which finds this unique least solution. The details of why this is so are beyond the scope of this book, and the interested reader is referred to [59, 60, 61, 64] for a detailed discussion.

A little thought reveals that Y needs to have the following property:

```
Y f = f (Y f)
```

Let us try this on our solution to map above:

```
map = Y  H
```

gives

```
map = H  (Y  H)
```

If we substitute the first H by its definition, we get

```
map = λf.λx.if null xs then Nil else
           Cons (f (head xs))
                ((Y  H) f (tail xs))
```

If we repeat the process for the inner $(Y\ H)$, we get

```
map = λf.λx.if null xs then Nil else
          Cons (f (head xs))
              (if null (tail xs) then Nil else
              Cons (f (head (tail xs)))
                   ((Y  H) f (tail (tail xs)))))
```

That is, we see that we are obtaining exactly the same infinite unfolding with which we began this section on recursion.

We are left with just one question: What is this mysterious Y function? Here is a definition for Y:

$$Y = \lambda f.(\lambda x.f\ (x\ x))\ (\lambda x.f\ (x\ x))$$

In the literature this is known as the Y combinator.

Exercise A.4   Verify that the Y, as defined above, indeed has the property

```
Y f = f (Y f)
```

Exercise A.5   Here is another definition for Y:

$$Y = (\lambda x.\lambda y.y\ (x\ x\ y))\ (\lambda x.\lambda y.y\ (x\ x\ y))$$

Verify that this definition also has the property

```
Y f = f (Y f)
```

In summary, recursion also can be modeled purely within the λ-calculus. Given a recursive function definition, with an arbitrary number of occurrences of the function name in the right-hand side:

```
f = (...f...f...)
```

we can first convert it into a fixpoint equation with a unique occurrence of f on the right-hand side:

```
f = G f                     where  G = λf'.(...f'...f'...)
```

and we can then write the "solution" to this equation without any recursion:

```
f = Y G
```

Exercise A.6 Here is the definition of `foldr` from Section 6.3.1:

```
foldr f z []     = z
foldr f z (x:xs) = f x (foldr f z xs)
```

Give a nonrecursive definition for `foldr` using Y. ∎

The definition of Y above contains instances of self-application—the term $(\lambda x.f(x\ x))$ is applied to itself, and there are two instances where the term x is applied to itself. If unrestrained, self-application can lead to strange paradoxes, analogous to Bertrand Russell's famous paradox arising out of statements like "In a certain village, the barber shaves every person who does not shave himself." Who shaves the barber? If he shaves himself, the statement implies that he is not shaved by the barber (i.e., himself). If he does not shave himself, the statement implies that he is shaved by the barber (i.e., himself).

Consider the function

$$u = \lambda y.\textbf{if } (y\ y) = a \textbf{ then } b \textbf{ else } a$$

Now consider the term $(u\ u)$ and its reduction:

$$(u\ u) \longrightarrow \textbf{if } (u\ u) = a \textbf{ then } b \textbf{ else } a$$

According to this, if $(u\ u) = a$, then the result is b, but this is supposed to be the value of the original expression, which is $(u\ u)$! Similarly, if $(u\ u) \neq a$, then the result is a, but this is supposed to be the value of the original expression, which is $(u\ u)$! We get a paradoxical contradiction.

The resolution of such paradoxes is again outside the scope of this book; suffice it to say that it kept eminent mathematicians such as Bertrand Russell occupied for quite some time. In outline, the resolution involves preventing self-applications such as the one in the definition of u. It is not enough simply to ban a syntactic form such as $(u\ u)$: the syntactic form may appear only after some steps of computation, and in any case the self-application may have a more complex syntactic form (as in *Y*).

Type systems were originally invented precisely to deal with this problem. The Hindley-Milner type system, which is used in *pH*, Haskell, and ML, does not admit self-application—the definition of *u* or *Y* would simply be rejected by the type checker as ill-typed.

How, then, do we deal with recursion in practice? Instead of using such heavy hammers as self-application and the *Y* combinator, we use much more restricted forms that are sufficient for our purposes. We introduce recursive **let**-blocks into the syntax of the language and design special type rules to deal with recursion in such blocks. We are able to define directly the semantics of recursion so defined without encountering any nasty paradoxes. As it happens, it is also possible to implement the recursion expressed in such direct constructs more efficiently than using the general mechanisms of the *Y* combinator.

A.4.4   Integers: Church's Representation

We have already seen how lists and list functions can be encoded in the λ-calculus: empty lists, conses, tests for empty lists, conditionals, and recursion. Similarly, we can also encode numbers and functions on numbers. The encoding of a number *n* is a function that takes two arguments *x* and *y* and applies *x* *n* times, beginning with *y*:

$$0 \equiv \lambda x.\lambda y.y$$
$$1 \equiv \lambda x.\lambda y.(x\ y)$$
$$2 \equiv \lambda x.\lambda y.(x(x\ y))$$
$$n \equiv \lambda x.\lambda y.(x(x(x \ldots (x\ y)\ldots)))$$

The "incrementing" (or "successor") function takes a number *n* as argument and returns a number, a "$\lambda x.\lambda y.\cdots$" term, that applies *x* to *y* one more time than *n* would:

$$\mathsf{succ} \equiv \lambda n.\lambda x.\lambda y.(x(n\ x\ y))$$

The "plus" or "addition" function, when applied to two numbers *x* and *y*, just has to apply the successor function *x* times to *y*:

$$\mathsf{plus} \equiv \lambda x.\lambda y.(x\ \mathsf{succ}\ y)$$

How do we test for zero? Here is a definition:

$$\mathsf{isZero} \equiv \lambda n.n\ (\lambda y.\mathsf{False})\ \mathsf{True}$$

It causes the number *n* to apply the function-that-always-returns-the-constant-False *n* times to the constant True. If applied zero times, it just returns True, but if applied even once, it returns the constant False.

In this manner it is possible to define arbitrary functions on numbers. More generally, the λ-calculus is capable of expressing *any* computable function whatsoever. In this sense, the λ-calculus is theoretically equivalent in expressive power to a Turing machine.

Exercise A.7 Write a λ-term corresponding to the multiplication function. ■

Exercise A.8 Write two λ-terms corresponding to the exponentiation function, one using the multiplication term from Exercise A.7 and one without using it. ■

Exercise A.9 Write a λ-term corresponding to the function isOne that tests whether a number is equal to 1 or not. (*Hint:* Consider a function that, when applied *n* times to the pair (Cons False True), produces results

(Cons False True)	when $n = 0$
(Cons True False)	when $n = 1$
(Cons False False)	when $n = 2$
(Cons False False)	when $n = 3$
(Cons False False)	when $n = 4$
⋮	

Notice that each term can be obtained from the previous one by "shifting in" the term False from the right. Also notice that the head of these terms is True only when $n = 1$.) ■

Exercise A.10 Write a λ-term corresponding to the "decrementing" (or "predecessor") function. Assume the argument is ≥ 1 (i.e., the result does not matter for a zero argument). (*Hint:* A trick similar to that in Exercise A.9 will work. Consider the sequence of terms:

(Cons *anything* 0)	when $n = 0$
(Cons 0 1)	when $n = 1$
(Cons 1 2)	when $n = 2$
(Cons 2 3)	when $n = 3$
(Cons 3 4)	when $n = 4$
⋮	

Notice that the head of the *n*th term is $n - 1$.) ■

Exercise A.11   Is it possible to write a term T for which "succ T" reduces to the term for 0 (so that T might therefore represent "negative one")? If so, give such a term; if not, explain why.   ■

A.5   The Church-Rosser Property and Interpreters for the λ-Calculus

When implementing the λ-calculus (i.e., when implementing a representation for λ-terms and code to execute the rewrite rules), the code will often have a choice of multiple redexes on which it can operate. Which one should it choose? Does it matter which one it chooses?

The most serious way in which something could go wrong is if different choices of redexes led to different answers, for example, if one choice resulted in the answer 5 whereas another choice resulted in the answer 23. Fortunately, the λ-calculus has the *Church-Rosser* property, which states that if $E \longrightarrow E_1$ and $E \longrightarrow E_2$, then there exists an E_3 such that $E_1 \longrightarrow E_3$ and $E_2 \longrightarrow E_3$. In other words if, starting with E, different choices of redexes led us to two different terms E_1 and E_2, then there is always a way to bring them back together to a common term E_3. This property is also known as *confluence*. This property precludes the bad behavior described earlier; it is impossible for two different choices of redex to lead to the answers 5 and 23.

The second way in which things could go wrong is that one choice of redexes may result in a concrete answer, while another choice may result in looping forever without ever producing an answer. For example, consider the term

$(\lambda x.5) \ (Y \ f)$

If the interpreter concentrated on the outermost application, it would instantly produce the result 5. If, on the other hand, it concentrated on the application $(Y \ f)$, it could loop forever, expanding it to $(f \ (Y \ f))$ and then to $(f \ (f \ (Y \ f)))$ and so on, never producing a answer.

To consider this question carefully, we need to be precise about three things:

- ◆ The definition of an *answer*
- ◆ The *reduction strategy* (i.e., a method for choosing which redexes in an expression to reduce)
- ◆ A criterion for *terminating* the reduction process

There are several interesting term structures that we may consider to be *answers:*

- *Normal Form* (NF): An expression containing no redexes at all.
- *Head Normal Form* (HNF): This is defined as follows:

    x is in HNF
    $(\lambda x.E)$ is in HNF if E is in HNF
    $(x \; E_1 \cdots E_n)$ is in HNF

- *Weak Head Normal Form (WHNF):* This is defined as follows:

    x is in WHNF
    $(\lambda x.E)$ is in WHNF   (Note: E does not have to be in WHNF.)
    $(x \; E_1 \cdots E_n)$ is in WHNF

NF is the tightest form. HNF is weaker (it can contain redexes, according to the last clause in its definition), but is semantically the most interesting because it represents the fundamental "information content" of the term. WHNF is the weakest—only the leftmost term is not a redex, but it is in practice the most interesting because it represents the maximum useful information we can print in an answer. Most actual implementations use WHNF for answers.

Two well-known reduction strategies are

- *Normal Order:* Always choose the leftmost outermost redex.
- *Applicative Order:* Always choose the leftmost innermost redex.

When used on the term described earlier, $((\lambda x.5) \; (Y \; f))$, a normal order interpreter would reduce the outermost redex and immediately produce the answer 5, whereas an applicative order interpreter would loop forever, trying to reduce $(Y \; f)$. In fact, the normal order strategy is an example of a *normalizing strategy*—any strategy that terminates and produces an answer whenever the expression indeed has an answer (these are also known as *standard reduction strategies*).

Here is a so-called *Call By Name* interpreter that generally follows the normal order strategy but does not look inside λ-abstractions.

Answers: WHNF
Strategy: leftmost redex, but not inside a λ-abstraction

$$
\begin{array}{lcl}
\mathrm{cn}[\![x]\!] & = & x \\
\mathrm{cn}[\![\lambda x.E]\!] & = & \lambda x.E \\
\mathrm{cn}[\![(E_1 \; E_2)]\!] & = & \textbf{let} \; f = \mathrm{cn}[\![E_1]\!]
\end{array}
$$

                                in
                          case f of
                          $\lambda x.E_3$ -> $cn[\![E_3[E_2/x]]\!]$
                            _   -> $(f\ E_2)$

Note that for applications, it first reduces only the function part (the result must be in WHNF). If it is a λ-expression, we have a redex, and it performs the reduction; otherwise the application is now in WHNF and this is just returned. This strategy can cause expressions to be replicated (in an application, E_2 is substituted for each of possibly many occurrences of x).

In contrast, here is a so-called *Call By Value* interpreter that generally follows the applicative order strategy, but does not look inside λ-abstractions.

Answers: WHNF
Strategy: leftmost innermost redex, but not inside a λ-abstraction

$cv[\![x]\!]$ = x
$cv[\![\lambda x.E)]\!]$ = $\lambda x.E$
$cv[\![(E_1\ E_2)]\!]$ =   **let** $f =\ cv[\![E_1]\!]$
                             $a =\ cv[\![E_2]\!]$
                      in
                          case f **of**
                          $\lambda x.E_3$ -> $cv[\![E_3[a/x]]\!]$
                                 -> $(f\ a)$

Note that for applications, it first reduces both the function part and the argument part (the results must be in WHNF). Then it examines the function part, and if it is a λ-expression, we have a redex, and it performs the reduction; otherwise the application is now in WHNF and this is just returned. In particular, if the argument part of the application is a looping term like $(Y\ f)$, then the interpreter will loop forever trying to reduce it, even though the argument may never actually be used by the function. However, note that it mostly avoids the expression replication behavior of the Call By Name interpreter since, in applications, E_2 is first reduced to WHNF a before being substituted for possibly many occurrences of x. Of course, if the WHNF a has internal redexes, they will still be replicated.

For an application $(E_1\ E_2)$, the Call By Value interpreter does not specify any particular order in which to evaluate E_1 and E_2—they could even be done in parallel. However, many real languages (e.g., ML and Scheme) tighten this strategy: the function and the argument are evaluated one at a time, often in a specific order. In this case, the reduction strategy becomes completely sequential. Once the strategy is sequential, it then becomes easy to add side-effecting operations to the language meaningfully; the meaning of the "state" of updatable storage cells is unambiguous in a sequential interpreter. Indeed both ML and Scheme have side-effecting operations.

Exercise A.12   Show the reduction of the following term using the Call By Name interpreter:

$$(\lambda x.\lambda y.x \ (\lambda g.(g \ x)(g \ y)(g \ y))(\lambda x.x))(\lambda x.\lambda y.x \ y)(\lambda z.z)$$

If it does not terminate, indicate this.   ■

Exercise A.13   The Call By Name interpreter generally follows the normal order strategy, except that it does not reduce inside λ-abstractions. Show the reduction of the following term using the Call By Name interpreter and using the normal order strategy:

$$(\lambda x.\lambda y.x)(\lambda z.(\lambda x.\lambda y.x) \ z \ ((\lambda x.x \ x)(\lambda x.x \ x)))$$

If it does not terminate, indicate this.   ■

Exercise A.14   Write an interpreter "lo$[\![E]\!]$" (for "leftmost outermost") implementing normal order reduction. Show its behavior it on the following term:

$$((\lambda x.x)(\lambda f.f \ (\lambda x.x) \ \Omega))(\lambda x.(\lambda y.x))$$

where Ω is any expression that will loop forever, such as the following: $(\lambda x.(x \ x))(\lambda x.(x \ x))$.   ■

Exercise A.15   The Call By Value interpreter generally follows the applicative order strategy, except that it does not reduce inside λ-abstractions. Show the reduction of the following term using the Call By Value interpreter and using the applicative order strategy:

$$(\lambda x.\lambda y.x)(\lambda z.(\lambda x.\lambda y.x) \ z \ ((\lambda x.z \ x)(\lambda x.z \ x)))$$

If it does not terminate, indicate this.   ■

Exercise A.16   Write an interpreter "li$[\![E]\!]$" (for "leftmost innermost") implementing applicative order reduction.   ■

A.6   From the λ-Calculus to Practical Programming Languages

The λ-calculus is a truly amazing system. With just three syntactic forms (variables, abstractions, and applications) and essentially one computation rule (β-reduction), it is capable of expressing every computable function. Its utter minimalism and clear separation of concerns (e.g., expressing function values versus binding of values to names) make it an excellent and essential tool in the study and comparison of programming languages and their semantics.

However, the λ-calculus is too austere a language to be a comfortable programming language for humans. We have already discussed some ways in which we inject semantic and practical concerns. First, we add special notations to express recursion (recursive **let**-blocks) and type systems that avoid the paradoxes arising out of self-application. These special notations also allow more efficient implementation of recursion. Next, instead of encoding everything in λ-terms, we directly add to the language constants such as booleans and numbers, data structures such as arrays and lists, and control structures like conditionals, and we add rewrite rules that directly express computation on such terms (such rewrite rules are known as δ rules).

In *pH* we go further. The β-reduction rule in the λ-calculus can cause the argument expression to be replicated. In particular, there is no concept in the λ-calculus of *sharing* of expressions. In *pH*, on the other hand, the β rule is carefully crafted to avoid duplication of expressions and to preserve sharing, without forcing early evaluation of arguments (the *pH* β rule is described in Chapter 4 and Appendix B).

In the λ-calculus there is no notion of *sequencing* (other than the fact that a redex cannot be reduced until it actually appears in the expression). A particular reduction strategy may introduce a certain order in which reductions are performed. In *pH* we introduced the notion of localized explicit sequencing (in Chapter 8). It is localized in the sense that each sequencing construct only describes sequencing of its components and has no sequencing relationship with other sequencing constructs elsewhere in the expression.

Finally, building on the fact that *pH*'s reduction system has sequencing and specifies sharing precisely, we are able to introduce side-effecting operations (I- and M-structures) in a meaningful, understandable, and controllable way in the presence of abundant implicit parallelism.

Collected Rewrite Rules for *pH*

We reserve the right to rewrite these terms at any time.

—*From a service agreement*

Rewrite rules for *pH* constitute a formal semantics for *pH*, specifying precisely the execution model and, in particular, parallelism and sharing. Rewrite rules for the basic functional subset of *pH* were introduced in Chapter 4. That chapter also covered general concepts about rewrite rules, determinacy, reduction strategies, parallelism, answers, and termination. In each subsequent chapter we augmented the rewrite rules to cover the constructs introduced therein, such as tuples, lists and algebraic types, arrays, sequencing, I-structures, and M-structures. The staged presentation also necessitated some incompleteness; for example, the renaming rules in Chapter 4 did not address expressions and statements introduced in subsequent chapters. In this appendix we present the complete set of rules for convenient reference.

B.1   Core Abstract Syntax

An arbitrary *pH* program containing convenient *pH* notations such as pattern matching, algebraic types, list and array comprehensions, arrays with bounds, and can be "desugared" into the core abstract syntax. The desugarings are described in each chapter along with each notation and are not repeated here, where we focus only on the core syntax.

Expressions:

E	$::=$	x	Identifiers
	$\mid$	$\backslash x\ \text{->}\ E$	λ-abstractions
	$\mid$	$E_1\ E_2$	Applications
	$\mid$	**let** S **in** E	**Let**-blocks
	$\mid$	**Cond**$(E_p,\ E_t,\ E_f)$	Conditionals
	$\mid$	$\text{PF}_k(E_1,\cdots,E_k)$	Application of primitive functions
	$\mid$	CN_0	Constants
	$\mid$	$\text{CN}_k(SE_1,\cdots,SE_k)$	Constructed terms, $k \geq 1$
	$\mid$	O_j	Heap object identifiers
	$\mid$	`allocate()`	Cell allocation

Statements:

S	$::=$	ϵ	Empty statements
	$\mid$	$x\ \text{=}\ E$	Bindings
	$\mid$	$S_1;\ S_2$	Parallel statements
	$\mid$	$S_1\ \text{>>>}\ S_2$	Sequential statements
	$\mid$	`alloc_trig`	Heap allocation trigger
	$\mid$	$\text{sStore}(E,\ E)$	Synchronized cell store
	$\mid$	$\text{empty}(\text{O}_j)$	Empty cells
	$\mid$	$\text{error}(\text{O}_j)$	Error cells
	$\mid$	$\text{full}(\text{O}_j,\ V)$	Full cells
	$\mid$	$\text{arraySStore}(E,E,E)$	Synchronized array store
	$\mid$	$\text{arrayEmpty}(\text{O}_j,\ V)$	Empty array elements
	$\mid$	$\text{arrayError}(\text{O}_j,\ V)$	Error array elements
	$\mid$	$\text{arrayFull}(\text{O}_j,\ V,\ V)$	Full array elements

Primitive functions of various arities, and constants:

PF_1	$::=$	`negate` $\mid$ `not` $\mid\ \cdots$	Primitive functions of arity 1
	$\mid$	$\text{proj}_1\ \mid\ \text{proj}_2\ \mid\ \cdots$	Algebraic type selectors (projection)
	$\mid$	`iFetch`	I-structure cell fetch
	$\mid$	`mFetch`	M-structure cell fetch
	$\mid$	`arrayAllocate`	Array allocation
PF_2	$::=$	`+` $\mid$ `-` $\mid\ \cdots$	Primitive functions of arity 2

|	`arrayIFetch`	I-structure array fetch
|	`arrayMFetch`	M-structure array fetch

$$CN_0 ::= \quad \textit{Integer} \mid \textit{Boolean} \mid \cdots$$

Symbols not in monospaced font represent syntactic classes. For example, E represents the class of expressions and S represents the class of statements. Symbols in monospaced fonts represent literal program text. The symbols "::=" and "|" are metasymbols (i.e., part of the grammar's notation), not *pH* notation.

Constructed terms $CN_k(\cdots)$ contain only simple expressions (SE), not arbitrary expressions. The last four heap statements contain only values (V).

The term `alloc_trig` was discussed in Section 8.5.2. It is not part of *pH* source programs, but is introduced in an outermost **let**-block during desugaring. The number of occurrences of `alloc_trig` in the program directly controls how many updatable cells or arrays can be allocated in parallel.

Parallel statement composition (";") has the following equivalence properties:

$$
\begin{aligned}
s_1 ;\ s_2 \quad &\equiv\quad s_2 ;\ s_1 \\
s_1 ;\ (s_2 ;\ s_3) \quad &\equiv\quad (s_1 ;\ s_2) ;\ s_3 \\
\epsilon ;\ s \quad &\equiv\quad s
\end{aligned}
$$

B.1.1   Values, Simple Expressions, and Heap Terms

These are expressions and statements that do not contain any exposed computation.

Values:

V	::=	CN_0	Constants
	|	$\backslash x \ \text{->}\ E$	λ-abstractions
	|	$CN_k(SE_1, \cdots, SE_k)$	Constructed terms
	|	0_j	Cell identifiers

Note that the body of a λ-abstraction can be an arbitrary expression.

Simple Expressions:

SE	::=	x	Identifiers
	|	V	Values

Heap terms:

$$
\begin{aligned}
H \quad ::= \quad & x = V \mid H;\ H & & \text{Value bindings} \\
\mid \quad & \texttt{alloc\_trig} & & \text{Heap allocation trigger} \\
\mid \quad & \texttt{empty}(O_j) & & \text{Empty cells} \\
\mid \quad & \texttt{error}(O_j) & & \text{Error cells} \\
\mid \quad & \texttt{full}(O_j,\ V) & & \text{Full cells} \\
\mid \quad & \texttt{arrayEmpty}(O_j,\ V) & & \text{Empty array elements} \\
\mid \quad & \texttt{arrayError}(O_j,\ V) & & \text{Error array elements} \\
\mid \quad & \texttt{arrayFull}(O_j,\ V,\ V) & & \text{Full array elements}
\end{aligned}
$$

B.2 α-Renaming

α-renaming is used to avoid free variable capture, particularly in the β and block flattening rewrite rules.

An *environment* is an ordered sequence of mappings of identifiers to new identifiers:

$$
(x_n \rightarrow t_n) : \cdots : (x_0 \rightarrow t_0) : \phi
$$

Each mapping $(x_j \rightarrow t_j)$ maps an existing bound variable x_j to an identifier t_j. The sequence is read from left to right, so that if there are two mappings $(y \rightarrow t_i)$ and $(y \rightarrow t_j)$ for the same variable y, the left one takes precedence. An environment is always extended from the left with new bindings. We use the symbol ρ for environments and start the process with ϕ, the empty environment.

The following function renames an identifier x according to a given environment ρ:

$$
\begin{aligned}
\text{RenId}[\![x]\!]\,\phi & = x \\
\text{RenId}[\![x]\!]\,((x \rightarrow x') : \rho_1) & = x' \\
\text{RenId}[\![x]\!]\,((y \rightarrow y') : \rho_1) & = \text{RenId}[\![x]\!]\,\rho_1 & & x \neq y
\end{aligned}
$$

The following function renames all bound variables in an arbitrary expression:

$$
\begin{aligned}
\text{Ren}[\![x]\!]\,\rho & = \text{RenId}[\![x]\!]\,\rho \\
\text{Ren}[\![\backslash x \text{->} e]\!]\,\rho & = \backslash t \text{->} (\text{Ren}[\![e]\!]\,\rho_1) \\
& \quad \text{where } \rho_1 = (x \rightarrow t) : \rho \\
& \quad \text{and } t \text{ is a fresh identifier that does} \\
& \quad \text{not otherwise occur in the program} \\
\text{Ren}[\![e_1\ e_2]\!]\,\rho & = (\text{Ren}[\![e_1]\!]\,\rho)\ (\text{Ren}[\![e_2]\!]\,\rho)
\end{aligned}
$$

$$\text{Ren}[\![\textbf{let } s \textbf{ in } e]\!]\,\rho \quad = \textbf{let } \text{Ren}_S[\![s]\!]\,\rho_1 \textbf{ in } \text{Ren}[\![e]\!]\,\rho_1$$
$$\text{where } \rho_1 = \text{ExtendEnv}_S[\![s]\!]\,\rho$$
$$\text{Ren}[\![\textbf{Cond}(e_p, e_t, e_f)]\!]\,\rho = \textbf{Cond}(\text{Ren}[\![e_p]\!]\,\rho,\ \text{Ren}[\![e_t]\!]\,\rho,\ \text{Ren}[\![e_f]\!]\,\rho)$$
$$\text{Ren}[\![\text{PF}_k(e_1, \cdots, e_k)]\!]\,\rho = \text{PF}_k(\text{Ren}[\![e_1]\!]\,\rho,\ \cdots,\ \text{Ren}[\![e_k]\!]\,\rho)$$
$$\text{Ren}[\![\text{CN}_0]\!]\,\rho = \text{CN}_0$$
$$\text{Ren}[\![\text{CN}_k(e_1, \cdots, e_k)]\!]\,\rho = \text{CN}_k(\text{Ren}[\![e_1]\!]\,\rho,\ \cdots,\ \text{Ren}[\![e_k]\!]\,\rho)$$
$$\text{Ren}[\![0_j]\!]\,\rho = 0_j$$
$$\text{Ren}[\![\texttt{allocate}()]\!]\,\rho = \texttt{allocate}()$$

The following function is used during renaming of **let**-blocks to extend an environment with bindings of all the bound variables of the block to new names:

$$\text{ExtendEnv}_S[\![\epsilon]\!]\,\rho = \rho$$
$$\text{ExtendEnv}_S[\![x = e]\!]\,\rho = (x \rightarrow t) : \rho$$
$$\text{ExtendEnv}_S[\![s_1;\ s_2]\!]\,\rho = \text{ExtendEnv}_S[\![s_1]\!]$$
$$(\text{ExtendEnv}_S[\![s_2]\!]\,\rho)$$
$$\text{ExtendEnv}_S[\![s_1 \text{ >>> } s_2]\!]\,\rho = \text{ExtendEnv}_S[\![s_1]\!]$$
$$(\text{ExtendEnv}_S[\![s_2]\!]\,\rho)$$
$$\text{ExtendEnv}_S[\![\texttt{alloc\_trig}]\!]\,\rho = \rho$$
$$\text{ExtendEnv}_S[\![\texttt{sStore}(e_1,\ e_2)]\!]\,\rho = \rho$$
$$\text{ExtendEnv}_S[\![\texttt{empty}(0_j)]\!]\,\rho = \rho$$
$$\text{ExtendEnv}_S[\![\texttt{error}(0_j)]\!]\,\rho = \rho$$
$$\text{ExtendEnv}_S[\![\texttt{full}(0_j,\ v)]\!]\,\rho = \rho$$
$$\text{ExtendEnv}_S[\![\texttt{arraySStore}(e_1,\ e_2,\ e_3)]\!]\,\rho = \rho$$
$$\text{ExtendEnv}_S[\![\texttt{arrayEmpty}(0_j,\ j)]\!]\,\rho = \rho$$
$$\text{ExtendEnv}_S[\![\texttt{arrayError}(0_j,\ j)]\!]\,\rho = \rho$$
$$\text{ExtendEnv}_S[\![\texttt{arrayFull}(0_j,\ j,\ v)]\!]\,\rho = \rho$$

The following function renames the statement in a block; it renames both the left-hand side variables and the right-hand side expressions:

$$\text{Ren}_S[\![\epsilon]\!]\,\rho = \epsilon$$
$$\text{Ren}_S[\![x = e]\!]\,\rho = \text{Ren}[\![x]\!]\,\rho = \text{Ren}[\![e]\!]\,\rho$$
$$\text{Ren}_S[\![s_1;\ s_2]\!]\,\rho = \text{Ren}_S[\![s_1]\!]\,\rho;\ \text{Ren}_S[\![s_2]\!]\,\rho$$
$$\text{Ren}_S[\![s_1 \text{ >>> } s_2]\!]\,\rho = \text{Ren}_S[\![s_1]\!]\,\rho \text{ >>> } \text{Ren}_S[\![s_2]\!]\,\rho$$
$$\text{Ren}_S[\![\texttt{alloc\_trig}]\!]\,\rho = \texttt{alloc\_trig}$$
$$\text{Ren}_S[\![\texttt{sStore}(e_1,\ e_2)]\!]\,\rho = \texttt{sStore}(\text{Ren}[\![e_1]\!]\,\rho,\ \text{Ren}[\![e_2]\!]\,\rho)$$
$$\text{Ren}_S[\![\texttt{empty}(0_j)]\!]\,\rho = \texttt{empty}(0_j)$$
$$\text{Ren}_S[\![\texttt{error}(0_j)]\!]\,\rho = \texttt{error}(0_j)$$
$$\text{Ren}_S[\![\texttt{full}(0_j,\ e)]\!]\,\rho = \texttt{full}(0_j,\ \text{Ren}[\![e]\!]\,\rho)$$
$$\text{Ren}_S[\![\texttt{arraySStore}(e_1, e_2, e_3)]\!]\,\rho = \texttt{arraySStore}(\text{Ren}[\![e_1]\!]\,\rho,$$
$$\text{Ren}[\![e_2]\!]\,\rho,$$
$$\text{Ren}[\![e_3]\!]\,\rho)$$
$$\text{Ren}_S[\![\texttt{arrayEmpty}(0_j,\ \underline{n})]\!]\,\rho = \texttt{arrayEmpty}(0_j,\ \underline{n})$$

$$\text{Ren}_S [\![\text{arrayError}(0_j, \underline{n})]\!] \rho = \text{arrayError}(0_j, \underline{n})$$
$$\text{Ren}_S [\![\text{arrayFull}(0_j, \underline{n}, e)]\!] \rho = \text{arrayFull}(0_j, \underline{n}, \text{Ren}[\![e]\!]\rho)$$

The following notational conventions are followed:

- e' and s' are renamed versions of expression e and statement s, respectively, in order to avoid name conflicts.
- t is always a fresh identifier that does not otherwise occur in the program.
- $e[t/x]$ represents expression e with all free occurrences of identifier x substituted by identifier t. It can be defined as

$$e[t/x] = \text{Ren}[\![e]\!] ((x \rightarrow t) : \phi)$$

Equivalences under α-renaming:

$$\begin{array}{lll} \backslash x \; \text{->} \; e & \equiv \; \backslash t \; \text{->} \; e[t/x] & (\alpha\text{-}\lambda) \\ \textbf{let } x = e; \; s \; \textbf{in} \; e_0 & \equiv \; \textbf{let } t = e[t/x]; \; s[t/x] \; \textbf{in} \; e_0[t/x] & (\alpha\text{-let}) \end{array}$$

Alternatively,

$$e \qquad\qquad \equiv \; \text{Ren}[\![e]\!] \, \phi \qquad\qquad (\alpha)$$

B.3   Rewrite Rules

The rewrite rules are organized by major syntactic classes.

B.3.1   Primitive Functions (δ Rules)

δ rules (rules for built-in primitive functions):

$$\underline{x} + \underline{y} \qquad\qquad\qquad \longrightarrow \; \underline{x + y} \qquad\qquad (+)$$

    . . . and similarly for other arithmetic primitives, etc.

δ rule for algebraic type selectors:

$$\text{proj}_j \; \text{CN}_k(\cdots, e_j, \cdots) \qquad \longrightarrow \; e_j \qquad\qquad (\text{Proj})$$

δ rules for operations on I-structure cells and arrays are covered in Sections B.3.7 and B.3.8, respectively.

B.3.2   Conditionals

$$\begin{array}{lll} \textbf{Cond}(\text{True}, \; e_1, \; e_2) & \longrightarrow \; e_1 & (\text{CondT}) \\ \textbf{Cond}(\text{False}, \; e_1, \; e_2) & \longrightarrow \; e_2 & (\text{CondF}) \end{array}$$

B.3.3 Function Application (β-Reduction)

$$(\backslash x \; \text{->} \; e_1) \; e_2 \qquad\qquad \longrightarrow \quad \textbf{let } t \; = \; e_2 \; \textbf{ in } \; e_1[t/x] \qquad (\beta)$$

t is a fresh identifier and $e_1[t/x]$ represents a renaming of all free occurrences of x in e_1 by t; see Section B.2 for details.

B.3.4 Instantiation (a.k.a. Substitution)

Expression contexts:

$$
\begin{array}{lll}
C[\,] & ::= & [\,] \\
 & | & \backslash x \; \text{->} \; C[\,] \\
 & | & C[\,] \; E \qquad\qquad | \quad E \; C[\,] \\
 & | & \textbf{let } S \textbf{ in } C[\,] \quad | \quad \textbf{let } SC[\,] \textbf{ in } E \\
 & | & \text{Cond}(C[\,], E_t, E_f) \quad | \quad \text{Cond}(E_p, C[\,], E_f) \quad | \quad \text{Cond}(E_p, E_t, C[\,]) \\
 & | & \text{PF}_k(\cdots, \; C[\,], \; \cdots) \\
 & | & \text{CN}_k(\cdots, \; C[\,], \; \cdots)
\end{array}
$$

Statement contexts:

$$
\begin{array}{lll}
SC[\,] & ::= & x = C[\,] \qquad\qquad | \quad SC[\,]; \; S \\
 & | & SC[\,] \; \text{>>>} \; S \qquad | \quad S \; \text{>>>} \; SC[\,] \\
 & | & \text{sStore}(C[\,], \; E) \quad | \quad \text{sStore}(E, \; C[\,]) \\
 & | & \text{arraySStore}(C[\,], E, E) \\
 & | & \text{arraySStore}(E, C[\,], E) \\
 & | & \text{arraySStore}(E, E, C[\,])
\end{array}
$$

We omit the symmetric clause "$S; \; SC[\,]$" because the semicolon is always symmetric.

Rewrite rules for instantiation (x in $C[x]$ must be free in $C[x]$, and a must be a Simple Expression):

$$
\begin{array}{lll}
\textbf{let } x \; = \; a; \; s \textbf{ in } C[x] & \longrightarrow \textbf{let } x \; = \; a; \; s \textbf{ in } C'[a] & (\text{Inst1}) \\
\textbf{let } x \; = \; a \; \text{>>>} \; s \textbf{ in } C[x] & \longrightarrow \textbf{let } x \; = \; a \; \text{>>>} \; s \textbf{ in } C'[a] & (\text{Inst1a}) \\
x \; = \; a; \; y \; = \; C[x] & \longrightarrow x \; = \; a; \; y \; = \; C'[a] & (\text{Inst2}) \\
x \; = \; a \; \text{>>>} \; y \; = \; C[x] & \longrightarrow x \; = \; a \; \text{>>>} \; y \; = \; C'[a] & (\text{Inst2a}) \\
x \; = \; C[x] & \longrightarrow x \; = \; C'[C[x]] & (\text{Inst3})
\end{array}
$$

A C' in the right-hand side indicates that the context needs to be α-renamed to avoid capturing free variables of the term being substituted into the context.

B.3.5   Block Flattening and Expression Lifting

In order to avoid the possibility of infinite sequences of reductions (in which instantiation immediately cancels lifting), all these rules except the first two are inapplicable when e is a simple expression.

$$x = \textbf{let } s \textbf{ in } e \qquad \longrightarrow \quad x = e'; \; s' \qquad\qquad \text{(Flat1)}$$
$$\textbf{let } \epsilon \textbf{ in } e \qquad \longrightarrow \quad e \qquad\qquad\qquad\quad \text{(Flat2)}$$

In the lift rules below, $e \notin SE$:

$$\textbf{let } s \textbf{ in } e \qquad \longrightarrow \quad \textbf{let } s; \; t = e \qquad\qquad \text{(LiftB)}$$
$$\textbf{in } t$$

$$(e \; e_2) \qquad\qquad \longrightarrow \quad \textbf{let } t = e \qquad\qquad\qquad \text{(LiftAp1)}$$
$$\textbf{in } t \; e_2$$

$$(e_1 \; e) \qquad\qquad \longrightarrow \quad \textbf{let } t = e \qquad\qquad\qquad \text{(LiftAp2)}$$
$$\textbf{in } e_1 \; t$$

$$\textbf{Cond}(e, \; e_1, \; e_2) \qquad \longrightarrow \quad \textbf{let } t = e \qquad\qquad\qquad \text{(LiftCond)}$$
$$\textbf{in } \textbf{Cond}(t, \; e_1, \; e_2)$$

$$\text{PF}_k(\cdots, \; e, \; \cdots) \qquad \longrightarrow \quad \textbf{let } t = e \qquad\qquad\qquad \text{(LiftPF)}$$
$$\textbf{in } \text{PF}_k(\cdots, \; t, \; \cdots)$$

$$\text{CN}_k(\cdots, \; e, \; \cdots) \qquad \longrightarrow \quad \textbf{let } t = e \qquad\qquad\qquad \text{(LiftCN)}$$
$$\textbf{in } \text{CN}_k(\cdots, \; t, \; \cdots)$$

$$\text{sStore}(e, e_2) \qquad\qquad \longrightarrow \quad t = e; \qquad\qquad\qquad\quad \text{(LiftsStore1)}$$
$$\text{sStore}(t, e_2)$$

$$\text{sStore}(e_1, e) \qquad\qquad \longrightarrow \quad t = e; \qquad\qquad\qquad\quad \text{(LiftsStore2)}$$
$$\text{sStore}(e_1, t)$$

$$\text{arraySStore}(e, e_2, e_3) \quad \longrightarrow \quad t = e; \qquad\qquad\qquad\quad \text{(LiftsArraySStore1)}$$
$$\text{arraySStore}(t, e_2, e_3)$$

$$\text{arraySStore}(e_1, e, e_3) \quad \longrightarrow \quad t = e; \qquad\qquad\qquad\quad \text{(LiftsArraySStore2)}$$
$$\text{arraySStore}(e_1, t, e_3)$$

$$\text{arraySStore}(e_1, e_2, e) \quad \longrightarrow \quad t = e; \qquad\qquad\qquad\quad \text{(LiftsArraySStore3)}$$
$$\text{arraySStore}(e_1, e_2, t)$$

Note: We do not lift the arms e_2 and e_3 from a conditional, nor do we lift expressions out of λ-bodies.

B.3.6   Sequentialization (Barriers)

Sequential statement composition ("$>>>$") has the following equivalence property with respect to heap terms (it can be used as a rewrite rule in either direction):

$$(h; \; s_1) \; >>> \; s_2 \qquad \equiv \; h; \; (s_1 \; >>> \; s_2)$$

It can be shown that ">>>", just like "; ", is associative:

$$(s_1 \ggg s_2) \ggg s_3 \equiv s_1 \ggg (s_2 \ggg s_3)$$

But note that ">>>" is not commutative like "; ":

$$s_1 \ggg s_2 \quad\quad\quad \not\equiv s_2 \ggg s_1$$

The rewrite rules for ">>>" show that ϵ is a "unit" for ">>>" just like "; ":

$$
\begin{array}{lll}
\epsilon \ggg S & \longrightarrow S & \text{(SEQ1)} \\
S \ggg \epsilon & \longrightarrow S & \text{(SEQ2)}
\end{array}
$$

B.3.7   I-structure and M-structure Cells

Cell allocation:

```
alloc_trig;            ⟶   alloc_trig;            (Alloc)
x = allocate()             empty(O_j)
                           x = O_j
```

Cell assignment:

```
empty(O_j);            ⟶   full(O_j,v)            (SStore)
sStore(O_j, v)
```

```
full(O_j,v);           ⟶   full(O_j,v);           (SStoreErr)
sStore(O_j, w)             error(O_j)
```

Cell selection:

```
full(O_j,v);           ⟶   full(O_j,v);           (iFetch)
x = iFetch(O_j)            x = v
```

```
full(O_j,v);           ⟶   empty(O_j);            (mFetch)
x = mFetch(O_j)            x = v
```

B.3.8   I-structure and M-structure Arrays

Array allocation:

```
alloc_trig;            ⟶   alloc_trig;            (ArrayAlloc)
x = arrayAllocate(n)       x = O_a;
                           arrayEmpty(O_a,0);
                           ...;
                           arrayEmpty(O_a,n − 1)
```

Array assignment:

$$\begin{aligned} &\texttt{arrayEmpty}(0_a,j)\texttt{;} &&\longrightarrow &&\texttt{arrayFull}(0_a,j,v) &&\text{(ArraySStore)}\\ &\texttt{arraySStore}(0_a,j,v) \end{aligned}$$

$$\begin{aligned} &\texttt{arrayFull}(0_a,j,v)\texttt{;} &&\longrightarrow &&\texttt{arrayFull}(0_a,j,v)\texttt{;} &&\text{(ArraySStoreErr)}\\ &\texttt{arraySStore}(0_a,j,w) && &&\texttt{arrayError}(0_a,j) \end{aligned}$$

Array selection:

$$\begin{aligned} &\texttt{arrayFull}(0_a,j,v)\texttt{;} &&\longrightarrow &&\texttt{arrayFull}(0_a,j,v)\texttt{;} &&\text{(ArrayIFetch)}\\ &x = \texttt{arrayIFetch}(0_a,j) && &&x = v \end{aligned}$$

$$\begin{aligned} &\texttt{arrayFull}(0_a,j,v)\texttt{;} &&\longrightarrow &&\texttt{arrayEmpty}(0_a,j)\texttt{;} &&\text{(ArrayMFetch)}\\ &x = \texttt{arrayMFetch}(0_a,j) && &&x = v \end{aligned}$$

References

[1] H. Abelson and G. J. Sussman (with Julie Sussman). *Structure and Interpretation of Computer Programs*. MIT Press, Cambridge, MA, 1985.

[2] S. Aditya and A. Caro. Compiler-Directed Type Reconstruction for Polymorphic Languages. In *Proc. Functional Programming Languages and Computer Architecture (FPCA)*, Copenhagen, Denmark, June 1993.

[3] S. Ahuja, N. Carriero, and D. Gelernter. Linda and Friends. *IEEE Computer*, 19(8): 26–34, August 1986.

[4] Z. Ariola and Arvind. Properties of a First-Order Functional Language with Sharing. *Theoretical Computer Science*, 146(1–2):69–108, July 1995.

[5] Z. M. Ariola. Notes on the Confluence Property of Term Rewriting Systems and the λ-Calculus. Technical Report CSG Memo 321, Computation Structures Group, MIT Lab. for Computer Science, Cambridge, MA, November 7, 1990.

[6] J. Armstrong. The Development of Erlang. In *Proc. Intl. Conf. on Functional Programming (ICFP)*, Amsterdam, The Netherlands, pages 196–203, 1997.

[7] J. Armstrong, R. Virding, and M. Williams. *Concurrent Programming in Erlang*. Prentice Hall, Englewood Cliffs, NJ, 1993.

[8] K. Arnold and J. Gosling. *The Java Programming Language, second edition*. Addison-Wesley, Reading, MA, 1998.

[9] Arvind, A. Caro, J.-W. Maessen, and S. Aditya. A Multithreaded Substrate and Compilation Model for the Implicitly Parallel Language pH. In *Proc. Wkshp. on Languages and Compilers for Parallel Computing (LCPC)*, August 1996.

[10] Arvind, K. P. Gostelow, and W. Plouffe. The (Preliminary) Id Report. Technical Report 114, Dept. of Information and Computer Science, Univ. of California, Irvine, CA, 1978.

[11]   Arvind and R. S. Nikhil. Executing a Program on the MIT Tagged-Token Dataflow Architecture. *IEEE Trans. on Computers*, 39(3):300–318, March 1990.

[12]   H. P. Barendregt. *The Lambda Calculus, Its Syntax and Semantics*. North Holland, Amsterdam, The Netherlands, 1981.

[13]   B. Blanchet. Escape Analysis: Correctness Proof, Implementation and Experimental Results. In *Proc. 25th ACM Symp. on Principles of Programming Languages (POPL)*, San Diego, CA, pages 25–37, January 1998.

[14]   G. E. Blelloch, S. Chatterjee, J. C. Hardwick, J. Sipelstein, and M. Zagha. Implementation of a Portable Nested Data-Parallel Language. In *Proc. 4th ACM Symp. on Principles and Practice of Parallel Programming (PPoPP)*, pages 102–111, May 19–22, 1993.

[15]   R. D. Blumofe, C. F. Joerg, B. C. Kuszmaul, C. E. Leiserson, K. H. Randall, and Y. Zhou. Cilk: An Efficient Multithreaded Runtime System. In *Proc. 5th ACM Symp. on Principles and Practice of Parallel Programming (PPoPP)*, Santa Barbara, CA, pages 207–216, July 19–21, 1995.

[16]   A. Church. *The Calculi of Lambda Conversion*. Princeton University Press, Princeton, NJ, 1941.

[17]   A. Church. *Introduction to Mathematical Logic*. Princeton University Press, Princeton, NJ, 1956.

[18]   A. Colmerauer. Prolog in 10 Figures. *Communications of the ACM*, 28(12):1296–1310, December 1985.

[19]   D. E. Culler, A. Dusseau, S. C. Goldstein, A. Krishnamurthy, S. Lumetta, T. von Eicken, and K. Yelick. Parallel Programming in Split-C. In *Proc. Supercomputing 93*, Portland, OR, November 1993.

[20]   M. Feeley. An Efficient and General Implementation of Futures on Large Scale Shared-Memory Multiprocessors, April 1993. Ph.D. thesis. Available at *http://www.iro.umontreal.ca/~feeley/papers/futures.ps.gz*.

[21]   S. Finne, D. Leijen, E. Meijer, and S. L. Peyton Jones. H/Direct: A Binary Foreign Language Interface for Haskell. In *Proc. Intl. Conf. on Functional Programming (ICFP)*, Baltimore, MD, 1998.

[22]   S. Finne, D. Leijen, E. Meijer, and S. L. Peyton Jones. Calling Hell from Heaven and Heaven from Hell. In *Proc. Intl. Conf. on Functional Programming (ICFP)*, Paris, France, 1999.

[23]   C. Flanagan and R. S. Nikhil. pHluid: The Design of a Parallel Functional Language Implementation on Workstations. In *Proc. Intl. Conf. on Functional Programming (ICFP)*, Philadelphia, PA, pages 169–179, May 24–26, 1996.

[24] A. Geist, A. Begeulin, J. Dongarra, W. Jiang, R. Manchek, and V. S. Sundaram. *PVM: Parallel Virtual Machine. A User's Guide and Tutorial for Network Parallel Computing.* MIT Press, Cambridge, MA, 1994. *http://www.epm.ornl.gov/pvm.*

[25] B. Goldberg and M. Gloger. Polymorphic Type Reconstruction for Garbage Collection without Tags. In *Proc. ACM Symp. on LISP and Functional Programming (LFP)*, pages 53–65, June 1992.

[26] S. C. Goldstein, K. E. Schauser, and D. E. Culler. Lazy Threads: Implementing a Fast Parallel Call. *J. of Parallel and Distributed Computing*, 37(1):5–20, 1996.

[27] M. J. Gordon, R. Milner, L. Morris, M. Newey, and C. Wadsworth. A Metalanguage for Interactive Proof in LCF. In *Proc. 5th ACM Symp. on Principles of Programming Languages (POPL)*, pages 119–130, 1978.

[28] R. H. Halstead. Multilisp: A Language for Concurrent Symbolic Computation. *ACM Trans. on Programming Languages and Systems (TOPLAS)*, 7(4):501–539, October 1985.

[29] High Performance Fortran Forum. High Performance Fortran Language Specification, Version 1.0. Technical Report CRPC-TR92225, Center for Research on Parallel Computation, Rice University, Houston, TX, May 3, 1993. *http://www.crpc.rice.edu/HPFF/home.html.*

[30] C. Hoare. Monitors: An Operating System Structuring Concept. *Communications of the ACM*, 17(10):549–557, October 1974.

[31] R. Hughes. Lazy Memo-functions. Technical Report Programming Methodology Group Report PMG-42, Department of Computer Science, Chalmers University of Technology and University of Göteborg, Göteborg, Sweden, January 1985.

[32] R. Hughes. Why Functional Programming Matters. *The Computer Journal*, 32(2):98–107, 1989.

[33] IEEE. Threads Standard POSIX 1003.1c-1995 (also ISO/IEC 9945-1:1996), 1996.

[34] R. Jones and R. Lins. *Garbage Collection : Algorithms for Automatic Dynamic Memory Management.* John Wiley & Sons, New York, August 1996.

[35] R. Kelsey, W. Clinger, and J. Rees (eds.). Revised[5] Report on the Algorithmic Language Scheme. *Higher-Order and Symbolic Computation*, 11(1):7–105, August 1998. Available at *http://www.brics.dk/~hosc/11-1/168705.html* and in ACM SIGPLAN Notices 33:3, September 1998, pages 26–76.

[36] D. Knuth. *The Art of Computer Programming, Volume 1: Fundamental Algorithms.* Addison-Wesley, Reading, MA, 1973.

[37] P. J. Landin. A Correspondence between ALGOL 60 and Church's Lambda-Notation: Part I. *Communications of the ACM*, 8(2):89–101, February 1965.

[38]   P. J. Landin. A Correspondence between ALGOL 60 and Church's Lambda-Notation: Part II. *Communications of the ACM*, 8(3):158–165, March 1965.

[39]   X. Leroy. Unboxed Objects and Polymorphic Typing. In *Proc. 19th ACM Symp. Principles of Programming Languages (POPL)*, pages 177–188. ACM Press, New York, 1992.

[40]   Message Passing Interface Forum. MPI: A Message-Passing Interface Standard, May 1994. *http://www.mpi-forum.org*.

[41]   R. Milner. A Theory of Type Polymorphism in Programming. *J. of Computer and System Sciences*, 17:348–375, 1978.

[42]   R. Milner, M. Tofte, and R. Harper. *The Definition of Standard ML*. MIT Press, Cambridge, MA, 1990.

[43]   R. S. Nikhil. Id (Version 90.1) Language Reference Manual. Technical Report CSG Memo 284-2, MIT Laboratory for Computer Science, Cambridge, MA, July 15, 1991.

[44]   R. S. Nikhil. A Multithreaded Implementation of Id using P-RISC Graphs. In *Proc. 6th Ann. Wkshp. on Languages and Compilers for Parallel Computing (LCPC)*, Portland, OR (Springer Verlag LNCS 768), pages 390–405, August 12–14, 1993.

[45]   R. S. Nikhil. *Cid*: A Parallel "Shared-Memory" C for Distributed Memory Machines. In *Proc. 7th Ann. Wkshp. on Languages and Compilers for Parallel Computing (LCPC)*, Ithaca, NY (Springer Verlag LNCS 892), pages 376–390, August 8–10, 1994.

[46]   R. S. Nikhil and Arvind. Id: A Language with Implicit Parallelism. In *A Comparative Study of Parallel Programming Languages: The Salishan Problems*, John Feo (ed.), pages 169–215. North Holland, Amsterdam, The Netherlands, 1992.

[47]   R. S. Nikhil, K. Pingali, and Arvind. Id Nouveau. Technical Report CSG Memo 265, Computation Structures Group, MIT Lab. for Computer Science, Cambridge, MA, July 1986.

[48]   OpenMP Architecture Review Board. OpenMP Specifications, 1997 (Fortran), 1998 (C/C++). *http://www.openmp.org*.

[49]   G. M. Papadopoulos and D. E. Culler. Monsoon: An Explicit Token Store Architecture. In *Proc. 17th Intl. Symp. on Computer Architecture (ISCA)*, Seattle, WA, May 1990.

[50]   Y. G. Park and B. Goldberg. Escape Analysis on Lists. In *Proc. ACM SIGPLAN Conf. on Programming Language Design and Implementation (PLDI)*, San Francisco, CA, pages 116–127, June 1992.

[51]   S. L. Peyton Jones. *The Implementation of Functional Programming Languages*. Prentice-Hall, Englewood Cliffs, NJ, 1987.

[52] S. L. Peyton Jones and J. Launchbury. Unboxed Values as First Class Citizens. In *Proc. Functional Programming Languages and Computer Architecture (FPCA)*, Boston, MA (Springer Verlag LNCS 523), pages 636–666, September 1991.

[53] S. L. Peyton Jones (ed.), J. Hughes (ed.), L. Augustsson, D. Barton, B. Boutel, W. Burton, J. Fasel, K. Hammond, R. Hinze, P. Hudak, T. Johnsson, M. Jones, J. Launchbury, E. Meijer, J. Peterson, A. Reid, C. Runciman, and P. Wadler. Haskell 98: A Non-strict, Purely Functional Language, February 1999. *http://www.haskell.org*.

[54] W. Press, B. Flannery, S. Teukolsky, and W. Vettering. *Numerical Recipes: The Art of Scientific Computing*. Cambridge University Press, Cambridge, England, 1986.

[55] J. Reynolds. Types, Abstraction and Parametric Polymorphism. In *Information Processing 83*, pages 513–523, 1983.

[56] M. C. Rinard and P. C. Diniz. Commutativity Analysis: A New Analysis Framework for Parallelizing Compilers. *ACM Trans. on Programming Languages and Systems (TOPLAS)*, 19(6):942–991, November 1997.

[57] M. C. Rinard, D. J. Scales, and M. S. Lam. Jade: A High-Level, Machine-Independent Language for Parallel Programming. *IEEE Computer*, 26(6):28–38, June 1993.

[58] K. E. Schauser. *Compiling Lenient Languages for Parallel Asynchronous Execution*. PhD Thesis, Computer Science Division, University of California, Berkeley, CA, May 1994.

[59] D. Scott. Outline of a Mathematical Theory of Computation. In *Proc. of the 4th Annual Princeton Conf. on Information Systems*, pages 169–176, 1970.

[60] D. Scott. Data Types as Lattices. *SIAM Journal on Computing*, 5, 1976.

[61] D. Scott. Logic and Programming Languages. *Communications of the ACM*, 20(9):634–641, September 1977.

[62] G. Smolka, M. Henz, and J. Würtz. Object-Oriented Concurrent Constraint Programming in Oz. In *Proc. Principles and Practice of Constraint Programming*, P. van Hentenryck and V. Saraswat (eds.), pages 29–48, MIT Press, Cambridge, MA, 1995.

[63] G. L. Steele Jr. *Common Lisp: The Language*. Digital Press, Billerica, MA, 1984.

[64] J. E. Stoy. *Denotational Semantics: The Scott-Strachey Approach to Programming Language Theory*. MIT Press, Cambridge, MA, 1977.

[65] C. Strachey. *Fundamental Concepts in Programming Languages*. Oxford University Press, Oxford, England, 1967.

[66] K. Taura, K. Tabata, and A. Yonezawa. StackThreads/MP: Integrating Futures into Calling Standards. In *Proc. ACM Sigplan Symp. on Principles and Practice of Parallel Programming (PPoPP)*, Atlanta, GA, pages 60–71, May 4–6, 1999.

[67] K. R. Traub. A Compiler for the MIT Tagged-Token Dataflow Architecture. Technical Report LCS TR-370, MIT Laboratory for Computer Science, Cambridge, MA, August 1986.

[68] D. Turner. The Semantic Elegance of Applicative Languages. In *Proc. Functional Programming Languages and Computer Architecture (FPCA)*, Portsmouth, NH, pages 85–92, October 1981.

[69] K. Ueda and T. Chikayama. Design of the Kernel Language for the Parallel Inference Machine. *The Computer Journal*, 33(6):494–500, 1990.

[70] D. Ungar. Generation Scavenging: A Non-disruptive High Performance Storage Reclamation Algorithm. In *Proc. ACM SIGSOFT/SIGPLAN Software Engineering Symp. on Practical Software Development Environments*, Peter Henderson (ed.), Pittsburgh, PA, April 23–25, 1984, pages 157–167.

[71] P. Wadler. Listlessness Is Better than Laziness: Lazy Evaluation and Garbage Collection at Compile Time. In *Proc. ACM Symp. on Lisp and Functional Programming (LFP)*, Austin, TX, pages 45–52, August 6–8, 1984.

[72] P. Wadler. Deforestation: Transforming Programs to Eliminate Trees. In *European Symp. on Programming*, Nancy, France, pages 344–358, January 1988.

[73] P. Wadler. Theorems for Free! In *Proc. Functional Programming and Computer Architecture (FPCA)*, London, England, September 1989.

[74] P. Wadler. Linear Types Can Change the World! In M. Broy and C. Jones (eds.), *Programming Concepts and Methods, Sea of Galilee, Israel*. North Holland, Amsterdam, The Netherlands, April 1990. IFIP TC 2 Working Conference.

[75] P. Wadler. Monads for functional programming. In *Advanced Functional Programming*, J. Jeuring and E. Meijer (eds.) (LNCS 925). Springer Verlag, Berlin, 1995.

[76] D. Warren. DAI Research Report 141. Technical Report, University of Edinburgh, 1980.

[77] N. Wirth. *Programming in Modula-2*. Springer Verlag, Berlin, 1982.

Index